Final Roll Call

Confederate Losses during the 1865 Carolinas Campaign

Volume I: North Carolina

Wade Sokolosky
with
Stacey Jones

Final Roll Call Confederate Losses during the 1865 Carolinas Campaign, Volume I: North Carolina by Wade Sokolosky and Stacey Jones

© 2025 The Scuppernong Press

First Printing
The Scuppernong Press
PO Box 1724
Wake Forest, NC 27588
www.scuppernongpress.com

Cover design by Frank B. Powell, III

About the front cover. March 10, 1865, battle scene of Wise's Forks courtesy of Stephen McCall (artist).
About the back cover: Surgeon Ralph B. Hanahan's Casualty Return for Hagood's Brigade at the Battle of Wise's Forks (Collection of Wade Sokolosky).

All rights reserved and printed in the United States of America.

No part of this book may be reproduced or transmitted in any form or by any means, electronic or mechanical, including photocopying, recording, or by any information and storage and retrieval system, without written permission from the publisher.

International Standard Book Number ISBN 978-1-942806-73-8

Library of Congress Control Number: 2025933093

This Book is Dedicated
to the Men that it Entails

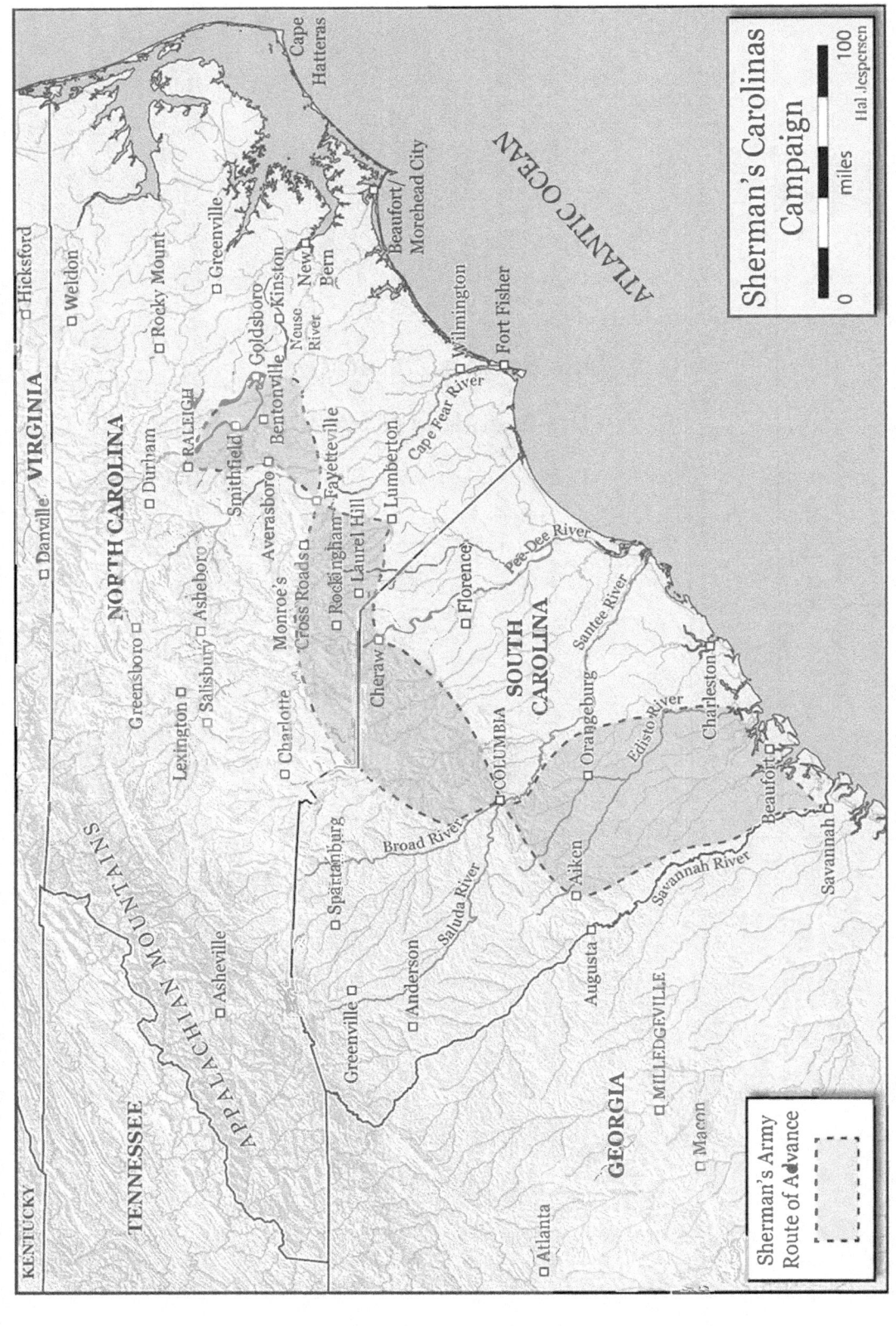

Table of Contents

Preface	iii
Guide to Abbreviations and Symbols	vii
Additional Notes	ix
Part I: Artillery	1
1st Battalion North Carolina Heavy Artillery	3
10th Regiment North Carolina State Troops	
(1st Regiment North Carolina Artillery)	23
36th Regiment North Carolina Troops	
(2nd Regiment North Carolina Artillery)	27
3rd Battalion North Carolina Light Artillery	33
40th Regiment North Carolina Troops	
(3rd Regiment North Carolina Light Artillery)	37
10th Battalion North Carolina Heavy Artillery	61
13th Battalion North Carolina Light Artillery	67
Captain Abner A. Moseley's Company	
(Sampson Artillery)	71
Part II: Cavalry	73
65th Regiment North Carolina Troops	
(6th Regiment North Carolina Cavalry)	75
Part III: Infantry	81
2nd Battalion North Carolina Local Defense Troops	83
8th Regiment North Carolina State Troops	87
17th Regiment North Carolina Troops (2nd Organization)	91
31st Regiment North Carolina Troops	123
42nd Regiment North Carolina Troops	127
50th Regiment North Carolina Troops	157
51st Regiment North Carolina Troops	163
58th Regiment North Carolina Troops	169
60th Regiment North Carolina Troops	177
61st Regiment North Carolina Troops	179
66th Regiment North Carolina Troops	185
67th Regiment North Carolina Troops	203
68th Regiment North Carolina Troops	211
Captain James M. McDougald's Company	215
Part IV: Reserve Units	217
1st Battalion North Carolina Junior Reserves	219
1st Regiment North Carolina Junior Reserves	
(70th Regiment North Carolina)	221
2nd Regiment North Carolina Junior Reserves	
(71st Regiment North Carolina)	227
3rd Regiment North Carolina Junior Reserves	
(72nd Regiment North Carolina)	233
7th Regiment North Carolina Senior Reserves	
(77th Regiment North Carolina)	239

Bibliography	240
Index	243
About the Authors	263
Additional Information Not Previously Found	265
Additional Information Submission	265

Preface and Acknowledgements

On February 1, 1865, Major General William T. Sherman and his more than 60,000 U.S. Army veterans began their northward march out of the South Carolina Low Country toward Goldsboro, North Carolina. Along the Lower Cape Fear River, Major General John M. Schofield's Federal troops supported Sherman's advance as they sought to follow up their victory at Fort Fisher by capturing North Carolina's largest city, Wilmington. Throughout February and March 1865, Confederate forces within the Carolinas would desperately try to halt this juggernaut, but to no avail.

In February 1865, the opposing forces in South Carolina skirmished almost daily, with serious fighting along the rivers in the Low Country, Columbia, and Cheraw. As Sherman marched northward through the Palmetto State, simultaneously, in North Carolina, the battles of Fort Anderson, Town Creek, Forks Road, and the fall of Wilmington occurred. However, March 1865 proved to be the Old North State's bloodiest month of the entire war, where, during a brief 14-day span, "Two Weeks of Fury," General Joseph E. Johnston's outnumbered Confederates fought four desperate battles: Wise's Forks; Monroe's Crossroads; Averasboro, and Bentonville. The ultimate cost of these battles is found in existing North Carolina Confederate hospital records, prison registries, Confederate pension applications, and the unmarked graves found at the various battlefields.

The more than 1,300 individual names listed in *Final Roll Call* are not absolute, as the compilers acknowledge the shortcomings of Confederate casualty reporting during the war's final months. Those who died or were hospitalized for non-battle-related injuries during this period are not included in this work. To do so goes far beyond the scope of this study, as I sought to gain a better understanding of the losses tied directly to the fighting. I made one exception regarding cases of desertion, as it provides insight into the state of morale of Confederate forces during these final months.

An invaluable source for Tar Heel soldiers, and the base information for all material contained within this work, is the multi-volume series, *North Carolina Troops 1861-1865 A Roster*. *Final Roll Call* supplements the *North Carolina Troops* series with new information when available. Additional resources included National Archives Record Group 109, Compiled Service Records of Confederate Soldiers, Confederate Medical Department Hospital Records, and Prisoner of War Records. Material obtained from the National Archives was supplemented by casualty lists, such as Surgeon Isaac S. Tanner's record of wounded from Hoke's Division; Surgeon Ralph B. Hanahan's record of wounded from Hagood's Brigade; hospital listings and obituaries in wartime newspapers; *The War of the Rebellion: A Compilation of the Official Records of the Union and Confederate Armies*; Confederate pension applications filed by veterans and their wives; soldier letters, diaries, and journals; and postwar unit histories.

None of this would have been possible without the help of others. First, Stacey Jones, whose research expertise helped solve the mysteries surrounding many of the soldier's names that grace this work. To Phillip Martin for sharing his excellent research on the Confederate hospitals at High Point. Skip Riddle, who never fails to share information. And to the great staff at North Carolina's various historic sites, who never wavered to help with information when I called. Finally, I believe there will never be a final closure on the overall Confederate losses during the 1865 Carolinas Campaign. Only the Good Lord knows the exact fate of the men who never returned home after the war. So, I took on this task with an open mind and a clear objective to capture as much information as possible. This is just one small measure of honoring these men. Despite the many years of work and effort, I know I have likely made errors for which I am responsible alone.

Wade Sokolosky
Beaufort, NC

Wade Sokolosky's desire to highlight and, when possible, define further the fates of the Confederate soldiers killed, injured, and captured during Sherman's Carolinas Campaign in 1865 was an ambitious and worthy study. This deep dive into this historical subject will provide curious readers and serious students of the period with a fresh understanding of what happened to these men. This work will be a desired read for many interest groups, from curious enthusiasts to respected Civil War researchers and novice family historians to seasoned genealogists.

Wade has honored me by allowing my research services to help in this endeavor. Finding and creating the most accurate narratives possible for the Tar Heel soldiers in this volume was challenging. Modern research tools have allowed us to expand on what was compiled previously about these men, help determine and correct errors, and resolve many situations left inconclusive in the past.

I hope we have accurately represented the soldiers in this volume according to the sacrifices made by each of them during February and March of 1865. Although errors were found and corrected, some may still be present. Hopefully, there will be fewer errors, and they can be corrected as new sources become available for further research. Secondly, I pray that future generations will not forget the sacrifices and struggles made by the soldiers in this conflict. Thirdly, I am excited to move forward with upcoming volumes of the *Final Roll Call* involving the troops from other states present during the Carolinas Campaign.

Stacey Jones
Pikeville, NC

Guide to Abbreviations and Symbols Used in the Source Notes and Text

6/281	National Archives, Record Group 109, Chapter 6, Confederate Medical Department Records, Patient Registry for General Hospital No. 3.
6/290	National Archives, Record Group 109, Chapter 6, Confederate Medical Department Records, Patient Registry for General Hospital No. 13.
AIANCT	Purser, Charles E., Jr., *Additional Information and Amendments to the North Carolina Troops, 1861-1865*, 2 vols.
Barbee	Barbee Wayside Hospital (High Point, NC)
CV	*Confederate Veteran Magazine*
DC	*Daily Conservative* (Raleigh) Newspaper
DConf	*Daily Confederate* (Raleigh) Newspaper
DJ	*Daily Journal* (Wilmington, NC) Newspaper
DP	*Daily Progress* (Raleigh) Newspaper
GH	General Hospital, e.g., GH No. 3
Hanahan (BV)	Surgeon Ralph B. Hanahan's "Return of Wounded for Hagood's Brigade" at Bentonville
Hanahan (WF)	Surgeon Ralph B. Hanahan's "Return of Wounded for Hagood's Brigade" At Wise's Forks
Histories	Walter G. Clark, *Histories of the Several Regiments and Battalions from North Carolina in the Great War 1861-'65*. 5 vols.
M251	Compiled Service Records of Confederate Soldiers from Florida
M270	Compiled service records of Confederate Soldiers from North Carolina
M1761	Muster Rolls and Lists of Confederate Soldiers Paroled in North Carolina
NA	National Archives and Records Administration, Washington, D.C.
NC	North Carolina
NCOAH	North Carolina Office of Archives and History
NC Troops or *NCT*	Manarin, Louis H., comp., et al., *North Carolina Troops, 1861-1865: A Roster*, 22 volumes to date
NCS	*North Carolina Standard* (Raleigh) Newspaper
OR	*The War of Rebellion: A Compilation of the Official Records of the Union and Confederate Armies*. 128 vols., Washington, D.C.
RG109	Record Group 109, War Department Collection of Confederate Records, National Archives, Washington, D.C.
SC	South Carolina
SHA	Southern Historical Association
Tanner (BV)	"Return of Wounded for Hoke's Division" at Bentonville
Tanner (WF)	"Return of Wounded for Hoke's Division" at Kinston (Wise's Forks)
WD	*Western Democrat* (Charlotte) Newspaper

Symbols Used in the Text

- ♦ Inconclusive – insufficient information to determine if an individual was captured, killed, or wounded at a specific battle.
- ▲ Change to information listed in *NC Troops* or a soldier's compiled service records.
- ♦▲ Inconclusive-with Changes – Although additional source material was discovered, insufficient information still exists to identify where an individual was captured, killed, or wounded.

Additional Notes

I have written the names of North Carolina towns, cities, and counties without the comma, then NC. All out-of-state locations are marked as such. The town of Washington is the one from North Carolina, unless otherwise identified with D.C. North Carolinians used to spell city names differently, such as Goldsborough/Goldsboro, New Bern/Newberne, Tarboro/Tarborough, etc.; I have chosen to use the contemporary spelling, only retaining the former spelling when part of a directly quoted source. I have attempted to keep the writings from letters, diaries, and journals as unaltered as possible. When necessary, I added words in brackets for clarity.

Bentonville Battlefield Monument Area

(Courtesy of Bentonville Battlefield State Historic Site)

PART I

(Artillery)

Funeral Notice for Capt. John W. Taylor, 1st Battalion NC Heavy Artillery. Severely wounded at Bentonville on March 19, 1865, and died in Raleigh on April 4, 1865. Captain Taylor's lock of hair was sent home to his wife.

(Courtesy of Mike Taylor)

1st Battalion North Carolina Heavy Artillery

♦Alderman, John E., Private, Company B
Bentonville (Inconclusive)
According to Lt. Richard P. Allen's 1st Battalion NC casualty list from the battle of Bentonville, Pvt. J. A. Alderman, Co. B, was wounded and reported missing. Private J. A. Alderman is not in the National Archives Compiled Service Records for North Carolina Confederate soldiers. However, a Jno. E. Alderman, Co. B, 1st Battalion NC, filed a Confederate pension application in 1901 seeking disability for his time as a prisoner at Point Lookout, Maryland. Interestingly, his name does not appear either in *NC Troops*. Further research is required.
Source: *DC* (Raleigh), April 7, 1865; M270; NC Confederate Pension (Sampson County).

Baker, John W., Private, Company A
Fayetteville
Captured in Fayetteville on March 11, 1865. Based on the location of his capture, Baker was absent from his command at the time of the battle of Wise's Forks (March 7-11, 1865). Confined at Newport News, Virginia, and released upon taking the Oath of Allegiance on June 30, 1865.
Source: *NCT*, I:3; M270.

▲Barden, William E., Private, Company A
Fort Anderson
According to Wilmington's *Daily Journal*, Pvt. Wm. E. Barden, Co. A, 1st Battalion NC, was wounded in the neck during the engagement at Fort Anderson and admitted to GH No. 4 in the port city on February 19, 1865, and transferred the following day to an unspecified hospital. *NC Troops* does not specify Fort Anderson as the location. No further records.
Source: *DJ* (Wilmington, NC), February 20, 1865; *NCT*, I:3; M270.

♦Best, J. W., Private, Company B
Bentonville (Inconclusive)
According to Surgeon Hanahan's "Return of Wounded for Hagood's Brigade" at Bentonville, Pvt. J. W. Best, Co. B, 1st Battalion NC, was slightly wounded in the right leg on March 19, 1865. There is no individual with the surname of Best listed on the unit rolls with the first and middle initials of "J. W." Additionally, a Pvt. J. W. Best was not listed in the battalion's publicized casualty list. Surgeon Hanahan probably misspelled the initials and may have been the same soldier as Pvt. William H. Best of Co. B of 1st Battalion. See William H. Best.
Source: Hanahan (BV), 4; M270.

♦Best, William H., Private, Company B
Bentonville (Inconclusive)
According to Lt. Richard P. Allen's 1st Battalion NC casualty list from the battle of Bentonville, Pvt. W. H. Best, Co. B, was wounded. Pvt. William H. Best, Co. B, is probably the same soldier as Pvt. W. H. Best. Neither Best's service records nor *NC Troops* note the wound he received at the battle of Bentonville. 1865. The *NC Standard* listed a Pvt. W. H. Burt of Co. B, 1st Battalion NC, was wounded at Bentonville on March 19, 1865, and present in Raleigh's Baptist Church Hospital with a wound to the "left leg." No W. H. Burt is listed in the unit rolls, so he is probably the same as William H. Best, who was later paroled at Goldsboro on May 24, 1865. Further research is required.
Source: *DC* (Raleigh), April 7, 1865; *DP* (Raleigh), March 27, 1865; *NCS* (Raleigh), March 24, 1865; *NCT*, I:11; M270.

▲Biggs, Absalom D., Private, Company A
Bentonville
According to Lt. Richard P. Allen's 1st Battalion NC casualty list from the battle of Bentonville, Pvt. A. D. Biggs, Co. A, was reported missing. Private Absalom D. Biggs, Co. A, is the same soldier as Pvt. A. D. Biggs. However, Biggs's service records do not indicate that U.S. Army forces captured him during the battle.

Allen either erroneously reported Biggs as missing, or the soldier rejoined the unit at some point after the battle. Biggs's service records indicate that he was at GH No. 13 (Pettigrew) in Raleigh on April 8, 1865, for unspecified reasons and captured there as a patient on April 13, 1865. A. D. Biggs's Confederate pension application indicates that he was wounded at Bentonville. *NC Troops* does not note that he was wounded at Bentonville.
Source: *DC* (Raleigh), April 7, 1865; M270; NC Confederate Pension (Robeson County); *NCT*, I:3.

Bishop, Riley M., Private, Company B
Bentonville
According to Lt. Richard P. Allen's 1st Battalion NC casualty list from the battle of Bentonville, Pvt. R. Bishop, Co. B, was wounded and reported missing. R. M. Bishop stated on his Confederate pension that he was wounded at Bentonville on March 19, 1865, from gunshots in both thighs, and his right index finger was shot off. Bishop was admitted to GH No. 13 (Pettigrew) in Raleigh on April 5, 1865, with no ailment specified, and later captured and paroled at the same hospital while a patient on April 13, 1865.
Source: *DC* (Raleigh), April 7, 1865; *NCT*, I:11; M270; NC Confederate Pension (Duplin County).

▲Blackman, William, Sergeant, Company C
[Correction to *NC Troops* and Sgt. William Blackman's Compile Service Records]
Sgt. William Blackman of Co. C, 1st Battalion NC, was not admitted to GH No. 3 in High Point on account of a gunshot wound to the head, nor did he die of said wounds on March 26, 1865. That individual was Sgt. W. W. Blackburn of Co. C, 1st Florida Infantry, who was probably wounded at the battle of Bentonville, was admitted to GH No. 3 in High Point. W. W. Blackburn's records indicating his death at High Point are erroneously filed within Sgt. William Blackman's National Archives Compiled Service Records of 1st Battalion NC Heavy Artillery. The No. 3 Patient Registry indicates that Sgt. W. W. Blackburn, entry no. 2495, of Co. C, 1st Florida, was admitted for unspecified reasons between March 21 and April 7, 1865. A GH No. 3 report, "Discharges on Surgeon's Certificates and Deaths," lists that Blackburn died on March 26, 1865, due to a gunshot wound to the head. Sergeant W. W. Blackburn is buried in the Confederate Section of Oakwood Cemetery, High Point. Additionally, Sgt. William Blackman's name is not listed on the casualty returns of Surgeons Hanahan or Tanner for either Wise's Forks or Bentonville, nor is his name present on Lt. Richard P. Allen's compiled casualty list from the battle of Bentonville for 1st Battalion NC Heavy Artillery.
Source: *NCT*, I:23, 695; M270; M251; RG109, 6/291:49; *DC* (Raleigh), April 7, 1865.

♦Brown, Duncan, Sergeant, Company A
Bentonville (Inconclusive)
According to Lt. Richard P. Allen's 1st Battalion NC casualty list from the battle of Bentonville, Sgt. D. Brown, Co. A, was wounded. Sergeant Duncan Brown of Co. A is the same soldier as Sgt. D. Brown. Brown's name does not appear on either Hanahan or Tanner's casualty returns from the battle. Neither Brown's service records nor *NC Troops* note the wounds he received at the battle of Bentonville. His service records indicate that he was captured as a patient at a Raleigh hospital on April 13, 1865. However, the June 3, 1894, edition of the *Goldsboro Daily Argus* reported that Duncan Brown, Co. A, 1st Battalion NC Heavy Artillery, died from wounds at Bentonville's Harper House. Sergeant Brown's name appears on a monument at Bentonville Battlefield State Historic Site, leading some to assume he is buried in the Confederate mass grave located there. His noticeable absence from Hanahan's listing of casualties from Hagood's Brigade suggests he may have initially been treated as a wounded prisoner by U.S. Army medical personnel at the Harper House (XIV Corps Field Hospital) and left behind when the Federals departed. Further research is required.
Source: *DC* (Raleigh), April 7, 1865; M270; *NCT*, I:4; *Goldsboro Daily Argus* (NC), June 3, 1894.

♦Brown, William A., Private, Company A
Bentonville (Inconclusive)
According to Surgeon Hanahan's "Return of Wounded for Hagood's Brigade" at Bentonville, Pvt. W. A. Brown, Co. A, 1st Battalion NC, was severely wounded in his right leg on March 19, 1865. Private W. A.

Brown also appears in Surgeon Tanner's "Return of Casualties in Hoke's Div. near Bentonville" and Lt. Richard P. Allen's compiled casualty list for 1st Battalion NC. Private William A. Brown of Co. A is probably the same soldier listed as Pvt. W. A. Brown. A Pvt. W. A. Brown of Co. A, 1st Battalion NC, was hospitalized at GH No. 3 in High Point for unspecified reasons between March 21 and April 7, 1865 (see patient registry entry no. 2519). Further research is required because *NC Troops* notes that William A. Brown was discharged on April 23, 1864, while stationed at Fort Pender.
Source: Hanahan (BV), 3; Tanner (BV), 146; *DC* (Raleigh), April 7, 1865; *NCT*, I:4; RG109, 6/291:50; M270.

▲Brown, William Henry, Captain, Company C
Bentonville
According to Surgeon Hanahan's "Return of Wounded for Hagood's Brigade" at Bentonville, Capt. W. H. Brown, Co. C, 1st Battalion NC, was slightly wounded in the breast on March 19, 1865. Captain Brown also appears in Surgeon Tanner's "Return of Casualties in Hoke's Div. near Bentonville" and Lt. Richard P. Allen's compiled casualty list for 1st Battalion NC. *NC Troops* notes that Brown was hospitalized in Greensboro on an unspecified date in March 1865, where he was paroled in May 1865. However, his service records do not indicate his hospitalization in March 1865 or his parole later in May.
Source: Hanahan (BV), 3; Tanner (BV), 146; *DC* (Raleigh), April 7, 1865; *NCT*, I:22; M270.

▲Cobb, Alexander M., Corporal, Company C
Bentonville
According to Surgeon Hanahan's "Return of Wounded for Hagood's Brigade" at Bentonville, Pvt. A. M. Cobb, Co. C, 1st Battalion NC, was slightly wounded in the right arm above the elbow on March 20, 1865. Corporal A. M. Cobb also appears in Surgeon Tanner's "Return of Casualties in Hoke's Div. near Bentonville" and Lt. Richard P. Allen's compiled casualty list for 1st Battalion NC. Corporal Alexander M. Cobb of Co. C is the same soldier as A. M. Cobb. Neither Cobb's service records nor *NC Troops* note the wound he received at the battle of Bentonville.
Source: Hanahan (BV), 1; Tanner (BV), 146; *DC* (Raleigh), April 7, 1865; *NCT*, I:24; M270.

▲Colvin, Aaron M., Private, Company B
Fort Anderson
According to Wilmington's *Daily Journal*, Pvt. A. M. Colvin, Co. B, 1st Battalion NC, had his arm broken during the engagement at Fort Anderson and was admitted to GH No. 4 in the port city on February 19, 1865, with a shell wound to the right arm. *NC Troops* does not identify Colvin as having been wounded at Fort Anderson. Received a 60-day furlough on February 20, 1865. His Confederate pension indicates that he was "severely wounded" with his arm broken at Fort Anderson.
Source: *DJ* (Wilmington, NC), February 20, 1865; *NCT*, I:13; M270; NC Confederate Pension (Pender County).

▲Cowan, Thomas W., Private, Company B
Wise's Forks
According to Surgeon Hanahan's "List of Killed and Wounded in Hagood's Brigade" at Wise's Forks, Corp. T. W. Cowen, Co. B, 1st Battalion NC, was "killed on the field" between March 7 – 10, 1865. Private T. W. Cowen also appears in Surgeon Tanner's "Return of Casualties near Kinston, March 8 & 10, 1865," as killed. Private Thomas W. Cowan is probably the same soldier as Corp. T. W. Cowen. Neither his service records nor *NC Troops* note his death at Wise's Forks.
Source: Hanahan (WF), 1; Tanner (WF), 137; *NCT*, I:13; M270.

♦Eakins, Robert, Private, Company B
Bentonville (Inconclusive)
According to Lt. Richard P. Allen's 1st Battalion NC casualty list from the battle of Bentonville, Pvt. R. Eakins, Co. B, was wounded and reported missing between March 19 – 21, 1865. Neither Eakins's service records nor *NC Troops* note that he was wounded and captured at Bentonville. His noticeable absence from Surgeon Hanahan's casualty return for Hagood's Brigade suggests he may have initially been treated as a wounded prisoner by U.S. Army medical personnel at the Harper House (XIV Corps Field Hospital) and left behind when the Federals departed. Further research is required.

Source: *DC* (Raleigh), April 7, 1865; *NCT*, I:14; M270.

▲Ellis, Zacheus, 1st Lieutenant, Company B
Bentonville
According to Lt. Richard P. Allen's 1st Battalion NC casualty list from the battle of Bentonville, Lt. Z. Ellis was wounded and reported missing. Ellis was serving as the battalion's acting adjutant at his death. Ellis's noticeable absence from Surgeon Hanahan's casualty return for Hagood's Brigade suggests he may have initially been treated as a wounded prisoner by U.S. Army medical personnel at the Harper House (XIV Corps Field Hospital) and left behind when the Federals departed. *NC Troops* indicates that he was killed at Bentonville on March 19, 1865. Lieutenant Ellis's name appears on a monument at Bentonville Battlefield State Historic Site, leading some to assume he is buried in the Confederate mass grave located there.
Source: *DC* (Raleigh), April 7, 1865; *NCT*, I:11; SHA, *Memoirs of Georgia*, 2:386; M270.

♦Flowers, Hugh, Private, Company D
Bentonville (Inconclusive)
According to Lt. Richard P. Allen's 1st Battalion NC casualty list from the battle of Bentonville, Pvt. Hugh Flowers was wounded and reported missing. Flowers's noticeable absence from Surgeon Hanahan's casualty return for Hagood's Brigade suggests he may have initially been treated as a wounded prisoner by U.S. Army medical personnel at the Harper House (XIV Corps Field Hospital) and left behind when the Federals departed. Flowers's name appears on a list of prisoners of war who were present in a Raleigh hospital on April 13, 1865, when the city was captured. Neither Flowers's service records nor *NC Troops* notes his wounding or possible capture at the battle of Bentonville. Further research is required.
Source: *DC* (Raleigh), April 7, 1865; *NCT*, I:33; M270.

▲French, Beverly Tucker, Sergeant, Company D
Wise's Forks
According to Surgeon Hanahan's "List of Killed and Wounded in Hagood's Brigade" at Wise's Forks, Sgt. B. Tucker French, Co. C, 1st Battalion NC, was wounded in the left side of the back and severely in the left foot. *NC Troops* notes that he transferred from Co. C of the battalion in January 1864. GH No. 3 "Register of Wounded and Operations" indicates Sgt. B. T. French, Co. D, 1st NC Artillery, was wounded on March 9, 1865, suffering from a gunshot wound to the left foot. His service records and *NC Troops* incorrectly note that French was transferred from Kinston to GH No. 3 in Greensboro on March 9, 1865. In National Archives Confederate Record Group 109, GH No. 3's location is erroneously identified as Greensboro. Goldsboro is the correct location. Confederate authorities began relocating GH No. 3 from Goldsboro to High Point on March 11, 1865, as part of the town's evacuation. The hospital resumed operations in High Point on or about March 19, 1865. The GH No. 3 Patient Registry lists a Sgt. B. T. French, entry no. 1833, of "Co. D, 1st NC Artillery." The hospital erred in recording his proper unit identification.
Source: Hanahan (WF), 1; GH No. 3 Ledger B, entry no. 48; *NCT*, I:33; M270; Sokolosky, *NC's Confederate Hospitals*, vol. 2; RG109, 6/291:36.

Gilchrist, John A., 1st Lieutenant, Company C
Bentonville
According to Lt. Richard P. Allen's 1st Battalion NC casualty list from the battle of Bentonville, Lt. J. A. Gilchrist was wounded. *NC Troops* notes that Lt. John A. Gilchrist was wounded in the battle of Bentonville on March 19, 1865. According to Gilchrist's service records, he was transferred from Weldon's Way Hospital No. 1 to GH No. 1 in Kittrell Springs during the first week of April 1865.
Source: *DC* (Raleigh), April 7, 1865; *NCT*, I:22; Clark, *Histories*, IV:312; M270.

♦Gilchrist, William C., Private, Company C
Bentonville (Inconclusive)
According to Lt. Richard P. Allen's 1st Battalion NC casualty list from the battle of Bentonville, Corp. W. C. Gilchrist was wounded and reported missing. Neither Gilchrist's service records nor *NC Troops* note that he was wounded and possibly captured at Bentonville. Gilchrist's noticeable absence from Surgeon Hanahan's casualty return for Hagood's Brigade suggests he may have initially been treated as a wounded

prisoner by U.S. Army medical personnel at the Harper House (XIV Corps Field Hospital) and left behind when the Federals departed. Further research is required.
Source: *DC* (Raleigh), April 7, 1865; *NCT*, I:25; M270.

♦Gillespie, D., Private, Company A
Bentonville (Inconclusive)
According to Lt. Richard P. Allen's 1st Battalion NC casualty list from the battle of Bentonville, three soldiers from Co. A were killed in the battle; Pvt. D. Gillespie was one. There is no D. Gillespie listed on the rolls. However, there is a Pvt. G. D. Gillespie, who served in Co. A, 1st Battalion NC, but Allen identified him as wounded at Bentonville. Further research is required.
Source: *DC* (Raleigh), April 7, 1865; M270.

▲Gillespie, G. D., Private, Company A
Bentonville
According to Surgeon Hanahan's "Return of Wounded for Hagood's Brigade" at Bentonville, Pvt. G. D. Gillespie, Co. A, 1st Battalion NC, was slightly wounded in the right cheek on March 19, 1865. His name also appears on Surgeon Tanner's "Return of Casualties in Hoke's Div. near Bentonville" and Lt. Richard P. Allen's compiled 1st Battalion casualty list from the battle. Additionally, both the *Daily Progress* and *NC Standard* listed a Pvt. __ Gillespie of Co. B, 1st Battalion as having been wounded in the "right cheek" on March 19, 1865, at Bentonville, and present in Raleigh's Baptist Church Hospital. Private G. D. Gillespie of Co. A is probably the same soldier listed by the newspapers as Pvt. Gillespie. Neither G. D. Gillespie's service records nor *NC Troops* note the wound he received at the battle of Bentonville or his hospitalization.
Source: Hanahan (BV), 2: Tanner (BV), 146; *DC* (Raleigh), April 7, 1865; *DP* (Raleigh), March 27, 1865; *NCS* (Raleigh), March 24, 1865; *NCT*, I:5; M270.

Gillespie, John W., Corporal, Company D
Bentonville
Captured at the battle of Bentonville on March 19, 1865. According to Lt. Richard P. Allen's 1st Battalion NC casualty list from the battle of Bentonville, Pvt. J. Gillespie, Co. B, was wounded and missing. Confined at Point Lookout, Maryland, and released upon taking the Oath of Allegiance on June 27, 1865. *NC Troops* notes that Gillespie transferred from Co. B of the battalion to D on January 13, 1864.
Source: *DC* (Raleigh), April 7, 1865; *NCT*, I:14, 33; M270.

▲Graham, Hugh, Private, Company A
Bentonville
According to Lt. Richard P. Allen's 1st Battalion NC casualty list from the battle of Bentonville, Pvt. H. Graham, Co. A, 1st Battalion NC, was wounded. Additionally, the *NC Standard* reported that Private Graham, 1st Battalion NC, whose given name was not listed, was admitted to Raleigh's Baptist Church Hospital with a wounded right arm. Private Hugh Graham of Co. A was probably the same soldier as Pvt. H. Graham. Neither Graham's service records nor *NC Troops* note the wound he received at the battle of Bentonville.
Source: *DC* (Raleigh), April 7, 1865; *NCS* (Raleigh), March 29, 1865; *DP* (Raleigh), March 27, 1865; *NCT*, I:5; M270.

▲Graham, Thomas S., Private, Company D
Bentonville
According to Surgeon Hanahan's "Return of Wounded for Hagood's Brigade" at Bentonville, Pvt. T. S. Graham, Co. C, 1st Battalion NC, was severely wounded in his jaw (fracture) on March 19, 1865. His name also appears on Surgeon Tanner's "Return of Casualties in Hoke's Div. near Bentonville." Thomas S. Graham's service records indicate that he was admitted to GH No. 13 (Pettigrew) in Raleigh on March 22, 1865, suffering from a gunshot wound to his mouth. Allen's compiled casualty list from the battle of Bentonville for 1st Battalion NC reported that Pvt. T. S. Graham, Co. D, was killed. Thomas S. Graham of Co. C is the same soldier as Pvt. T. S. Graham. The hospital registry notes that Graham died the next day. *NC Troops* does not note his wounding and death.

Source: Hanahan (BV), 4; Tanner (BV), 146; *NCS* (Raleigh), March 29, 1865; *DP* (Raleigh), March 27, 1865; M270; *DC* (Raleigh), April 7, 1865; *NCT*, I:25, 34.

♦▲Harris, Joseph P., 1st Sergeant, Company C
Bentonville

According to Lt. Richard P. Allen's 1st Battalion NC casualty list from the battle of Bentonville, Sgt. J. P. Harris, Co. C, was wounded and reported missing. Neither Harris's service records nor *NC Troops* note that he was wounded and captured at Bentonville. Harris's noticeable absence from Surgeon Hanahan's casualty return for Hagood's Brigade suggests he may have initially been treated as a wounded prisoner by U.S. Army medical personnel at the Harper House (XIV Corps Field Hospital) and left behind when the Federals departed. Further research is required.
Source: *DC* (Raleigh), April 7, 1865; *NCT*, I:25; M270.

Heath, William A., Private, Company B
Fort Anderson

Captured at Fort Anderson on February 19, 1865. Confined at Point Lookout, Maryland, and released upon taking the Oath of Allegiance on June 13, 1865.
Source: *NCT*, I:15; M270; NC Confederate Pension (Duplin County).

♦▲Henry, James A., Private, Company B
Wise's Forks

NC Troops notes that he was killed on March 8, 1865, at Kinston. However, according to Surgeon Hanahan's "List of Killed and Wounded in Hagood's Brigade" at Wise's Forks, Pvt. J. A. Henry, Co. B, 1st Battalion NC, was slightly wounded in the head. Private J. A. Henry also appears in Surgeon Tanner's "Return of Casualties near Kinston, March 8 & 10, 1865," as slightly wounded as well. Further research is required.
Source: *NCT*, I:15, 703; Hanahan (WF), 1; Tanner (WF), 137; M270.

▲Herring, John D., Private, Company B
Bentonville

According to Surgeon Hanahan's "Return of Wounded for Hagood's Brigade" at Bentonville, Pvt. J. D. Herring, Co. B, 1st Battalion NC, was slightly wounded in the head on March 20, 1865. Private J. D. Herring's name also appears on Surgeon Tanner's "Return of Casualties in Hoke's Div. near Bentonville" and Lt. Richard P. Allen's compiled 1st Battalion casualty list from the battle. Furthermore, the *Daily Progress* reported that Pvt. J. D. Herring, 1st Battalion NC, was at Raleigh's Baptist Church Hospital, suffering from a head wound. Private John D. Herring of Co. B is the same soldier as Pvt. J. D. Herring. Neither Herring's service records nor *NC Troops* note the wound he received at the battle of Bentonville.
Source: Hanahan (BV), 1; Tanner (BV), 146; *DC* (Raleigh), April 7, 1865; *NCS* (Raleigh), March 24, 1865; *DP* (Raleigh), March 27, 1865; *NCT*, I:15; M270.

Hines, William S., Private, Company B
Piney Grove

Captured at Piney Grove on March 18, 1865. Confined at Point Lookout, Maryland, and released upon taking the Oath of Allegiance on June 27, 1865. *NC Troops* notes that Hines resided in Sampson County at the time of his initial enlistment, which suggests he may have been home on furlough or other military duties at the time of his capture.
Source: *NCT*, I:15; M270.

♦Hodges, D., Private, Company A
Bentonville (Inconclusive)

According to Lt. Richard P. Allen's 1st Battalion NC casualty list from the battle of Bentonville, Pvt. D. Hodges, Co. A, was wounded. The battalion rolls do not list any Hodges with a given name beginning with the letter "D." Also, neither Hanahan nor Tanner list a D. Hodges on their casualty returns. Lieutenant Allen likely erred in his report, and Pvt. William T. Hodges of Co. A is probably the same soldier as Pvt. D. Hodges. See William T. Hodges below.
Source: *DC* (Raleigh), April 7, 1865; M270.

▲**Hodges, William T.**, Private, Company A,
Bentonville
According to Surgeon Hanahan's "Return of Wounded for Hagood's Brigade" at Bentonville, Pvt. W. T. Hodges, Co. A, 1st Battalion NC, was severely wounded in the right shoulder on March 19, 1865. Private W. T. Hodges's name also appears on Surgeon Tanner's "Return of Casualties in Hoke's Div. near Bentonville." Private William T. Hodges of Co. A is the same soldier as Pvt. W. T. Hodges. His service records and *NC Troops* incorrectly note that Hodges was hospitalized at GH No. 3 in Greensboro on an unspecified date in March 1865. In National Archives Confederate Record Group 109, General Hospital No. 3's location is erroneously identified as Greensboro. High Point is the correct location. Confederate authorities began relocating GH No. 3 from Goldsboro to High Point on March 11, 1865, as part of the town's evacuation. The hospital resumed operations in High Point on or about March 19, 1865. The No. 3 Patient Registry lists a Pvt. W. T. Hodges, entry no. 2337, of Co. A, admitted for unspecified reasons between March 21 and April 7, 1865. He was paroled there as a patient in May 1865.
Source: Hanahan (BV), 3; Tanner (BV), 146; *NCT*, I:6; M270; Sokolosky, *NC's Confederate Hospitals*, vol. 2; RG109, 6/291:46.

♦**Hughes, N. A.**, Private, Company C
Bentonville (Inconclusive)
According to Lt. Richard P. Allen's 1st Battalion NC casualty list from the battle of Bentonville, Pvt. N. A. Hughes, Co. C, was wounded. Unit rolls show no record of an N. A. Hughes. Further research is required.
Source: *DC* (Raleigh), April 7, 1865; M270.

♦**Hughes, Robert**, Private, Company C
Bentonville (Inconclusive)
According to Lt. Richard P. Allen's 1st Battalion NC casualty list from the battle of Bentonville, Pvt. Robert Hughes, Co. C, was wounded and reported missing. Neither his service records nor *NC Troops* note his wounding and possible capture at Bentonville. His noticeable absence from Hanahan's listing of casualties from Hagood's Brigade suggests he may have initially been treated as a wounded prisoner by U.S. Army medical personnel at the Harper House (XIV Corps Field Hospital) and left behind when the Federals departed. Further research is required.
Source: *DC* (Raleigh), April 7, 1865; M270.

Jackson, Lewis, Private, Company B
Bentonville
Captured at the battle of Bentonville on March 19, 1865. Confined at Point Lookout, Maryland, and released upon taking the Oath of Allegiance on June 14, 1865. According to Lt. Richard P. Allen's 1st Battalion NC casualty list from the battle of Bentonville, Pvt. L. Jackson, Co. B, was wounded and reported missing.
Source: M270; *NCT*, I:16; *DC* (Raleigh), April 7, 1865.

▲**James, John W.**, Private, Company A
Bentonville
According to Lt. Richard P. Allen's 1st Battalion NC casualty list from the battle of Bentonville, Pvt. J. W. James, Co. A, was reported missing. Private John W. James of Co. A is probably the same soldier as Pvt. J. W. James. Neither John W. James's service records nor *NC Troops* specify where James was captured; however, both sources do show that he was confined to several locations in Virginia at the end of the war. Based on Allen's report, Pvt. John W. James was captured in the battle of Bentonville.
Source: *DC* (Raleigh), April 7, 1865; *NCT*, I:6; M270.

Jewett, Richard B., Sergeant Major, Field & Staff
Bentonville
Captured at the battle of Bentonville on March 19, 1865. Confined at Point Lookout, Maryland, and released upon taking the Oath of Allegiance on June 4, 1865. According to Lt. Richard P. Allen's 1st Battalion NC casualty list from the battle of Bentonville, Sgt. R. B. Jewett, Field and Staff, was reported missing.

Source: M270; *NCT*, I:1, 25; *DC* (Raleigh), April 7, 1865.

♦Johnson, A., Private, Company B
Bentonville (Inconclusive)
According to Lt. Richard P. Allen's 1st Battalion NC casualty list from the battle of Bentonville, Pvt. A. Johnson, Co. B, was wounded and reported missing. There is no Pvt. A. Johnson in the National Archives Compiled Service Records for North Carolina Confederate soldiers.
Source: *DC* (Raleigh), April 7, 1865; M270.

▲Jones, George R., Private, Company C
Bentonville
According to Lt. Richard P. Allen's 1st Battalion NC casualty list from the battle of Bentonville, Pvt. G. R. Jones, Co. C, was wounded. Private George R. Jones is the same soldier as Pvt. G. R. Jones. His service records indicate that he was paroled at Thomasville on May 1, 1865. The actual location of his parole was the Thomasville General Hospital, where he was paroled as a patient.
Source: *NCT*, I:25; *DC* (Raleigh), April 7, 1865; M270; M1761, Thomasville General Hospital Paroles.

Jones, William T., Private, Company B
Clinton
William T. Jones's service records indicate he was captured in Clinton on March 20, 1865. Based on the location of his capture, Jones was absent from his command at the time of the battle of Bentonville. Confined at Hart's Island, New York, and released upon taking the Oath of Allegiance on June 19, 1865.
Source: *NCT*, I:16; M270.

▲Judge, Stephen M., Private, Company B
Bentonville
According to Surgeon Hanahan's "Return of Wounded for Hagood's Brigade" at Bentonville, Pvt. S. M. Judge, Co. B, was severely wounded in the right shoulder on March 19, 1865. Private S. M. Judge's name also appears on Surgeon Tanner's "Return of Casualties in Hoke's Div. near Bentonville" and Allen's compiled casualty list from the battle of Bentonville for 1st Battalion NC Heavy Artillery. Tanner listed Judge's wound as having impacted his "right arm." The *Daily Progress* reported that a Private Judge, with no first name noted, was at Raleigh's Baptist Church Hospital with a wounded right arm and eye. Private Stephen M. Judge of Co. B is probably the same soldier as Pvt. S. M. Judge. Hanahan and Tanner mistakenly list Private Judge as a member of Co. B, 40th NC State Troops (3rd NC Artillery). Neither Judge's service records nor *NC Troops* notes the wound he received at the battle of Bentonville.
Source: Hanahan (BV), 3; Tanner (BV), 147; *DC* (Raleigh), April 7, 1865*NCT*, I:16; *NCS* (Raleigh), March 24, 1865; *DP* (Raleigh), March 27, 1865; M270.

▲Kelly, Henry H., Private, Company C
Bentonville
According to Lt. Richard P. Allen's 1st Battalion NC casualty list from the battle of Bentonville, Pvt. H. H. Kelly, Co. C, was wounded and reported missing. *NC Troops* notes that Pvt. Henry H. Kelly was wounded in the right thigh at Bentonville on March 19, 1865. His service records do not indicate that he was wounded in March 1865.
Source: *DC* (Raleigh), April 7, 1865; *NCT*, I:25, 706; M270.

♦Kennedy, L., Private, Company B
Bentonville (Inconclusive)
According to Lt. Richard P. Allen's 1st Battalion NC casualty list from the battle of Bentonville, Pvt. L. Kennedy, Co. B, was wounded and reported missing. Besides Levi T. Kennedy, who was captured at Fort Anderson, no other soldiers with the same surname and first initial of "L" served in the battalion. Further research is required.
Source: *DC* (Raleigh), April 7, 1865; *NCT*, I:16; M270.

Kennedy, Levi T., Private, Company B

Fort Anderson
Wounded and captured on February 18, 1865, probably at or near Fort Anderson. He was later admitted to a U.S. Army hospital in Wilmington on March 5, 1865. No further records. Levi Thomas Kennedy survived the war and died on April 1, 1919. He is buried in the Kennedy Family Cemetery in Turkey, North Carolina.
Source: M270; *NCT*, I:16; Find a Grave.

▲**King, Everett**, Private, Company B
Bentonville
According to Lt. Richard P. Allen's 1st Battalion NC casualty list from the battle of Bentonville, Pvt. E. King, Co. B, was wounded and reported missing. Neither his service records nor *NC Troops* indicate that he was wounded and possibly captured at Bentonville. King's noticeable absence from Surgeon Hanahan's casualty return for Hagood's Brigade suggests he may have initially been treated as a wounded prisoner by U.S. Army medical personnel at the Harper House (XIV Corps Field Hospital) and left behind when the Federals departed. Everett King's name appears on a monument at Bentonville Battlefield State Historic Site, leading some to assume he is buried in the Confederate mass grave located there. Further research is required.
Source: *DC* (Raleigh), April 7, 1865; *NCT*, I:16, 706; M270.

♦▲**King, Solomon O.**, Private, Company C
Bentonville (Inconclusive)
According to Surgeon Hanahan's "Return of Wounded for Hagood's Brigade" at Bentonville, Pvt. S. B. King, Co. C, 1st Battalion NC, was slightly wounded in the left thigh on March 19, 1865. Private S. B. King's name also appears on Surgeon Tanner's "Return of Casualties in Hoke's Div. near Bentonville" and Allen's compiled casualty list from the battle 1st Battalion NC Heavy Artillery. Battalion rolls show no record of S. B. King; however, the rolls include the name of Solomon O. King. Solomon O. King is probably the soldier listed on Hanahan and Tanner's casualty returns. Neither King's service records nor *NC Troops* notes his wounding at Bentonville.
Source: Hanahan (BV), 3; Tanner (BV), 146; *DC* (Raleigh), April 7, 1865; *NCT*, I:26; M270.

Kitchen, John, Private, Company D
Bentonville
Captured at the battle of Bentonville on March 19, 1865. Confined at Point Lookout, Maryland, and released upon taking the Oath of Allegiance on June 28, 1865. Bentonville. According to Lt. Richard P. Allen's 1st Battalion NC casualty list from the battle of Bentonville, Pvt. J. Kitchen, Co. A, was reported missing.
Source: M270; *NCT*, I:34; *DC* (Raleigh), April 7, 1865.

▲**Lamb, William R.**, Private, Company B
Bentonville
According to Surgeon Hanahan's "Return of Wounded for Hagood's Brigade" at Bentonville, Pvt. W. R. Lamb, Co. B, 1st Battalion NC, was wounded in the little finger of his left hand on March 20, 1865, requiring amputation up to the first joint. Private W. R. Lamb is also listed in Surgeon Tanner's "Return of Casualties in Hoke's Div. near Bentonville" and Allen's compiled casualty list from the battle for 1st Battalion NC Heavy Artillery. The *Daily Progress* reported that a Private Lamb, with no first name noted, was at Raleigh's Baptist Church Hospital with a wounded finger. Private William R. Lamb of Co. B, 1st Battalion NC, is probably the same soldier as Pvt. W. R. Lamb. Neither Lamb's service records nor *NC Troops* note the wound he received at the battle of Bentonville.
Source: Hanahan (BV), 1; Tanner (BV), 146; *DC* (Raleigh), April 7, 1865; *DP* (Raleigh), March 27, 1865; *NCT*, I:16; M270.

▲**Larkins, Eli**, Private, Company B
Bentonville
Captured at Bentonville on March 19, 1865. Confined at Point Lookout, Maryland, and released upon taking the Oath of Allegiance on June 28, 1865. According to Lt. Richard P. Allen's 1st Battalion NC casualty list from the battle of Bentonville, Pvt. L. Larkins, Co. B, was wounded and reported missing.

Source: M270; *DC* (Raleigh), April 7, 1865; *NCT*, I:17.

♦Lesley, L., Private, Company A
Bentonville (Inconclusive)

According to Lt. Richard P. Allen's 1st Battalion NC casualty list from the battle of Bentonville, Pvt. L. Lesley, Co. A, was killed. There is no L. Lesley on the battalion rolls. Private Neil Leslie of Co. A may be the same soldier as Pvt. L. Leslie; however, neither Neil Leslie's service records nor *NC Troops* note his death at the battle of Bentonville. Further research is required.

Source: *NCT*, I:6; *DC* (Raleigh), April 7, 1865; Purser, *AIANCT*, II:1; M270.

▲McCall, Duncan D., Private, Company A,
Bentonville

According to Surgeon Hanahan's "Return of Wounded for Hagood's Brigade" at Bentonville, Pvt. D. D. McCall, Co. A, 1st Battalion NC, was slightly wounded in the chest on March 19, 1865. His name also appears on Surgeon Tanner's "Return of Casualties in Hoke's Div. near Bentonville" and Allen's compiled casualty list from the battle for 1st Battalion NC. Private Duncan D. McCall of Co. A is probably the same soldier as Pvt. D. D. McCall. His service records and *NC Troops* incorrectly note that McCall was hospitalized at GH No. 3 in Greensboro on an unspecified date in March 1865. In National Archives Confederate Record Group 109, General Hospital No. 3's location is erroneously identified as Greensboro. High Point is the correct location. Confederate authorities began relocating GH No. 3 from Goldsboro to High Point on March 11, 1865, as part of the town's evacuation. The hospital resumed operations in High Point on or about March 19, 1865. The No. 3 Patient Registry lists a Pvt. D. D. McCall, entry no. 2526, of Co. A, admitted for unspecified reasons between March 21 and 31, 1865. No further records.

Source: Hanahan (BV), 4; Tanner (BV), 146; *NCT*, I:6; M270; Sokolosky, *NC's Confederate Hospitals*, vol. 2; *DC* (Raleigh), April 7, 1865; RG109, 6/291:50.

▲McCall, John T., Private, Company A
Bentonville

Captured at the battle of Bentonville on March 19, 1865. Confined at Point Lookout, Maryland, and released upon taking the Oath of Allegiance on June 29, 1865. Lt. Richard P. Allen compiled a casualty list from the battle of Bentonville for 1st Battalion NC and erroneously reported Pvt. John S. McCall as missing.

Source: M270; *NCT*, I:6; *DC* (Raleigh), April 7, 1865.

▲McCoy, Kenneth, Private, Company A,
Bentonville

According to Surgeon Hanahan's "Return of Wounded for Hagood's Brigade" at Bentonville, Pvt. K. McCoy, Co. A, 1st Battalion NC, was severely wounded in the left side on March 20, 1865. Private K. McCoy's name also appears on Surgeon Tanner's "Return of Casualties in Hoke's Div. near Bentonville" and Allen's compiled casualty list from the battle for 1st Battalion NC. Private Kenneth McCoy of Co. A is the same soldier as Pvt. K. McCoy. Neither McCoy's service records nor *NC Troops* note the wound he received at the battle of Bentonville. McCoy's service records incorrectly note that he was admitted to GH No. 3 in Greensboro on an unspecified date in March 1865. In National Archives Confederate Record Group 109, General Hospital No. 3's location is erroneously identified as Greensboro. High Point is the correct location. Confederate authorities relocated GH No. 3 from Goldsboro to High Point on or about March 11, 1865, as part of the town's evacuation. The hospital resumed operations in High Point on or about March 19, 1865. The No. 3 Patient Registry lists a Pvt. Kenneth McCoy, 1st NC, entry no. 2523, of Co. A, admitted for unspecified reasons between March 21 and 31, 1865. McCoy was paroled as a patient in the hospital on May 1, 1865.

Source: Hanahan (BV), 1; Tanner (BV), 146; *NCT*, I:6; M270; Sokolosky, *NC's Confederate Hospitals*, vol. 2; *DC* (Raleigh), April 7, 1865; RG109, 6/291:50.

▲McDuffie, Luther Calvin, Private, Company B
Bentonville

NC Troops indicates that Pvt. Luther C. McDuffie was wounded on March 19, 1865, at Bentonville. According to Surgeon Hanahan's "Return of Wounded for Hagood's Brigade" at Bentonville, Pvt. B. McDuffy, Co. B, 1st Battalion NC, was slightly wounded in the head on March 20, 1865. Private B. McDuffy is also listed in Surgeon Tanner's "Return of Casualties in Hoke's Div. near Bentonville" and Allen's compiled casualty list from the battle for 1st Battalion NC. The March 29, 1865, edition of the *NC Standard* reported that Pvt. C. McDuffie was at GH No. 8 (Peace Institute) (Raleigh) suffering from a head wound. L. C. McDuffie's Confederate pension application indicates that he was wounded at Bentonville, "gunshot wound on right side of Frontal bone, and now suffers from Paralysis of left side." Private Luther C. McDuffie of Co. B is the same soldier listed by Hanahan and Tanner as Pvt. B. McDuffy. McDuffie was captured in a Raleigh hospital on April 13, 1865. Paroled in May 1865.
Source: *NCT*, I:17; Hanahan (BV), 1; Tanner (BV), 146; *DC* (Raleigh), April 7, 1865; *NCS* (Raleigh), March 29, 1865; M270; NC Confederate Pension (Pender County).

McDuffie, Robert John, Private, Company B
Fort Anderson
Captured at Fort Anderson on February 19, 1865. Confined at Point Lookout, Maryland, and released upon taking the Oath of Allegiance on June 29, 1865.
Source: M270; *NCT*, I:17; NC Confederate Widow's Pension (Cumberland County).

♦▲McEachin, Evander, Private, Company C
Wise's Forks (Inconclusive)
According to Surgeon Hanahan's "Killed and Wounded in Hagood's Brigade" at Wise's Forks, Pvt. V. McAchin, Co. C, 1st Battalion NC, was slightly wounded in the left breast. Private V. McAchin also appears in Surgeon Tanner's "Return of Casualties near Kinston, March 8 & 10, 1865." Private McEachin was admitted to GH No. 13 (Pettigrew) in Raleigh on March 10, 1865, for a non-battle-related illness and returned to duty on March 14, 1865. Private Evander McEachin may be the same soldier as Pvt. V. McAchin. Further research is required.
Source: Hanahan (WF), 1; Tanner (WF), 137; *NCT*, I:26; M270.

McGuire, John K., Private, Company A
Bentonville
Captured at the battle of Bentonville on March 19, 1865. Confined at Point Lookout, Maryland, and released upon taking the Oath of Allegiance on June 11, 1865. According to Lt. Richard P. Allen's 1st Battalion NC casualty list from the battle of Bentonville, Pvt. J. K. McGuire, Co. A, was reported missing.
Source: M270; *NCT*, I:7; *DC* (Raleigh), April 7, 1865.

♦▲McKay, James A., Private, Company C
Bentonville (Inconclusive)
According to Lt. Richard P. Allen's 1st Battalion NC casualty list from the battle of Bentonville, Pvt. J. A. McKay, Co. C, was wounded and reported missing. Private James A. McKay of Co. C is probably the same soldier as Pvt. J. A. McKay. Neither McKay's service records nor *NC Troops* note that he was wounded and captured at Bentonville. McKay's noticeable absence from Surgeon Hanahan's casualty return for Hagood's Brigade suggests he may have initially been treated as a wounded prisoner by U.S. Army medical personnel at the Harper House (XIV Corps Field Hospital) and left behind when the Federals departed. James McKay of Whiteville in Columbus County was admitted to an unspecified Confederate hospital in Raleigh on April 8, 1865. The Ladies Memorial Association of Raleigh records note that James McKay served in the 1st Battalion SC Reserves. No further records. Further research is required.
Source: *DC* (Raleigh), April 7, 1865; *NCT*, I:26; M270; Purser, *AIANCT*, I:1.

McKellar, James, Private, Company A
Bentonville (Inconclusive)
According to Surgeon Hanahan's "Return of Wounded for Hagood's Brigade" at Bentonville, Pvt. B. McKeller, Co. A, 1st Battalion NC, was severely wounded in the right arm on March 19, 1865. Private B. McKeller is also listed in Surgeon Tanner's "Return of Casualties in Hoke's Div. near Bentonville." Allen's

compiled casualty list from the battle of Bentonville for 1st Battalion NC Heavy Artillery reported that a soldier with a similar surname from Co. A, Private P. McKeiler, was wounded at Bentonville. The wounded soldier was probably Pvt. James McKellar of Co. A. Neither McKellar's service records nor *NC Troops* note the wound he received at the battle of Bentonville. Further research is required.
Source: Hanahan (BV), 4; Tanner (BV), 146; *DC* (Raleigh), April 7, 1865; *NCT*, I:7; M270.

McLaughlin, Archibald J., Private, Company A
Bentonville
Captured at the battle of Bentonville on March 19, 1865. Confined at Point Lookout, Maryland, and released upon taking the Oath of Allegiance on June 29, 1865. Lieutenant Richard P. Allen's compiled casualty list from the battle of Bentonville for 1st Battalion NC, Pvt. A. J. McLaughlin, Co. A, erroneously reported McLaughlin as killed.
Source: M270; *NCT*, I:7; *DC* (Raleigh), April 7, 1865.

McLean, Daniel L., Private, Company A
Bentonville
Captured at the battle of Bentonville on March 19, 1865. Confined at Point Lookout, Maryland, and released upon taking the Oath of Allegiance on June 29, 1865. According to Lt. Richard P. Allen's 1st Battalion NC casualty list from the battle of Bentonville, Pvt. D. S. McLean, Co. A, was reported missing. *NC Troops* notes that the middle initial is "L."
Source: M270; *NCT*, I:7; *DC* (Raleigh), April 7, 1865.

▲McNeill, Daniel Evander, Private, Company C
Wise's Forks
According to Surgeon Hanahan's "Killed and Wounded in Hagood's Brigade" at Wise's Forks, Pvt. D. E. McNeel, Co. C, 1st Battalion NC, was slightly wounded in the right breast. Private D. E. McNeil also appears in Surgeon Tanner's "Return of Casualties near Kinston, March 8 & 10, 1865." Neither McNeill's service records nor *NC Troops* note his wounding at Wise's Forks. McNeill survived the war but was murdered in August 1878. He is buried in the McNeill Cemetery, Red Springs, NC.
Source: Hanahan (WF), 1; Tanner (WF), 137; *NCT*, I:27; M270; Find a Grave; NC Confederate Widow's Pension (Robeson County).

▲McPhaul, John A., Private, Company C
Bentonville
According to Lt. Richard P. Allen's 1st Battalion NC casualty list from the battle of Bentonville, Pvt. J. A. McPhaul, Co. C, was wounded and reported missing. Private John A. McPhaul of Co. C is probably the same soldier as Corp. J. A. McPhaul. Neither McPhaul's service records nor *NC Troops* note that he was mortally wounded at Bentonville. McPhaul's noticeable absence from Surgeon Hanahan's casualty return for Hagood's Brigade suggests he may have initially been treated as a wounded prisoner by U.S. Army medical personnel at the Harper House (XIV Corps Field Hospital) and left behind when the Federals departed. Based on an 1866 listing of Confederate dead buried on the John Harper farm, published in Wilmington's *Daily Journal*, a Pvt. J. A. Methauls of 1st Battalion NC was interred there. As reported in the paper, J. A. Methauls is probably the same soldier as John A. McPhaul. J. A. McPhaul's name appears on a monument at Bentonville Battlefield State Historic Site, leading some to assume he is buried in the Confederate mass grave located there.
Source: *DC* (Raleigh), April 7, 1865; *NCT*, I:27, 709; M270; *DJ* (Wilmington, NC), August 8, 1866.

♦▲McPhaul, Maloy, Sergeant, Company A
Bentonville (Inconclusive)
The June 3, 1894, edition of the *Goldsboro Argus* reported that Pvt. Maloy A. McPhaul, Co. A, 1st Battalion NC, died at Bentonville's Harper House after being wounded during the battle. Neither McPhaul's service records nor *NC Troops* note his death. The name M. McPhaul appears on a monument at Bentonville Battlefield State Historic Site, leading some to assume he is buried in the Confederate mass grave located there. Further research is required.

Source: *NCT*, I:7; *Argus* (Goldsboro), June 3, 1894; M270.

♦Miller, M., Private, Company A
(Inconclusive)
The March 24, 1865, edition of the *NC Standard* reported that Pvt. M. Miller, Co. A, 1st Battalion NC, was admitted to Raleigh's Baptist Church Hospital with a wounded left arm. The name M. Miller also appears in the *Daily Progress*. There is no Pvt. M. Miller listed in the unit rolls. Both newspapers may have incorrectly listed M. Miller's unit as the 1st Battalion. A Pvt. Mack Miller of Co. A, 58th NC, was wounded at the battle of Bentonville. See Mack Miller listed under the 58th NC, page 173.
Source: *NCS* (Raleigh), March 24, 1865; *DP* (Raleigh), March 27, 1865; M270.

♦▲Moore, Hezekiah W., Drummer (Private), Company B
Bentonville (Inconclusive)
According to Surgeon Hanahan's "Return of Wounded for Hagood's Brigade" at Bentonville. Pvt. H. W. Moore, Co. B, 1st Battalion NC, was slightly wounded in the right knee on March 19, 1865. Additionally, Lt. Richard P. Allen's casualty list for 1st Battalion NC from the battle of Bentonville reported Pvt. H. W. Moore, Co. B, was wounded during the battle. Neither Hezekiah W. Moore's service records nor *NC Troops* note that he was wounded at Bentonville. Hezekiah W. Moore was a resident of New Hanover County when he first enlisted into the 1st Battalion in June 1862. A Hezekiah W. Moore of New Hanover County appears on the 41st NC (3rd NC Cavalry) rolls, who joined the unit in October 1861 but was later discharged in June 1862. A Confederate pension filed by H. W. Moore of Sampson County in 1908, indicates that he served in the 3rd NC Cavalry before being discharged in 1862. He further noted that "he was not wounded in the war." Further research is required.
Source: Hanahan (BV), 4; Tanner (BV), 146; *DC* (Raleigh), April 7, 1865; *NCT*, I:18; *NCT*, II:187; M270; NC Confederate Pension (Sampson County).

▲Murray, Murdock W., Private, Company B
Bentonville
Captured at the battle of Bentonville on March 19, 1865. Confined at Point Lookout, Maryland, and released upon taking the Oath of Allegiance on June 29, 1865. According to Lt. Richard P. Allen's 1st Battalion NC casualty list from the battle of Bentonville, Pvt. M. W. Murry, Co. B, was wounded and reported missing.
Source: M270; *NCT*, I:18.

Newton, Nathan W., Private, Company B
Fort Anderson
Captured at Fort Anderson on February 19, 1865. Confined at Point Lookout, Maryland, and released upon taking the Oath of Allegiance on June 29, 1865.
Source: M270; *NCT*, I:19.

▲Phillips, James W., Private, Company D
Bentonville
According to Surgeon Hanahan's "Return of Wounded for Hagood's Brigade" at Bentonville, Pvt. J. W. Phillips, Co. C, 1st Battalion NC, was slightly wounded in the right shoulder on March 19, 1865. Private J. W. Phillips is also listed in Surgeon Tanner's "Return of Casualties in Hoke's Div. near Bentonville." Private James W. Phillips of Co. C is probably the same soldier as Pvt. J. W. Phillips. *NC Troops* does not note the wound he received at the battle of Bentonville. His service records indicate that Phillips was admitted to GH No. 3 in High Point on an unspecified date in March 1865, and he was paroled there as a patient on May 1, 1865. The No. 3 Patient Registry lists a Pvt. J. W. Phillips, entry no. 2429, of Co. C, admitted for unspecified reasons between March 21 and 31, 1865. Phillips was paroled as a patient in the hospital on May 1, 1865. The April 7, 1865, edition of the *Daily Confederate* mistakenly reported that Phillips was killed at Bentonville.
Source: Hanahan (BV), 3; Tanner (BV), 146; *NCT*, I:36; M270; RG109, 6/291:48; *DConf* (Raleigh), April 7, 1865.

▲Potter, A. Gustavus, Private, Company C

Bentonville
According to Surgeon Hanahan's "Return of Wounded for Hagood's Brigade" at Bentonville, Pvt. A. G. Potter, Co. C, 1st Battalion NC, was severely wounded in the right thigh on March 19, 1865. Private A. G. Potter is also listed in Surgeon Tanner's "Return of Casualties in Hoke's Div. near Bentonville" and Allen's compiled casualty list from the battle for 1st Battalion NC. The unit rolls do not list a Potter with a first name beginning with the letter A. However, Gustavus Potter, Co. C, 1st Battalion NC, is listed as having no middle name. Neither Gustavus Potter's service records nor *NC Troops* note that he was wounded at the battle of Bentonville. A. G. Potter's Confederate pension application, listed as having served in Co. C, 1st Battalion NC, indicates that he was wounded in the right hip at Bentonville. A. G. Potter is the soldier listed on Hanahan and Tanner's returns.
Source: Hanahan (BV), 4; Tanner (BV), 146; *DC* (Raleigh), April 7, 1865; *NCT*, I:28; M270; NC Confederate Pension (Bladen County).

▲**Powers, George G.**, Private, Company B
Bentonville
Captured at the battle of Bentonville on March 19, 1865. According to Lt. Richard P. Allen's 1st Battalion NC casualty list from the battle of Bentonville, Pvt. G. G. Powers, Co. B, was wounded and reported missing. Confined at Point Lookout, Maryland, where he died of pneumonia on May 24, 1865.
Source: *NCT*, I:19; M270.

▲**Powers, Kitchen F.**, Corporal, Company B
Bentonville
Captured at the battle of Bentonville on March 19, 1865. According to Lt. Richard P. Allen's 1st Battalion NC casualty list from the battle of Bentonville Heavy Artillery, Corp. Corp. K. F. Powers, Co. B, was wounded and reported missing. Confined at Point Lookout, Maryland, and released upon taking the Oath of Allegiance on June 16, 1865.
Source: *NCT*, I:19; M270; NC Confederate Pension (Pender County).

▲**Powers, Nicaner William**, Private, Company B
Bentonville
Captured at the battle of Bentonville on March 19, 1865. According to Lt. Richard P. Allen's 1st Battalion NC casualty list from the battle of Bentonville, Pvt. N. W. Powers, Co. B, was wounded and reported missing. Confined at Point Lookout, Maryland, and released upon taking the Oath of Allegiance on June 14, 1865.
Source: *NCT*, I:19; M270.

♦▲**Rabon, Armand**, Private, Company C
Bentonville (Inconclusive)
According to Lt. Richard P. Allen's 1st Battalion NC casualty list from the battle of Bentonville, Pvt. A. Rabon, Co. C, was killed. Neither Rabon's service records nor *NC Troops* note that he died at the battle of Bentonville. A Pvt. Arnold Rabon's name appears on a monument at Bentonville Battlefield State Historic Site, leading some to assume he is buried in the Confederate mass grave at the site. It is unclear whether Armand is the same soldier as Arnold; further research is required.
Source: *NCT*, I:28, 714; *DC* (Raleigh), April 7, 1865; Purser, *AIANCT*, II:1; M270.

Rankin, John T., Lieutenant, Company D
Town Creek
Wounded and captured at the battle of Town Creek on February 20, 1865. Confined at Fort Delaware, Delaware, and released upon taking the Oath of Allegiance on May 26, 1865. "At Town Creek Lieutenant John T. Rankin . . . greatly distinguished himself, fighting his guns until shot down and his section and men surrounded and captured by the enemy." John T. Rankin is the oldest son of Capt. Robert G. Rankin of 1st Battalion NC. Lieutenant Rankin is buried at Oakdale Cemetery in Wilmington, North Carolina.
Source: *NCT*, I:31, 714; M270; Clark, *Histories*, IV:311; Find a Grave.

Rankin, Robert George, Captain, Company A
Bentonville
Wounded at the battle of Bentonville on March 19, 1865, while commanding the battalion. According to Surgeon Hanahan's "Return of Wounded for Hagood's Brigade" at Bentonville, Capt. R. G. Rankin, Co. A, 1st Battalion NC, was severely wounded in the "lower third right thigh" on March 19, 1865. His name also appears in Surgeon Tanner's "Return of Casualties in Hoke's Div. near Bentonville" and Lt. Richard P. Allen's compiled casualty list from the battle for 1st Battalion NC. The *Daily Confederate* reported Rankin's coat was "pierced in eleven places by balls," and he had "three wounds on his person." The March 29, 1865, edition of the *NC Standard* published that Rankin died in Raleigh on March 26. Captain Rankin's name appears on a monument at Bentonville Battlefield State Historic Site, leading some to assume he is buried in the Confederate mass grave there. However, he is buried at Oakdale Cemetery in Wilmington, North Carolina.
Source: Hanahan (BV), 4; Tanner (BV), 146; Clark, *Histories*, IV:312; *NCT*, I:2, 714; *DC* (Raleigh), March 24, 1865, and April 7, 1865; *NCS* (Raleigh), March 29, 1865; Purser, *AIANCT*, I:1; M270; Find a Grave.

◆**Ray, W.**, Private, Company C
Bentonville (Inconclusive)
According to Surgeon Hanahan's "Return of Wounded for Hagood's Brigade" at Bentonville, Pvt. W. Ray, Co. C, 1st Battalion NC, was slightly wounded on the left side on March 19, 1865. Private S. B. King's name also appears on Surgeon Tanner's "Return of Casualties in Hoke's Div. near Bentonville" and Lt. Richard P. Allen's compiled casualty list from the battle for 1st Battalion NC Heavy Artillery. The battalion rolls do not include a soldier with the surname Ray, whose given name begins with the letter W. Further research is required.
Source: Hanahan (BV), 4; Tanner (BV), 146; *DC* (Raleigh), April 7, 1865; M270.

▲**Reasons, Joseph T.**, Private, Company B
Fort Anderson
According to Wilmington's *Daily Journal*, J. G. Reason, Co. B, 1st Battalion NC, was wounded in the hand during the engagement at Fort Anderson and admitted to GH No. 4 in the port city on February 19, 1865. Private Joseph T. Reasons is probably the same soldier as Pvt. J. G. Reason. *NC Troops* does not identify Reasons as having been wounded at Fort Anderson. Received a 60-day furlough on February 20, 1865.
Source: *DJ* (Wilmington, NC), February 20, 1865; *NCT*, I:19; M270.

◆**Reynolds, Lewis**, Private, Company B
Wise's Forks (Inconclusive)
According to Surgeon Hanahan's "List of Killed and Wounded in Hagood's Brigade" at Wise's Forks, Pvt. E. B. Reynolds, Co. B, 1st Battalion NC, was slightly wounded in the left temple. No Reynolds is listed on the rolls, with the first and middle names beginning with E and B. Further research is required.
Source: Hanahan (WF), 1; M270.

▲**Rivenbark, Matthew J.**, Sergeant, Company B
Bentonville
According to Surgeon Hanahan's "Return of Wounded for Hagood's Brigade" at Bentonville, Sgt. M. J. Rivenbark, Co. B, 1st Battalion NC, was severely wounded in the right hand on March 19, 1865. Sergeant M. J. Rivenbark is also listed in Surgeon Tanner's "Return of Casualties in Hoke's Div. near Bentonville" and Allen's compiled casualty list from the battle for 1st Battalion NC Heavy Artillery. The *Daily Progress* reported that a Sgt. M. J. Rivenbank was a patient in Raleigh's Baptist Church Hospital with an injured left hand. The newspaper misspelled his surname in the listing. Sergeant Matthew J. Rivenbark of Co. B is the same soldier as Sgt. M. J. Rivenbark. Neither Rivenbark's service records nor *NC Troops* note the wound he received at the battle of Bentonville.
Source: Hanahan (BV), 2; Tanner (BV), 146; *DC* (Raleigh), April 7, 1865; *DP* (Raleigh), March 27, 1865; *NCS* (Raleigh), March 24, 1865; *NCT*, I:20, 715; M270.

Robeson, David G., 2nd Lieutenant, Company A

Piney Grove
Captured in Piney Grove on March 19, 1865. Based on the location of his capture, Robeson was absent from his command at the time of the battle of Bentonville. Confined at Johnson's Island, Ohio, and released upon taking the Oath of Allegiance on June 17, 1865.
Source: *NCT*, I:2; M270.

▲**Rodgers, William B.**, Private, Company C
Bentonville
According to Lt. Richard P. Allen's 1st Battalion NC casualty list from the battle of Bentonville, Pvt. W. B. Rodgers, Co. C, was wounded and reported missing. Private William B. Rodgers of Co. C is probably the same soldier as Pvt. W. B. Rogers. Neither Rodgers's service records nor *NC Troops* note that he was wounded and captured at the battle of Bentonville. Rodgers's noticeable absence from Surgeon Hanahan's casualty return for Hagood's Brigade suggests he may have initially been treated as a wounded prisoner by U.S. Army medical personnel at the Harper House (XIV Corps Field Hospital) and left behind when the Federals departed. Further research is required.
Source: *DC* (Raleigh), April 7, 1865; *NCT*, I:29; M270.

▲**Russ, William Henry**, Private, Company C
Bentonville
Captured near Bentonville on March 19, 1865. According to Lt. Richard P. Allen's 1st Battalion NC casualty list from the battle of Bentonville, Pvt. W. H. Russ, Co. C, was wounded and reported missing. Russ's noticeable absence from Surgeon Hanahan's casualty return for Hagood's Brigade suggests he may have initially been treated as a wounded prisoner by U.S. Army medical personnel at the Harper House (XIV Corps Field Hospital) before being turned over to authorities. Confined at Point Lookout, Maryland, and released upon taking the Oath of Allegiance on June 17, 1865.
Source: *NCT*, I:29; *DC* (Raleigh), April 7, 1865; M270; NC Confederate Pension (Bladen County).

▲**Sikes, George W.**, Private, Company C
Bentonville
Captured at the battle of Bentonville on March 19, 1865. According to Lt. Richard P. Allen's 1st Battalion NC casualty list from the battle of Bentonville, Pvt. G. W. Sikes, Co. C, was wounded and reported missing. Sikes's noticeable absence from Surgeon Hanahan's casualty return for Hagood's Brigade suggests he may have initially been treated as a wounded prisoner by U.S. Army medical personnel at the Harper House (XIV Corps Field Hospital) before being turned over to authorities. His service records indicate that Sikes was later confined at Point Lookout, Maryland, and released upon taking the Oath of Allegiance on June 20, 1865.
Source: *NCT*, I:29; *DC* (Raleigh), April 7, 1865; M270.

▲**Simpson, John O.**, Private, Company C
Bentonville
According to Lt. Richard P. Allen's 1st Battalion NC casualty list from the battle of Bentonville, Pvt. J. O. Simpson, Co. C, was wounded and reported missing. Private John O. Simpson of Co. C is probably the same soldier as Pvt. J. O. Simpson. Neither Simpson's service records nor *NC Troops* note that he was wounded and captured at the battle of Bentonville. Simpson's noticeable absence from Surgeon Hanahan's casualty return for Hagood's Brigade suggests he may have initially been treated as a wounded prisoner by U.S. Army medical personnel at the Harper House (XIV Corps Field Hospital) and left behind when the Federals departed. Further research is required.
Source: *DC* (Raleigh), April 7, 1865; *NCT*, I:29, 716; M270.

♦**Stewart [Steward], C. E.**, Private, Company A
Bentonville (Inconclusive)
According to Surgeon Hanahan's "Return of Wounded for Hagood's Brigade" at Bentonville, Pvt. C. E. Stewart, Co. A, 1st Battalion NC, was slightly wounded in the right wrist on March 19, 1865. Private C. E. Stewart is also listed in Surgeon Tanner's "Return of Casualties in Hoke's Div. near Bentonville" and Allen's

compiled casualty list from the battle for 1st Battalion NC. Additionally, both the *Daily Progress* and *NC Standard* reported a Pvt. C. E. Steward of Co. A, 1st Battalion, wounded in the "right wrist" in Raleigh's Baptist Church Hospital. Battalion rolls show no record of a C. E. Stewart or Steward. Further research is required.
Source: Hanahan (BV), 2; Tanner (BV), 146; *DC* (Raleigh), April 7, 1865; *DP* (Raleigh), March 27, 1865; *NCS* (Raleigh), March 24, 1865; M270.

▲Stone, Duncan E., Private, Company C
Bentonville
According to Surgeon Hanahan's "Return of Wounded for Hagood's Brigade" at Bentonville, Pvt. D. Stone, Co. C, 1st Battalion NC, was severely wounded in the right parietal bone on March 19, 1865, at Bentonville. Private D. Stone is also listed in Surgeon Tanner's "Return of Casualties in Hoke's Div. near Bentonville" and Allen's compiled casualty list from the battle for 1st Battalion NC. Private Duncan E. Stone of Co. C is probably the same soldier as Pvt. D. Stone. Stone's service records note he was admitted to Raleigh's GH No. 13 (Pettigrew) on March 23, 1865, with a gunshot wound to the right side of his head and meningitis. However, *NC Troops* does not note that Stone's wound occurred at the battle of Bentonville. Stone later died from his wounds on March 29, 1865, and is buried at Oakwood Cemetery in Raleigh, North Carolina.
Source: Hanahan (BV), 2; Tanner (BV), 146; *DC* (Raleigh), April 7, 1865; *NCT*, I:29; M270.

Sutton, John A., Private, Company D
Bentonville
Captured at the battle of Bentonville on March 19, 1865. Confined at Point Lookout, Maryland, and released upon taking the Oath of Allegiance on June 19, 1865.
Source: *NCT*, I:37; M270; NC Confederate Pension (Bladen County).

▲Taylor, Gilbert C., Corporal, Company A
Bentonville
According to Lt. Richard P. Allen's 1st Battalion NC casualty list from the battle of Bentonville, Corp. D. C. Taylor, Co. A, was wounded. Corporal Gilbert C. Taylor of Co. A is probably the same soldier as Corp. D. C. Taylor. The June 3, 1894, edition of the *Goldsboro Argus* reported that Pvt. Gilbert C. Taylor died at Bentonville's Harper House after being wounded during the battle. Neither Taylor's service records nor *NC Troops* note the wound he received at the battle of Bentonville. G. C. Taylor's name appears on a monument at Bentonville Battlefield State Historic Site, leading some to assume he is buried in the Confederate mass grave at the site. Further research is required.
Source: *NCT*, I:9; *DC* (Raleigh), April 7, 1865; *Argus* (Goldsboro), June 3, 1894; M270.

Taylor, Jacob W., 1st Lieutenant, Company B
Bentonville
Captured at the battle of Bentonville on March 19, 1865. Confined at Johnson's Island, Ohio, and released upon taking the Oath of Allegiance on June 17, 1865. Jacob was the brother of Capt. John William Taylor. According to Lt. Richard P. Allen's 1st Battalion NC casualty list from the battle of Bentonville, Lt. J. W. Taylor, Co. B, was wounded and reported missing.
Source: M270; *NCT*, I:11.

▲Taylor, John William, Captain, Company B
Bentonville
According to Surgeon Hanahan's "Return of Wounded for Hagood's Brigade" at Bentonville, Capt. J. W. Taylor, Co. B, 1st Battalion NC, suffered a severe fracture of his left shoulder joint on March 19, 1865. The injury proved mortal. According to Lt. Richard P. Allen's 1st Battalion NC casualty list from the battle of Bentonville, Capt. J. W. Taylor, Co. B, was wounded. *NC Troops* incorrectly notes that Taylor died at home in New Hanover County on April 4, 1865. He died on the same date at Mr. Willie J. Palmer's residence in Raleigh. Palmer, the superintendent of the North Carolina Institute for the Deaf, Dumb, and Blind, was an old acquaintance of Taylor and had him removed from the Officer's Hospital to his home. Oral family

history maintains that Captain Taylor's widowed wife, Phebe, sent their son Knox and a farmhand to Raleigh to return his remains home to their New Hanover County farm.
Source: Hanahan (BV), 4; Clark, *Histories*, IV:312; *NCT*, I:11, 718; *DC* (Raleigh), April 7, 1865; M270; W. J. Palmer to Mrs. Taylor, April 11, 1865, Taylor Papers, Bentonville Battlefield State Historic Site; ibid.

▲Taylor, Lewis, Private, Company B
Wise's Forks
According to Surgeon Hanahan's "List of Killed and Wounded in Hagood's Brigade" at Wise's Forks, Pvt. L. Taylor, Co. B, 1st Battalion NC, was severely wounded in the right groin. Private L. Taylor also appears in Surgeon Tanner's "Return of Casualties near Kinston, March 8 & 10, 1865." *NC Troops* notes that Pvt. Lewis Taylor was wounded at Kinston on March 8, 1865. Taylor's service records indicate that he was admitted to GH No. 13 (Pettigrew) in Raleigh on March 11, 1865, suffering from a gunshot in his right thigh. On an undetermined date, Pvt. Lewis Taylor was transferred to GH No. 3 in High Point, where he was admitted for unspecified reasons. Taylor was later paroled there as a patient on May 1, 1865. Lewis Taylor's Confederate pension states that he was wounded at Kinston on or about March 8, 1865. His physician's statement described his wound as a "gunshot wound in [the] right hip joint, ball there yet, cannot discover its whereabouts, which renders him totally unfit for labor."
Source: Hanahan (WF), 1; Tanner (WF), 137; *NCS* (Raleigh), March 29, 1865; *NCT*, I:20; M270; RG109, 6/291:50; NC Confederate Pension (Duplin County).

▲Taylor, Major J., Private, Company B
Bentonville
According to Lt. Richard P. Allen's 1st Battalion NC casualty list from the battle of Bentonville, Pvt. M. Taylor, Co. B, was wounded and reported missing. Private Major J. Taylor is the same soldier as Pvt. M. Taylor. Neither *NC Troops* nor his service records indicate that he was wounded and captured at Bentonville. His noticeable absence from Hanahan's listing of casualties from Hagood's Brigade suggests he may have initially been treated as a wounded prisoner by U.S. Army medical personnel at the Harper House (XIV Corps Field Hospital) and left behind when the Federals departed. He later died at an undetermined location on April 5, 1865. M. J. Taylor's name appears on a monument at Bentonville Battlefield State Historic Site, leading some to assume he is buried in the Confederate mass grave located there. However, Taylor is buried in Linton Cemetery, Magnolia, North Carolina. Major J. Taylor was the brother of Capt. John William Taylor of 1st Battalion. Further research is required.
Source: *NCT*, I:20, 718; *DC* (Raleigh), April 7, 1865; *Argus* (Goldsboro), June 3, 1894; M270; Find a Grave.

Thornton, Moore Lee, Private, Company A
Clinton
Moore Lee Thornton's service records note that he was captured in Clinton on March 22, 1865, which implies he was absent during the battle of Bentonville. Confined at Hart's Island, New York, and released upon taking the Oath of Allegiance on June 19, 1865. His name does not appear in Lt. Richard P. Allen's compiled casualty list from the battle for 1st Battalion NC Heavy Artillery.
Source: M270; *NCT*, I:10; M270.

▲Underhill, John, Private, Company C
Bentonville
According to Surgeon Hanahan's "Return of Wounded for Hagood's Brigade" at Bentonville, Pvt. J. Underhill, Co. C, 1st Battalion NC, was wounded in his left leg on March 20, 1865, requiring amputation up to his upper thigh. Private J. Underhill is also listed in Surgeon Tanner's "Return of Casualties in Hoke's Div. near Bentonville" and Allen's compiled casualty list from the battle for 1st Battalion NC. Private John Underhill of Co. C is probably the same soldier as Pvt. J. Underhill. Underhill was admitted to GH No. 13 (Pettigrew) in Raleigh with an amputated hip on March 24, 1865, and died there the same day. Underhill is buried at Oakwood Cemetery in Raleigh, North Carolina. *NC Troops* does not indicate that the mortal wound was received at the battle of Bentonville. Susan Underhill's pension application includes two sworn statements from individuals who witnessed Pvt. John Underhill's terrible fate at Bentonville. One soldier, Pvt. Mordecai Albertson of Co. G, 40th NC, recalled during the retreat from Bentonville that he witnessed

Underhill "in an ambulance with his leg amputated and was in a dying condition." Another soldier from Co. G, 40th NC, Pvt. Benjamin S. Barwick observed the wounded Underhill "with his leg off above the knee."
Source: Hanahan (BV), 1; Tanner (BV), 146; *DC* (Raleigh), April 7, 1865; *NCT*, I:30; M270; NC Widow's Pension (Lenoir County).

♦▲Watts, Lewis, Private, Company C
Bentonville (Inconclusive)
According to Lt. Richard P. Allen's 1st Battalion NC casualty list from the battle of Bentonville, Pvt. L. Watts, Co. C, was wounded. Private Lewis Watts of Co. C is probably the same soldier as Pvt. L. Watts. Neither Watts's service records nor *NC Troops* note his wounding at the battle of Bentonville. Additionally, Surgeon Hanahan and Tanner's casualty returns both list a Pvt. L. Wadkins, Co. D, slightly wounded in the left leg. However, unit rolls show no record of L. Wadkins. This may have been a transcription error on Hanahan and Tanner's part, and that Pvt. Lewis was the same wounded soldier treated by the surgeons. Lewis Watts's Confederate pension application does not refer to having been wounded at Bentonville, only that he "suffers from infirmity of age."
Source: *DC* (Raleigh), April 7, 1865; *NCT*, I:30; M270; NC Confederate Pension (Robeson County).

▲Wilson, Amzi R., Private, Company B
Bentonville
NC Troops indicates that Pvt. Amzi R. Wilson presumably was killed in action at the battle of Bentonville on March 19, 1865. According to Lt. Richard P. Allen's 1st Battalion NC casualty list from the battle of Bentonville, Pvt. A. Wilson, Co. B, was wounded and reported missing. Private Amzi R. Wilson of Co. B is probably the same soldier as Pvt. A. R. Wilson. Wilson's noticeable absence from Surgeon Hanahan's casualty return for Hagood's Brigade suggests he may have initially been treated as a wounded prisoner by U.S. Army medical personnel at the Harper House (XIV Corps Field Hospital) and left behind when the Federals departed. *NC Troops* notes that he died at Bentonville on March 19, 1865. However, another source indicates that Pvt. Amzi R. Wilson died on April 19, 1865, and is buried in the Merritt Cemetery in Clinton, North Carolina.
Source: *NCT*, I:21, 721; *DC* (Raleigh), April 7, 1865; M270; https://www.familysearch.org/ark:/61903/3:1:3Q9M-CST7-S7CS-P?view=index.

▲Wilson, Francis M., Private, Company B
Bentonville
According to Surgeon Hanahan's "Return of Wounded for Hagood's Brigade" at Bentonville, Pvt. F. M. Wilson, Co. B, 1st Battalion NC, was severely wounded on March 20, 1865, in the right breast, fracturing his clavicle, requiring amputation up to the first joint. Private F. M. Wilson is also listed in Surgeon Tanner's "Return of Casualties in Hoke's Div. near Bentonville" and Allen's compiled casualty list from the battle for 1st Battalion NC. The *NC Standard* reported Wilson was at GH No. 8 (Peace Institute) in Raleigh, wounded in the shoulder. No further records.
Source: Hanahan (BV), 1; Tanner (BV), 146; *DC* (Raleigh), April 7, 1865; *NCS* (Raleigh), March 29, 1865; *NCT*, I:21; M270.

♦Winfry, J. G., Private, Company A
(Inconclusive)
According to Lt. Richard P. Allen's 1st Battalion NC casualty list from the battle of Bentonville, Pvt. J. G. Winfry, Co. A, was reported missing. A file for J. G. Winfry is not found in the National Archives Compiled Service Records for North Carolina Confederate soldiers. Further research is required.
Source: *DC* (Raleigh), April 7, 1865; M270.

Captain Robert G. Rankin
Mortally Wounded on March 19, 1865, at Bentonville
Died March 26, 1865, in Raleigh
Acting Commander, 1st Battalion NC Heavy Artillery

(Courtesy of Bentonville Battlefield State Historic Site)

10th Regiment North Carolina State Troops (1st North Carolina Artillery)

Best, Richard W., Private, Company F
Neuse River Bridge
Captured at Neuse River Bridge on March 19, 1865. Confined at Hart's Island, New York, and released upon taking the Oath of Allegiance on June 19, 1865. Based on the date and location of Best's capture, he was probably taken by advance elements of Maj. Gen. Oliver O. Howard's Right Wing. In August 1914, Richard W. Best applied for admission to the North Carolina Soldier's Home in Raleigh.
Source: *NCT*, I:103; M270; NC Confederate Pension (Wayne County).

Best, W. T., Corporal, Company F
Goldsboro
Captured at Goldsboro on March 19, 1865. Confined at Hart's Island, New York, and released upon taking the Oath of Allegiance on June 19, 1865. Based on the date and location of Best's capture, he was probably taken by advance elements of Maj. Gen. Oliver O. Howard's Right Wing.
Source: *NCT*, I:103; M270; NC Confederate Pension (Wayne County).

Brafford, Nathan, Private, Company F
Goldsboro
Captured at Goldsboro on March 20, 1865. Confined at Hart's Island, New York, and released upon taking the Oath of Allegiance on June 18, 1865. Based on the date and location of Brafford's capture, he was probably taken by advance elements of Maj. Gen. Oliver O. Howard's Right Wing.
Source: *NCT*, I:103; M270.

Brewer, Munro, Private, Company B
Goldsboro (Post Bentonville)
Captured at Goldsboro on March 28, 1865. Confined at Hart's Island, New York, and released upon taking the Oath of Allegiance on June 19, 1865.
Source: *NCT*, I:53; M270; NC Confederate Pension (Wayne County).

Britt, Noah, Private, Company F
Goldsboro
Captured at Goldsboro on March 19, 1865. Confined at Point Lookout, Maryland, where he died on May 2, 1865, of scurvy. Based on the date and location of Britt's capture, he was probably taken by advance elements of Maj. Gen. Oliver O. Howard's Right Wing.
Source: *NCT*, I:103; M270.

Britt, Thomas, Private, Company F
Unspecified Location
U.S. Army records indicated that he was captured in Charleston County, NC, on March 19, 1865. Probably captured in Johnston County. Confined at Point Lookout, Maryland, and released upon taking the Oath of Allegiance on June 23, 1865.
Source: *NCT*, I:103; M270.

▲**Brockwell, Hutson**, Private, Company F
Unspecified Location
According to the Barbee Wayside Hospital patient registry in High Point, Pvt. H. Brockwell of Co. F, 10th NC, was admitted on March 9, 1865, suffering from a gunshot wound to the face. Neither Brockwell's service records nor *NC Troops* note his wounding and hospitalization at High Point. Further research is required.
Source: Barbee Wayside Hospital Registry, no. 5750; *NCT*, I:103; M270.

Capps, Henry G., Private, Company F

Goldsboro
Captured at Goldsboro on March 20, 1865. Confined at Hart's Island, New York, and released upon taking the Oath of Allegiance on June 18, 1865. Based on the date and location of Capp's capture, he was probably taken by advance elements of Maj. Gen. Oliver O. Howard's Right Wing. On his Confederate pension application, he used the middle initial "G."
Source: *NCT*, I:104; M270; NC Confederate Pension (Johnston County).

Hampson, Joseph M., Private, Company F
Goldsboro
Captured in a Goldsboro hospital on March 19, 1865, probably the former GH No. 3. Following the battle of Wise's Forks, on March 11, 1865, General Hospital No. 3 staff relocated to High Point to reopen the hospital there, leaving behind Dr. Benjamin F. Cobb to care for those patients unable to survive transfer to other hospitals. Confined at Military Prison, Camp Hamilton, Virginia, and released upon taking the Oath of Allegiance on May 29, 1865.
Source: *NCT*, I:106; Sokolosky, *NC's Confederate Hospitals*, vol. 2; M270.

Hollowell, Marshall H., Private, Company F
Goldsboro
Captured at Goldsboro on March 19, 1865. Confined at Hart's Island, New York, and released upon taking the Oath of Allegiance on June 19, 1865. Based on the date and location of Hollowell's capture, he was probably taken by advance elements of Maj. Gen. Oliver O. Howard's Right Wing.
Source: *NCT*, I:106; M270; NC Confederate Pension (Wayne County).

Hood, Robert B., Private, Company F
Goldsboro
Captured at Goldsboro on March 19, 1865. Confined at Hart's Island, New York, where he was released upon taking the Oath of Allegiance on June 18, 1865. Based on the March 19 date and location of Hood's capture, he was probably taken by advance elements of Maj. Gen. Oliver O. Howard's Right Wing. However, within Hood's service records exists a U.S. Army of the Ohio record that indicates Pvt. Robert B. Hood, Co. F, 10th NC, was a deserter, captured on March 28, 1865. Further research is required.
Source: *NCT*, I:106; M270.

Hood, Solomon P., Private, Company F
Goldsboro
Captured at Goldsboro on March 20, 1865. Confined at Hart's Island, New York, and released upon taking the Oath of Allegiance on June 18, 1865. Based on the date and location of Hood's capture, he was probably taken by advance elements of Maj. Gen. Oliver O. Howard's Right Wing.
Source: *NCT*, I:106; M270.

Howell, Kedar, Private, Company F
Goldsboro (Post Bentonville)
Captured at Goldsboro on March 28, 1865. U.S. Army of the Ohio records identified Kedar Howell as a deserter when captured. Confined first at Hart's Island, New York Harbor, and later transferred to Davis Island, New York Harbor, in July 1865, where he died on July 9, 1865, of consumption.
Source: *NCT*, I:107; M270.

Howell, Robert, Private, Company F
Goldsboro (Post Bentonville)
Captured at Goldsboro on March 24, 1865, and took the Oath of Allegiance that same day. U.S. Army of the Ohio records identified Robert Howell as a deserter when captured.
Source: *NCT*, I:107; M270.

Johnson, James, Private, Company F
Goldsboro (Post Bentonville)

Captured at Goldsboro on March 23, 1865, and took the Oath of Allegiance that same day. U.S. Army of the Ohio records identified Johnson as a deserter when captured.
Source: *NCT*, I:107; M270.

King, James S., Private, Company B
Pikeville (Post Bentonville)
Captured at Pikeville on March 28, 1865. Confined at Hart's Island, New York, and released upon taking the Oath of Allegiance on June 19, 1865.
Source: *NCT*, I:57; M270; NC Confederate Pension (Forsyth County).

Langston, John, Private, Company I (2nd)
Goldsboro (Post Bentonville)
Captured at Goldsboro on March 22, 1865, and administered the oath that same day. Company rolls indicate that John Langston was absent without leave as of December 31, 1864. U.S. Army of the Ohio records identified Langston as a deserter when captured.
Source: *NCT*, I:154; M270.

Pate, James A., Private, Company B
Goldsboro (Post Bentonville)
Captured at Goldsboro on March 24, 1865. Confined in Washington, D.C., and released upon taking the Oath of Allegiance on May 13, 1865.
Source: *NCT*, I:58; M270.

Robinson, Henry, Private, Company F
Goldsboro (Post Bentonville)
Captured at Goldsboro on March 22, 1865. Confined at Hart's Island, New York, and released upon taking the Oath of Allegiance on June 6, 1865.
Source: *NCT*, I:110; M270.

Simpkins, John, Private, Company H
Goldsboro (Post Bentonville)
U.S. Army Provost Marshal records indicate that Simpkins was captured at Goldsboro on March 22, 1865, and took the Oath of Allegiance that same day. Included in the remarks section was the letter "D," which probably designated him as a deserter.
Source: *NCT*, I:135; M270.

Strickland, J. H., Private, Company F
Goldsboro (Post Bentonville)
Captured at Goldsboro on March 25, 1865, and took the Oath of Allegiance that same day.
Source: *NCT*, I:111; M270.

Thornton, Isaac Ingram, Private, Company F
Goldsboro
Captured at Goldsboro on March 19, 1865. Confined at Point Lookout, Maryland, and released upon taking the Oath of Allegiance on June 21, 1865. Based on the date and location of Thornton's capture, he was probably taken by advance elements of Maj. Gen. Oliver O. Howard's Right Wing.
Source: *NCT*, I:111; M270; NC Confederate Widow's Pension (Sampson County).

Vinson, Nathan, Private, Company F
Goldsboro (Post Bentonville)
Captured at Goldsboro on March 23, 1865. U.S. Army of the Ohio records identified Vinson as a deserter when captured and sent to the Provost Marshall at New Bern that same day.
Source: *NCT*, I:112; M270.

Walsh, William A., Private, Company F

Goldsboro
Captured at Goldsboro on March 19, 1865. Confined at Hart's Island, New York, and released upon taking the Oath of Allegiance on June 6, 1865. Based on the date and location of Walsh's capture, he was probably taken by advance elements of Maj. Gen. Oliver O. Howard's Right Wing.
Source: *NCT*, I:112; M270.

Williams, Patrick J., Bugler, Private, Company I (2nd)
Kinston (Post Wise's Forks)
Captured at Kinston on March 15, 1865. Company rolls indicate that Patrick J. Williams was absent without leave as of December 31, 1864. U.S. Army of the Ohio records indicate that Williams was forwarded to the Provost Marshall at New Bern, but no further record.
Source: *NCT*, I:157; M270; NC Confederate Pension (Wake County).

Private Henry C. Maultsby
36th Regiment NC Troops
Severely wounded in the left leg during the battle of Bentonville, Maultsby died at General Hospital No. 3 in High Point on April 8, 1865, and is buried in Oakwood Cemetery there.

(Courtesy of Phillip Martin)

36th Regiment North Carolina Troops (2nd North Carolina Artillery)

Anders, Franklin James, Private, Company H
Bentonville
Captured at the battle of Bentonville on March 19, 1865. Confined at Point Lookout, Maryland, and released upon taking the Oath of Allegiance on June 4, 1865.
Source: *NCT*, I:291; M270.

▲**Baldwin, John K.**, Company B (3rd)
Bentonville
According to Surgeon Hanahan's "Return of Wounded for Hagood's Brigade" at Bentonville, Pvt. J. R. Baldwin, Co. D, 36th NC, was slightly wounded in the left arm on March 21, 1865. A Lt. J. R. Baldwin, Co. D, also appears on Surgeon Tanner's "Return of Casualties in Hoke's Div. near Bentonville," with a slight wound to the left arm. Private John K. Baldwin is probably the same J. R. Baldwin Surgeon Hanahan listed as wounded. Baldwin's service records and *NC Troops* incorrectly note that Baldwin was hospitalized at GH No. 3 in Greensboro on an unspecified date in March 1865 for unspecified reasons. In National Archives Confederate Record Group 109, General Hospital No. 3's location is erroneously identified as Greensboro. High Point is the correct location. Confederate authorities began relocating GH No. 3 from Goldsboro to High Point on March 11, 1865, as part of the town's evacuation. The hospital resumed operations in High Point on or about March 19, 1865. The No. 3 Patient Registry lists a Pvt. J. R. Baldwin, entry no. 2330, of Co. B, 36th NC, admitted for unspecified reasons between March 21 and April 7, 1865. Baldwin's middle initial may be the letter K. Further information is required.
Source: Hanahan (BV), 5; *NCT*, I:208; M270; Sokolosky, *NC's Confederate Hospitals*, vol. 2; RG109, 6/291:46.

▲**Brooks, William F.**, Captain, Company K
Bentonville
According to Surgeon Hanahan's "Return of Wounded for Hagood's Brigade," Capt. __ Brooks, Co. K, 36th NC, was severely wounded in the right arm on March 19, 1865, at Bentonville, requiring amputation above the elbow. His name also appears on Surgeon Tanner's "Return of Casualties in Hoke's Div. near Bentonville" as Capt. __ Brooks. *NC Troops* notes that Capt. William F. Brooks was wounded at Bentonville on March 19, 1865. The March 24, 1865, edition of the *NC Standard* reported Capt. J. Brooks of the 36th NC Troops was a patient at the Haywood House Hospital (Officer's Hospital) in Raleigh with an amputated arm. The newspaper likely erred in reporting Brooks's initial for his given name. Brooks's service records do not note his hospitalization in Raleigh. No further records.
Source: Hanahan (BV), 4; Tanner (BV), 147; Clark, *Histories*, II: 651; *NCT*, I:326; *NCS* (Raleigh), March 24, 1865; *DP* (Raleigh), March 27, 1865; M270.

Bullock, Henry G., Corporal, Company C (2nd)
Near Fayetteville
A resident of Cumberland County at the time of his enlistment, Henry G. Bullock, was captured near Fayetteville on March 12, 1865. Confined at Point Lookout, Maryland, and released upon taking the Oath of Allegiance on June 24, 1865.
Source: *NCT*, I:228; M270.

▲**Burney, Daniel H.**, Private, Company B (3rd)
Bentonville
According to Surgeon Hanahan's "Return of Wounded for Hagood's Brigade" at Bentonville, Pvt. D. H. Burney, Co. B, 36th NC, was slightly wounded in the left side and a flesh wound to the left hand on March 19, 1865. Private D. H. Burney also appears in Surgeon Tanner's "Return of Casualties in Hoke's Div. near Bentonville," slightly wounded on the left side. The March 24, 1865, edition of the *NC Standard* reported that Pvt. D. H. Burney, 36th NC, was at the Episcopal Church Hospital in Raleigh, wounded in his left hand

and side. Private Daniel H. Burney of Co. B is the same soldier as Pvt. D. H. Burney. Neither Burney's service records nor *NC Troops* note the wound he received at the battle of Bentonville.
Source: Hanahan (BV), 2; Tanner (BV), 147; *NCS* (Raleigh), March 24, 1865; *DP* (Raleigh), March 27, 1865; *NCT*, I:209; M270.

▲Dyson, William J., Private, Company E
Bentonville
According to Surgeon Hanahan's "Return of Wounded for Hagood's Brigade," Pvt. W. J. Dyson of Co. K, 1st Battalion NC, was slightly wounded in the right hand on March 20, 1865, at Bentonville. Private W. J. Dyson also appears in Surgeon Tanner's "Return of Casualties in Hoke's Div. near Bentonville," listed under Co. K, 1st Battalion NC. Private William J. Dyson of Co. E, 36th NC Troops, is probably the same soldier as Pvt. W. J. Dyson. Either Hanahan and Tanner erred in reporting Private Dyson as a member of the 1st Battalion NC, or Dyson's Co. E was temporarily attached to the 1st Battalion on March 20, 1865. Neither Dyson's service records nor *NC Troops* note the wound he received at the battle of Bentonville.
Source: Hanahan (BV), 1; Tanner (BV), 146; *NCT*, I:250; M270.

Feutrel, Lawrence, Private, Company D (2nd)
Piney Grove
Captured at Piney Grove on March 18, 1865. Confined at Point Lookout, Maryland, and released upon taking the Oath of Allegiance on June 27, 1865.
Source: *NCT*, I:240; M270.

Gore, Christopher, Private, Company K
Sugar Loaf
Captured near Fort Fisher on February 11-16, 1865. Confined at Point Lookout, Maryland, and released upon taking the Oath of Allegiance on May 13, 1865.
Source: *NCT*, I:329; M270.

Griffin, William C., Private, Company C (2nd)
Fayetteville
A resident of Cumberland County at the time of his enlistment, William C. Griffin, was captured at Fayetteville on March 11, 1865, the day U.S. forces occupied the town. Confined at Hart's Island, New York Harbor, and released upon taking the Oath of Allegiance on June 14, 1865.
Source: *NCT*, I:229; M270.

♦Guthrie, Thomas C., Private, Company K
(Inconclusive)
Captured, date and location undetermined. Admitted to Foster General Hospital in New Bern on March 30, 1865, as a prisoner of war and died there on April 19, 1865, at 2:30 p.m., of acute diarrhea. NC Troops indicates that he is buried at New Bern.
Source: *NCT*, I:329; M270.

Hall, Calton, Private, Company B (3rd)
Sampson County
A resident of Sampson County at the time of his enlistment, Calton Hall was captured in Sampson County on March 17, 1865. Confined at Point Lookout, Maryland, and released upon taking the Oath of Allegiance on June 14, 1865.
Source: *NCT*, I:212, 702; M270.

Higgs, Joseph Benjamin, Private, Company F
Bentonville
Captured at the battle of Bentonville on March 19, 1865. Confined at Point Lookout, Maryland, and released upon taking the Oath of Allegiance on June 27, 1865.
Source: *NCT*, I:263; M270.

Horne [Horn], John, Private, Company C (2nd)
Piney Grove
Captured at Piney Grove on March 19, 1865. Confined at New Port News, Virginia, and released upon taking the Oath of Allegiance on June 30, 1865. He signed his Confederate pension application using the surname Horn.
Source: *NCT*, I:231; M270; NC Confederate Pension (Cumberland County).

Hunter, Samuel Benjamin, Captain, Company F
Bentonville
NC Troops notes that he was wounded at the battle of Bentonville on March 19, 1865. His service records do not indicate that he was hospitalized on account of his wound.
Source: Clark, *Histories*, II: 651; *NCT*, I:257; M270.

▲**Kelly, James A.,** 2nd Lieutenant, Company B (3rd)
Bentonville
According to Surgeon Hanahan's "Return of Wounded for Hagood's Brigade," at Bentonville, Lt. J. Kelly, Co. B, 36th NC, was slightly wounded in the left arm on March 19, 1865. Kelly also appears in Surgeon Tanner's "Return of Casualties in Hoke's Div. near Bentonville," wounded slightly in the left arm. The March 24, 1865, edition of the *NC Standard* reported that Kelly was wounded at Bentonville on March 19, 1865, and was a patient at Haywood House Hospital (Officer's Hospital) in Raleigh. Kelly's service records and *NC Troops* do not note the wound he received at the battle of Bentonville. No further information.
Source: Hanahan (BV), 4; Tanner (BV), 147; *NCS* (Raleigh), March 24, 1865; *NCT*, I:208, 706; M270.

Layton, John A., Private, Company A (2nd)
Sampson County
Captured in Sampson County on March 18, 1865. Confined at Point Lookout, Maryland, on March 30, 1865. No further information.
Source: *NCT*, I:191, 707; M270.

▲**Maultsby, Henry C.,** Private, Company B (3rd)
Bentonville
According to Surgeon Hanahan's "Return of Wounded for Hagood's Brigade," at Bentonville, Pvt. H. C. Maultsby, Co. B, 36th NC, was severely wounded in the left leg on March 19, 1865. Private H. C. Maultsby also appears in Surgeon Tanner's "Return of Casualties in Hoke's Div. near Bentonville," wounded severely in the left leg. Private Henry C. Maultsby of Co. B is the same soldier listed by both surgeons. Maultsby's service records and *NC Troops* incorrectly note that he was hospitalized at GH No. 3 in Greensboro on an unspecified date in March 1865. In National Archives Confederate Record Group 109, General Hospital No. 3's location is erroneously identified as Greensboro. High Point is the correct location. Confederate authorities began relocating GH No. 3 from Goldsboro to High Point on March 11, 1865, as part of the town's evacuation. The hospital resumed operations in High Point on or about March 19, 1865. The No. 3 Patient Registry lists a Pvt. H. Maultsby, entry no. 2540, of Co. B, admitted for unspecified reasons between March 21 and April 7, 1865. Neither Maultsby's service records nor *NC Troops* note the wound he received at the battle of Bentonville. Private Henry C. Maultsby died on April 8, 1865, while still a patient at the hospital and is buried in the Confederate Section of Oakwood Cemetery, High Point.
Source: Hanahan (BV), 3; Tanner (BV), 147; *NCS* (Raleigh), March 24, 1865; *NCT*, I:213; M270; Sokolosky, *NC's Confederate Hospitals*, vol. 2; RG109, 6/291:50; Barbee Wayside Hospital Registry, no. 5824.

♦**McDonald, L.,** Private, Company B (3rd)
Bentonville (Inconclusive)
The April 4, 1865, edition of the *Western Democrat* reported that Pvt. L. McDonald, 36th NC, was at the Episcopal Church Hospital in Raleigh wounded in the stomach. There is no L. McDonald listed on the 36th NC rolls.
Source: *Western Democrat* (Charlotte), April 4, 1865; *DP* (Raleigh), March 27, 1865.

◆**McFadyen, H. L.,** Private, Company B (3rd)
Bentonville (Inconclusive)
The March 24, 1865, edition of the *NC Standard* reported that Pvt. H. S. McFadgen, Co. B, 36th NC, was at the Episcopal Church Hospital in Raleigh suffering from a contusion. Private H. S. McFadgen is not listed in either Hanahan or Tanner's casualty returns from the battle of Bentonville. Private H. L. McFadyen of Co. B may be the same soldier as Pvt. H. S. McFadgen. Further research is required.
Source: *NCT*, I:213; *NCS* (Raleigh), March 24, 1865; *DP* (Raleigh), March 27, 1865; M270.

▲**McKee, David James,** Private, Company H
Bentonville
According to Surgeon Hanahan's "Return of Wounded for Hagood's Brigade," at Bentonville, Pvt. D. J. McKee of Co. H, 1st Battalion NC, was severely wounded in the left hip on March 20, 1865. Private D. J. McKee also appears in Surgeon Tanner's "Return of Casualties in Hoke's Div. near Bentonville," listed under Co. H, 1st Battalion. Hanahan and Tanner mistakenly listed Private McKee's unit as the 1st Battalion NC. Private David J. McKee of Co. H, 36th NC, is the same soldier as Pvt. D. J. McKee. The March 24, 1865, edition of the *NC Standard* reported Pvt. D. J. McKee of the 36th NC was a patient at the Episcopal Church Hospital in Raleigh wounded in the left thigh. David James McKee, Co. H, 36th NC, indicated in his Confederate pension that he was wounded in the thigh and his "hearing was affected by firing of cannon." Private David James McKee is the same soldier Hanahan and *NC Standard* listed as Pvt. D. J. Mckee. Neither McKee's service records nor *NC Troops* (Volume I) note the wound he received at the battle of Bentonville.
Source: Hanahan (BV), 1; Tanner (BV), 146; *NCS* (Raleigh), March 24, 1865; *DP* (Raleigh), March 27, 1865; NC Confederate Pension (Bladen County); M270; *NCT*, I:296.

McLaughlin, Kenneth, Private, Company H
Bentonville
Captured at the battle of Bentonville on March 19, 1865. Confined at Point Lookout, Maryland, and released upon taking the Oath of Allegiance on June 29, 1865.
Source: *NCT*, I:296; M270.

▲**Melvin, Joseph M.,** Private, Company H
Bentonville
According to Surgeon Hanahan's "Return of Wounded for Hagood's Brigade" at Bentonville, Pvt. J. L. Melvin, Co. F, 36th NC, was severely wounded in his left leg below the knee on March 20, 1865. Private J. L. Melvin also appears in Surgeon Tanner's "Return of Casualties in Hoke's Div. near Bentonville," listed under Co. F. Private Joseph M. Melvin of Co. H is the same soldier as Pvt. J. L. Melvin. Private Joseph M. Melvin's service records indicate he was admitted to GH No. 13 (Pettigrew Hospital) in Raleigh on March 21, 1865, wounded in the left leg, and later captured at the hospital as a patient on April 13, 1865. *NC Troops* notes that Melvin was admitted to a Raleigh hospital, wounded from an unspecified battle.
Source: Hanahan (BV), 1; Tanner (BV), 147; *DC* (Raleigh), March 29, 1865; *NCS* (Raleigh), March 29, 1865; *NCT*, I:296, 710; M270.

◆▲**Millard, Luther R.,** Sergeant, Company C (2nd)
Bentonville (Inconclusive)
Sergeant Luther R. Millard's service records indicate he was admitted to GH No. 13 (Pettigrew Hospital) on March 24, 1865, suffering from a gunshot wound in his left side. Several days later, the March 29, 1865, edition of the *NC Standard* reported L. R. Millard, Co. F, 36th NC, was a patient at the Wayside Hospital (Ladies' Wayside) in Raleigh suffering from a wound to his left side. Millard's service records and *NC Troops* incorrectly note that he was hospitalized at GH No. 3 in Greensboro on an unspecified date in April 1865. In National Archives Confederate Record Group 109, General Hospital No. 3's location is erroneously identified as Greensboro. High Point is the correct location. Confederate authorities began relocating GH No. 3 from Goldsboro to High Point on March 11, 1865, as part of the town's evacuation. The hospital resumed operations in High Point on or about March 19, 1865. The No. 3 Patient Registry lists a Sgt. L. R. Millard, entry no. 2633, of Co. C, 36th NC, admitted for unspecified reasons between March 21 and April

7, 1865. The timing of Millard's hospital admittance in Raleigh several days after the battle of Bentonville makes it probable that he was wounded at some point during the battle. However, his absence from either Hanahan or Tanner's casualty returns raises the question of his wounding from possibly another battle or skirmish. Further research is required.
Source: *NCT*, I: 233; M270; Sokolosky, *NC's Confederate Hospitals*, vol. 2; RG109, 6/291:52.

▲Pigott, James F., Private, Company K
Bentonville
According to Surgeon Hanahan's "Return of Wounded for Hagood's Brigade," Pvt. J. F. Pigott of Co. K, 1st Battalion NC, was severely wounded in the right breast on March 19, 1865, at Bentonville. Private J. F. Pigott also appears in Surgeon Tanner's "Return of Casualties in Hoke's Div. near Bentonville," listed under Co. K, 1st Battalion. Hanahan and Tanner mistakenly list Private Pigott as a 1st Battalion NC Heavy Artillery soldier. Neither Pigott's service records nor *NC Troops* note the wound he received at Bentonville. James F. Pigott's Confederate pension indicates that he was wounded at Bentonville, "struck by a minnie ball in the left side, penetrating through to the skin from whence the doctor cut it out."
Source: Hanahan (BV), 2; Tanner (BV), 146; *NCT*, I:332; M270; NC Confederate Pension (Brunswick County).

▲Raybon, Richard, Private, Company E
Bentonville
According to Surgeon Hanahan's "Return of Wounded for Hagood's Brigade," Pvt. R. Rabon of Co. K, 1st Battalion NC, was slightly wounded in the right hip on March 20, 1865, at Bentonville. Private R. Rabon also appears in Surgeon Tanner's "Return of Casualties in Hoke's Div. near Bentonville," listed under Co. K, 1st Battalion NC. Private Richard Raybon of Co. E, 36th NC, is probably the same soldier as Pvt. R. Rabon. Hanahan and Tanner erred in reporting Private Rabon, belonging to 1st Battalion NC, or Raybon's Co. E, was temporarily attached to the 1st Battalion NC on March 20, 1865. Neither Raybon's service records nor *NC Troops* note the wound he received at the battle of Bentonville.
Source: Hanahan (BV), 1; Tanner (BV), 146; *NCT*, I:253; M270.

Robinson, Frederick G., Sergeant, Company C (2nd)
Bentonville
Captured at the battle of Bentonville on March 19, 1865. Confined at Point Lookout, Maryland, and released upon taking the Oath of Allegiance on June 7, 1865.
Source: *NCT*, I:233; M270.

Russ, William, Private, Company K
Wise's Forks (Inconclusive)
William Russ indicated on his Confederate pension application that he was wounded in battle, on or about March 9, 1865, "by the bursting of a shell," which struck him in the right hip. However, he notes the location as Fort Fisher. Private Russ's name is not listed on Surgeon Hanahan's casualty roster from the battle of Wise's Forks. Neither his service records nor *NC Roster* note that he was wounded in the battle. Further research is required.
Source: *NCT*, I:333; M270; NC Confederate Pension (Brunswick County).

Simmons, Wiley King, Private, Company A (2nd)
Piney Grove
Captured at Piney Grove on March 18, 1865. Confined at Point Lookout, Maryland, and released upon taking the Oath of Allegiance on June 20, 1865.
Source: *NCT*, I:195; M270.

Stevenson, James C., Private, Company A (2nd)
Bentonville
Captured at the battle of Bentonville on March 19, 1865. Confined at Point Lookout, Maryland, and released upon taking the Oath of Allegiance on June 20, 1865.
Source: *NCT*, I:195, 717; M270.

▲**Taylor, John Douglas**, Lieutenant Colonel, Field and Staff
Bentonville
According to Surgeon Hanahan's "Return of Wounded for Hagood's Brigade," at Bentonville, Col. J. D. Taylor, 36th NC, was wounded in the left arm on March 19, 1865, requiring amputation. Taylor also appears in Surgeon Tanner's "Return of Casualties in Hoke's Div. near Bentonville," wounded dangerously in the left arm, requiring amputation. Taylor recalled in his "War Recollections" that he arrived at Raliegh in a train carrying Confederate wounded on March 21, 1865, and authorities transferred him to the private residence of Mr. T. C. McIlhenny, where he was cared for until returning home in May 1865. However, Taylor's service records indicate that he was admitted to GH No. 13 (Pettigrew Hospital) on April 12, 1865, where he was transferred to an unspecified location on April 16, 1865.
Source: Hanahan (BV), 4; Tanner (BV), 147; Clark, *Histories*, II: 651; *NCT*, I:173; M270. Taylor, "War Recollections," 8, 11.

▲**Weathersbee, Francis Joseph**, Private, Company F
Bentonville
According to Surgeon Hanahan's "Return of Wounded for Hagood's Brigade," at Bentonville, Pvt. F. J. Wetherby, Co. F, 36th NC, was severely wounded in the left thigh on March 19, 1865. Private F. J. Weatherby also appears in Surgeon Tanner's "Return of Casualties in Hoke's Div. near Bentonville," wounded severely in the left thigh. *NC Troops* notes that Pvt. Francis J. Weathersbee was wounded at Bentonville on March 19, 1865. Private Francis J. Weathersbee is the same soldier. His service records and *NC Troops* incorrectly note that Weathersbee was hospitalized at GH No. 3 in Greensboro on an unspecified date in March 1865. In National Archives Confederate Record Group 109, General Hospital No. 3's location is erroneously identified as Greensboro. High Point is the correct location. Confederate authorities began relocating GH No. 3 from Goldsboro to High Point on March 11, 1865, as part of the town's evacuation. The hospital resumed operations in High Point on or about March 19, 1865. The No. 3 Patient Registry lists a Pvt. F. J. Weathersber, entry no. 2472, of Co. F, 36th NC, admitted for unspecified reasons between March 21 and April 7, 1865. The hospital erred in the spelling of his surname. No further information.
Source: Hanahan (BV), 5; Tanner (BV), 147; *NCT*, I:268; M270; Sokolosky, *NC's Confederate Hospitals*, vol. 2; RG109, 6/291:49.

Williamson, Obediah H., 1st Lieutenant, Company E
Bentonville
Captured at the battle of Bentonville on March 19, 1865. Confined at Johnson's Island, Ohio, and released upon taking the Oath of Allegiance on June 17, 1865.
Source: *NCT*, I:247; M270.

▲**Wood, Thomas**, Private, Company F
Bentonville
According to Surgeon Hanahan's "Return of Wounded for Hagood's Brigade" at Bentonville, Pvt. T. Wood, Co. F, 36th NC, was mortally wounded in the head on March 19, 1865. Private T. Wood also appears in Surgeon Tanner's "Return of Casualties in Hoke's Div. near Bentonville" with a dangerous head wound. Private Thomas Wood of Co. F is probably the same soldier as Pvt. T. Wood. Neither Wood's service records nor *NC Troops* note the mortal wound he received at the battle of Bentonville. No further records.
Source: Hanahan (BV), 2; Tanner (BV), 147; *NCT*, I:268; M270.

3rd Battalion North Carolina Light Artillery

Brickhouse, Franklin L., Corporal, Company B
Town Creek
Captured at the battle of Town Creek on February 20, 1865. Confined at Point Lookout, Maryland, and released upon taking the Oath of Allegiance on June 23, 1865.
Source: *NCT*, I:348; M270.

Bush, Abram T., Private, Company B
Town Creek
Captured at the battle of Town Creek on February 20, 1865. Confined at Point Lookout, Maryland, and released upon taking the Oath of Allegiance on June 23, 1865.
Source: *NCT*, I:349; M270; NC Confederate Pension (Chowan County).

Chippewater, Joseph F., Private, Company B
Town Creek
Captured at the battle of Town Creek on February 20, 1865. Confined at Point Lookout, Maryland, and released upon taking the Oath of Allegiance on June 26, 1865.
Source: *NCT*, I:349; M270.

Dodd, W. M., Private, Company C
Town Creek
Captured at Fayetteville on March 14, 1865. Confined at Point Lookout, Maryland, and released upon taking the Oath of Allegiance on May 15, 1865.
Source: *NCT*, I:362; M270.

Gibson, Thomas L., Private, Company B
Town Creek
Captured at the battle of Town Creek on February 20, 1865. Confined at Point Lookout, Maryland, and released upon taking the Oath of Allegiance on June 27, 1865. Gibbon's Confederate pension application indicates that he was wounded in the head; however, it does not specify the date and location.
Source: *NCT*, I:350; M270; NC Confederate Pension (Martin County).

Hodges, Thomas B., Private, Company A
Sugar Loaf
NC Troops notes that Pvt. Thomas B. Hodges was killed along the Sugar Loaf Line on February 11, 1865. His widow, Rebecca C. Hodges, indicated on her widow's pension application that Thomas B. Hodges was killed near Fort Fisher.
Source: *NCT*, I:341; Keith, *3rd Battalion*, 304; M270; NC Confederate Widow's Pension (Northampton), 1885 and 1901.

Hunter, Benjamin F., Sergeant, Company B
Town Creek
Captured at the battle of Town Creek on February 20, 1865. Confined at Point Lookout, Maryland, and released upon taking the Oath of Allegiance on June 28, 1865.
Source: *NCT*, I:352; M270.

▲**Larkins, James R.**, Private, Company B
Town Creek
Wounded at Town Creek on February 20, 1865. A week after the battle, Captain William Badham Jr. penned a letter informing his wife that Private Larkins had been wounded during the fight at Town Creek. Paroled at Greensboro on April 28, 1865, with the remark: "Absent at home wounded." No further records.
Source: *NCT*, I:352; M270; William J. Badham to Wife, February 28, 1865, see Keith, *3rd Battalion*, 305.

Leonard, John W., Private, Company B
Town Creek

Captured at the battle of Town Creek on February 20, 1865. Confined at Point Lookout, Maryland, and released upon taking the Oath of Allegiance on June 29, 1865.
Source: *NCT*, I:353; M270.

Littleton, Edward J., Private, Company B
Fort Anderson
Deserted at Fort Anderson in February 1865. Sent to Washington, D.C., where he took the Oath of Amnesty on March 1, 1865. Granted passage to Norfolk, Virginia. No further records.
Source: *NCT*, I:353; M270.

Mizell, William, Private, Company B
Fort Anderson
Parole muster roll from Greensboro, dated April 28, 1865, contains the remark: "Deserted at Clayton Depot in March 1865." No further records.
Source: *NCT*, I:353; M270.

Monds, Lemuel, Private, Company B
Town Creek
Captured at the battle of Town Creek on February 20, 1865. Confined at Point Lookout, Maryland, and released upon taking the Oath of Allegiance on June 29, 1865.
Source: *NCT*, I:354; M270.

Monds, William M., Private, Company B
Fort Anderson
Parole muster roll from Greensboro, dated April 28, 1865, contains the remark: "Deserted at Clayton Depot in March 1865." No further records.
Source: *NCT*, I:354; M270; NC Confederate Widow's Pension.

Newberry, Demetrius W., Private, Company B
Town Creek
NC Troops notes that at the time of his parole, Pvt. Demetrius W. Newberry was "[a]bsent wounded at Town Creek." Captain William Badham Jr., in a letter to his wife, dated February 28, 1865, noted that Private Newberry had been wounded at the battle of Town Creek. No further information.
Source: *NCT*, I:354; M270; Keith, *3rd Battalion*, 305.

Nixon, James A., Private, Company B
Town Creek
Captured at the battle of Town Creek on February 20, 1865. Confined at Point Lookout, Maryland, and released upon taking the Oath of Allegiance on June 29, 1865.
Source: *NCT*, I:354; M270.

Nixon, John E., Private, Company B
Town Creek
Captured at the battle of Town Creek on February 20, 1865. Confined at Point Lookout, Maryland, and released upon taking the Oath of Allegiance on June 29, 1865.
Source: *NCT*, I:354; M270; NC Confederate Widow's Pension (Bertie County).

Only, Richard M., Private, Company B
Town Creek
Captured at the battle of Town Creek on February 20, 1865. Confined at Point Lookout, Maryland, and released upon taking the Oath of Allegiance on June 29, 1865.
Source: *NCT*, I:354; M270.

Privett, Samuel, Private, Company B
Town Creek

Captured at the battle of Town Creek on February 20, 1865. Confined at Point Lookout, Maryland, and released upon taking the Oath of Allegiance on June 17, 1865.
Source: *NCT*, I:355; M270.

Riddick, Job, Private, Company B
Town Creek
Captured at the battle of Town Creek on February 20, 1865. Confined at Point Lookout, Maryland, and released upon taking the Oath of Allegiance on May 14, 1865.
Source: *NCT*, I:355; M270.

Webb, William Jeptha, Private, Company B
Town Creek
Captured at the battle of Town Creek on February 20, 1865. Confined at Point Lookout, Maryland, and released upon taking the Oath of Allegiance on June 21, 1865.
Source: *NCT*, I:357; M270.

Williams, Hezekiah, Private, Company C
Sugar Loaf Line
NC Troops notes that Pvt. Hezekiah Williams, Co. C, was wounded along the Sugar Loaf Line in February 1865. Hezekiah Williams stated in his Confederate pension application that he was wounded in February 1865 "by the explosion of a shell in my right side[?] and elbow." Author H. James Keith erroneously listed that Pvt. Hezekiah Williams of Co. A was killed while defending the Sugar Loaf Line on February 15, 1865.
Source: *NCT*, I:370; NC Confederate Pension (Harnett County); Keith, *3rd Battalion*, 304; M270.

John Cobb House
Battle of Wise's Forks
Served as a field hospital for both wounded Confederate and U.S. Army soldiers.

(Courtesy of Skip Riddle)

Colonel John J. Hedrick
Commander, 40th Regiment NC Troops (3rd NC Artillery)
Wounded at the Battle of Wise's Forks

(Histories of Several Regiments and Battalions from North Carolina in the Great War)

40th Regiment North Carolina Troops
(3rd North Carolina Artillery)

Albertson, Joshua L., Sergeant, Company A
Kinston (Post Wise's Forks)
U.S. Army Provost Marshal records indicate that Sgt. Joshua L. Albertson was captured at Kinston on March 19, 1865. Included in the remarks section was the letter "D," which probably designated him as a deserter. No further information. *NC Troops* notes that he was captured and paroled on March 19, 1865.
Source: *NCT*, I:376; M270; NC Confederate Pension (Lenoir County).

▲**Ball, G. W.**, Private, Company H (2nd)
Wise's Forks
According to Surgeon Hanahan's "List of Killed and Wounded in Hagood's Brigade" at Wise's Forks, Pvt. G. W. Ball, Co. H, 40th NC, was wounded in the right leg. Neither *NC Troops* nor his service records note his wounding. Further research is required.
Source: Hanahan (WF), 1; Tanner (WF), 137; *NCT*, I:480; M270.

▲**Ball, J. W.**, Private, Company H (2nd)
Bentonville
According to Surgeon Hanahan's "Return of Wounded for Hagood's Brigade" at Bentonville, Pvt. J. W. Ball, Co. H, 40th NC, was slightly wounded in the right foot on March 19, 1865. His name also appears on Surgeon Tanner's "Return of Casualties in Hoke's Div. near Bentonville." Neither Ball's service records nor *NC Troops* note the wound he received at Bentonville.
Source: Hanahan (BV), 3; Tanner (BV), 147; *NCT*, I:480; M270.

Ball, Niles, Private, Company C
Fort Anderson
Deserted from Fort Anderson on February 16, 1865. He was sent to Washington, D.C., where he took the Oath of Allegiance.
Source: *NCT*, I:397; M270; NC Confederate Pension (Beaufort County).

Barnes, Christopher C., Private, Company B
Fort Anderson
NC Troops indicates that he was wounded at Fort Anderson on February 19, 1865. Barnes was admitted to GH No. 4 in Wilmington that same day and, according to hospital records, was transferred to GH No. 2 in Wilson. On an undetermined date and location, he was captured and Confined at Elmira, New York, where he died on April 23, 1865. Buried in Woodlawn National Cemetery, Elmira.
Source: *NCT*, I:387; M270.

Barnes, John, Sergeant, Company H (2nd)
Bentonville
Captured at the battle of Bentonville on March 19, 1865. Confined at Point Lookout, Maryland, and released upon taking the Oath of Allegiance on June 3, 1865.
Source: *NCT*, I:480; M270.

▲**Barnhart, J. M.**, Private, Company L
Bentonville (Inconclusive)
According to Surgeon Hanahan's "Return of Wounded for Hagood's Brigade" at Bentonville, Pvt. J. M. Barnhart, Co. L, 40th NC, was severely wounded in the right hand (first finger, first joint amputated) on March 20, 1865. Private J. M. Barnhart also appears in Surgeon Tanner's "Return of Casualties in Hoke's Div. near Bentonville." Further research is required.
Source: Hanahan (BV), 1; Tanner (BV), 148; M270.

Berry, Christopher S., Private, Company I

Bentonville

Captured at the battle of Bentonville on March 19, 1865. Confined at Point Lookout, Maryland, and released upon taking the Oath of Allegiance on June 24, 1865.
Source: *NCT*, I:491; M270.

Boney, Gabriel J., Private, Company H (2nd)
Bentonville

Captured at the battle of Bentonville on March 19, 1865. Confined at Point Lookout, Maryland, and released upon taking the Oath of Allegiance on June 3, 1865.
Source: *NCT*, I:480, 695; M270.

Bonner, Macon, 1st Lieutenant, Company B
Fort Anderson

Captured at Fort Anderson on February 19, 1865. Confined at Fort Delaware, Delaware, and released upon taking the Oath of Allegiance on June 17, 1865.
Source: *NCT*, I:386, 695; M270.

Bowers, John, Sergeant, Company H (2nd)
Bentonville

Captured at the battle of Bentonville on March 19, 1865. Confined at Point Lookout, Maryland, and released upon taking the Oath of Allegiance on June 3, 1865.
Source: *NCT*, I:480; M270.

Bradford, William, Private, Company I
Bentonville

NC Troops notes Pvt. William Bradford was wounded in the knee on March 21, 1865, at Bentonville. According to Wilson's service records, he was admitted to GH No. 13 in Raleigh on March 21, 1865, with a gunshot wound on the left side of his knee. Bradford was furloughed on March 23, 1865, for 60 days. Further research is required.
Source: *NCT*, I:491, 696; *DP* (Raleigh), March 28, 1865; M270.

Bridgeman, John L., Private, Company B
Fort Anderson

Captured at Fort Anderson on February 19, 1865. Confined at Point Lookout, Maryland, and released upon taking the Oath of Allegiance on June 24, 1865.
Source: *NCT*, I:388; M270.

▲**Britt, George C.**, Private, Company B
Bentonville

According to Surgeon Hanahan's "Return of Wounded for Hagood's Brigade" at Bentonville, Pvt. G. Britt, Co. B, 40th NC, was slightly wounded in the left hand on March 19, 1865. Private G. Britt also appears in Surgeon Tanner's "Return of Casualties in Hoke's Div. near Bentonville." Private George C. Britt of Co. B is probably the same soldier as Pvt. G. Britt. Neither Britt's service records nor *NC Troops* note the wound he received at the battle of Bentonville.
Source: Hanahan (BV), 2; Tanner (BV), 147; *NCT*, I:388; M270.

Brooks, Iverson J. W., Private, Company C
Wilmington

Captured near Wilmington on March 1, 1865. Confined at Point Lookout, Maryland, and released upon taking the Oath of Allegiance on June 23, 1865.
Source: *NCT*, I:397; M270.

Brown, Henry C., Private, Company H (2nd)
Bentonville

▲**Brown, William H.**, Corporal, Company A
Wise's Forks
According to Surgeon Hanahan's "List of Killed and Wounded in Hagood's Brigade" at Wise's Forks, Corp. W. H. Brown, Co. A, was killed during the battle. *NC Troops*, based on information obtained from Julia Brown's application for a widow's pension, notes William H. Brown was wounded near Kinston on March 8, 1865, and died of wounds in a Kinston hospital on March 15, 1865. A fellow soldier in Co. A, Pvt. William E. Hill provided a sworn statement that indicated he witnessed "Wm. H. Brown when he fell wounded . . . and saw him carried from the battlefield and has never seen him since."
Source: Hanahan (WF), 1; *NCT*, I:377; M270; NC Confederate Widow's Pension (Lenoir County).

♦**Bullock, Henry C.**, Sergeant, Company F
Bentonville or Wise's Forks (Inconclusive)
The March 29, 1865, edition of the *NC Standard* reported that Lt. H. C. Bullock of Co. F, 40th NC, was suffering from a thigh wound at GH No. 8 (Peace Institute) in Raleigh. Neither Hanahan nor Tanner listed Bullock as having been wounded at Wise's Forks or Bentonville. *NC Troops* indicates that Henry C. Bullock was wounded in the thigh on an unspecified date between March 7 and April 5, 1865 and that he was hospitalized in Raleigh. Paroled at Goldsboro on May 23, 1865. Further research is required.
Source: *NCS* (Raleigh), March 29, 1865; *NCT*, I:430, 697; M270.

Byrd, Josiah Miller, Private, Company A
Moseley Hall
Captured at Moseley Hall on March 31, 1865. Confined at Hart's Island, New York Harbor, where he died on May 22, 1865, of typhoid fever.
Source: *NCT*, I:377; M270; NC Confederate Pension (Lenoir and Wake Counties).

▲**Calhoun, O. D.**, Private, Company F
Bentonville
According to Surgeon Hanahan's "Return of Wounded for Hagood's Brigade" at Bentonville, Pvt. O. D. Calhoun, Co. F, 40th NC, suffered a concussion on March 19, 1865. Private O. D. Calhoun also appears in Surgeon Tanner's "Return of Casualties in Hoke's Div. near Bentonville." Neither Calhoun's service records nor *NC Troops* note his concussion received at the battle of Bentonville. No further information.
Source: Hanhan (BV), 2; Tanner (BV), 147; *NCT*, I:430; M270.

Callaway, Elijah E., Private, Company B
Fort Anderson
Captured at Fort Anderson on February 19, 1865. Confined at Point Lookout, Maryland, and released upon taking the Oath of Allegiance on June 4, 1865.
Source: *NCT*, I:388; M270.

♦▲**Callaway, Jesse R.**, Private, Company B
Bentonville (Inconclusive)
U.S. Army records indicate that Pvt. Jesse R. Callaway was captured in Smithfield on March 19, 1865. Either the date or location of capture is incorrect, as Confederate forces occupied the town through the first week of April 1865. Confined at Point Lookout, Maryland, and released upon taking the Oath of Allegiance on June 24, 1865. Possibly Bentonville. *NC Troops* incorrectly identifies Smithville (present-day Southport) as the capture location. Further Research is required.
Source: *NCT*, I:388; M270.

Carter, Amos, Private, Company H (2nd)
Fort Anderson

Captured at Fort Anderson on February 19, 1865. Confined at Point Lookout, Maryland, and released upon taking the Oath of Allegiance on May 13, 1865.
Source: *NCT*, I:481; M270.

♦▲Chambers, James F., Private, Company B
Bentonville (Inconclusive)
Based on an 1866 listing of Confederate dead buried on the John Harper farm, published in Wilmington's *Daily Journal*, a J. F. Chambers of the 40th NC was interred there. As reported in the paper, J. F. Chambers is probably the same soldier as James F. Chambers. *NC Troops* does not note his wounding or later death at Bentonville. Further research is required.
Source: *NCT*, XII:388; M270; *DJ* (Wilmington, NC), August 8, 1866.

Chewning, Thomas, Private, Company C
Bentonville
Captured at the battle of Bentonville on March 19, 1865. Confined at Point Lookout, Maryland, and released upon taking the Oath of Allegiance on June 26, 1865.
Source: *NCT*, I:398; M270.

Clapp, Peter, Private, Company H (2nd)
Bentonville
Captured at the battle of Bentonville on March 19, 1865. Confined at Point Lookout, Maryland, and released upon taking the Oath of Allegiance on June 26, 1865.
Source: *NCT*, I:481; M270.

♦Clark, Robert G., Private, Company I
Bentonville (Inconclusive)
Service records indicate that he was captured in Smithfield, North Carolina on March 19, 1865. Confined at Point Lookout, Maryland, and released upon taking the Oath of Allegiance on June 26, 1865. Smithfield remained under Confederate control until mid-April 1865. The location or date of capture is incorrect.
Source: *NCT*, I:492; M270.

Clark, William, Private, Company I
Fort Anderson
Captured at Fort Anderson on February 19, 1865. Confined at Point Lookout, Maryland, and released upon taking the Oath of Allegiance on June 26, 1865.
Source: *NCT*, I:492; M270.

Coble, Elias, Private, Company H (2nd)
Bentonville
Captured at the battle of Bentonville on March 19, 1865. Confined at Point Lookout, Maryland, and released upon taking the Oath of Allegiance on June 10, 1865.
Source: *NCT*, I:481; M270; NC Confederate Widow's Pension (Richmond County).

▲Collins, Benjamin F., Private, Company B
Bentonville
According to Surgeon Hanahan's "Return of Wounded for Hagood's Brigade" at Bentonville. Pvt. B. F. Collins, Co. B, 40th NC, was slightly wounded in the left side of his neck on March 21, 1865. His name also appears on Surgeon Tanner's "Return of Casualties in Hoke's Div. near Bentonville." Private Benjamin F. Collins of Co. B is the same soldier as Pvt. B. F. Collins. Private Benjamin F. Collins had previously served in the 12th NC before being discharged in July 1862 on account of being underage. In August 1863, he enlisted in the 40th NC, first serving in Co. A and later transferred to Co. B in early 1865. Collins indicated on his pension application that he was "wounded through the neck." *NC Troops* does not note his wounding at Bentonville.
Source: Hanahan (BV), 5; Tanner (BV), 147; *NCT*, V:198; *NCT*, I:388; M270; NC Confederate Pension (Nash County).

Congleton, Ashley, 1st Lieutenant, Company C
Bentonville
Captured at the battle of Bentonville on March 19, 1865. Confined at Johnson's Island, Ohio, and released upon taking the Oath of Allegiance on June 18, 1865.
Source: *NCT*, I:396; M270.

Cook, David A., Private, Company I
Bentonville
Captured at the battle of Bentonville on March 19, 1865. Confined at Point Lookout, Maryland, and released upon taking the Oath of Allegiance on June 26, 1865.
Source: *NCT*, I:492; M270.

Cox, Abram R., Private, Company I
Fort Anderson
Captured at Fort Anderson on February 19, 1865. Confined at Point Lookout, Maryland, and released upon taking the Oath of Allegiance on June 26, 1865.
Source: *NCT*, I:492; M270.

▲**Craft, Richard A.**, Private, Company H (2nd)
Wise's Forks
According to Surgeon Hanahan's "List of Killed and Wounded in Hagood's Brigade" at Wise's Forks, Pvt. R. Craft, Co. H, 40th NC, had his "4th finger amputated." Private R. Craft of Co. H is also listed in Tanner's "Return of Casualties near Kinston." GH No. 3 "Register of Wounded and Operations" indicates Pvt. R. Craft, Co. H, 40th NC, was wounded on March 10, 1865, suffering from a gunshot wound to the right hand. Neither *NC Troops* nor his service records note his wounding. Both sources also incorrectly note that Craft was transferred from Kinston to GH No. 3 in Greensboro on March 10, 1865, for unspecified reasons. In National Archives Confederate Record Group 109, General Hospital No. 3's location is erroneously identified as Greensboro. Goldsboro is the correct location. Confederate authorities began relocating GH No. 3 from Goldsboro to High Point on March 11, 1865, as part of the town's evacuation. The hospital resumed operations in High Point on or about March 19, 1865. Confederate pension records indicate that he was "wounded at Kinston about the close of the war in 1865 in the right hand, causing the loss of one finger." The pension records state the loss of the "right third finger," which conflicts with Hanahan's "4th finger amputated" note.
Source: Hanahan (WF), 1; Tanner (WF), 137; GH No. 3 Ledger B, entry no. 64; *NCT*, I:482; M270; Sokolosky, *NC's Confederate Hospitals*, vol. 2; NC Confederate Pension (Pitt County).

Davis, John Z., 1st Lieutenant, Company A
Fort Anderson
Wounded mortally in the stomach by an exploding naval shell on February 18, 1865 at Fort Anderson. According to Wilmington's *Daily Journal*, Lt. J. Z. Davis, Co. A, 40th NC, was admitted to GH No. 4 in the port city, where he died of wounds on February 19, 1865.
Source: Fonvielle, *Fort Anderson*, 72; *Daily Journal* (Wilmington, NC), February 20, 1865; *NCT*, I:375, 699; M270.

▲**Deneale, William H.**, Sergeant Major, Field and Staff
Bentonville
According to Surgeon Hanahan's "Return of Wounded for Hagood's Brigade" at Bentonville, Sgt. Maj. W. Deneal, Field and Staff, 40th NC, was slightly wounded in the right hand on March 19, 1865. His name also appears on Surgeon Tanner's "Return of Casualties in Hoke's Div. near Bentonville." Neither Deneale's service records nor *NC Troops* note the wound he received at Bentonville.
Source: Hanahan (BV), 4; Tanner (BV), 147; *NCT*, I:374; M270.

Doughty, Charles H., Sergeant, Company C
Near Town Creek

Captured near Town Creek on February 20, 1865. Confined at Point Lookout, Maryland, and released upon taking the Oath of Allegiance on June 26, 1865.
Source: *NCT*, I:399; M270; NC Confederate Pension (Edgecombe County).

♦Dowdy, Harman H., Private, Company B
Wise's Forks (Inconclusive)
Service records indicate that he was admitted to GH No. 13 (Pettigrew Hospital) for a fractured tibia (right leg) on March 11, 1865, and returned to duty on March 18, 1865. Unable to determine if Dowdy's fracture was non-battle related or due to combat. His Confederate pension application does not specify he was wounded in battle, only that he is disabled.
Source: M270; *NCS* (Raleigh), March 29, 1865; *NCT*, I:389; NC Confederate Pension (Craven County).

Eagles, Benjamin F., Private, Company H (2nd)
Bentonville
Captured at the battle of Bentonville on March 19, 1865. Confined at Point Lookout, Maryland, and released upon taking the Oath of Allegiance on June 12, 1865.
Source: *NCT*, I:483; M270.

▲Eason, Willis, Corporal, Company F
Bentonville
According to Surgeon Hanahan's "Return of Wounded for Hagood's Brigade" at Bentonville, Corp. W. Eason, Co. F, 40th NC, was severely wounded in the back on March 19, 1865. His name also appears on Surgeon Tanner's "Return of Casualties in Hoke's Div. near Bentonville." Corporal Willis Eason of Co. F is the same soldier as Corp. W. Eason. The March 29, 1865, edition of the *NC Standard* reported that Corp. W. Eason was at GH No. 8 (Peace Institute) in Raleigh, suffering from a wound to his left side. Neither Eason's service records nor *NC Troops* note the wound he received at the battle of Bentonville. No further information.
Source: Hanahan (BV), 4; Tanner (BV), 147; *NCS* (Raleigh), March 29, 1865; *NCT*, I:431; M270.

▲Ermul, Paschal H., Corporal, Company B
Bentonville
According to Surgeon Hanahan's "Return of Wounded for Hagood's Brigade" at Bentonville, Corp. P. H. Ermul, Co. B, 40th NC, was severely wounded on the right side on March 19, 1865. His name also appears on Surgeon Tanner's "Return of Casualties in Hoke's Div. near Bentonville." Corporal Paschal H. Ermul of Co. B is the same soldier as Corp. P. H. Ermul. Neither Ermul's service records nor *NC Troops* note the wound he received at the battle of Bentonville. On an undetermined date following the battle, Corporal Ermul was evacuated to Thomasville General Hospital, where he was paroled as a patient on May 1, 1865.
Source: Hanahan (BV), 3; Tanner (BV), 147; *NCT*, I:389; M270; M1761, Thomasville General Hospital Paroles.

Farmer, John D., Private, Company F
Greene County
A resident of Greene County at the time of his enlistment, John D. Farmer was captured in Greene County on March 10, 1865. Confined at Hart's Island, New York Harbor, and released upon taking the Oath of Allegiance on June 19, 1865.
Source: *NCT*, I:431; M270.

Farmer, Moses, Private, Company H (2nd)
Bentonville
Captured at the battle of Bentonville on March 19, 1865. Confined at Point Lookout, Maryland, and released upon taking the Oath of Allegiance on June 3, 1865.
Source: *NCT*, I:483; M270.

▲Farmer, Samuel B., Corporal, Company H (2nd)
Wise's Forks

According to Surgeon Hanahan's "List of Killed and Wounded in Hagood's Brigade" at Wise's Forks, Sgt. S. B. Farmer, Co. H, 40th NC, was wounded in the right hip. Neither *NC Troops* nor his service records note his wounding.
Source: Hanahan (WF), 1; Tanner (WF), 137; *NCT*, I:483; M270.

▲Felton, Howell, Private, Company F
Bentonville
According to Surgeon Hanahan's "Return of Wounded for Hagood's Brigade" at Bentonville, Pvt. H. Felton, Co. F, 40th NC, was slightly wounded in the right arm on March 20, 1865. Private H. Felton also appears in Surgeon Tanner's "Return of Casualties in Hoke's Div. near Bentonville." Private Howell Felton of Co. F is probably the same soldier as Pvt. H. Felton. Paroled at Goldsboro on May 9, 1865. Neither Felton's service records nor *NC Troops* note the wound he received at the battle of Bentonville.
Source: Hanahan (BV), 1; Tanner (BV), 147; *NCT*, I:431; M270.

Flowers, Abner, Private, Company I
Anson County
Captured in Anson County on March 5, 1865, while on furlough. Confined at Point Lookout, Maryland, and released upon taking the Oath of Allegiance on June 26, 1865.
Source: *NCT*, I:493; M270.

Flowers, Robert W., Private, Company H (2nd)
Bentonville
Captured at the battle of Bentonville on March 19, 1865. Confined at Point Lookout, Maryland, and released upon taking the Oath of Allegiance on June 26, 1865.
Source: *NCT*, I:483; M270; NC Confederate Pension (Brunswick County).

Fodry, A. Fulford, Private, Company G (3rd)
Bentonville
Captured at the battle of Bentonville on March 20, 1865. Confined at Hart's Island, New York Harbor, and released upon taking the Oath of Allegiance on June 18, 1865.
Source: *NCT*, I:456; M270.

Frank, Philip, Private, Company C
Bentonville
Captured at the battle of Bentonville on March 19, 1865. Confined at Point Lookout, Maryland, and released upon taking the Oath of Allegiance on June 26, 1865.
Source: *NCT*, I:399; M270.

Gallagher, James, Private, Company H (2nd)
Bentonville
Captured at the battle of Bentonville on March 19, 1865. Confined at Point Lookout, Maryland, and released upon taking the Oath of Allegiance on June 27, 1865.
Source: *NCT*, I:483; M270.

Garrison, Robert J., Private, Company C
Bentonville
Captured at the battle of Bentonville on March 19, 1865. Confined at Point Lookout, Maryland, and released upon taking the Oath of Allegiance on June 27, 1865.
Source: *NCT*, I:400; M270.

▲Gordon, W., Private, Company L
Bentonville (Inconclusive)
According to Surgeon Hanahan's "Return of Wounded for Hagood's Brigade" at Bentonville, Pvt. W. Gordon, Co. F, 40th NC, was severely wounded in the left leg below the knee on March 20, 1865. Private

W. Gordon also appears in Surgeon Tanner's "Return of Casualties in Hoke's Div. near Bentonville." Further research is required.
Source: Hanahan (BV), 1; Tanner (BV), 148; M270.

▲Greene, Robert, Private, Company B
Fort Anderson
Private Robert Greene and five other soldiers from Co. B were wounded on February 3, 1865, by a single shell fired from the USS *Tacony* on Fort Anderson. The men happened to be lounging in their quarters when the round impacted. Admitted to GH No. 4 in Wilmington with a fractured skull on February 5, 1865. Received a 60-day furlough on February 8, 1865.
Source: Fonvielle, *Fort Anderson*, 43-44; *NCT*, I:390; M270.

♦Gulledge, Elisha, Private, Company C
Bentonville (Inconclusive)
Wounded on an undetermined date and location. His service records and NC Troops incorrectly note that he was admitted to GH No. 3 in Greensboro from Wilmington on February 21, 1865 [NC Troops states February 23], with a gunshot wound. Transferred to Charlotte, where he was admitted to GH No. 11 on April 21, 1865, suffering from a right arm amputation. Further research is required.
Source: *NCT*, I:400; M270.

♦Gulledge, W. D., Private, Company C
Bentonville (Inconclusive)
Surgeon Hanahan's "Return of Wounded for Hagood's Brigade" at Bentonville, Pvt. W. D. Gulledge, Co. C, 40th NC, was wounded with the remarks, "right arm amputated." According to Surgeon Tanner's "Return of Casualties in Hoke's Div. near Bentonville," Pvt. W. D. Gulledge, Co. C, suffered a dangerous wound in the right arm and required amputation. The March 24, 1865, edition of the *Daily Progress* reported Pvt. W. D. Gulledge was wounded in the right arm, requiring amputation, at the battle of Bentonville and was later admitted to GH No. 13 (Pettigrew) in Raleigh. The service records for Pvt. Elisha Gulledge, Co. C, 40th NC, contains an entry for a Pvt. W. D. Gulledge, Co. C, 40th NC, which indicates that he was admitted to GH No. 13 due to a gunshot wound to his right arm requiring amputation. *NC Troops* does not list any Gulledge with a given name beginning with the letter W. Further research is required.
Source: Hanahan (BV), 2; Tanner (BV), 147; *DP* (Raleigh), March 24, 1865; M270.

Ham, Benjamin, Private, Company F
Goldsboro (Post Bentonville)
Captured at Goldsboro on March 30, 1865. Confined at Hart's Island, New York Harbor, and released upon taking the Oath of Allegiance on June 219, 1865.
Source: *NCT*, I:431; M270; NC Confederate Pension (Greene County).

Hansley, Thomas, Private, Company H (2nd)
Fort Anderson
Captured at Fort Anderson on February 19, 1865. Confined at Point Lookout, Maryland, and released upon taking the Oath of Allegiance on May 13, 1865.
Source: *NCT*, I:484; M270.

Harris, Taylor, Private, Company I
Fort Anderson
Taylor Harris deserted from Fort Anderson on February 18, 1865. Sent to Washington, D.C., where he took the Oath of Allegiance.
Source: *NCT*, I:494; M270; NC Confederate Pension (Pitt County).

▲Hedrick, John J., Colonel, Field and Staff
Wise's Forks
Colonel John J. Hedrick was wounded at the battle of Wise's Forks "while gallantly leading his regiment in a charge." Neither Hanahan nor Tanner's casualty returns from the battle of Wise's Forks, note Colonel

Hedrick among the wounded. The GH No. 13 (Pettigrew Hospital) Patient Registry indicates Colonel Hedrick was admitted for a gunshot wound in his left thigh on March 11, 1865, and transferred to Charlotte on March 16, 1865. However, Charlotte's GH No. 11 Patient Registry indicates he wasn't admitted until April 9, 1865. His name also appears in the March 29, 1865, edition of the *NC Standard* as a patient at GH No. 13 (Pettigrew Hospital) in Raleigh. *NC Troops* does not identify Wise's Forks as the location of wounding.
Source: Clark, *Histories*, II:762; Sokolosky and Smith, *To Prepare for Sherman's Coming*, 131; NCT, I:391; M270.

Hellen, Joseph F., 1st Lieutenant, Company H (2nd)
Bentonville
Captured at the battle of Bentonville on March 19, 1865. Confined at Johnson's Island, Ohio, and released upon taking the Oath of Allegiance on June 17, 1865.
Source: *NCT*, I:479; M270.

Higgins, John M., Private, Company A
Kinston (Post Wise's Forks)
U.S. Army Provost Marshal records indicate that Pvt. John M. Higgins was captured at Kinston on March 16, 1865, with the letter "D" included in the remarks section, which probably designated him as a deserter. Paroled on March 16, 1865.
Source: *NCT*, I:379; M270.

Hill, John Hampden, 2nd Lieutenant, Company H (2nd)
Bentonville
According to *NC Troops*, Lt. John Hampden Hill was wounded in the left leg at the battle of Bentonville on March 19, 1865. Hill's service records do not note the wounded he received at the battle of Bentonville. John H. Hill, at age 71, received a Confederate pension.
Source: *NCT*, I:480, 704; M270; NC Confederate Pension (Wayne County).

Hill, William E., Private, Company A
Kinston (Post Wise's Forks)
Captured and paroled at Kinston on March 17, 1865. No further information.
Source: *NCT*, I:379; M270.

Hines, Benjamin H., Private, Company G (3rd)
Bentonville
Captured at the battle of Bentonville on March 20, 1865. Confined at Hart's Island, New York Harbor, and released upon taking the Oath of Allegiance on June 18, 1865.
Source: *NCT*, I:458; M270.

▲Hines, James A., Sergeant, Company A
Wise's Forks
According to Surgeon Hanahan's "List of Killed and Wounded in Hagood's Brigade" at Wise's Forks, Sgt. J. A. Hines, Co. A, was slightly wounded in the left hand. Neither *NC Troops* nor his service records indicate his wounding at the battle.
Source: Hanahan (WF), 1; Tanner (WF), 137; *NCT*, I:380; M270.

Howell, Calvin, Private, Company H (2nd)
Bentonville
Captured at the battle of Bentonville on March 19, 1865. Confined at Point Lookout, Maryland, and released upon taking the Oath of Allegiance on June 3, 1865.
Source: *NCT*, I:484; M270.

▲Hoyle, J. C., Private, Company F
Wise's Forks

According to Surgeon Hanahan's "List of Killed and Wounded in Hagood's Brigade" at Wise's Forks, Pvt. J. L. Hoyle, Co. F, 40th NC, was wounded in the right hip. Neither *NC Troops* nor his service records note his wounding. His service records indicate he was admitted to GH No. 10 in Salisbury on March 12, 1865, for unspecified reasons. No further records.
Source: Hanahan (WF), 1; Tanner (WF), 137; *NCT*, I:432; M270.

Hudnell, Willis B., Private, Company B
Bentonville
Captured at the battle of Bentonville on March 19, 1865. Confined at Point Lookout, Maryland, and released upon taking the Oath of Allegiance on June 27, 1865.
Source: *NCT*, I:391; M270; NC Confederate Pension (Beaufort County).

▲Hunter, Henry D., Private, Company F
Wise's Forks
According to Surgeon Hanahan's "List of Killed and Wounded in Hagood's Brigade" at Wise's Forks, Pvt. H. D. Hunter, Co. F, 40th NC, was wounded in the right hip. Neither *NC Troops* nor his service records note his wounding. The Barbee Wayside Hospital (High Point) Patient Registry lists a Pvt. H. D. Hunter, entry no. 5745, of Co. F, 40th NC, was admitted for a gunshot wound to his right hip on March 9, 1865. No further records.
Source: Hanahan (WF), 1; Tanner (WF), 137; *NCT*, I:432; M270.

Jackson, Asa, Private, Company I
Fort Anderson
Captured at Fort Anderson on February 19, 1865. Confined at Point Lookout, Maryland, and released upon taking the Oath of Allegiance on June 28, 1865.
Source: *NCT*, I:495; M270.

▲Jackson, Bracy E., Private, Company B
Fort Anderson
Private Bracy E. Jackson and five other soldiers from Co. B were wounded on February 3, 1865, by a single shell fired from the USS *Tacony* on Fort Anderson. The men happened to be lounging in their quarters when the round impacted. Admitted to GH No. 4 in Wilmington with a "shell wound of [the] left side" on February 5, 1865. Received a 60-day furlough on February 14, 1865. His Confederate pension records, which goes the first name of Bracey, indicates that he was wounded by a piece of shell, cutting his hip and head.
Source: Fonvielle, *Fort Anderson*, 43-44; *NCT*, I:391; M270; NC Confederate Pension (Beaufort County).

▲Jackson, Cornelius, Private, Company B
Bentonville
According to Surgeon Hanahan's "Return of Wounded for Hagood's Brigade" at Bentonville, Pvt. C. Jackson, Co. B, 40th NC, was severely wounded in the left thigh (fracture) on March 19, 1865. His name also appears on Surgeon Tanner's "Return of Casualties in Hoke's Div. near Bentonville." Private Cornelius Jackson of Co. B is the same soldier as Pvt. C. Jackson. Cornelius Jackson stated in his Confederate pension application that he was wounded at Bentonville on March 19, 1865, while on the skirmish line, "shot through the thigh near [the] hip joint." *NC Troops* noted his wounding at Bentonville on March 19, 1865. On an undetermined date following the battle, Private Jackson was evacuated to Greensboro, where he was paroled as a patient at the Garrett House Hospital, a temporary ward of GH No. 12, on May 2, 1865.
Source: Hanahan (BV), 4; Tanner (BV), 147; *NCT*, I:391; M270; NC Confederate Pension (Beaufort County).

▲Jackson, Thomas, Private, Company F
Bentonville
According to Surgeon Hanahan's "Return of Wounded for Hagood's Brigade" at Bentonville, Pvt. T. Jackson, Co. F, 40th NC, was slightly wounded in the left thigh on March 19, 1865. His name also appears on Surgeon Tanner's "Return of Casualties in Hoke's Div. near Bentonville." Thomas Jackson, Co. F, 40th NC, stated in his Confederate pension application that he was wounded at Bentonville "in the thigh and

the ball still in me." The physician's statement in his 1901 pension request indicated that "the ball is now slowly moving towards the knee." Private Thomas Jackson of Co. F is the same soldier as Pvt. T. Jackson. Neither Jackson's service records nor *NC Troops* note the wound he received at the battle of Bentonville.
Source: Hanhan (BV), 3; Tanner (BV), 147; *NCT*, I:432, 458; NC Confederate Pension (Nash County); M270.

Jones, Calvin E., Private, Company A
Kinston (Post Wise's Forks)
Captured and paroled at Kinston on March 18, 1865. No further records.
Source: *NCT*, I:380, 706; M270.

▲Jones, George W., Private, Company A
Wise's Forks
According to Surgeon Hanahan's "List of Killed and Wounded in Hagood's Brigade" at Wise's Forks, Pvt. G. W. Jones, Co. A, 40th NC, was killed during the battle. Neither *NC Troops* nor his service records note his death. His widow, Paulina C. Jones, applied for a Widow's Pension in December 1906 but did not note her husband's death.
Source: Hanahan (WF), 1; Tanner (WF), 137; *NCT*, I:381; M270; NC Confederate Widow's Pension (Lenoir County).

Jones, Haywood, Private, Company F
Bentonville
Captured at the battle of Bentonville on March 19, 1865. Confined at Point Lookout, Maryland, and released upon taking the Oath of Allegiance on June 28, 1865.
Source: *NCT*, I:432; M270.

Jones, Robert B., Corporal, Company I
Bentonville
Captured at the battle of Bentonville on March 19, 1865. Confined at Point Lookout, Maryland, and released upon taking the Oath of Allegiance on June 28, 1865.
Source: *NCT*, I:495; M270.

Jones, Thaddeus L., Private, Company I
Bentonville
Captured at the battle of Bentonville on March 19, 1865. Confined at Point Lookout, Maryland, and released upon taking the Oath of Allegiance on June 28, 1865.
Source: *NCT*, I:495, 706; M270.

Jones, Walter J., Private, Company H (2nd)
Bentonville
Captured at the battle of Bentonville on March 19, 1865. Confined at Point Lookout, Maryland, and released upon taking the Oath of Allegiance on June 3, 1865.
Source: *NCT*, I:484; M270.

▲Jordan, William H., Private, Company F
Fort Anderson
According to Wilmington's *Daily Journal*, Pvt. W. H. Jordan, 40th NC, was severely wounded in the thigh during the engagement at Fort Anderson and admitted to GH No. 4 in the port city on February 19, 1865. *NC Troops* does not identify Jordan as having been wounded at Fort Anderson. He was transferred on February 20, 1865, to another hospital.
Source: *Daily Journal* (Wilmington, NC), February 20, 1865; *NCT*, I:432; M270; NC Confederate Pension (Cumberland County).

Kennedy, Richard M., Private, Company A
Iredell County
Captured and paroled in Iredell County on March 15, 1865. No further information.
Source: *NCT*, I:381; M270; NC Confederate Pension (Pitt County).

▲**Kerman, James M.**, Corporal, Company I
Bentonville
According to Surgeon Hanahan's "Return of Wounded for Hagood's Brigade" at Bentonville, Pvt. J. M. Kerman, Co. I, 40th NC, was severely wounded in the left arm, requiring amputation, on March 19, 1865. His name also appears on Surgeon Tanner's "Return of Casualties in Hoke's Div. near Bentonville." Corporal James M. Kerman, Co. I, is probably the same soldier as Pvt. J. M. Kerman. Neither Kerman's service records nor *NC Troops* note the wound he received at the battle of Bentonville. On an undetermined date following the battle, Corporal Kerman was evacuated to Greensboro, where he was paroled as a patient at the Garrett House Hospital, a temporary ward of GH No. 12, on May 2, 1865.
Source: Hanahan (BV), 3; Tanner (BV), 148; *NCT*, I:495, 706; M270.

Ketchum, Christopher, Private, Company B
Near Wilmington
Captured near Wilmington on February 19, 1865. Confined at Point Lookout, Maryland, and released upon taking the Oath of Allegiance on June 28, 1865.
Source: *NCT*, I:391; M270.

♦**Kick, George**, Private, Company B
Near Goldsboro (Possibly Bentonville)
Captured near Goldsboro on March 19, 1865. Confined at Point Lookout, Maryland, and released upon taking the Oath of Allegiance on June 28, 1865.
Source: *NCT*, I:391; M270.

▲**Lancaster, Lawrence**, Private, Company F
Fort Anderson
Private Lawrence Lancaster, Co. F, 40th NC, was wounded in the right arm at Fort Anderson on February 18, 1865, requiring amputation. Lawrence was admitted to GH No. 4 in the port city on February 19, 1865, receiving a furlough of 60 days the following day. *NC Troops* does not identify Lawrence as having been wounded at Fort Anderson.
Source: Fonvielle, *Fort Anderson*, 72; *Daily Journal* (Wilmington, NC), February 20, 1865; *NCT*, I:433; M270.

Lee, Elam, Private, Company I
Johnston County
Captured in Johnston County on March 18, 1865. Confined at Point Lookout, Maryland, and released upon taking the Oath of Allegiance on June 28, 1865.
Source: *NCT*, I:496; M270.

Lee, James W., Private, Company I
Johnston County
Captured in Johnston County on March 18, 1865. Confined at Point Lookout, Maryland, and released upon taking the Oath of Allegiance on June 28, 1865.
Source: *NCT*, I:496; M270; NC Confederate Pension (Johnston County).

Lee, Joel, Private, Company I
Wilmington
Deserted to the enemy at Wilmington on February 22, 1865. No further record.
Source: *NCT*, I:496; M270; NC Confederate Pension (Sampson County).

Lee, Sedulus D., Private, Company I
North East Station
Deserted to the enemy at North East Station on February 22, 1865. No further record.
Source: *NCT*, I:496; M270; NC Confederate Pension (Johnston County).

Leggett, John E., Captain, Company C
Bentonville

Captured at the battle of Bentonville on March 19, 1865. Confined at Johnson's Island, Ohio, and released upon taking the Oath of Allegiance on June 17, 1865.
Source: *NCT*, I:396; M270.

Locke, William, Private, Company I
Lenoir – Wayne Counties
Captured between Kinston and Goldsboro on March 19, 1865. Confined at Point Lookout, Maryland, and released upon taking the Oath of Allegiance on June 28, 1865.
Source: *NCT*, I:496; M270.

Long, Edward, 2nd Lieutenant, Company C
Bentonville
Captured at the battle of Bentonville on March 19, 1865. Confined at Johnson's Island, Ohio, and released upon taking the Oath of Allegiance on June 17, 1865.
Source: *NCT*, I:396; M270.

▲Long, Wilson N., Private, Company I
Bentonville
Captured at the battle of Bentonville on March 19, 1865. Confined at Point Lookout, Maryland, and released upon taking the Oath of Allegiance on June 28, 1865. Wilson N. Long's Confederate Pension application states that he was wounded as well at Bentonville with a gunshot wound in the right hip joint.
Source: *NCT*, I:496, 708; M270; NC Confederate Pension (Beaufort County).

Lucas, Henry D., Private, Company H (2nd)
Bentonville
Captured at the battle of Bentonville on March 19, 1865. Confined at Point Lookout, Maryland, and released upon taking the Oath of Allegiance on June 3, 1865.
Source: *NCT*, I:485; M270; NC Confederate Pension (Sampson County).

Mason, William T., Private, Company I
Fort Anderson
The Wilmington *Daily Journal* reported a Pvt. Mason, no first name provided, of Co. I, 40th NC, was mortally wounded in the head during the engagement at Fort Anderson. The soldier is Pvt. William T. Mason of Co. I. Mason was admitted to GH No. 4 in the port city on February 19, 1865, where he died two days later. The company roll for January-February 1865 noted that he had been in the hospital in Wilmington since February 12 with a mortal wound from the battle of Fort Anderson.
Source: *Daily Journal* (Wilmington, NC), February 20, 1865; Fonvielle, *Fort Anderson*, 72; *NCT*, I:496; M270.

Maurice, Samuel, Private, Company I
Fort Anderson
Captured at Fort Anderson on February 19, 1865. Confined at Point Lookout, Maryland, and released upon taking the Oath of Allegiance on May 15, 1865. His Confederate pension records note the middle initial of "L."
Source: *NCT*, I:496; M270; NC Confederate Pension (Richmond County).

♦▲Mayo, Charles E. S., Private, Company B
Bentonville (Inconclusive)
According to Surgeon Hanahan's "Return of Wounded for Hagood's Brigade" at Bentonville, Pvt. C. Mayo, Co. B, 40th NC, was slightly wounded in the right cheek on March 19, 1865. Private Charles E. S. Mayo of Co. B is probably the same soldier as Pvt. C. Majo. Neither Mayo's service records nor *NC Troops* note the wound he received at the battle of Bentonville.
Source: Hanahan (BV), 2; *NCT*, I:392; M270.

McCauley, John A., Corporal, Company C
Bentonville

Captured at the battle of Bentonville on March 19, 1865. Confined at Point Lookout, Maryland, and released upon taking the Oath of Allegiance on June 29, 1865.
Source: *NCT*, I:402; M270.

McCullen, Lewis M., Private, Company G (3rd)
Kinston (Post Wise's Forks)
U.S. Army Provost Marshal records indicate that Pvt. Lewis M. McCullen was captured at Kinston on March 14, 1865. The letter "D" was included in the remarks section, which probably designated him a deserter. *NC Troops* notes that he was captured and paroled on March 14, 1865.
Source: *NCT*, I:460; M270.

McLauchlin, James W., Private, Company D
Bentonville
Captured at Fayetteville on March 11, 1865. Confined at Fort Monroe, Virginia, and released upon taking the Oath of Allegiance on April 5, 1865.
Source: *NCT*, I:423; M270.

McNeill, John B., Private, Company E
Bentonville
Captured at the battle of Bentonville on March 19, 1865. Confined at Point Lookout, Maryland, and released upon taking the Oath of Allegiance on June 29, 1865.
Source: *NCT*, I:423, 708; M270.

▲McPhaul, James, Private, Company E
Bentonville
According to Surgeon Hanahan's "Return of Wounded for Hagood's Brigade" at Bentonville, Pvt. J. McPhaul, Co. E, 40th NC, was mortally wounded in the head on March 19, 1865. J. McPhaul also appears in Surgeon Tanner's "Return of Casualties in Hoke's Div. near Bentonville." Private James McPhaul of Co. E is probably the same soldier as Pvt. J. McPhaul. Neither McPhaul's service records nor *NC Troops* notes his death as the result of the wound he received at Bentonville.
Source: Hanahan (BV), 2; Tanner (BV), 147; *NCT*, I:423; M270.

Mock, David, Private, Company I
Bentonville
Captured at the battle of Bentonville on March 19, 1865. Confined at Point Lookout, Maryland, and released upon taking the Oath of Allegiance on June 29, 1865.
Source: *NCT*, I:497; M270.

Murphey, William D., Private, Company F
Kinston (Post Wise's Forks)
U.S. Army Provost Marshal records indicate that Pvt. William D. Murphey was captured at Kinston on March 15, 1865, with the letter "D" included in the remarks section, which probably designated him as a deserter. No further information. Paroled on March 19, 1865.
Source: *NCT*, I:434; M270.

▲Murray, Alphonso H., Private, Company C
Bentonville
According to Surgeon Hanahan's "Return of Wounded for Hagood's Brigade" at Bentonville, Pvt. A. H. Murry, Co. C, 40th NC, was wounded in the right hand (first finger, first joint amputated) on March 19, 1865. His name also appears on Surgeon Tanner's "Return of Casualties in Hoke's Div. near Bentonville." Private Alphonso H. Murray of Co. C is probably the same soldier as Pvt. A. H. Murry. Neither Murray's service records nor *NC Troops* note the wound he received at the battle of Bentonville.
Source: Hanahan (BV), 2; Tanner (BV), 147; *NCT*, I:402; M270; NC Confederate Widow's Pension (Guilford County).

Newell, Samuel T., Corporal, Company H (2nd)

Bentonville
Captured at the battle of Bentonville on March 19, 1865. Confined at Point Lookout, Maryland, and released upon taking the Oath of Allegiance on June 3, 1865.
Source: *NCT*, I:486; M270.

▲Newman, William S., Private, Company A
Bentonville
According to Surgeon Hanahan's "Return of Wounded for Hagood's Brigade" at Bentonville, Pvt. W. Newman, Co. F, 40th NC, was slightly wounded in the head on March 19, 1865. W. Newman also appears in Surgeon Tanner's "Return of Casualties in Hoke's Div. near Bentonville." Private William S. Newman of Co. A is probably the same soldier as Pvt. W. Newman. Neither Newman's service records nor *NC Troops* note the wound he received at the battle of Bentonville. Additionally, both sources incorrectly note that he was hospitalized at GH No. 3 in Greensboro on an unspecified date in March 1865. In National Archives Confederate Record Group 109, General Hospital No. 3's location is erroneously identified as Greensboro. High Point is the correct location. Confederate authorities began relocating GH No. 3 from Goldsboro to High Point on March 11, 1865, as part of the town's evacuation. The hospital resumed operations in High Point on or about March 19, 1865. The No. 3 Patient Registry lists a Pvt. W. S. Newman, entry no. 2577, of Co. A, 40th NC, admitted for unspecified reasons between March 21 and April 7, 1865.
Source: Hanahan (BV), 3; Tanner (BV), 147; *NCT*, I:382; M270; Sokolosky, *NC's Confederate Hospitals*, vol. 2; RG109, 6/291:51.

▲Nivens, Dunkin, Private, Company C
Bentonville
According to Surgeon Hanahan's "Return of Wounded for Hagood's Brigade" at Bentonville, Pvt. D. Niven, Co. C, 40th NC, was slightly wounded in the scalp on March 19, 1865. D. Niven also appears in Surgeon Tanner's "Return of Casualties in Hoke's Div. near Bentonville." Private Dunkin Nivens of Co. C is probably the same soldier as Pvt. D. Niven. Neither Niven's service records nor *NC Troops* note the wound he received at the battle of Bentonville. Niven's service records and *NC Troops* incorrectly note that he was hospitalized at GH No. 3 in Greensboro on an unspecified date in March 1865. In National Archives Confederate Record Group 109, General Hospital No. 3's location is erroneously identified as Greensboro. High Point is the correct location. Confederate authorities began relocating GH No. 3 from Goldsboro to High Point on March 11, 1865, as part of the town's evacuation. The hospital resumed operations in High Point on or about March 19, 1865. The No. 3 Patient Registry lists a Pvt. D. Niven, entry no. 2419, of Co. C, 40th NC, admitted for unspecified reasons between March 21 and April 7, 1865
Source: Hanahan (BV), 3; Tanner (BV), 147; *NCT*, I:402; M270; Sokolosky, *NC's Confederate Hospitals*, vol. 2; RG109, 6/291:48.

♦▲Oast, W. T., Private, Company F
Goldsboro (Inconclusive)
U.S. Army prisoner of war records indicate that Pvt. W. T. Oast was captured at Goldsboro on March 15, 1865. Either the date of capture or location is incorrect. Federal forces did not occupy Goldsboro for another week. Based on the date, it is probable that Kinston was the location of the capture. Confined at Hart's Island, New York Harbor, and released upon taking the Oath of Allegiance on June 19, 1865. *NC Troops* incorrectly identifies the date of capture as May 15, 1865.
Source: *NCT*, I:434; M270.

O'Connell, John, First Sergeant, Company H (2nd)
Bentonville
Captured at the battle of Bentonville on March 19, 1865. Confined at Point Lookout, Maryland, and released upon taking the Oath of Allegiance on June 6, 1865.
Source: *NCT*, I:486; M270; NC Confederate Widow's Pension (Chatham County).

Owen, David A., Private, Company I
Bentonville

Captured at the battle of Bentonville on March 19, 1865. Confined at Point Lookout, Maryland, and released upon taking the Oath of Allegiance on June 29, 1865.
Source: *NCT*, I:497; M270; NC Confederate Widow's Pension (Hertford County).

Owen, Jacob S., Private, Company I
Bentonville
Captured at the battle of Bentonville on March 19, 1865. Confined at Point Lookout, Maryland, and released upon taking the Oath of Allegiance on June 29, 1865.
Source: *NCT*, I:497; M270.

Pate, Robert, Private, Company F
Kinston (Post Wise's Forks)
U.S. Army Provost Marshal records indicate that Pvt. Robert Pate was captured at Kinston on March 18, 1865, with the letter "D" included in the remarks section, which probably designated him as a deserter. No further information. Paroled on March 19, 1865.
Source: *NCT*, I:434; M270.

Philips, Reuben, Private, Company C
Bentonville
Captured at the battle of Bentonville on March 19, 1865. Confined at Point Lookout, Maryland, and released upon taking the Oath of Allegiance on June 16, 1865.
Source: *NCT*, I:403, 713; M270.

Phillips, Frank, Private, Company C
Bentonville
Captured at the battle of Bentonville on March 19, 1865. Confined at Point Lookout, Maryland, and released upon taking the Oath of Allegiance on June 26, 1865.
Source: *NCT*, I:403; M270.

▲Potter, John L., Private, Company B
Fort Anderson
Private John L. Potter and five other soldiers from Co. B were wounded on February 3, 1865, by a single shell fired from the USS *Tacony* on Fort Anderson. The men happened to be lounging in their quarters when the round impacted. Potter was only slightly wounded. *NC Troops* does not note his wounding at Fort Anderson.
Source: Fonvielle, *Fort Anderson*, 43-44; *NCT*, I:392; M270.

♦Pullin, J. L., Private, Company I
Wise's Forks (Inconclusive)
According to Surgeon Hanahan's "List of Killed and Wounded in Hagood's Brigade" at Wise's Forks, Pvt. J. L. Pullin, Co. I, 40th NC, was wounded in the left hand. No J. L. Pullin is listed on the unit rolls. However, there are Pullens: Pvt. J. C. (Co. H) and Pvt. John C. (Co. I). One of these two soldiers may be the soldier identified as Pvt. J. L. Pullin. Further research is required.
Source: Hanahan (WF), 1; Tanner (WF), 137; *NCT*, I:487, 497; M270.

▲Purser, James R., Private, Company B
Bentonville
According to Surgeon Hanahan's "Return of Wounded for Hagood's Brigade" at Bentonville, Pvt. J. R. Purser, Co. B, 40th NC, was slightly wounded in the back on March 19, 1865. His name also appears on Surgeon Tanner's "Return of Casualties in Hoke's Div. near Bentonville." Private James R. Purser of Co. B is the same soldier as Pvt. J. R. Purser. Neither Purser's service records nor *NC Troops* note the wound he received at the battle of Bentonville.
Source: Hanahan (BV), 3; Tanner (BV), 147; *NCT*, I:392; M270.

▲Purser, Jesse D., Private, Company B

Wise's Forks
NC Troops indicate that Pvt Jesse D. Purser was wounded at Kinston on March 8, 1865. Paroled at Greensboro on May 2, 1865. Purser's Confederate pension application indicates that he was wounded in the "knee and eye" at "the last Battle of Kinston." The application further stated, "left eyesight gone from injury," and a bullet caused the injury to his right knee.
Source: *NCT*, I:392; M270; NC Confederate Pension (Carteret County).

▲**Ramsey, William J.**, Private, Company I
Bentonville
According to Surgeon Hanahan's "Return of Wounded for Hagood's Brigade" at Bentonville, Pvt. W. J. Raysey, Co. I, 40th NC, was slightly wounded in the right leg on March 19, 1865. A W. J. Racey also appears in Surgeon Tanner's "Return of Casualties in Hoke's Div. near Bentonville." The company rolls list no soldier with the surnames of Raysey or Racey; however, there is a Pvt. William J. Ramsey. Hanahan and Tanner probably transcribed the surname incorrectly, and Private William J. Ramsey of Co. I is the soldier. Neither Ramsey's service records nor *NC Troops* note the wound he received at the battle of Bentonville; however, he was paroled as a patient in Tate House Hospital, a temporary ward of GH No. 12 in Greensboro, at the war's conclusion.
Source: Hanahan (BV), 3; Tanner (BV), 148; *NCT*, I:497; M270.

Rasberry, Alex J., Private, Company F
Greene County (Post Bentonville)
U.S. Army provost records indicate that Pvt. Alex J. Rasberry was captured in Greene County on March 27, 1865. Confined at Hart's Island, New York Harbor, and released upon taking the Oath of Allegiance on June 19, 1865.
Source: *NCT*, I:435; M270.

▲**Ray, C. L.**, Private, Company H (2nd)
Wise's Forks
According to Surgeon Hanahan's "List of Killed and Wounded in Hagood's Brigade" at Wise's Forks, Pvt. C. L. Ray, Co. H, 40th NC, was severely wounded in the abdomen. Private C. L. Ray of Co. H is also listed in Tanner's "Return of Casualties near Kinston." GH No. 3 "Register of Wounded and Operations" indicates Pvt. C. Ray, Co. H, 40th NC, was wounded on March 10, 1865, suffering from a gunshot wound to the right thigh. Neither *NC Troops* nor his service records note his wounding. His service records and *NC Troops* incorrectly note that Ray was transferred from Kinston to GH No. 3 in Greensboro on March 10, 1865, for unspecified reasons. In National Archives Confederate Record Group 109, General Hospital No. 3's location is erroneously identified as Greensboro. Goldsboro is the correct location. Confederate authorities began relocating GH No. 3 from Goldsboro to High Point on March 11, 1865, as part of the town's evacuation. The hospital resumed operations in High Point on or about March 19, 1865. No further records.
Source: Hanahan (WF), 1; Tanner (WF), 137; GH No. 3 Ledger B, entry no. 65; *NCT*, I:487; M270; Sokolosky, *NC's Confederate Hospitals*, vol. 2.

▲**Rich, Lewis W.**, Private, Company H (2nd)
Fort Anderson
According to Wilmington's *Daily Journal*, Pvt. L. M. Rich, Co. H, 40th NC, was severely wounded in the hip and thigh during the engagement at Fort Anderson and was admitted to GH No. 4 in the port city on February 19, 1865, and transferred the following day to another hospital. *NC Troops* does not identify Rich as having been wounded at Fort Anderson.
Source: *Daily Journal* (Wilmington, NC), February 20, 1865; *NCT*, I:487, 715; M270.

▲**Ricks, A. E.**, Private, Company H (2nd)
Bentonville
According to Surgeon Hanahan's "Return of Wounded for Hagood's Brigade" at Bentonville, Pvt. A. E. Ricks, Co. H, 40th NC, was severely wounded in the right shoulder on March 19, 1865. His name also

appears on Surgeon Tanner's "Return of Casualties in Hoke's Div. near Bentonville." Neither Ricks's service records nor *NC Troops* note the wound he received at the battle of Bentonville.
Source: Hanahan (BV), 3; Tanner (BV), 148; *NCT*, I:487; M270.

♦Ricks, R., Private, Company H (2nd)
Bentonville (Inconclusive)
According to Surgeon Hanahan's "Return of Wounded for Hagood's Brigade" at Bentonville, Pvt. R. Ricks, Co. H, 40th NC, was slightly wounded in the right arm on March 19, 1865. There is no R. Ricks listed in Co. H or any other unit in the regiment. A Pvt. R. H. Ricks previously served in Co. G but transferred to Co. A, 10th NC Troops (1st Artillery) in October 1862. Further research is required.
Source: Hanahan (BV), 3; Tanner (BV), 148; *NCT*, I:442; M270.

▲Robason, Alfred, Private, Company B
Fort Anderson
Private Alfred Robason and five other soldiers from Co. B were wounded on February 3, 1865, by a single shell fired by the USS *Tacony* on Fort Anderson. The men happened to be lounging in their quarters when the round impacted. Robason was "torn up" by the shell's shrapnel. Robason died of wounds on February 5, 1865. Location of death not provided. His widow's pension application included a sworn statement from Harmon Cory, who was present at the time of Robason's death, indicating that he died at "Fort Anderson in the hospital on the 6th day of February 1865." His widow signed her pension application as Prudence Roberson.
Source: Fonvielle, *Fort Anderson*, 43-44; *NCT*, I:393; M270; NC Confederate Widow's Pension (Martin County.)

Roberts, Joseph L., Private, Company C
Goldsboro
Captured at Goldsboro on March 22, 1865, and released the next day upon taking the Oath of Allegiance.
Source: *NCT*, I:403, 713; M270.

Robertson, John C., Captain, Company F
Bentonville
Captured at the battle of Bentonville on March 19, 1865. Confined at Johnson's Island, Ohio, and released upon taking the Oath of Allegiance on June 17, 1865.
Source: *NCT*, I:428; M270.

Ross, John Riley, Sergeant, Company B
Bentonville
Wounded at the battle of Bentonville on March 19, 1865. Ross's service records do not note the wound received at Bentonville. No further information.
Source: *NCT*, I:393; M270.

Rushing, Elijah J., Private, Company H (2nd)
Bentonville
Captured at the battle of Bentonville on March 19, 1865. Confined at Point Lookout, Maryland, and released upon taking the Oath of Allegiance on June 3, 1865.
Source: *NCT*, I:487; M270.

Russell, Nicholas A., Private, Company H (2nd)
Town Creek
Captured at Town Creek on February 20, 1865. Confined at Point Lookout, Maryland, and released upon taking the Oath of Allegiance on June 17, 1865.
Source: *NCT*, I:487; M270.

Ryland, Noah, Company F
Bentonville

NC Troops notes that Pvt. Noah Ryland was wounded at Bentonville on March 19, 1865. Ryland indicated on his Confederate pension application that he was shot by a "rifle ball through his right foot" at the battle of Bentonville on March 19, 1865. Ryland's service records do not note the wound he received at Bentonville. He was later paroled at Greensboro on April 29, 1865.
Source: *NCT*, I:435; NC Confederate Pension (Greene County); M270.

Sikes, James T., Private, Company H (2nd)
Bentonville
Captured at the battle of Bentonville on March 19, 1865. Confined at Point Lookout, Maryland, and released upon taking the Oath of Allegiance on June 19, 1865.
Source: *NCT*, I:487; M270.

Simmons, Lemuel, Private, Company A
Kinston (Post Wise's Forks)
U.S. Army Provost Marshal records indicate that Pvt. Lemuel Simmons was captured at Kinston on March 16, 1865, with the letter "D" included in the remarks section, which probably designated him as a deserter. No further information.
Source: *NCT*, I:383; M270.

Southerland, Wiley T., Private, Company H (2nd)
Fort Anderson
Captured at Fort Anderson on February 19, 1865. Confined at Point Lookout, Maryland, and released upon taking the Oath of Allegiance on May 14, 1865.
Source: *NCT*, I:488; M270.

Stafford, William W., Private, Company F
Moseley Hall (Post Bentonville)
U.S. Army Provost Marshal records indicate that Pvt. William W. Stafford was captured at Moseley Hall on March 29, 1865. Confined at Hart's Island, New York Harbor, and released upon taking the Oath of Allegiance on June 19, 1865.
Source: *NCT*, I:435; M270; NC Confederate Pension (Harnett County).

Stokes, George A., Private, Company A
Bentonville
NC Troops notes that Pvt. George A. Stokes was wounded at Bentonville on March 19, 1865. Stokes indicated on his Confederate pension application that he was wounded in the right hip "by a spent ball and knocked down" at the battle of Bentonville. Stokes's service records do not note the wound he received at Bentonville.
Source: *NCT*, I:383; NC Confederate Pension (Duplin County); M270.

♦▲Strayhorn, Isaac R., Sergeant, Company H (2nd)
Bentonville (Inconclusive)
According to Surgeon Hanahan's "Return of Wounded for Hagood's Brigade" at Bentonville, Sgt. J. R. Strayhorn, Co. H, 40th NC, was slightly wounded in the scalp on March 19, 1865. Strayhorn is also listed in Surgeon Tanner's "Return of Casualties in Hoke's Div. near Bentonville," but also as Pvt. J. R. Strayhorn. Paroled in Greensboro on an unspecified date. Isaac R. Strayhorn is probably the same soldier as J. R. Strayhorn. Neither Strayhorn's service records nor *NC Troops* note the wound he received at the battle of Bentonville. Further research is required.
Source: Hanahan (BV), 2; Tanner (BV), 147; *NCT*, I:488; M270.

Sugg, George W., Private, Company F
Bentonville
Captured at the battle of Bentonville on March 19, 1865. Confined at Point Lookout, Maryland, where he died of pneumonia on May 28, 1865.
Source: *NCT*, I:436; M270.

♦**Sutton, William Hardy**, Private, Company A
(Inconclusive)
William Henry Sutton's service records erroneously note that he was admitted to GH No. 3 in Greensboro on March 2, 1865, suffering from a gunshot wound to his left arm. In National Archives Confederate Record Group 109, General Hospital No. 3's location is erroneously identified as Greensboro. Goldsboro is the correct location. Confederate authorities began relocating GH No. 3 from Goldsboro to High Point on March 11, 1865, as part of the town's evacuation. The hospital resumed operations in High Point on or about March 19, 1865. At some point, Sutton was transferred from Goldsboro to a Raleigh hospital, where he was captured as a patient on April 13, 1865. There are no further records.
Source: *NCT*, I:383; M270; Sokolosky, *NC's Confederate Hospitals*, vol. 2.

▲**Tarlton, John W.**, Private, Company C
Bentonville
According to Surgeon Hanahan's "Return of Wounded for Hagood's Brigade at Bentonville," Pvt. J. W. Darlton, Co. C, 40th NC, was severely wounded in the left hip on March 19, 1865. J. W. Darlton also appears in Surgeon Tanner's "Return of Casualties in Hoke's Div. near Bentonville." The company rolls list no soldier with the surname of Darlton; however, there is a Pvt. John W. Tarlton on the rolls that the *NC Troops* notes as having been wounded in March 1865. Hanahan and Tanner probably transcribed the surname incorrectly, and Private John W. Tarlton of Co. C is the same soldier as Pvt. J. W. Darlton. Tarlton's service records and *NC Troops* incorrectly note that he was hospitalized at GH No. 3 in Greensboro on an unspecified date in March 1865. In National Archives Confederate Record Group 109, General Hospital No. 3's location is erroneously identified as Greensboro. High Point is the correct location. Confederate authorities began relocating GH No. 3 from Goldsboro to High Point on March 11, 1865, as part of the town's evacuation. The hospital resumed operations in High Point on or about March 19, 1865. The No. 3 Patient Registry lists a Pvt. J. W. Tarlton, entry no. 2520, of Co. C, 40th NC, admitted for unspecified reasons between March 21 and April 7, 1865.
Source: Hanahan (BV), 4; Tanner (BV), 147; *NCT*, I:404; M270; RG109, 6/291:50; Sokolosky, *NC's Confederate Hospitals*, vol. 2; NC Confederate Widow's Pension (Anson County).

Tate, William N., Private, Company C
Near Town Creek
Captured near Town Creek on February 20, 1865. Confined at Point Lookout, Maryland, and released upon taking the Oath of Allegiance on June 21, 1865.
Source: *NCT*, I:404; M270; NC Confederate Pension (Alamance County).

▲**Thomas, John A., Jr.**, 1st Sergeant, Company B
Fort Anderson
Sergeant John A. Thomas and five other soldiers from Co. B were wounded on February 3, 1865, by a single shell fired from the USS *Tacony* on Fort Anderson. The men happened to be lounging in their quarters when the round impacted. Thomas was only slightly wounded. *NC Troops* does not note his wounding at Fort Anderson.
Source: Fonvielle, *Fort Anderson*, 43-44; *NCT*, I:393; M270.

▲**Tommer, Alexander**, Sergeant, Company B
Wise's Forks
According to Surgeon Hanahan's "List of Killed and Wounded in Hagood's Brigade" at Wise's Forks, Sgt. Alex Toomer, Co. B, 40th NC, was killed during the battle. Neither *NC Troops* nor his service records note his death.
Source: Hanahan (WF), 1; Tanner (WF), 137; *NCT*, I:393; M270.

Tuten, Thomas A. E., 2nd Lieutenant, Company I
Bentonville

Captured at the battle of Bentonville on March 19, 1865. Confined at Johnson's Island, Ohio, and released upon taking the Oath of Allegiance on June 17, 1865.
Source: *NCT*, I:491; M270.

Tuten, Wilson, Private, Company B
Fort Anderson
Captured at Fort Anderson on February 19, 1865. Confined at Point Lookout, Maryland, and released upon taking the Oath of Allegiance on June 21, 1865. His widow's pension includes the middle initial "B."
Source: *NCT*, I:393; M270; NC Confederate Pension (Beaufort County).

▲Vann, Albert C., Private, Company B
Bentonville
U.S. Army records indicate that Pvt. Albert C. Vann was captured on March 19, 1865, at two different locations, Bentonville and Smithill [sic]. Confined at Point Lookout, Maryland, and released upon taking the Oath of Allegiance on June 3, 1865. *NC Troops* incorrectly identifies Smithville (present-day Southport) as the capture location. Based on the date, Bentonville is the probable location of capture.
Source: *NCT*, I:394; M270.

Vause, Robert Bond, 2nd Lieutenant, Company A
Fort Anderson
Lieutenant Robert B. Vause was killed instantly at Fort Anderson on February 18, 1865, by the concussion from an overhead exploding naval shell "without a single fragment having struck him." Vause was buried along the west bank of the Cape Fear River upriver from the fort, where, according to family history, he still rests. The family later placed a headstone in the Vause Family Cemetery in Lenoir County, North Carolina, to memorialize his sacrifice. His home, a significant wartime structure on the Wise's Forks battlefield, stood until its demolition in 2018.
Source: *NCT*, I:376, 719; M270; Fonvielle, *Fort Anderson*, 72.

♦Vick, William B., Private, Company F
(Inconclusive)
Discharge from GH No. 13 (Pettigrew) in Raleigh on February 27, 1865. On an unspecified date and location, Vick was captured. Confined at Point Lookout, Maryland, and released upon taking the Oath of Allegiance on June 21, 1865.
Source: *NCT*, I:436; M270.

Waters, George W., Corporal, Company I
Fort Anderson
Captured at Fort Anderson on February 19, 1865. Confined at Point Lookout, Maryland, and released upon taking the Oath of Allegiance on June 22, 1865.
Source: *NCT*, I:499; M270.

Watson, Guilford H., Guilford, Company A
Kinston (Post Wise's Forks)
Captured and paroled at Kinston on March 15, 1865. No further records.
Source: *NCT*, I:384; M270.

Watts, Josiah T., Private, Company H (2nd)
Fayetteville
Captured at Fayetteville on March 14, 1865. Confined at Point Lookout, Maryland, and released upon taking the Oath of Allegiance on June 11, 1865.
Source: *NCT*, I:489; M270; NC Confederate Widow's Pension (Wake County).

Webb, David, Private, Company H (2nd)
Bentonville

Captured at the battle of Bentonville on March 19, 1865. Confined at Point Lookout, Maryland, and released upon taking the Oath of Allegiance on June 22, 1865.
Source: *NCT*, I:489; M270; NC Confederate Widow's Pension (Wilson County).

▲Whitaker, William, Private, Company B
Fort Anderson
Private William Whitaker and five other soldiers from Co. B were wounded on February 3, 1865, by a single shell fired from the USS *Tacony* on Fort Anderson. The men happened to be lounging in their quarters when the round impacted. Whitaker was wounded "right bad" in the leg. He was admitted to Wilmington's GH No. 4 on February 5, 1865, with a gunshot wound to the left leg, and transferred to GH No. 3 in Goldsboro on February 12, 1865. Another medical record notes that he was transferred to GH No. 6 in Fayetteville on February 20, 1865. The references to No. 6 and a later date are probably incorrect, and they highlight the confusion in Wilmington in the days before the Confederate evacuation on February 22, 1865. William Whitaker was paroled in Goldsboro on May 5, 1865. His Confederate pension indicates that he was wounded in the left leg below the knee by "a piece of bomb shell," fracturing the bone.
Source: Fonvielle, *Fort Anderson*, 43-44; *NCT*, I:394; M270; NC Confederate Pension (Martin County).

♦Whitehurst, Charles C., Captain, Company I
Wise's Forks (Inconclusive)
Captain Charles C. Whitehurst's service records indicate that he was admitted to GH No. 13 (Pettigrew Hospital) for a contusion on March 11, 1865, and transferred to the Officer's Hospital (Haywood House) on March 27, 1865. His name also appears in the March 29, 1865, edition of the *NC Standard* as a patient at GH No. 13 (Pettigrew Hospital) in Raleigh. On an undetermined date, medical authorities transferred Captain Whitehurst to Greensboro, where he was admitted to Tate House Hospital, a temporary ward of GH No. 12. He was later paroled as a patient at the hospital on April 28, 1865.
Source: M270; *NCS* (Raleigh), March 29, 1865; *NCT*, I:490.

▲Willis, John W., Private, Company C
Bentonville
According to Surgeon Hanahan's "Return of Wounded for Hagood's Brigade" at Bentonville, Pvt. J. W. Willis, Co. C, 40th NC, was slightly wounded in the left leg on March 19, 1865. His name also appears on Surgeon Tanner's "Return of Casualties in Hoke's Div. near Bentonville." Private John W. Willis of Co. C is the same soldier as Pvt. J. W. Willis. Willis's service records note that he was admitted to GH No. 13 (Raleigh) on March 21, 1865, and furloughed from there for 60 days beginning March 27, 1865.
Source: Hanahan (BV), 2; Tanner (BV), 147; *NCT*, I:404, 721; *DP* (Raleigh), March 28, 1865.

▲Wilson, Calvin D., Private, Company H (2nd)
Bentonville
According to Surgeon Hanahan's "Return of Wounded for Hagood's Brigade" at Bentonville, Sgt. C. D. Wilson, Co. H, 40th NC, was severely wounded in the abdomen on March 19, 1865. His name also appears on Surgeon Tanner's "Return of Casualties in Hoke's Div. near Bentonville." Sergeant Calvin D. Wilson of Co. H is the same soldier as Pvt. C. D. Wilson listed in *NC Troops*. Wilson's service records, which also notes the rank of private, indicate that he was admitted to GH No. 13 (Pettigrew) in Raleigh on March 21, 1865, with a gunshot wound to his testicles, and later transferred to a hospital in Salisbury, probably GH No. 10, on March 26, 1865. *NC Troops* erred in noting his date of hospital admittance as March 25, 1865. Calvin D. Wilson's Alamance County Confederate Pension application reported he was wounded in the "left testicle" at the battle of Bentonville. In a sworn statement submitted on Wilson's behalf, Lt. John H. Hill described Calvin Wilson as a "true & brave Confederate soldier...wounded at Bentonville."
Source: Hanahan (BV), 4; Tanner (BV), 147; *NCT*, I:489; *COB*, March 26, 1865; *NCS*, (Raleigh), March 24, 1865; M270; NC Confederate Pension (Alamance County).

Wilson, Peter, Private, Company H (2nd)
Bentonville

Captured at the battle of Bentonville on March 19, 1865. Confined at Point Lookout, Maryland, and released upon taking the Oath of Allegiance on June 3, 1865.
Source: *NCT*, I:489; M270.

▲Winborn, Woodard, Private, Company F
Bentonville
According to Surgeon Tanner's "Return of Casualties in Hoke's Div. near Bentonville," Private W. Winman, Co. F, 40th NC, was slightly wounded in the head. The March 29, 1865, edition of the *NC Standard* reported that Woodard Winborn of Co. F, 40th NC, was suffering from a head wound at GH No. 8 (Peace Institute) in Raleigh. Surgeon Hanahan erred in the correct spelling of the surname, but the unit identification and description of the wound are the same. Woodward Winborn's Confederate pension application indicates that he was "wounded in the head and left side" at Bennettsville [sic] in May 1865, which Winborn incorrectly recalled. Private Woodard Winborn of Co. F is the same soldier listed by Tanner as Pvt. W. Winman. On an undetermined date, he was admitted to Odd Fellows Lodge Hospital, a temporary ward of GH No. 12 in Greensboro, where he received his parole on May 2, 1865.
Source: Tanner (BV), 147; *NCT*, I:437, 721; *NCS* (Raleigh), March 29, 1865; M270; NC Confederate Pension (Edgecombe County).

Windley, James T., First Sergeant, Company I
Bentonville
Captured at the battle of Bentonville on March 19, 1865. Confined at Point Lookout, Maryland, and released upon taking the Oath of Allegiance on June 22, 1865.
Source: *NCT*, I:499; M270.

Winningham, James N., Private, Company H (2nd)
Bentonville
Captured at the battle of Bentonville on March 19, 1865. Confined at Point Lookout, Maryland, and released upon taking the Oath of Allegiance on June 22, 1865.
Source: *NCT*, I:489; M270.

Workman, George W., Private, Company I
Fort Anderson
Captured at Fort Anderson on February 19, 1865. Confined at Point Lookout, Maryland, and released upon taking the Oath of Allegiance on May 14, 1865.
Source: *NCT*, I:500; M270.

Lt. Robert Bond Vause
Co. A, 40th Regiment NC Troops (3rd NC Artillery)
Killed at Fort Anderson on February 18, 1865.

(Courtesy of John Vause)

Sr. Surgeon Ralph B. Hanahan
Casualty Return for Hagood's Brigade battle of Wise's Forks

(Wade Sokolosky Collection)

10th Battalion North Carolina Heavy Artillery

▲**Austin, John E. W.**, Sergeant, Company C
Bentonville
According to Asst. Surgeon T. W. Bickett's compiled casualty list from the battle of Bentonville for 10th Battalion NC, Sgt. J. E. W. Austin, Co. C, was slightly wounded in the hand on March 19, 1865. The March 27, 1865, edition of the *Daily Progress* reported that Sgt. J. E. W. Austin of Co. C, 10th NC, was at Raleigh's Baptist Church Hospital with a wounded hand. Austin was later paroled at Charlotte with his unit on May 3, 1865.
Source: *WD* (Charlotte), April 4, 1865; *NCT*, I:532, 693; *DP* (Raleigh), March 274, 1865; M270.

▲**Baucom, Henry T.**, Private, Company C
Bentonville
According to Asst. Surgeon T. W. Bickett's compiled casualty list from the battle of Bentonville for 10th Battalion NC, Pvt. H. M. Baucom suffered a "very slight" wound to his hand on March 19, 1865. Private Henry T. Baucom is probably the same soldier as Pvt. H. M. Baucom. *NC Troops* notes that his correct middle initial may be M.
Source: *NCT*, I:532, 694; M270.

▲**Baucom, Lewis R.**, Private, Company C
Bentonville
According to Asst. Surgeon T. W. Bickett's compiled casualty list from the battle of Bentonville for 10th Battalion NC, Pvt. L. R. Baucom was wounded in the arm on March 19, 1865, resulting in its amputation. Baucom's service records note that he was admitted to GH No. 13 in Raleigh on March 24, 1865, with an amputated right arm caused by a gunshot wound. He was later paroled at Charlotte on May 3, 1865. Lewis R. Baucom stated in his 1885 Confederate pension that he was "shot through the right arm between the elbow and shoulder, in consequence of which his right arm was amputated, about three inches from the shoulder joint." A second pension application filed in 1901 indicated that Baucom's arm was amputated on the battlefield.
Source: *WD* (Charlotte), April 4, 1865; *NCT*, I:532, 694; M270; NC Confederate Pension (Anson County), 1885 and 1901.

▲**Benton, Jesse Morris**, Corporal, Company D
Bentonville
According to Asst. Surgeon T. W. Bickett's compiled casualty list from the battle of Bentonville for 10th Battalion NC, Corp. J. M. Benton was slightly wounded in the head on March 19, 1865. *NC Troops* notes that he may have been slightly wounded in the head at Bentonville. The March 27, 1865, edition of the *Daily Progress* reported that A. Benton of Co. D, 10th NC, was at Raleigh's Baptist Church Hospital suffering from a concussion. Corporal Jesse M. Benton is probably the same soldier as A. Benton. *NC Troops* notes that Benton may have been wounded at Bentonville on March 19, 1865.
Source: *WD* (Charlotte), April 4, 1865; *DP* (Raleigh), March 27, 1865; *NCT*, I:533, 543, 695; M270.

▲**Bivens, William**, Private, Company C
Bentonville
According to Asst. Surgeon T. W. Bickett's compiled casualty list from the battle of Bentonville for 10th Battalion NC, Pvt. Wm. Bivens, Co. C, was severely wounded in the hand on March 19, 1865. The March 27, 1865, edition of the *Daily Progress* reported that Pvt. W. Brevins of Co. C, 10th NC, was at Raleigh's Baptist Church Hospital with a wounded hand. Private William Bivens is the same soldier as Pvt. W. Brevins. His service records do not note the wound he received at the battle of Bentonville.
Source: *WD* (Charlotte), April 4, 1865; *DP* (Raleigh), March 27, 1865; *NCT*, I:533, 695; M270.

▲**Conder, William**, Private, Company C
Bentonville

According to Asst. Surgeon T. W. Bickett's compiled casualty list from the battle of Bentonville for 10th Battalion NC, Pvt. Wm. Conder, Co. C, was severely wounded in the arm and thigh on March 19, 1865. The March 27, 1865, edition of the *Daily Progress* reported that Pvt. W. Conder of Co. C, 10th NC, was at Raleigh's Baptist Church Hospital with a wound to the face, not his arm and thigh. His service records do not note the wound he received at the battle of Bentonville.
Source: *WD* (Charlotte), April 4, 1865; *DP* (Raleigh), March 27, 1865; *NCT*, I:534, 698; M270.

▲Forbis, Larkin, V., Private, Company C
Bentonville
According to Asst. Surgeon T. W. Bickett's compiled casualty list from the battle of Bentonville for 10th Battalion NC, Pvt. L. V. Forbis, Co. C, was severely wounded in the hip on March 19, 1865. His service records and *NC Troops* incorrectly note that Forbis was hospitalized at GH No. 3 in Greensboro on an unspecified date in March 1865. In National Archives Confederate Record Group 109, General Hospital No. 3's location is erroneously identified as Greensboro. High Point is the correct location. Confederate authorities began relocating GH No. 3 from Goldsboro to High Point on March 11, 1865, as part of the town's evacuation. The hospital resumed operations in High Point on or about March 19, 1865. The No. 3 Patient Registry lists a Pvt. L. B. Forbeth, Co. C, 10th NC, entry no. 2535, was admitted between March 21 - April 7, 1865, for unspecified reasons. Because the hospital misspelled Forbis and incorrectly abbreviated his unit, Pvt. Larkin V. Forbis is probably the same soldier as Pvt. L. B. Forbeth. Forbis was later transferred and admitted to GH No. 11 (Charlotte) with a gunshot wound in the left hip. He was paroled at Charlotte on May 3, 1865.
Source: *WD* (Charlotte), April 4, 1865; *NCT*, I:534, 700; M270; Sokolosky, *NC's Confederate Hospitals*, vol. 2; RG109, 6/291:50; NC Confederate Widow's Pension (Mecklenburg County).

▲Fowler, William S., Private, Company D
Bentonville
According to Asst. Surgeon T. W. Bickett's compiled casualty list from the battle of Bentonville for 10th Battalion NC, Pvt. W. S. Fowler, Co. D, was wounded in the leg on March 19, 1865. His service records indicate he was admitted to GH No. 13 (Pettigrew) in Raleigh on March 24, 1865, suffering from a gunshot wound to his left knee joint, which required amputation to the left thigh. Fowler died four days later, on March 29, 1865. The place of the burial is unknown.
Source: *WD* (Charlotte), April 4, 1865; *NCT*, I:544, 701; M270.

▲Goodson, Peter M., Private, Company D
Bentonville
According to Asst. Surgeon T. W. Bickett's compiled casualty list from the battle of Bentonville for 10th Battalion NC, Pvt. P. M. Goodson, Co. D, was mortally wounded on March 19, 1865, and later died before April 4, 1865. The place and date of death are unknown. *NC Troops* notes his wounding at Bentonville.
Source: *WD* (Charlotte), April 4, 1865; *NCT*, I:544, 702; Purser, *AIANCT*, II:10; M270.

Gregory, James N., Private, Company B
Averasboro (Post Battle)
Captured at Averasboro on March 18, 1865. According to his service records, Gregory was a resident of Harnett County before the war. The capture date is two days after the battle of Averasboro and a day before Bentonville. Gregory may have been captured as a straggler or one of an undetermined number of Confederate wounded left behind following the battle. Confined at Point Lookout, Maryland, and released upon taking the Oath of Allegiance on June 4, 1865.
Source: *NCT*, I:526; M270; NC Confederate Pension (Harnett County).

▲Harris, Calvin G., Private, Company A
Bentonville
Note: *NC Troops* and National Archives Compiled Service Records for North Troops incorrectly list Calvin Harris's middle initial as C. It should read Calvin G. Harris. According to Asst. Surgeon T. W. Bickett's compiled casualty list from the battle of Bentonville for 10th Battalion NC, Pvt. C. G. Harris was

slightly wounded in the hip (contusion) on March 19, 1865. *NC Troops* notes that he was wounded in the hip (contusion) at Bentonville. Harris's service records do not note the wound he received at the battle of Bentonville. The patient registry for GH No. 3 in High Point lists a Pvt. G. C. Harris, Co. B, 10th NC, entry no. 2316, admitted between March 21 - April 7, 1865, for unspecified reasons. This is Pvt. Calvin G. Harris of Co. A, 10th NC Battalion. C. G. Harris indicated on his Confederate pension that he was wounded at Bentonville while serving in Co. A, 10th Battalion NC. Harris noted that "a bombshell" struck him "high on the right hip."
Source: *WD* (Charlotte), April 4, 1865; *NCT*, I:517, 703; M270; RG109, 6/291:46; NC Confederate Pension (Davidson County).

Harris, James Edward, Sergeant, Company A
Bentonville
Wounded and captured at the battle of Bentonville on March 19, 1865. Confined at the hospital on David's Island, New York Harbor, until released in early May 1865.
Source: *NCT*, I:571, 703; M270; NC Confederate Pension (Davidson County).

▲Helms, John, Private, Company D
Bentonville
According to Asst. Surgeon T. W. Bickett's compiled casualty list from the battle of Bentonville for 10th Battalion NC, Pvt. John Helms, Company D, was mortally wounded on March 19, 1865, and later died before April 4, 1865. The place and date of death are unknown.
Source: *WD* (Charlotte), April 4, 1865; *NCT*, I:545, 703; Purser, *AIANCT*, II:10; M270.

▲Hemby, Amos, Private, Company D
Bentonville
According to Asst. Surgeon T. W. Bickett's compiled casualty list from the battle of Bentonville for 10th Battalion NC, Pvt. Amos Hemby, Co. D, was severely wounded in the hand on March 19, 1865.
Source: *WD* (Charlotte), April 4, 1865; *NCT*, I:545, 703; M270.

▲Leach, Henry C., Private, Company A
Bentonville
According to Asst. Surgeon T. W. Bickett's compiled casualty list from the battle of Bentonville for 10th Battalion NC, Pvt. Clay Leach, Co. A, was slightly wounded in the finger on March 19, 1865. Clay Leach is the same soldier as Henry C. Leach. The March 27, 1865, edition of the *Daily Progress* reported that Pvt. H. C. Leach of Co. A was at Raleigh's Baptist Church Hospital suffering from a wounded finger. *NC Troops* notes that he was wounded in the finger at Bentonville and hospitalized in Raleigh. Leach's service records do not note the wound received at the battle of Bentonville.
Source: *WD* (Charlotte), April 4, 1865; *NCT*, I:518, 707; *DP* (Raleigh), March 27, 1865; M270.

▲McCauley, Samuel S. S., 2nd Lieutenant, Company C
Bentonville
According to Asst. Surgeon T. W. Bickett's compiled casualty list from the battle of Bentonville for 10th Battalion NC, Lt. S. S. S. McCauley, Co. C, was slightly wounded in the side on March 19, 1865. The March 24, 1865 edition of the *NC Standard* listed a wounded Lt. S. S. S. McAubey of the 10th Battalion present in the Officer's Hospital (Haywood House) in Raleigh. The newspaper erred in the spelling of the surname. Neither *NC Troops* nor his service records note his presence in the Raleigh hospital. Additionally, his service records and *NC Troops* incorrectly note that McCauley was hospitalized at GH No. 3 in Greensboro on an unspecified date in March 1865. In National Archives Confederate Record Group 109, General Hospital No. 3's location is erroneously identified as Greensboro. High Point is the correct location. Confederate authorities began relocating GH No. 3 from Goldsboro to High Point on March 11, 1865, as part of the town's evacuation. The hospital resumed operations in High Point on or about March 19, 1865. The No. 3 Patient Registry lists Lt. S. S. S. McCauley, Co. I, 10th NC Battalion, entry no. 2365, was admitted between March 31 and April 7, 1865, for unspecified reasons. The hospital erroneously listed McCauley's unit as Co. I. He was paroled at Charlotte on May 3, 1865, with the remark: "at home."

Source: *WD* (Charlotte), April 4, 1865; *NCS* (Raleigh), March 24, 1865; *DP* (Raleigh), March 27, 1865; *NCT*, I:532, 708; M270; Sokolosky, *NC's Confederate Hospitals*, vol. 2; RG109, 6/291:47.

Mendenhall, Julian C., Private, Company A
Bentonville

According to Asst. Surgeon T. W. Bickett's compiled casualty list from the battle of Bentonville for 10th Battalion NC, Sgt. J. C. Mendenhall, Co. A, was slightly wounded in the face on March 19, 1865. Paroled at Greensboro May 4-5, 1865. No further records.
Source: *WD* (Charlotte), April 4, 1865; *NCT*, I:519, 710; M270; NC Confederate Widow's Pension (Davidson County).

▲Moore, Jordan M., Private, Company D
Averasboro (Post Battle)

Captured at Averasboro on March 18, 1865. According to his service records, Moore was a resident of Harnett County before the war. The capture date is two days after the battle of Averasboro and a day before Bentonville. Moore may have been captured as a straggler or one of an undetermined number of Confederate wounded left behind following the battle. Confined at Point Lookout, Maryland, and released upon taking the Oath of Allegiance on June 29, 1865. In 1894, Jordan M. Moore's application for admittance to the North Carolina Soldiers' Home was approved.
Source: *NCT*, I:546; M270; NC Confederate Pension (Harnett County).

▲Parks, Harvey Baxter, Private, Company C
Bentonville

According to Asst. Surgeon T. W. Bickett's compiled casualty list from the battle of Bentonville for 10th Battalion NC, Pvt. H. B. Parks, Co. A, suffered a flesh wound in his thigh on March 19, 1865. His service records and *NC Troops* incorrectly note that Parks was hospitalized at GH No. 3 in Greensboro on an unspecified date in March 1865. In National Archives Confederate Record Group 109, General Hospital No. 3's location is erroneously identified as Greensboro. High Point is the correct location. Confederate authorities began relocating GH No. 3 from Goldsboro to High Point on March 11, 1865, as part of the town's evacuation. The hospital resumed operations in High Point on or about March 19, 1865. The No. 3 Patient Registry lists a Pvt. H. B. Parks, Co. C, 10th NC, entry no. 2550, was admitted between March 31 – April 7, 1865, for unspecified reasons. The hospital erroneously listed Parks' unit as 10th NC without the battalion designation.
Source: *WD* (Charlotte), April 4, 1865; *NCT*, I:538, 712; M270; Sokolosky, *NC's Confederate Hospitals*, vol. 2; RG109, 6/281:50.

Quaite, William, Private, Company A
Bentonville

Captured at the battle of Bentonville on March 19, 1865. According to Asst. Surgeon T. W. Bickett's compiled casualty list from the battle of Bentonville for 10th Battalion NC, Pvt. W. Quate, Co. A, was missing. Confined at Point Lookout, Maryland, and released upon taking the Oath of Allegiance on June 17, 1865.
Source: *WD* (Charlotte), April 4, 1865; *NCT*, I:520; M270.

Spry, Gregory, Private, Company B
Bentonville

Captured at the battle of Bentonville on March 21, 1865. Confined at Hart's Island, New York, and released upon taking the Oath of Allegiance on June 18, 1865.
Source: *NCT*, I:530; M270.

Staten, William, Corporal, Company C
Bentonville

According to Asst. Surgeon T. W. Bickett's compiled casualty list from the battle of Bentonville for 10th Battalion NC, Corp. Wm. Staton, Co. C, was wounded in the left arm on March 19, 1865, requiring amputation. His service records note that he was admitted to GH No. 13 in Raleigh on March 24, 1865, with

an amputated left arm caused by a gunshot wound. He was captured as a patient at the Raleigh hospital on April 13, 1865. *NC Troops* also identifies the surname as "Staton." However, William spelled the surname as "Staten" on his Confederate pension application, which noted that he was wounded at Bentonville on March 19, 1865, "in the left arm, which caused said limb to be amputated at the shoulder."
Source: *WD* (Charlotte), April 4, 1865; *NCT*, I:540, 717; M270; NC Confederate Pension (Mitchell County).

♦Thigpen, A. Marion, Private, Company D
Bentonville (Inconclusive)
According to Asst. Surgeon T. W. Bickett's compiled casualty list from the battle of Bentonville for 10th Battalion NC, Lt. Thigpen, first name not given, Co. D, was slightly wounded in the hip on March 19, 1865. Lieutenant Thigpen is probably Pvt. A. Marion Thigpen of Co. A, 10th Battalion. Neither Pvt. A. M. Thigpen's service records nor *NC Troops* note that he was wounded in the battle of Bentonville. Further research is required.
Source: *WD* (Charlotte), April 4, 1865; *NCT*, I:548, 717; M270.

♦Turner, James, Private, Company C
Bentonville (Inconclusive)
According to Asst. Surgeon T. W. Bickett's compiled casualty list from the battle of Bentonville for 10th Battalion NC, Pvt. Jas. Turner was missing on March 19, 1865. Service records indicate that he was paroled at Charlotte on May 3, 1865.
Source: *WD* (Charlotte), April 4, 1865; *NCT*, I:548, 717; M270.

▲Underwood, William M., Company D
Bentonville
According to Asst. Surgeon T. W. Bickett's compiled casualty list from the battle of Bentonville for 10th Battalion NC, Pvt. Wm. A. Underwood, Co. D, was wounded in the thigh and hip on March 19, 1865. Underwood was admitted to GH No. 11 in Charlotte on March 27, 1865, wounded, and later furloughed from there on April 4, 1865. *NC Troops* notes his wounding at Bentonville.
Source: *WD* (Charlotte), April 4, 1865; *NCT*, I:541, 719; M270.

Walton, George D., Private, Company A
Bentonville
Wounded in the forearm at the battle of Bentonville on March 19, 1865. The March 24, 1865, edition of the *Daily Progress* reported that Pvt. G. Walton of Co. A was at Raleigh's Baptist Church Hospital suffering from a wounded forearm. Walton's service records do not note the wound received at the battle of Bentonville. He was later paroled at Greensboro on May 10, 1865.
Source: *NCT*, I:522; *DP* (Raleigh), March 27, 1865; M270.

▲Welborn, James M., Private, Company A
Bentonville
According to Asst. Surgeon T. W. Bickett's compiled casualty list from the battle of Bentonville for 10th Battalion NC, Pvt. J. M. Wilburn, Co. A, was wounded in the right arm and lung dangerously on March 19, 1865. Private James M. Welborn, Co. A, is Pvt. J. M. Wilburn. *NC Troops* notes his wounding at Bentonville.
Source: *WD* (Charlotte), April 4, 1865; *NCT*, I:522, 720; M270.

▲Wolfe, John N., Company C
Bentonville
According to Asst. Surgeon T. W. Bickett's compiled casualty list from the battle of Bentonville for 10th Battalion NC, Pvt. John Wolfe, Co. C, was killed on March 19, 1865. *NC Troops* notes his death on March 19, 1865, at Bentonville.
Source: *WD* (Charlotte), April 4, 1865; *NCT*, I:541, 721; Purser, *AIANCT*, II:10; M270.

Private John H. Curtis
Company E, 13th NC Light Artillery
Mortally Wounded on March 19, 1865, at Bentonville
Died March 23, 1865

(Courtesy of Bentonville Battlefield State Historic Site)

13th Battalion North Carolina Light Artillery[1]

Barber, Murdock, Private, Company A
Rockingham County
Captured in Rockingham County on March 8, 1865, while home on authorized furlough. Confined at Point Lookout, Maryland, and released upon taking the Oath of Allegiance on June 24, 1865.
Source: *NCT*, I:552; M270.

Batchelor, James K. P., Private, Company D
Bentonville
Wounded at the battle of Bentonville on or about March 19, 1865. Batchelor noted in his Confederate pension application that he was shot in the right side that "passed entirely through, which broke three ribs and injured my lungs." Service records do not indicate that he was hospitalized because of his wound. *NC Troops* notes that he was wounded at Bentonville.
Source: *NCT*, I:577; M270.

Bowen, Martin Van Buren, Private, Company C
Kinston (Post Wise's Forks)
Captured at Kinston on March 15, 1865, and paroled. Company rolls for January-February 1865 note: "Temporarily detailed in the Quartermaster Department, Kinston."
Source: *NCT*, I:569; M270.

▲**Brantley, S.**, Private, Company D
Wise's Forks
According to Surgeon Hanahan's "List of Killed and Wounded in Hagood's Brigade" at Wise's Forks, Pvt. S. Brantley, Co. D, was slightly wounded in the right elbow. Neither his service records nor *NC Troops* note his wounding at Wise's Forks.
Source: Hanahan (WF), 1; Tanner (WF), 137; *NCT*, I:578; M270.

Brown, John L., Quartermaster Sergeant, Company D
Bentonville
Captured at the battle of Bentonville on March 19, 1865. Confined at Point Lookout, Maryland, and released upon taking the Oath of Allegiance on June 24, 1865. In 1906, John L. Brown's application for acceptance into the North Carolina Soldiers' Home was approved because of "bad health, unable to take care of himself."
Source: *NCT*, I:578; M270; NC Confederate Pension (Beaufort County).

Bryan, Joseph B., 2nd Lieutenant, Company D
Bentonville
Captured at the battle of Bentonville on March 19, 1865. Confined at Johnson's Island, Ohio, and released upon taking the Oath of Allegiance on June 17, 1865.
Source: *NCT*, I:577; M270.

♦**Coffield, Zachariah**, Corporal, Company B
(Inconclusive)
His service records report that he was admitted to GH No. 13 (Pettigrew) in Raleigh on March 22, 1865, with a "fractured" right arm. Received a 60-day furlough on April 3, 1865. Based on the date of his hospitalization, Coffield was probably wounded at Bentonville.
Source: *NCT*, I:561; M270.

---

[1] According to *NC Troops* (1:550), the battalion was erroneously referred to as the "5th Battalion NC Light Artillery by some State authorities and as the 14th Battalion NC Light Artillery by the Confederate authorities." Interestingly, several soldiers' NC Confederate pension records indicated on their application forms that they served in the 5th Battalion.

▲**Curtis, John H.**, Private, Company E
Bentonville
NC Troops notes that he was killed at the battle of Bentonville on March 20, 1865. However, the *Hillsborough Recorder* reported Curtis was mortally wounded on March 19, 1865, and later died on March 23, 1865. According to the newspaper, Curtis's remains were brought home and interred.
Source: *NCT*, I:587; *Hillsborough Recorder* (NC), March 29, 1865; M270.

▲**Curtis, Samuel A.**, Private, Company E
Kinston (Post Wise's Forks)
U.S. Army Provost Marshal records indicate that Pvt. Samuel A. Curtis deserted his unit and was captured at Kinston on March 14, 1865.
Source: *NCT*, I:587; M270.

▲**Evans, Smith**, Private, Company B
Bentonville
NC Troops notes that he was wounded in March 1865, date and location unknown. He survived the war and lived until he died in 1907. Evan Smith's Confederate pension application indicates that he was "wounded by piece of shell striking below calf of the leg" at "Bennettsville" [sic] in March 1865. His pension application also specifies that he served in the 5th Battalion Light Artillery, which was an erroneous identification according to *NC Troops*. He is buried in Mount Lebanon Primitive Baptist Church Cemetery, Lebanon Township, Durham County, North Carolina.
Source: *NCT*, I:201, 562; M270; NC Confederate Pension (Durham County); Find a Grave.

Everett, William C., Private, Company D
Bentonville
Captured at the battle of Bentonville on March 19, 1865. Confined at Point Lookout, Maryland, and released upon taking the Oath of Allegiance on May 12, 1865.
Source: *NCT*, I:579; M270.

Forbes, Samuel Harney, 1st Lieutenant, Company D
Bentonville
Captured at the battle of Bentonville on March 19, 1865. Confined at Johnson's Island, Ohio, and released upon taking the Oath of Allegiance on June 17, 1865. Forbes's widow, Catherine M., spelled his full name on her pension application as Samuel Harvey Forbes.
Source: *NCT*, I:577; M270; NC Confederate Widow's Pension (Beaufort County).

Job, William L., Private, Company E
Kinston (Post-Wise's Forks)
U.S. Army Provost Marshal records indicate that Pvt. William L. Job deserted his unit and was captured at Kinston on March 18, 1865. No further information.
Source: *NCT*, I:589; M270.

Lea, William A., Private, Company E
Wise's Forks
Captured near Kinston on March 8, 1865. Confined at Point Lookout, Maryland, and released upon taking the Oath of Allegiance on May 15, 1865.
Source: *NCT*, I:590; M270; NC Confederate Widow's Pension (Durham County).

Mayo, William, Sergeant, Company D
Bentonville
NC Troops notes that he was wounded at the battle of Bentonville on March 19, 1865. Admitted to GH No. 13 (Pettigrew) in Raleigh on April 5, 1865, for unspecified reasons, where he was captured as a patient on April 13, 1865. On May 11, 1865, Mayo was admitted to U.S. Army Foster GH in New Bern with a gunshot wound to his right thigh that he suffered at Bentonville.
Source: *NCT*, I:581; M270; RG94, Foster General Hospital Registry.

▲**Moore, D. F.**, Private, Company D
Bentonville
According to Surgeon Hanahan's "Return of Wounded for Hagood's Brigade," Pvt. D. F. Moore, Co. D, 1st Battalion NC, was severely wounded in the left arm (fracture) on March 19, 1865, at Bentonville. His name also appears on Surgeon Tanner's "Return of Casualties in Hoke's Div. near Bentonville." Both Hanahan and Taylor erred in Moore's unit identification. Private D. F. Moore of Company D, 13th Battalion NC Light Artillery is the same soldier as Pvt. D. F. Moore. According to *NC Roster* Pvt. D. F. Moore transferred to Co. D, 13th Battalion in August 1864. His service records and *NC Troops* incorrectly note that Moore was hospitalized at GH No. 3 in Greensboro on an unspecified date in March 1865. In National Archives Confederate Record Group 109, General Hospital No. 3's location is erroneously identified as Greensboro. High Point is the correct location. Confederate authorities began relocating GH No. 3 from Goldsboro to High Point on March 11, 1865, as part of the town's evacuation. The hospital resumed operations in High Point on or about March 19, 1865. The No. 3 Patient Registry lists a Pvt. D. F. Moore, entry no. 2500, of Co. D, 13th NC, admitted for unspecified reasons between March 21 and April 7, 1865. D. F. Moore's Confederate pension indicates that he was wounded at Bentonville on March 19, 1865, suffering a gunshot wound "through his left arm, lost six inches of one bone from the wrist up and the other bone was dislocated at the wrist, broken six inches above the wrist joint." No further records. *NC Troops* does not note his wounding at Bentonville.
Source: Hanahan (BV), 4; Tanner (BV), 146; *NCT*, I:277, 582; M270; Sokolosky, *NC's Confederate Hospitals*, vol. 2; RG109, 6/291:49; NC Confederate Pension (Pamlico County).

Murphy, John, Private, Company B
Bentonville
Wounded at the battle of Bentonville on or about March 19, 1865. He was admitted to GH No. 13 (Pettigrew) in Raleigh on March 22, 1865, where he died on April 14, 1865. His widow, Sue Murphy, stated in her application for a pension that Pvt. John Murphy, her husband, died as a result of his wounding at the battle of Bentonville.
Source: *NCT*, I:565, 711; M270; NC Confederate Widow's Pension (Cumberland County).

♦**Nance, James H.**, Private, Company B
Smithfield (Inconclusive)
U.S. Army Provost Marshal records in Nance's service file contradict the date and location of capture. One record indicates Nance was captured at Smithfield on March 8, 1865. A second, reported by the U.S. Army XVII Corps, notes that his capture occurred on April 12, 1865, "in the field." Further research is required.
Source: *NCT*, I:565; M270.

Noah, Humphrey, Private, Company D
Bentonville
Captured at the battle of Bentonville on March 19, 1865. Confined at Point Lookout, Maryland, and released upon taking the Oath of Allegiance on June 8, 1865.
Source: *NCT*, I:582; M270; NC Confederate Pension (Alamance County).

Odum, Benjamin D., Private, Company C
Kinston (Post Wise's Forks)
U.S. Army Provost Marshal records indicate that Pvt. Benjamin D. Odum deserted his unit and was captured at Kinston on March 15, 1865.
Source: *NCT*, I:573; M270.

▲**Parker, James N.**, Corporal, Company E
Bentonville
Wounded at the battle of Bentonville on or about March 19, 1865. Parker's Confederate pension application indicates that he was wounded by a shell at Bentonville, resulting in the loss of one eye. Captured and paroled in Chatham County on April 26, 1865. No further records.

Source: NC Confederate Pension (Orange County); *NCT*, I:591; M270.

Rowe, James M., 1st Lieutenant, Company C
Wise's Forks
Killed at the battle of Wise's Forks on March 8, 1865. The March 13, 1865, edition of Raleigh's *Weekly Conservative* reported that Lieutenant Rowe was killed at Wise's Forks on March 8, 1865. According to the newspaper's account, "Lieut. Rowe was killed by a minie ball while in the act of bringing off a piece of artillery belonging to Capt. Atkins's battery from the field to replenish the chest with ammunition." His service records do not reference his death.
Source: *NCT*, I:568; *Weekly Conservative* (Raleigh, NC), March 29, 1865; M270.

♦Sowers, Jacob, Private, Company D
Bentonville (Inconclusive)
Killed at the battle of Bentonville between March 19-21, 1865, or mortally wounded, dying at some point after the battle. The name Jacob Sours appears on a monument at Bentonville Battlefield State Historic Site, leading some to assume he is buried in the Confederate mass grave located there. The Jacob Sours identified on the monument is probably the same soldier as Jacob Sowers. Neither Sower's service records nor *NC Troops* note his death at Bentonville.
Source: *NCT*, I:583; M270.

Walters, John F., Private, Company A
Richmond County
Captured in Richmond County on March 8, 1865., while home on authorized furlough. Confined at Point Lookout, Maryland, and released upon taking the Oath of Allegiance on June 21, 1865.
Source: *NCT*, I:557; M270; NC Confederate Pension (Robeson County).

▲Watkins, Lewis A., Private, Company D
Wise's Forks and Bentonville

Wise's Forks
According to Surgeon Hanahan's "List of Killed and Wounded in Hagood's Brigade" at Wise's Forks, Pvt. L. Wadkins of Co. D, 13th NC, was slightly wounded in the right hip. Private L. Wadkins, Co. D, 13th NC, also appears in Surgeon Tanner's "Return of Casualties near Kinston," slightly wounded in the right hip. Private Lewis A. Watkins of Co. D is the same soldier as Pvt. L. Wadkins. Watkins recovered from the wound he received from Wise's Forks.

Bentonville
Less than two weeks later, at the battle of Bentonville, both surgeons Hanahan and Tanner reported that Pvt. L. Wadkins suffered a wound in the left leg on March 19, 1865, but interestingly, he was listed as serving in Co. D, 1st Battalion NC Heavy Artillery. Although Hanahan and Tanner may have incorrectly identified Watkins's unit, it suggests that Co. D, 13th Battalion NC Light Artillery may have served as "Red Infantry" (former artillery units converted to infantry) at Wise's Forks and Bentonville.

NC Troops notes that he was wounded in the battle of Bentonville on March 19, 1865, but does not mention his injury at Wise's Forks. Watkins indicated on his Confederate pension application that he was shot in the leg at Bentonville and sent to a hospital in Greensboro.
Source: Hanahan (WF), 1; Tanner (WF), 137; *NCT*, I:584; Hanahan (BV), 3; Tanner (BV), 146; M270; NC Confederate Pension (New Hanover).

Captain Abner A. Moseley's Company (Sampson Artillery)

Boone, David C., Corporal
Town Creek
Captured at the battle of Town Creek on February 19, 1865. Confined at Point Lookout, Maryland, and released upon taking the Oath of Allegiance on June 24, 1865.
Source: *NCT*, I:606; M270.

▲**Bryan [Bryant], Joseph E.**, Private
Fort Anderson (Probably Town Creek)
Joseph E. Bryan indicated on his Confederate pension that he was wounded at Fort Anderson on or about February 20, 1865. Unfortunately for Bryant, the ball was never removed. The recommending physician noted that the "bullet entered left knee joint on [the] left side, fracturing the patella and lower 3 or 4 inches of [the] femur . . . passing downward and lodged in the joint." *NC Troops* does not his wounding in February 1865. *NC Troops* spells the surname Bryant; based on pension records, the correct spelling is Bryan.
Source: *NCT*, I:606, 696; M270; NC Confederate Pension (Wayne County), 1885 and 1901.

Caison, Hillory R., Private
Clinton
A resident of Sampson County at the time of his enlistment, Pvt. Hillory R. Caison was captured at Clinton on March 20, 1865. Confined at Hart's Island, New York Harbor, and released upon taking the Oath of Allegiance on June 19, 1865.
Source: *NCT*, I:607; M270; NC Confederate Pension (Pender County).

Flythe, George Washington, Private
Town Creek
Captured at the battle of Town Creek on February 20, 1865. Confined at Point Lookout, Maryland, and released upon taking the Oath of Allegiance on June 27, 1865.
Source: *NCT*, I:607; M270.

Granger, William, Private
Town Creek
Captured at the battle of Town Creek on February 19, 1865. Confined at Point Lookout, Maryland. There is no record of release.
Source: *NCT*, I:608; M270.

Hargrove, John C., Private
Goldsboro
Captured at Goldsboro on March 21, 1865. Confined at Point Lookout, Maryland, and released upon taking the Oath of Allegiance on June 27, 1865.
Source: *NCT*, I:608; M270.

Harris, Henry F., Corporal
Town Creek
Captured at the battle of Town Creek on February 19, 1865. Confined at Point Lookout, Maryland, and released upon taking the Oath of Allegiance on May 15, 1865.
Source: *NCT*, I:608; M270.

Henry, James F., Sergeant
Town Creek
Captured at the battle of Town Creek on February 19, 1865. Confined at Point Lookout, Maryland, and released upon taking the Oath of Allegiance on June 13, 1865.
Source: *NCT*, I:608; M270.

Jones, Jonas, Private
Town Creek
Captured at the battle of Town Creek on February 19, 1865. Confined at Point Lookout, Maryland, and released upon taking the Oath of Allegiance on June 28, 1865.
Source: *NCT*, I:609; M270.

King, James, Private
Town Creek
Captured at the battle of Town Creek on February 19, 1865. Confined at Point Lookout, Maryland, and released upon taking the Oath of Allegiance on June 28, 1865.
Source: *NCT*, I:609, 706; M270.

McKinnon, Daniel, Private
Town Creek
Captured at the battle of Town Creek on February 19, 1865. Confined at Point Lookout, Maryland, and released upon taking the Oath of Allegiance on June 29, 1865.
Source: *NCT*, I:610; M270.

Peterson, Laban, Private
Town Creek
Captured at the battle of Town Creek on February 19, 1865. Confined at Point Lookout, Maryland, and released upon taking the Oath of Allegiance on June 17, 1865.
Source: *NCT*, I:610; M270.

Simmons, Saunders, Sergeant
Piney Grove
Captured at Piney Grove on March 19, 1865. Confined at Point Lookout, Maryland, and released upon taking the Oath of Allegiance on June 20, 1865. Simmons spelled his given name as Sanders in his NC Confederate Pension application.
Source: *NCT*, I:611; M270; NC Confederate Pension (Sampson County).

Smith, William S., Private
Town Creek
Captured at the battle of Town Creek on February 19, 1865. Confined at Point Lookout, Maryland, and released upon taking the Oath of Allegiance on June 19, 1865.
Source: *NCT*, I:611; M270.

Watts, Guilford, Private
Town Creek
Captured at the battle of Town Creek on February 19, 1865. Confined at Point Lookout, Maryland, and released upon taking the Oath of Allegiance on June 21, 1865.
Source: *NCT*, I:612; M270; NC Confederate Pension (Columbus County).

Watts, William, Private
Inconclusive
Captured, date and location not recorded, and confined at Point Lookout, Maryland, and released upon taking the Oath of Allegiance on June 21, 1865.
Source: *NCT*, I:612; M270.

PART II
(Cavalry)

Return of Wounded of Hagood's Brigade Near Bentonville N.C. March 22d

#	Name	Rank	Co.	Regt	Wound
1	H Anderson	Pvt	H	7th Batt S.C.	Flesh wound left side neck. Slight
2	J R Tew	"	Hamilton	Hall Arty	Left thigh & hand Mortal (shell)
3	C Mavo	"	B	40 Regt N.C.	Flesh wound right cheek. Slight
4	D Stone	"	C	1st Batt "	Right parietal bone. Severe
5	G D Gillespie	"	A	" " "	Flesh wound right cheek. Slight
6	C E Stewart	"	"	" " "	Flesh wound wrist right arm. Slight
7	P W Willis	"	C	40 Regt "	Flesh wound left leg. Slight
8	J A Hobbs	"	B	7th Batt S.C.	Abdomen Severe
9	G F Pigott	"	K	1st Batt N.C.	Right breast flesh wound severe
10	H Kennedy	"	Hart's	Battery S.C.	Concussion
11	A H Murry	"	C	40 Regt N.C.	1st finger 1st joint Ampt right hand. Contusion left arm
12	J T Gregory	"	C	27 Regt S.C.	Contusion left Arm
13	M J Rivenbark	Sgt	B	1st Batt N.C.	Right hand. Severe
14	J Wood	Pvt	F	36 Regt "	Head Mortal
15	L McPhaul	"	E	40 Regt "	" "
16	F D Gus	"	C	" " "	Right Arm Ampt.
17	J K ??	"	H	" " "	Scalp wound slight
18	J Fox	Pvt	"	7th Batt S.C.	Left Arm penetrating lung severe
19	J G Yarbough	"	F	" " "	Left leg flesh wound. Slight
20	O D Calhoun	"	"	40 Regt N.C.	Concussion
21	D Steadman	"	B	2nd Batt N.C.	Right scapula passing through Axila severe
22	C H Burney	"	"	36 Regt "	Left side & left hand flesh wounds Slight
23	C Bell	Lieut	C	7th Batt S.C.	Head Mortal
24	G Brett	Pvt	B	40 Regt N.C.	Left hand flesh wound Slight

Sr. Surgeon Ralph B. Hanahan
Casualty Return for Hagood's Brigade battle of Bentonville

(Friends of Bentonville Battlefield Association)

65th Regiment North Carolina Troops (6th Regiment NC Cavalry)

Allison, Joseph E., Private, Company C
Kinston
Captured at Kinston on March 10, 1865. Confined at Point Lookout, Maryland, and released upon taking the Oath of Allegiance on June 27, 1865.
Source: *NCT*, II:470, 791; M270.

Barlow, John, Private, Company B
Goldsboro (Post Bentonville)
Captured at Goldsboro on March 23, 1865, and took the Oath of Allegiance that same day. Sent to New Bern on March 26, no further records.
Source: *NCT*, II:464; M270.

Brown, Elam, Private, Company C
New Hope
Captured at New Hope, an area in eastern Wayne County, on March 17, 1865. Confined at Point Lookout, Maryland, where he died of scurvy on April 4, 1865.
Source: *NCT*, II:471; M270.

Burnett, Drew D., Private, Company C
New Hope
Captured at New Hope, an area in eastern Wayne County, on March 17, 1865. Confined at Point Lookout, Maryland, and released upon taking the Oath of Allegiance on June 23, 1865.
Source: *NCT*, II:471; M270.

♦▲**Dickson, John F.**, Private, Company B
New Bern (Inconclusive)
Deserted to the enemy, probably at New Bern, on an undetermined date. Sent to Washington, D.C., on March 10, 1865, where he took the Oath of Allegiance and was provided transportation to Cincinnati, Ohio. Throughout 1864, the 6th NC Cavalry had a terrible reputation for problems with discipline and desertion. The *New Berne Times* reported several occasions in January-February 1865 that groups of 6th NC cavalrymen crossed Federal lines on horseback. On one such instance in February, two officers and a large group, reportedly 69, although one must acknowledge the likelihood of exaggeration for propaganda purposes, "fully equipped" men deserted at New Bern.
Source: *NCT*, II:465; M270; Smith and Sokolosky, *To Prepare for Sherman's Coming*, 40; *NBT* (New Bern), January 24, 1865; ibid., February 28, 1865.

Early, Thomas, Private, Company D
Kinston (Post Wise's Forks)
Captured at Kinston on March 17, 1865. Confined at Point Lookout, Maryland, and released upon taking the Oath of Allegiance on June 12, 1865. Confederate pension records indicate that he suffered a fall from his horse, injuring his shoulder while charging the enemy at Kinston. Date not reported.
Source: *NCT*, II:477; M270; NC Confederate Pension (Polk County).

♦▲**Faw, Amos**, Private, Company B
New Bern (Inconclusive)
Deserted to the enemy, probably at New Bern, on an undetermined date. Sent to Washington, D.C., on March 10, 1865, where he took the Oath of Allegiance and was provided transportation to Cincinnati, Ohio. Throughout 1864, the 6th NC Cavalry had a terrible reputation for problems with discipline and desertion. The *New Berne Times* reported several occasions in January-February 1865 that groups of 6th NC cavalrymen crossed Federal lines on horseback. On one such instance in February, two officers and a large

group, reportedly 69, although one must acknowledge the likelihood of exaggeration for propaganda purposes, "fully equipped" men deserted at New Bern.
Source: *NCT*, II:465; M270; Smith and Sokolosky, *To Prepare for Sherman's Coming*, 40; *NBT* (New Bern), January 24, 1865; ibid., February 28, 1865.

Glazener, Benjamin N., Sr., Private, Company C
Kinston (Post Wise's Forks)
Captured at Kinston on March 17, 1865. Confined at Point Lookout, Maryland, and released upon taking the Oath of Allegiance on June 27, 1865.
Source: *NCT*, II:472; M270; NC Confederate Widow's Pension (Transylvania County).

♦▲Gosset, William J., Private, Company B
New Bern (Inconclusive)
Deserted to the enemy, probably at New Bern, on an undetermined date. Sent to Washington, D.C., on March 10, 1865, where he took the Oath of Allegiance and was provided transportation to Cincinnati, Ohio. Throughout 1864, the 6th NC Cavalry had a terrible reputation for problems with discipline and desertion. The *New Berne Times* reported several occasions in January-February 1865 that groups of 6th NC cavalrymen crossed Federal lines on horseback. On one such instance in February, two officers and a large group, reportedly 69, although one must acknowledge the likelihood of exaggeration for propaganda purposes, "fully equipped" men deserted at New Bern.
Source: *NCT*, II:465; M270; Smith and Sokolosky, *To Prepare for Sherman's Coming*, 40; *NBT* (New Bern), January 24, 1865; ibid., February 28, 1865.

♦▲Hardin, A., Private, (Company Unknown)
New Bern (Inconclusive)
Deserted to the enemy, probably at New Bern, on an undetermined date. Sent to Washington, D.C., on March 10, 1865, where he took the Oath of Allegiance and was provided transportation to Cincinnati, Ohio. Throughout 1864, the 6th NC Cavalry had a terrible reputation for problems with discipline and desertion. The *New Berne Times* reported several occasions in January-February 1865 that groups of 6th NC cavalrymen crossed Federal lines on horseback. On one such instance in February, two officers and a large group, reportedly 69, although one must acknowledge the likelihood of exaggeration for propaganda purposes, "fully equipped" men deserted at New Bern.
Source: *NCT*, II:514; M270; Smith and Sokolosky, *To Prepare for Sherman's Coming*, 40; *NBT* (New Bern), January 24, 1865; ibid., February 28, 1865.

♦▲Hardin, W., Private, (Company Unknown)
New Bern (Inconclusive)
Deserted to the enemy, probably at New Bern, on an undetermined date. Sent to Washington, D.C., on March 10, 1865, where he took the Oath of Allegiance and was provided transportation to Cincinnati, Ohio. Throughout 1864, the 6th NC Cavalry had a terrible reputation for problems with discipline and desertion. The *New Berne Times* reported several occasions in January-February 1865 that groups of 6th NC cavalrymen crossed Federal lines on horseback. On one such instance in February, two officers and a large group, reportedly 69, although one must acknowledge the likelihood of exaggeration for propaganda purposes, "fully equipped" men deserted at New Bern.
Source: *NCT*, II:514; M270; Smith and Sokolosky, *To Prepare for Sherman's Coming*, 40; *NBT* (New Bern), January 24, 1865; ibid., February 28, 1865.

Hill, Reuben A., Private, Company C
Kinston (Post Wise's Forks)
Captured at Kinston on March 16, 1865. Confined at Point Lookout, Maryland, and released upon taking the Oath of Allegiance on June 6, 1865.
Source: *NCT*, II:473; M270.

Jarrett, Obediah B., Private, Company I
Goldsboro

Captured at Goldsboro on March 23, 1865, and took the oath the same day.
Source: *NCT*, II:507; M270.

Lance, William H., Private, Company C
New Hope
Captured at New Hope, an area in eastern Wayne County, on March 17, 1865. Confined at Point Lookout, Maryland, and released upon taking the Oath of Allegiance on June 6, 1865.
Source: *NCT*, II:473; M270; NC Confederate Pension (Henderson County).

♦▲Latham, David C., Private, Company B
New Bern (Inconclusive)
Deserted to the enemy, probably at New Bern, on an undetermined date. Sent to Washington, D.C., on March 10, 1865, where he took the Oath of Allegiance and was provided transportation to Cincinnati, Ohio. Throughout 1864, the 6th NC Cavalry had a terrible reputation for problems with discipline and desertion. The *New Berne Times* reported several occasions in January-February 1865 that groups of 6th NC cavalrymen crossed Federal lines on horseback. On one such instance in February, two officers and a large group, reportedly 69, although one must acknowledge the likelihood of exaggeration for propaganda purposes, "fully equipped" men deserted at New Bern.
Source: *NCT*, II:467; M270; Smith and Sokolosky, *To Prepare for Sherman's Coming*, 40; *NBT* (New Bern), January 24, 1865; ibid., February 28, 1865; NC Confederate Pension (Ashe County).

♦▲Latham, James, Private, Company B
New Bern (Inconclusive)
Deserted to the enemy, probably at New Bern, on an undetermined date. Sent to Washington, D.C., on March 10, 1865, where he took the Oath of Allegiance and was provided transportation to Cincinnati, Ohio. Throughout 1864, the 6th NC Cavalry had a terrible reputation for problems with discipline and desertion. The *New Berne Times* reported several occasions in January-February 1865 that groups of 6th NC cavalrymen crossed Federal lines on horseback. On one such instance in February, two officers and a large group, reportedly 69, although one must acknowledge the likelihood of exaggeration for propaganda purposes, "fully equipped" men deserted at New Bern.
Source: *NCT*, II:467; M270; Smith and Sokolosky, *To Prepare for Sherman's Coming*, 40; *NBT* (New Bern), January 24, 1865; ibid., February 28, 1865.

Lawrence, William G., Private, Company D
Kinston (Post Wise's Forks)
Captured at Kinston on March 17, 1865. Confined at Point Lookout, Maryland, and released upon taking the Oath of Allegiance on June 28, 1865.
Source: *NCT*, II:479; M270; NC Confederate Pension (Henderson County).

♦Mitchell, E., Private, Company H
Goldsboro (Inconclusive)
Service records indicate captured at Goldsboro on February 22, 1865. Confined at Hart's Island, New York Harbor, and released upon taking the Oath of Allegiance on June 18, 1865. Either the location or date of capture is incorrect. Federal forces were not present at Goldsboro on the recorded date of capture. Further research is required.
Source: *NCT*, II:503; M270.

Morgan, Oliver C., Blacksmith, Company C
Kinston (Post Wise's Forks)
Captured at Kinston on March 16, 1865. No further records. He had previously deserted the company in February 1864. Confined at Point Lookout, Maryland, and released upon taking the Oath of Allegiance on June 23, 1865.
Source: *NCT*, II:474; M270.

Neagle, John P., Private, Company G (2nd)

White Hall
Captured at White Hall on March 20, 1865. Confined at Point Lookout, Maryland, and released upon taking the Oath of Allegiance on June 29, 1865.
Source: *NCT*, II:497; M270.

Neely, Albert Jefferson, Private, Company D
Kinston (Post Wise's Forks)
Captured at Kinston on March 17, 1865. Confined at Point Lookout, Maryland, and released upon taking the Oath of Allegiance on June 15, 1865.
Source: *NCT*, II:480; M270; NC Confederate Pension (Henderson County).

Parrish, Nathaniel H., Sergeant, Company G (2nd)
New Hope (Post Wise's Forks)
Captured at New Hope, an area in eastern Wayne County, on March 17, 1865. Confined at Point Lookout, Maryland, and released upon taking the Oath of Allegiance on June 16, 1865.
Source: *NCT*, II:497; M270; NC Confederate Widow's Pension (Macon County).

♦▲**Ray, A. H.**, Lieutenant, (Company Unknown)
New Bern (Inconclusive)
Deserted to the enemy, probably at New Bern, on an undetermined date. Sent to Washington, D.C., on March 10, 1865, where he took the Oath of Allegiance and was provided transportation to Cincinnati, Ohio. Throughout 1864, the 6th NC Cavalry had a terrible reputation for problems with discipline and desertion. The *New Berne Times* reported several occasions in January-February 1865 that groups of 6th NC cavalrymen crossed Federal lines on horseback. On one such instance in February, two officers and a large group, reportedly 69, although one must acknowledge the likelihood of exaggeration for propaganda purposes, "fully equipped" men deserted at New Bern.
Source: *NCT*, II:514; M270; Smith and Sokolosky, *To Prepare for Sherman's Coming*, 40; *NBT* (New Bern), January 24, 1865; ibid., February 28, 1865.

♦▲**Ray, George W.**, Private, Company B
New Bern (Inconclusive)
Deserted to the enemy, probably at New Bern, on an undetermined date. Sent to Washington, D.C., on March 10, 1865, where he took the Oath of Allegiance and was provided transportation to Cincinnati, Ohio. Throughout 1864, the 6th NC Cavalry had a terrible reputation for problems with discipline and desertion. The *New Berne Times* reported several occasions in January-February 1865 that groups of 6th NC cavalrymen crossed Federal lines on horseback. On one such instance in February, two officers and a large group, reportedly 69, although one must acknowledge the likelihood of exaggeration for propaganda purposes, "fully equipped" men deserted at New Bern.
Source: *NCT*, II:468; M270; Smith and Sokolosky, *To Prepare for Sherman's Coming*, 40; *NBT* (New Bern), January 24, 1865; ibid., February 28, 1865.

♦▲**Ray, Hilton H.**, 1st Lieutenant, Company B
New Bern (Inconclusive)
Deserted to the enemy, probably at New Bern, on an undetermined date. Sent to Washington, D.C., on March 10, 1865, where he took the Oath of Allegiance and was provided transportation to Cincinnati, Ohio. Throughout 1864, the 6th NC Cavalry had a terrible reputation for problems with discipline and desertion. The *New Berne Times* reported several occasions in January-February 1865 that groups of 6th NC cavalrymen crossed Federal lines on horseback. On one such instance in February, two officers and a large group, reportedly 69, although one must acknowledge the likelihood of exaggeration for propaganda purposes, "fully equipped" men deserted at New Bern.
Source: *NCT*, II:464; M270; Smith and Sokolosky, *To Prepare for Sherman's Coming*, 40; *NBT* (New Bern), January 24, 1865; ibid., February 28, 1865.

♦▲**Ray, James J.**, Private, Company B

New Bern (Inconclusive)
Deserted to the enemy, probably at New Bern, on an undetermined date. Sent to Washington, D.C., on March 10, 1865, where he took the Oath of Allegiance and was provided transportation to Cincinnati, Ohio. Throughout 1864, the 6th NC Cavalry had a terrible reputation for problems with discipline and desertion. The *New Berne Times* reported several occasions in January-February 1865 that groups of 6th NC cavalrymen crossed Federal lines on horseback. On one such instance in February, two officers and a large group, reportedly 69, although one must acknowledge the likelihood of exaggeration for propaganda purposes, "fully equipped" men deserted at New Bern.
Source: *NCT*, II:468; M270; Smith and Sokolosky, *To Prepare for Sherman's Coming*, 40; *NBT* (New Bern), January 24, 1865; ibid., February 28, 1865.

♦▲**Ray, James M.**, Private, Company B
New Bern (Inconclusive)
Deserted to the enemy, probably at New Bern, on an undetermined date. Sent to Washington, D.C., on March 10, 1865, where he took the Oath of Allegiance and was provided transportation to Cincinnati, Ohio. Throughout 1864, the 6th NC Cavalry had a terrible reputation for problems with discipline and desertion. The *New Berne Times* reported several occasions in January-February 1865 that groups of 6th NC cavalrymen crossed Federal lines on horseback. On one such instance in February, two officers and a large group, reportedly 69, although one must acknowledge the likelihood of exaggeration for propaganda purposes, "fully equipped" men deserted at New Bern.
Source: *NCT*, II:468; M270; Smith and Sokolosky, *To Prepare for Sherman's Coming*, 40; *NBT* (New Bern), January 24, 1865; ibid., February 28, 1865.

♦▲**Ray, John A.**, Private, Company B
New Bern (Inconclusive)
Deserted to the enemy, probably at New Bern, on an undetermined date. Sent to Washington, D.C., on March 10, 1865, where he took the Oath of Allegiance and was provided transportation to Cincinnati, Ohio. Throughout 1864, the 6th NC Cavalry had a terrible reputation for problems with discipline and desertion. The *New Berne Times* reported several occasions in January-February 1865 that groups of 6th NC cavalrymen crossed Federal lines on horseback. On one such instance in February, two officers and a large group, reportedly 69, although one must acknowledge the likelihood of exaggeration for propaganda purposes, "fully equipped" men deserted at New Bern.
Source: *NCT*, II:468; M270; Smith and Sokolosky, *To Prepare for Sherman's Coming*, 40; *NBT* (New Bern), January 24, 1865; ibid., February 28, 1865.

Reese, Aaron, Private, Company C
New Hope
Captured at New Hope, an area in eastern Wayne County, on March 17, 1865. Confined at Point Lookout, Maryland, where he died of fever on June 8, 1865. Buried in the Confederate Cemetery at Point Lookout.
Source: *NCT*, II:474; M270.

Rhea, Robert C., Contract Surgeon, Field and Staff
New Hope
Captured at New Hope, an area in eastern Wayne County, on March 17, 1865, and sent to New Bern. Contracted to serve in the regiment on April 1, 1863. No further records.
Source: *NCT*, II:458; M270; M331.

Sanders, John A. T., Private, Company G (2nd)
New Hope
Captured at New Hope, an area in eastern Wayne County, on March 17, 1865. Confined at Point Lookout, Maryland, and released upon taking the Oath of Allegiance on June 20, 1865.
Source: *NCT*, II:498; M270; NC Confederate Pension (Macon County).

♦▲**Shown, James W.**, Private, Company B
New Bern (Inconclusive)

Deserted to the enemy, probably at New Bern, on an undetermined date. Sent to Washington, D.C., on March 10, 1865, where he took the Oath of Allegiance and was provided transportation to Cincinnati, Ohio. Throughout 1864, the 6th NC Cavalry had a terrible reputation for problems with discipline and desertion. The *New Berne Times* reported several occasions in January-February 1865 that groups of 6th NC cavalrymen crossed Federal lines on horseback. On one such instance in February, two officers and a large group, reportedly 69, although one must acknowledge the likelihood of exaggeration for propaganda purposes, "fully equipped" men deserted at New Bern.
Source: *NCT*, II:469; M270; Smith and Sokolosky, *To Prepare for Sherman's Coming*, 40; *NBT* (New Bern), January 24, 1865; ibid., February 28, 1865.

Walsh, William, Private, Company C
New Hope
Captured at New Hope, an area in eastern Wayne County, on March 17, 1865. Confined at Point Lookout, Maryland, and released upon taking the Oath of Allegiance on June 22, 1865.
Source: *NCT*, II:475; M270; NC Confederate Pension (Wilkes County).

Harper House
The Harper House, ca. 1890s, served as the U.S. Army XIV Corps field hospital during the Battle of Bentonville. Post-battle, used to care for wounded Confederate soldiers left behind. John and Amy Harper are standing on the front porch.

(Courtesy of Bentonville Battlefield State Historic Site)

PART III
(Infantry)

Confederate Monument at Bentonville
March 20, 1895
Image taken by Parkers Studio, Dunn, NC

(Courtesy of Bentonville Battlefield State Historic Site)

2nd Battalion North Carolina Local Defense Troops[2]

Baggot, William, Private, Company B
Near Fayetteville
Captured near Fayetteville on March 7, 1865. Confined at Point Lookout, Maryland, and released upon taking the Oath of Allegiance on June 24, 1865.
Source: *NCT*, III:348; M270.

▲**Bradshaw, John Pope**, Private, Company B
Bentonville
According to Surgeon Hanahan's "Return of Wounded for Hagood's Brigade" at Bentonville, Pvt. J. P. Bedshaw, Co. B, 2nd Battalion NC, was slightly wounded in the scalp on March 19, 1865. Private J. P. Bedshaw also appears in Surgeon Tanner's "Return of Casualties in Hoke's Div. near Bentonville." Private John Pope Bradshaw of Co. B is the same soldier as Pvt. J. P. Bedshaw. Neither Bradshaw's service records nor *NC Troops* note the wound he received at the battle of Bentonville. Bradshaw described that his wound suffered at Bentonville "almost proved fatal," as it struck him "on the front of the skull."
Source: Hanahan (BV), 3; Tanner (BV), 146; *NCT*, III:348; M270; NC Confederate Pension (Chatham County).

▲**Bray, William**, Private, Company B
Bentonville
According to Surgeon Hanahan's "Return of Wounded for Hagood's Brigade" at Bentonville, Pvt. W. Bray, Co. B, 2nd Battalion NC, was severely wounded in the left hand on March 19, 1865. His name also appears in Surgeon Tanner's "Return of Casualties in Hoke's Div. near Bentonville." Private William Bray of Co. B is the same soldier as Pvt. W. Bray. Neither Bray's service records nor *NC Troops* note the wound he received at the battle of Bentonville.
Source: Hanahan (BV), 3; Tanner (BV), 146; *NCT*, III:348; M270.

Cromartie, Addison A., Private, Company F
Piney Grove
Captured at Piney Grove on March 19, 1865. Confined at Point Lookout, Maryland, and released upon taking the Oath of Allegiance on June 26, 1865.
Source: *NCT*, III:365; M270.

▲**DeRosset, Armand L.**, Captain, Company B
Averasboro
Wounded at the battle of Averasboro on March 16, 1865, while participating in a Confederate counterattack against U.S. Army XX Corps forces. DeRosset was later recovered off the battlefield by U.S forces and treated in a Federal field hospital, probably at Oak Grove. He survived the war.
Source: Smith and Sokolosky, *No Such Army*, 113-114; *NCT*, III:347, 678; M270.

Grice, William D., Private, Company B
Owensville
Captured at Owensville on March 16, 1865. Grice spent time in several U.S. Army hospitals until he was released upon taking the Oath of Allegiance on June 21, 1865, while a patient at Decamp General Hospital, David's Island, New York Harbor. See *NC Troops* for further information.
Source: *NCT*, III:350; M270.

Hall, James T., Corporal, Company E
Fayetteville

---

[2] The 2nd Battalion NC Local Defense Troops (official designation) was erroneously designated the 6th Battalion-Armory Guard in John W. Moore's *Roster of North Carolina Troops in the War Between the States*, 4 vols. and Clark's *Histories*.

Captured in Fayetteville on March 13, 1865. Confined at Hart's Island, New York Harbor, and released upon taking the Oath of Allegiance on June 18, 1865.
Source: *NCT*, III:362; M270.

Hall, Livingston, Private, Company B
Fayetteville
Captured at Fayetteville on March 18, 1865. Confined at Hart's Island, New York Harbor, and released upon taking the Oath of Allegiance on June 19, 1865.
Source: *NCT*, III:350; M270.

▲Herrington, John E., Private, Company B
Bentonville
According to Surgeon Hanahan's "Return of Wounded for Hagood's Brigade" at Bentonville, Pvt. J. E. Herrington, Co. B, 2nd Battalion NC, was severely wounded in the right hip on March 19, 1865. Private J. E. Herrington also appears in Surgeon Tanner's "Return of Casualties in Hoke's Div. near Bentonville." Private John E. Herrington of Co. E is the same soldier as Pvt. J. E. Herrington. Neither Herrington's service records nor *NC Troops* note the wound he received at the battle of Bentonville. Between March 21 and April 7, 1865, Pvt. J. E. Herrington was admitted to GH No. 3 in High Point for unspecified reasons (entry no. 2522). Hospital records incorrectly note his name as S. E. Harrington. Herrington later died at the hospital on an unspecified date and is buried in the Confederate Section of Oakwood Cemetery, High Point, North Carolina.
Source: Hanahan (BV), 3; Tanner (BV), 146; *NCT*, III:350; M270; RG109, 6/291:50.

Holland, Blueman, Private, Company B
Sampson County
Captured in his native Sampson County on March 18, 1865. Confined at Hart's Island, New York Harbor, and released upon taking the Oath of Allegiance on June 18, 1865.
Source: *NCT*, III:350; M270.

Johnson, Fleet, Private, Company D
Fayetteville
Captured in Fayetteville on March 12, 1865. Confined at Hart's Island, New York Harbor, where he died on May 29, 1865, of meningitis.
Source: *NCT*, III:359; M270.

McLeod, Archibald, Private, Company G
Piney Grove
Captured at Goldsboro on March 24, 1865. Sent to Washington, D.C., and released upon taking the Oath of Allegiance on April 5, 1865.
Source: *NCT*, III:369; M270.

Powell, Isham, Private, Company C
South River
Captured at South River on March 14, 1865. Isham Powell took the Oath of Allegiance on April 5, 1865, in Washington, D.C., and was provided transportation to Wilmington.
Source: *NCT*, III:356; M270.

Powell, James, Private, Company C
South River
Captured at South River on March 14, 1865. James Powell took the Oath of Allegiance on April 5, 1865, in Washington, D.C. Powell was later admitted to a U.S. Army hospital in New York City, where he died there on April 28, 1865.
Source: *NCT*, III:356; M270.

▲Robinson, Abner, Corporal, Company B

Bentonville

According to Surgeon Hanahan's "Return of Wounded for Hagood's Brigade" at Bentonville, Corp. A. Robinson, Co. B, 2nd Battalion NC, was slightly wounded in the head on March 19, 1865. Corporal A. Robinson also appears in Surgeon Tanner's "Return of Casualties in Hoke's Div. near Bentonville." Corporal Abner Robinson of Co. B is the same soldier as Corp. A. Robinson. Robinson's service records and *NC Troops* incorrectly note that he was admitted to a Greensboro hospital in April 1865. In National Archives Confederate Record Group 109, General Hospital No. 3's location is erroneously identified as Greensboro. High Point is the correct location. Confederate authorities began relocating GH No. 3 from Goldsboro to High Point on March 11, 1865, as part of the town's evacuation. The hospital resumed operations in High Point on or about March 19, 1865. The patient registry of GH No. 3 in High Point lists the admittance of Corp. A. Robinson of Co. B, 2nd NC Res. on an unspecified date in April 1865. This soldier is Corp. Abner Robinson of the 2nd Battalion NC. The hospital erred in the identification of Robinson's unit.

Source: Hanahan (BV), 4; Tanner (BV), 146; *NCT*, III:353; M270; Sokolosky, *NC Confederate Hospitals, vol. 2*; RG109, 6/291:55.

▲Stedman, David M., Private, Company B
Bentonville

According to Surgeon Hanahan's "Return of Wounded for Hagood's Brigade" at Bentonville, Pvt. D. Steadman, Co. B, 2nd Battalion NC, was severely wounded in the right scapula, passing through Axilla on March 19, 1865. Private D. Steadman also appears in Surgeon Tanner's "Return of Casualties in Hoke's Div. near Bentonville." Private David M. Stedman of Co. B is the same soldier as Pvt. D. Steadman. Present at Raleigh's GH No. 8 (Peace Institute) with a wound to his right shoulder. Neither Stedman's service records nor *NC Troops* note the wound he received at the battle of Bentonville.

Source: Hanahan (BV), 2; Tanner (BV), 146; *NCS* (Raleigh), March 29, 1865; *WD* (Charlotte), April 4, 1865; *NCT*, III:353; M270

Private John E. Herrington
2nd Battalion NC Local Defense Troops
The 2nd Battalion was attached to Hagood's Brigade, Hoke's Division, during the battle of Bentonville. Wounded in the right hip on March 19, 1865, Herrington later died at General Hospital No. 3 in High Point on an unspecified date. Buried in Oakwood Cemetery in High Point, North Carolina. Hospital records incorrectly noted the spelling of his name.

(Courtesy of Wade Sokolosky)

Dr. Stiles Kennedy, 8th Regiment NC Troops
Sr. Surgeon, Clingman's Brigade, Hoke's Division
Captured at Wise's Forks on March 8, 1865

(Wade Sokolosky Collection)

8th Regiment North Carolina State Troops

▲**Brothers, Richard T.**, Private, Company A
Bentonville
Wounded at the battle of Bentonville between March 19-21, 1865. According to Surgeon Tanner's "Return of Casualties in Hoke's Div. near Bentonville," Pvt. R. T. Brothers, Co. A, was severely wounded in the breast. Neither Brother's service records nor *NC Troops* note the wound he received at the battle of Bentonville.
Source: Tanner (BV), 140; *NCT*, IV:525; M270.

▲**Bundy, James A.**, Private, Company A
Wise's Forks
Wounded at the battle of Wise's Forks on March 10, 1865. According to Surgeon Tanner's "Return of Casualties near Kinston," Pvt. J. A. Bundy, Co. A, 8th NC, was severely wounded in both thighs on March 10, 1865. Admitted to GH No. 13 (Pettigrew) in Raleigh on March 11, 1865, with a gunshot wound in both thighs. His Confederate pension records indicate that he was wounded near Kinston in March 1865.
Source: Tanner (WF), 135; *NCS* (Raleigh), March 29, 1865; M270; *WD* (Charlotte), April 4, 1865; *NCT*, IV:525, 697; NC Confederate Pension (Pasquotank County).

▲**Clapp, David**, Sergeant, Company I
Wise's Forks
Wounded at the battle of Wise's Forks on March 8, 1865. According to Surgeon Tanner's "Return of Casualties near Kinston," Pvt. David Clapp, Co. I, 8th NC, was slightly wounded on the right side. The March 29, 1865, edition of the *NC Standard* listed Ensign David Clapp, Co. I, 8th NC, at GH No. 13, suffering a contusion from a shell. Admitted to Barbee Wayside Hospital in High Point on March 9, 1865.
Source: Tanner (WF), 135; *NCS* (Raleigh), March 29, 1865; *WD* (Charlotte), April 4, 1865; *NCT*, IV:605; M270; Barbee Wayside Registry, no. 5762; NC Confederate Pension (Alamance County).

Hawkins, James, Private, Company E
Fayetteville
Captured at Fayetteville on March 12, 1865. Confined at Point Lookout, Maryland, and released upon taking the Oath of Allegiance on June 28, 1865.
Source: *NCT*, III:567; M270.

▲**Hight, Alexander**, Private, Company F
Wise's Forks
Wounded at the battle of Wise's Forks on March 8, 1865. According to Surgeon Tanner's "Return of Casualties near Kinston," Pvt. A. Hight, Co. F, 8th NC, was dangerously wounded in the lungs. Neither his service records nor *NC Troops* note his wounding in March 1865.
Source: Tanner (WF), 135; *NCT*, IV:577; M270.

Hill, Atlas, Private, Company E
Fayetteville
Captured at Fayetteville on March 12, 1865. Confined at Hart's Island, New York Harbor, and released upon taking the Oath of Allegiance on June 18, 1865.
Source: *NCT*, III:568; M270.

Hobson, Richard, Private, Company E
Fayetteville
Captured at Fayetteville on March 12, 1865. Confined at Hart's Island, New York Harbor, and released upon taking the Oath of Allegiance on June 18, 1865.
Source: *NCT*, III:568; M270.

♦**Howell, W. S.**, Private, Company E
Columbia, SC (Inconclusive)

Captured at Columbia, South Carolina, on March 17, 1865. Confined at Hart's Island, New York Harbor, and released upon taking the Oath of Allegiance on June 20, 1865. If captured in Columbia, February is probably the month as it is the period that U.S. Army forces briefly occupied the city before continuing the march toward North Carolina.
Source: *NCT*, III:568; M270.

▲**Kennedy, Stiles**, Surgeon, Field and Staff
Wise's Forks
Captured at the battle of Wise's Forks on March 8, 1865. At the time of his capture, Kennedy served as the Senior Surgeon of Clingman's Brigade. His service records and *NC Troops* only note that he was captured in North Carolina on March 8, 1865. Confined at various prisons before being paroled on April 16, 1865.
Source: Sokolosky and Smith, *To Prepare for Sherman's Coming*, 133; *NCT*, III:522; M270.

Looper, Temolin, Private, Company C
Wise's Forks
Captured near Kinston on March 8, 1865. Confined at Point Lookout, Maryland, and released upon taking the Oath of Allegiance on May 15, 1865.
Source: *NCT*, III:547, 721; M270.

▲**Miller, John W.**, Private, Company K
Bentonville
Wounded at the battle of Bentonville between March 19-21, 1865. According to Surgeon Tanner's "Return of Casualties in Hoke's Div. near Bentonville," Pvt. J. W. Miller, Co. K, was slightly wounded in the scalp. The April 4, 1865, edition of the *Western Democrat* Pvt. J. W. Miller, 8th NC, was in a Raleigh hospital, wounded in the head. Private John W. Miller of Co. K is the same soldier as Pvt. J. W. Miller. *NC Troops* notes that he was wounded in the head at Bentonville on or about March 19, 1865.
Source: Tanner (BV), 140; *WD* (Charlotte), April 4, 1865; *NCT*, IV:620, 726; M270; NC Confederate Pension (Rowan County).

▲**Morse, James**, Private, Company I
Bentonville
Wounded at the battle of Bentonville between March 19-21, 1865. According to Surgeon Tanner's "Return of Casualties in Hoke's Div. near Bentonville," Pvt. Jas. Moore, Co. I, was slightly wounded in the right thigh. Paroled at Greensboro on May 14, 1865. *NC Troops* note the wound he received at the battle of Bentonville.
Source: Tanner (BV), 140; *NCT*, IV:610; M270.

▲**Page, W. Riley**, Private, Company H
Bentonville
Wounded at the battle of Bentonville between March 19-21, 1865. According to Surgeon Tanner's "Return of Casualties in Hoke's Div. near Bentonville," Pvt. Riley Page, Co. H, was dangerously wounded in the head. The April 4, 1865, edition of the *Western Democrat* reported that Pvt. Wm. Page, 8th NC, was in a Raleigh hospital suffering from a mortal wound to the head. *NC Troops* notes that he was killed at Bentonville, March 19-21, 1865.
Source: Tanner (BV), 140; *WD* (Charlotte), April 4, 1865; *NCT*, IV:600, 730; M270.

▲**Roberts, D. M.**, Private, Company D
Bentonville
Wounded at the battle of Bentonville between March 19-21, 1865. According to Surgeon Tanner's "Return of Casualties in Hoke's Div. near Bentonville," Pvt. D. Roberts, Co. D, was slightly wounded in the left forearm. Roberts's Confederate pension indicates that he was wounded in the left arm at Bentonville on March 19, 1865.
Source: Tanner (BV), 140; *NCT*, IV:558; M270; NC Confederate Pension (Wilson County).

▲**Stokely, Charles L.**, Sergeant, Company A

Bentonville
Wounded at the battle of Bentonville between March 19-21, 1865. According to Surgeon Tanner's "Return of Casualties in Hoke's Div. near Bentonville," Sgt. C. Stokely, Co. A, was slightly wounded in the right forearm. *NC Troops* does not indicate his wounding at Bentonville. Charles L. Stokely erred on his Confederate pension application by stating April 17, 1865. Additionally, Stokely noted that the wound to his right arm was near the shoulder, the ball "splitting the bone."
Source: Tanner (BV), 140; *NCT*, IV:531; M270; NC Confederate Pension Pasquotank County).

Unknown Soldier
Oakwood Cemetery
Raleigh, North Carolina

(Courtesy of Wade Sokolosky)

Confederate Monument
Riverside Cemetery in Smithfield, North Carolina
An unknown number of Bentonville wounded died in
Smithfield's temporary hospitals following the battle.

(Wade Sokolosky Collection)

17th Regiment North Carolina Troops (2nd Organization)

▲**Adams, J. H.**, Private, Company E
Sugar Loaf
Captured near Fort Fisher on February 11, 1865. No further records. Adams's capture likely occurred along with approximately 60 other 17th NC soldiers when the Federals advanced against the Sugar Loaf line. This strong Confederate defensive position stretched from the east bank of the Cape Fear River to the southern end of Myrtle Sound. The 17th NC occupied the far left of the line.
Source: M270; *NCT*, VI:239; Moore, *The Wilmington Campaign*, 97.

▲**Allison, John A.**, Private, Company L
Sugar Loaf
Services records indicate two captured dates, February 11, 1865 (near Fort Fisher) and February 16, 1865 (at Fort Fisher). Confined at Point Lookout, Maryland, and released upon taking the Oath of Allegiance on June 23, 1865. Allison's capture likely occurred on February 11, along with approximately 60 other 17th NC soldiers, when the Federals advanced against the Sugar Loaf line. This strong Confederate defensive position stretched from the east bank of the Cape Fear River to the southern end of Myrtle Sound. The 17th NC occupied the far left of the line. *NC Troops* incorrectly notes that he was captured at or near Fort Anderson on or about February 16, 1865. During the Wilmington Campaign, the 17th NC, part of Kirkland's Brigade, never served on the west side of the Cape Fear River.
Source: M270; Moore, *The Wilmington Campaign*, 97; *NCT*, VI:288.

▲**Andrews, George H.**, Private, Company E
Sugar Loaf
Services records indicate two captured dates, February 11, 1865 (near Fort Fisher) and February 16, 1865 (at Fort Fisher). Confined at Point Lookout, Maryland, and released upon taking the Oath of Allegiance on June 22, 1865. Andrew's capture likely occurred on February 11, along with approximately 60 other 17th NC soldiers, when the Federals advanced against the Sugar Loaf line. This strong Confederate defensive position stretched from the east bank of the Cape Fear River to the southern end of Myrtle Sound. The 17th NC occupied the far left of the line. *NC Troops* incorrectly notes that he was captured at or near Fort Anderson on or about February 16, 1865. During the Wilmington Campaign, the 17th NC, part of Kirkland's Brigade, never served on the west side of the Cape Fear River.
Source: M270; Moore, *The Wilmington Campaign*, 97; *NCT*, VI:239.

▲**Arrington, Benjamin R.**, Private, Company I
Sugar Loaf
Services records indicate two captured dates, February 11, 1865 (near Fort Fisher) and February 16, 1865 (at Fort Fisher). Confined at Point Lookout, Maryland, and released upon taking the Oath of Allegiance on June 3, 1865. Arrington's capture likely occurred on February 11, along with approximately 60 other 17th NC soldiers, when the Federals advanced against the Sugar Loaf line. This strong Confederate defensive position stretched from the east bank of the Cape Fear River to the southern end of Myrtle Sound. The 17th NC occupied the far left of the line. *NC Troops* incorrectly notes that he was captured at or near Fort Anderson on or about February 16, 1865. During the Wilmington Campaign, the 17th NC, part of Kirkland's Brigade, never served on the west side of the Cape Fear River.
Source: M270; Moore, *The Wilmington Campaign*, 97; *NCT*, VI:272; NC Confederate Pension (Nash County).

▲**Ausban, Jefferson J.**, Private, Company E
Sugar Loaf
Services records indicate that he was captured near Fort Fisher on February 19. Confined at Point Lookout, Maryland, and released upon taking the Oath of Allegiance on June 22, 1865. Ausban's capture on February 19 coincided with the Confederate withdrawal from the Sugar Loaf line to a new defensive position several miles back toward Wilmington. *NC Troops* incorrectly notes that he was captured at or near Fort Anderson

on or about February 16, 1865. During the Wilmington Campaign, the 17th NC, part of Kirkland's Brigade, never served on the west side of the Cape Fear River.
Source: M270; Moore, *The Wilmington Campaign*, 117; *NCT*, VI:240.

Ausbon, William James, Private, Company H
Wise's Forks
Captured at or near Wise's Forks on March 10, 1865. Confined at Point Lookout, Maryland, and released upon taking the Oath of Allegiance on June 22, 1865.
Source: *NCT*, VI:263; M270.

♦Avery, Jason, Private, Company H
Bentonville (Inconclusive)
Wounded at the battle of Bentonville between March 19-21, 1865. According to Surgeon Tanner's "Return of Casualties in Hoke's Div. near Bentonville," Pvt. Jason Avery, Co. H, 17th NC, was severely wounded in the left arm. No, Jason Avery is listed in the National Archives Compiled Service Records for North Carolina Soldiers belonging to the 17th NC. Further research is required.
Source: Tanner (WF), 148.

▲Baker, Bryant, Private, Company K
Sugar Loaf
Services records indicate two captured dates, February 11, 1865 (near Fort Fisher) and February 16, 1865 (at Fort Fisher). Confined at Point Lookout, Maryland, and released upon taking the Oath of Allegiance on May 12, 1865. Baker's capture likely occurred on February 11, along with approximately 60 other 17th NC soldiers, when the Federals advanced against the Sugar Loaf line. This strong Confederate defensive position stretched from the east bank of the Cape Fear River to the southern end of Myrtle Sound. The 17th NC occupied the far left of the line. *NC Troops* incorrectly notes that he was captured at or near Fort Anderson on or about February 16, 1865. During the Wilmington Campaign, the 17th NC, part of Kirkland's Brigade, never served on the west side of the Cape Fear River.
Source: M270; Moore, *The Wilmington Campaign*, 97; *NCT*, VI:282; NC Confederate Widow's Pension (Pitt County).

Barden, Arthur, Private, Company H
Wise's Forks
Captured at or near Wise's Forks on March 10, 1865. Confined at Point Lookout, Maryland, and released upon taking the Oath of Allegiance on June 23, 1865.
Source: *NCT*, VI:264; M270.

Barfield, Horace E., Private, Company I
Wise's Forks
Captured at or near Wise's Forks on March 10, 1865. Confined at Point Lookout, Maryland, and released upon taking the Oath of Allegiance on June 23, 1865.
Source: *NCT*, VI:273; M270.

▲Barfield, Thomas, Private, Company E
Sugar Loaf
Services records indicate two captured dates, February 11, 1865 (near Fort Fisher) and February 16, 1865 (at Fort Fisher). Confined at Point Lookout, Maryland, and released upon taking the Oath of Allegiance on June 23, 1865. Barfield's capture likely occurred on February 11, along with approximately 60 other 17th NC soldiers, when the Federals advanced against the Sugar Loaf line. This strong Confederate defensive position stretched from the east bank of the Cape Fear River to the southern end of Myrtle Sound. The 17th NC occupied the far left of the line. *NC Troops* incorrectly notes that he was captured at or near Fort Anderson on or about February 16, 1865. During the Wilmington Campaign, the 17th NC, part of Kirkland's Brigade, never served on the west side of the Cape Fear River.
Source: M270; Moore, *The Wilmington Campaign*, 97; *NCT*, VI:240.

▲Bass, Robert John, Private, Company I

Sugar Loaf
Services records indicate two captured dates, February 11, 1865 (near Fort Fisher) and February 16, 1865 (at Fort Fisher). Confined at Point Lookout, Maryland, and released upon taking the Oath of Allegiance on June 3, 1865. Bass's capture likely occurred on February 11, along with approximately 60 other 17th NC soldiers, when the Federals advanced against the Sugar Loaf line. This strong Confederate defensive position stretched from the east bank of the Cape Fear River to the southern end of Myrtle Sound. The 17th NC occupied the far left of the line. *NC Troops* incorrectly notes that he was captured at or near Fort Anderson on or about February 16, 1865. During the Wilmington Campaign, the 17th NC, part of Kirkland's Brigade, never served on the west side of the Cape Fear River.
Source: M270; Moore, *The Wilmington Campaign*, 97; NCT, VI:273.

Baum, Thomas T., Private, Company B
Kinston (Post Wise's Forks)
Captured at or near Kinston on March 16, 1865. Confined at Point Lookout, Maryland, and released upon taking the Oath of Allegiance on June 23, 1865.
Source: *NCT*, VI:216; M270; NC Confederate Pension (Currituck County).

Bennett, Calvin R., Private, Company A
Near Goldsboro
Captured near Goldsboro on March 20, 1865. Confined at Point Lookout, Maryland, and released upon taking the Oath of Allegiance on June 23, 1865.
Source: *NCT*, VI:208; M270; NC Confederate Widow's Pension (Martin County).

▲Bennett, Milton N., Private, Company F
Wise's Forks
Captured at or near Wise's Forks on March 10, 1865. Bennett was admitted to the U.S. Army Foster GH, patient registry no. 6355, in New Bern on March 11, 1865, for intermittent fever. Milton N. Bennett was later Confined at Point Lookout, Maryland, and released upon taking the Oath of Allegiance on June 23, 1865. *NC Troops* does not note his hospitalization at New Bern in March 1865.
Source: *NCT*, VI:247, 719; M270; RG94, Foster General Hospital Registry, 92.

Berry, William W., Private, Company B
Wise's Forks
Captured at Wise's Forks on March 10, 1865. Confined at Point Lookout, Maryland, and released upon taking the Oath of Allegiance on June 16, 1865.
Source: *NCT*, VI:217; M270; NC Confederate Pension (Hyde County).

▲Biggs, Levi W., Private, Company G
Sugar Loaf
Services records indicate he was captured near Fort Fisher on February 11, 1865. Confined at Point Lookout, Maryland, and released upon taking the Oath of Allegiance on June 24, 1865. Biggs's capture likely occurred with approximately 60 other 17th NC soldiers when the Federals advanced against the Sugar Loaf line. This strong Confederate defensive position stretched from the east bank of the Cape Fear River to the southern end of Myrtle Sound. The 17th NC occupied the far left of the line. *NC Troops* incorrectly notes that he was captured at or near Fort Anderson on or about February 11, 1865. During the Wilmington Campaign, the 17th NC, part of Kirkland's Brigade, never served on the west side of the Cape Fear River.
Source: M270; Moore, *The Wilmington Campaign*, 97; NCT, VI:255.

Blackwelder, William R., Private, Company L
Near Kinston (Post Wise's Forks)
Captured near Kinston on March 16, 1865. Confined at Point Lookout, Maryland, and released upon taking the Oath of Allegiance on June 24, 1865.
Source: *NCT*, VI:288; M270; NC Confederate Pension (Cabarrus County).

Blackwood, John Turner, Private, Company L
Near Goldsboro
Deserted to the enemy near Goldsboro on March 20, 1865. Confined at Point Lookout, Maryland, and released upon taking the Oath of Allegiance on May 12, 1865.
Source: *NCT*, VI:288; M270; NC Confederate Widow's Pension (Buncombe County).

▲**Bowers, William R.**, Private, Company E
Sugar Loaf
Services records indicate two captured dates, February 11, 1865 (near Fort Fisher) and February 16, 1865 (at Fort Fisher). Confined at Point Lookout, Maryland, and released upon taking the Oath of Allegiance on June 23, 1865. Bowers's capture likely occurred on February 11, along with approximately 60 other 17th NC soldiers, when the Federals advanced against the Sugar Loaf line. This strong Confederate defensive position stretched from the east bank of the Cape Fear River to the southern end of Myrtle Sound. The 17th NC occupied the far left of the line. *NC Troops* incorrectly notes that he was captured at or near Fort Anderson on or about February 16, 1865. During the Wilmington Campaign, the 17th NC, part of Kirkland's Brigade, never served on the west side of the Cape Fear River.
Source: M270; Moore, *The Wilmington Campaign*, 97; *NCT*, VI:240; NC Confederate Pension (Martin County).

▲**Bradley, W. Cornelius**, Private, Company I
Wise's Forks
Wounded at the battle of Wise's Forks between March 8-10, 1865. According to Surgeon Tanner's "Return of Casualties near Kinston," Pvt. C. Bradley, Co. I, 17th NC, was slightly wounded in the right leg. His service records indicate that he was admitted to GH No. 13 (Pettigrew) in Raliegh on March 11, 1865, with a gunshot wound to the right leg. *NC Troops* does not note his wounding at Wise's Forks.
Source: Tanner (WF), 138; *NCS* (Raleigh), March 29, 1865; *WD* (Charlotte), April 4, 1865; *NCT*, VI:273; M270; NC Confederate Widow's Pension (Edgecombe County).

▲**Briley, William Stephen**, Private, Company H
Bentonville
Wounded at the battle of Bentonville between March 19-21, 1865. According to Surgeon Tanner's "Return of Casualties in Hoke's Div. near Bentonville," Pvt. Stephen Bishop, Co. H, 17th NC, was slightly wounded in the left arm. No Stephen Bishop is listed on the unit rolls. Private William Stephen Briley is the same soldier Tanner incorrectly identified as Stephen Bishop. Briley was reported present in the Episcopal Church Hospital in Raleigh, wounded in the left arm. *NC Troops* indicates Pvt. William Stephen Briley was wounded at Bentonville on March 19, 1865.
Source: Tanner (BV), 148; *NCT*, VI:264, 721; M270; *Daily Progress* (Raleigh), March 27, 1865; *WD* (Charlotte), April 4, 1865; M270.

Brown, C., Private, (Company Unknown)
Sugar Loaf
Services records indicate that he was captured near Fort Fisher on February 19. No further records. Brown's capture on February 19 coincided with the Confederate withdrawal from the Sugar Loaf line to a new defensive position several miles back toward Wilmington. *NC Troops* incorrectly notes that he was captured at or near Fort Anderson on or about February 19, 1865. During the Wilmington Campaign, the 17th NC, part of Kirkland's Brigade, never served on the west side of the Cape Fear River.
Source: M270; Moore, *The Wilmington Campaign*, 117; *NCT*, VI:294.

▲**Brown, James M.**, Private, Company E
Sugar Loaf
Services records indicate two captured dates, February 11, 1865 (near Fort Fisher) and February 16, 1865 (at Fort Fisher). Confined at Point Lookout, Maryland, and released upon taking the Oath of Allegiance on June 24, 1865. Brown's capture likely occurred on February 11, along with approximately 60 other 17th NC soldiers, when the Federals advanced against the Sugar Loaf line. This strong Confederate defensive position stretched from the east bank of the Cape Fear River to the southern end of Myrtle Sound. The 17th

NC occupied the far left of the line. *NC Troops* incorrectly notes that he was captured at or near Fort Anderson on or about February 16, 1865. During the Wilmington Campaign, the 17th NC, part of Kirkland's Brigade, never served on the west side of the Cape Fear River.
Source: M270; Moore, *The Wilmington Campaign*, 97; *NCT*, VI:240; NC Confederate Pension (Martin County).

Cain, Joseph G., Private, Company I
Wise's Forks
Captured at or near Wise's Forks on March 10, 1865. Confined at Point Lookout, Maryland, and released upon taking the Oath of Allegiance on May 12, 1865.
Source: *NCT*, VI:274; M270; NC Confederate Pension (Halifax County).

▲Carawan, William M., Musician, Company B
Sugar Loaf
Captured near Fort Fisher on February 19, 1865. Carawan's capture coincided with the Confederate withdrawal from the Sugar Loaf line to a new defensive position several miles back toward Wilmington. Confined at Point Lookout, Maryland, and released upon taking the Oath of Allegiance on June 24, 1865.
Source: M270; *NCT*, VI:217; Moore, *The Wilmington Campaign*, 117.

♦▲Carney, Robert H., Private, Company K
(Inconclusive)
Service records indicate that he was reported absent due to wounds through March 8, 1865, and later paroled at Thomasville on May 1, 1865. The actual location of his parole was the Thomasville GH. His Confederate pension indicates that he was wounded in the knee at Shepherdsville (present-day Newport) in 1863.
Source: *NCT*, VI:282; M270; M1761, Thomasville General Hospital Paroles; NC Confederate Pension (Pitt County).

Causey, Frank, Private, Company I
Wise's Forks
Captured at or near Wise's Forks on March 8, 1865. Confined at Point Lookout, Maryland, and released upon taking the Oath of Allegiance on June 26, 1865.
Source: *NCT*, VI:274; M270.

▲Chappell, Benjamin, Private, Company L
Bentonville
Wounded at the battle of Bentonville between March 19-21, 1865. According to Surgeon Tanner's "Return of Casualties in Hoke's Div. near Bentonville," Pvt. Benj. Chappell, Co. L, 17th NC, was slightly wounded in the left thigh. *NC Troops* does not note his wounding at Bentonville. Paroled as a patient on May 1, 1865. Admitted to GH No. 3 in High Point on an unspecified date between March 21 and April 7, 1865, entry no. 2490.
Source: Tanner (BV), 148; RG109, 6/291:49; *NCT*, VI:182, 289; M270; NC Confederate Widow's Pension (Chowan County).

Cherry, John L., Private, Company A
Wise's Forks
Captured at Wise's Forks on March 10, 1865. Confined at Point Lookout, Maryland, and released upon taking the Oath of Allegiance on June 26, 1865.
Source: *NCT*, VI:208; M270; NC Confederate Pension (Martin County).

▲Cherry, William A., 2nd Lieutenant, Company K
Bentonville
Wounded at the battle of Bentonville between March 19-21, 1865. According to Surgeon Tanner's "Return of Casualties in Hoke's Div. near Bentonville," Lt. Wm. Cherry, Co. K, 17th NC, was slightly wounded in the right leg. *NC Troops* does not note his wounding at Bentonville.
Source: Tanner (BV), 148; *NCT*, VI:281; M270.

▲**Chesson, John B. J.**, Private, Company H
Wise's Forks
Wounded at the battle of Wise's Forks between March 8-10, 1865. According to Surgeon Tanner's "Return of Casualties near Kinston," Pvt. J. Chesson, Co. H, 17th NC, was severely wounded in the left lung. *NC Troops* does not note his wounding at Wise's Forks.
Source: Tanner (WF), 138; *NCT*, VI:265; M270.

Clark, Daniel, Private, Company H
Wise's Forks
Captured at or near Wise's Forks on March 10, 1865. Confined at Point Lookout, Maryland, and released upon taking the Oath of Allegiance on June 26, 1865.
Source: *NCT*, VI:265; M270.

▲**Clayton, Thomas T.**, Private, Company F
Bentonville
Wounded at the battle of Bentonville between March 19-21, 1865. According to Surgeon Tanner's "Return of Casualties in Hoke's Div. near Bentonville," Pvt. Thos. Clayton, Co. F, 17th NC, was slightly wounded in the head. His service records indicate that he was admitted to GH No. 11 in Charlotte on April 25, 1865, with a gunshot wound to the scalp. Paroled at Greensboro on April 29, 1865. *NC Troops* does not note his wounding at Bentonville.
Source: Tanner (BV), 148; *NCT*, VI:248, 725; M270; NC Confederate Pension (Person County).

▲**Coffield, Thomas Hunter**, Private, Company H
Sugar Loaf
Services records indicate two captured dates, February 11, 1865 (near Fort Fisher) and February 16, 1865 (at Fort Fisher). Confined at Point Lookout, Maryland, and released upon taking the Oath of Allegiance on June 24, 1865. Coffield's capture likely occurred on February 11, along with approximately 60 other 17th NC soldiers, when the Federals advanced against the Sugar Loaf line. This strong Confederate defensive position stretched from the east bank of the Cape Fear River to the southern end of Myrtle Sound. The 17th NC occupied the far left of the line. *NC Troops* incorrectly notes that he was captured at or near Fort Anderson on or about February 16, 1865. During the Wilmington Campaign, the 17th NC, part of Kirkland's Brigade, never served on the west side of the Cape Fear River.
Source: M270; Moore, *The Wilmington Campaign*, 97; *NCT*, VI:265; NC Confederate Pension (Martin County).

▲**Coltrain, Alfred M.**, Private, Company E
Wise's Forks
Wounded at the battle of Wise's Forks between March 8-10, 1865. According to Surgeon Tanner's "Return of Casualties near Kinston," Pvt. A. Coltrain, Co. E, 17th NC, was severely wounded in the right hip. Admitted to a Raleigh hospital on March 11, 1865, with a contusion of the right thigh. He was admitted to the Tate House Hospital, a temporary ward of GH No. 12 in Greensboro, on an unspecified date and later paroled as a patient on April 28, 1865.
Source: Tanner (WF), 138; *NCS* (Raleigh), March 29, 1865; *WD* (Charlotte), April 4, 1865; *NCT*, VI:241; M270.

▲**Cook, J. B.**, Private, (Company Unknown)
Sugar Loaf
Captured near Fort Fisher on February 19, 1865. No further records. Cook's capture coincided with the Confederate withdrawal from the Sugar Loaf line to a new defensive position several miles back toward Wilmington. *NC Troops* incorrectly notes that he was captured at or near Fort Anderson on February 19, 1865. During the Wilmington Campaign, the 17th NC, part of Kirkland's Brigade, never served on the west side of the Cape Fear River.
Source: M270; Moore, *The Wilmington Campaign*, 117; *NCT*, VI:294.

Cooper, Gilbert Y., Private, Company A
Wise's Forks

Captured at Wise's Forks on March 8, 1865. Confined at Point Lookout, Maryland, and released upon taking the Oath of Allegiance on June 24, 1865.
Source: *NCT*, VI:208; M270.

Copeland, Timothy Quincy, Private, Company C
Wise's Forks
Captured near Kinston on March 10, 1865. Confined at Point Lookout, Maryland, and released upon taking the Oath of Allegiance on June 26, 1865.
Source: *NCT*, VI:225; M270.

Cowen, William Henry, Private, Company A
Wise's Forks
Captured at Wise's Forks on March 10, 1865. Confined at Point Lookout, Maryland, and released upon taking the Oath of Allegiance on May 13, 1865.
Source: *NCT*, VI:208; M270.

♦▲Craddock, James H., Private, Company H
(Inconclusive)
Admitted to GH No. 13 (Pettigrew) in Raleigh on March 11, 1865, with a gunshot wound of the left leg. Received a 60-day furlough on March 23, 1865. Previously wounded in Virginia between May-August 1864. His hospitalization may be a result of an old wound.
Source: *NCT*, VI:265, 727; M270.

▲Craddock, William A., Private, Company H
Wise's Forks
Wounded at the battle of Wise's Forks between March 8-10, 1865. According to Surgeon Tanner's "Return of Casualties near Kinston," Sgt. W. Cratick [sic], Co. H, 17th NC, was severely wounded in the left hip. The *NC Standard* reported Pvt. W. A. Craddock, Co. H, 17th NC, was present in GH No. 13 (Pettigrew) wounded in the left hip in March 1865. *NC Troops* does not note his wounding at Wise's Forks; however, his Confederate pension records indicate he was wounded on April 1, 1865. Craddock stated on his pension application, "I have the ball that the Dr. cut out in my trunk."
Source: Tanner (WF), 138; *NCS* (Raleigh), March 29, 1865; *WD* (Charlotte), April 4, 1865; *NCT*, VI:265; M270; NC Confederate Pension (Beaufort County).

▲Craft, Elder James, Corporal, Company K
Sugar Loaf
Services records indicate two captured dates, February 11, 1865 (near Fort Fisher) and February 16, 1865 (at Fort Fisher). Confined at Point Lookout, Maryland, and released upon taking the Oath of Allegiance on May 13, 1865. Craft's capture likely occurred on February 11, along with approximately 60 other 17th NC soldiers, when the Federals advanced against the Sugar Loaf line. This strong Confederate defensive position stretched from the east bank of the Cape Fear River to the southern end of Myrtle Sound. The 17th NC occupied the far left of the line. *NC Troops* incorrectly notes that he was captured at or near Fort Anderson on or about February 16, 1865. During the Wilmington Campaign, the 17th NC, part of Kirkland's Brigade, never served on the west side of the Cape Fear River.
Source: M270; Moore, *The Wilmington Campaign*, 97; *NCT*, VI:282.

Cross, Lazarus, Private, Company E
Wise's Forks
Captured at or near Kinston on March 10, 1865. Confined at Point Lookout, Maryland, and released upon taking the Oath of Allegiance on June 26, 1865. In April 1898, Cross applied for admission to the North Carolina Soldiers' Home in Raleigh.
Source: *NCT*, VI:241; M270. NC Confederate Pension (Martin County).

♦▲Cross, William T., Private, Company E
Bentonville (Inconclusive)

Wounded at the battle of Bentonville between March 19-21, 1865. According to Surgeon Tanner's "Return of Casualties in Hoke's Div. near Bentonville," Pvt. W. P. Cross, Co. E, 17th NC, was severely wounded in the right arm. *NC Troops* does not note his wounding at Wise's Forks. William T. Cross may be the same soldier listed by Tanner as W. P. Cross. Confederate pension does note that he was wounded at any time during the war.
Source: Tanner (BV), 148; *NCT*, VI:241; M270; NC Confederate Pension (Martin County).

♦▲Cushing, William M., Private, Company E
Bentonville (Inconclusive)
Wounded at the battle of Bentonville between March 19-21, 1865. According to Surgeon Tanner's "Return of Casualties in Hoke's Div. near Bentonville," Pvt. Wm. Cushing, Co. E, 17th NC, was dangerously wounded in the abdomen. *NC Troops* does not note his wounding at Wise's Forks.
Source: Tanner (BV), 148; *NCT*, VI:241; M270.

Davenport, Hezekiah H., Private, Company G
Wise's Forks
Captured at or near Wise's Forks on March 10, 1865. Confined at Point Lookout, Maryland, and released upon taking the Oath of Allegiance on June 12, 1865.
Source: *NCT*, VI:257; M270; NC Confederate Widow's Pension (Tyrrell County).

Davenport, Jerome B., Private, Company G
Wise's Forks
Captured at or near Wise's Forks on March 10, 1865. Confined at Point Lookout, Maryland, and released upon taking the Oath of Allegiance on June 12, 1865.
Source: *NCT*, VI:257; M270; NC Confederate Pension (Halifax County).

Davis, Ashley, Private, Company D
Jamesville
Captured at or near Jamesville on or about February 11, 1865. Confined at Point Lookout, Maryland, and released upon taking the Oath of Allegiance on or about June 12, 1865.
Source: *NCT*, VI:234; M270; NC Confederate Widow's Pension (Beaufort County).

Davis, James L. G., Private, Company G
Wise's Forks
Wounded in the left leg (amputated) and captured at the battle of Wise's Forks on March 10, 1865. According to the U.S. Army Foster GH Patient Registry, a Pvt. James S. Davis, Co. G, 17th NC, was admitted (no. 6560) on March 15, 1865, for a gunshot in his side and left leg (amputated) that occurred on March 10, 1865. Private James L. G. Davis is the same soldier as Pvt. James S. Davis.
Source: *NCT*, VI:257; M270; RG94, Foster General Hospital Registry, 99; NC Confederate Pension (Edgecombe County); NC Confederate Widow's Pension (Martin County).

♦Duncan, Isaac T., Private, Company F
Near Raleigh (Inconclusive)
Captured near Raleigh on March 18, 1865. Confined at Point Lookout, Maryland, and released upon taking the Oath of Allegiance on June 26, 1865. No Federal forces were near Raleigh on March 18, 1865. Further research is required.
Source: *NCT*, VI:249; M270; NC Confederate Pension (Durham County).

Eastwood, William D., Private, Company B
Near Bentonville
Captured near Bentonville on March 22, 1865. Confined at Hart's Island, New York Harbor, and released upon taking the Oath of Allegiance on June 14, 1865.
Source: *NCT*, VI:218; M270.

▲English, Enoch D., Private, Company B

Sugar Loaf
Services records indicate two captured dates, February 11, 1865 (near Fort Fisher) and February 16, 1865 (at Fort Fisher). Confined at Point Lookout, Maryland, and released upon taking the Oath of Allegiance on June 26, 1865. English's capture likely occurred on February 11, along with approximately 60 other 17th NC soldiers, when the Federals advanced against the Sugar Loaf line. This strong Confederate defensive position stretched from the east bank of the Cape Fear River to the southern end of Myrtle Sound. The 17th NC occupied the far left of the line. *NC Troops* incorrectly notes that he was captured at or near Fort Anderson on or about February 16, 1865. During the Wilmington Campaign, the 17th NC, part of Kirkland's Brigade, never served on the west side of the Cape Fear River.
Source: M270; Moore, *The Wilmington Campaign*, 97; *NCT*, VI:218.

▲**Evans, Isaac**, Private, Company F
Bentonville
NC Troops notes that he died of disease while a prisoner at New Bern on March 1, 1865. In 1887, George B. Daniels, the former commander of Co. F, 17th NC, provided a sworn statement stating that Isaac Evans "was last seen going in the fight at Bentonville, N.C. in 1865, and has never been seen since." See "Widow's Claim for Pension," Mary A. E. Evans.
Source: *NCT*, VI:249, 731; M270; NC Confederate Widow's Pension (Granville County).

▲**Evans, J. Albert**, Private, Company E
Sugar Loaf
Captured at or near Fort Anderson on or about February 16, 1865. The 17th NC, part of Kirkland's Brigade, never served on the west side of the Cape Fear River during the Wilmington Campaign. Evans's capture likely occurred on February 11, along with approximately 60 other 17th NC soldiers, when the Federals advanced against the Sugar Loaf line, a strong Confederate defensive position that stretched from the east bank of the Cape Fear River to the southern end of Myrtle Sound. The 17th NC occupied the far left of the line. Confined at Point Lookout, Maryland, and released upon taking the Oath of Allegiance on June 12, 1865.
Source: *NCT*, VI:241; Moore, *The Wilmington Campaign*, 97; M270; NC Confederate Pension (Edgecombe County).

Evans, James M., Private, Company F
White Hall
Captured at or near White Hall on or about March 20, 1865. Confined at Point Lookout, Maryland, and released upon taking the Oath of Allegiance on June 26, 1865.
Source: *NCT*, VI:249; M270.

▲**Evans, Theophilus**, Private, Company K
Wise's Forks
Wounded at the battle of Wise's Forks between March 8-10, 1865. According to Surgeon Tanner's "Return of Casualties near Kinston," Pvt. T. Evans, Co. K, 17th NC, was dangerously wounded in the right leg. Paroled as a patient at GH No. 12 in Greensboro on April 28, 1865. *NC Troops* does not note his wounding at Wise's Forks.
Source: Tanner (WF), 138; *NCT*, VI:283, 745; M270; NC Confederate Pension (Wayne County).

▲**Everett, John H.**, Private, Company C
Wise's Forks
Wounded at the battle of Wise's Forks between March 8-10, 1865. According to Surgeon Tanner's "Return of Casualties near Kinston," Pvt. J. H. Everett, Co. C, 17th NC, was severely wounded in the right leg. The March 27, 1865 edition of the *Daily Progress* listed Pvt. J. H. Everit was a patient in the Baptist Church Hospital in Raleigh suffering from a wound to his right leg. No further records. *NC Troops* incorrectly notes that he was wounded at Bentonville on March 19, 1865,
Source: Tanner (WF), 137; *DP* (Raleigh), March 27, 1865; *WD* (Charlotte), April 4, 1865; *NCT*, VI:226, 731; M270; NC Confederate Widow's Pension (Halifax County).

Everett, Simon Turner, Private, Company E
Wise's Forks
Captured at or near Wise's Forks on March 10, 1865. Confined at Point Lookout, Maryland, and released upon taking the Oath of Allegiance on June 12, 1865.
Source: *NCT*, VI:242; M270.

▲**Everett, Staten**, Private, Company H
Wise's Forks
Wounded at the battle of Wise's Forks between March 8-10, 1865. According to Surgeon Tanner's "Return of Casualties near Kinston," Pvt. S. Everett, Co. H, 17th NC, was slightly wounded in the right forearm. His service records indicate that he was admitted to GH No. 13 (Pettigrew) in Raleigh on March 11, 1865, with a gunshot wound to the right arm. Received a 60-day furlough on March 16, 1865.
Source: Tanner (WF), 138; *NCS* (Raleigh), March 29, 1865; *WD* (Charlotte), April 4, 1865; *NCT*, VI:265; M270.

Foley, Staten W., Private, Company G
Wise's Forks
Captured at or near Wise's Forks on March 10, 1865. Confined at Point Lookout, Maryland, and released upon taking the Oath of Allegiance on June 27, 1865.
Source: *NCT*, VI:257; M270; NC Confederate Pension (Washington County).

Freeman, William T., Corporal, Company G
Wise's Forks
Captured at or near Wise's Forks on March 10, 1865. Confined at Point Lookout, Maryland, and released upon taking the Oath of Allegiance on June 27, 1865.
Source: *NCT*, VI:257; M270.

▲**Fronley, W. H.**, Private, (Company Unknown)
Sugar Loaf
Captured near Fort Fisher on February 19, 1865. No further records. Fronley's capture coincided with the Confederate withdrawal from the Sugar Loaf line to a new defensive position several miles back toward Wilmington. *NC Troops* incorrectly notes that he was captured at or near Fort Anderson on February 19, 1865. During the Wilmington Campaign, the 17th NC, part of Kirkland's Brigade, never served on the west side of the Cape Fear River.
Source: M270; Moore, *The Wilmington Campaign*, 117; *NCT*, VI:294.

▲**Gardiner, David C.**, Private, Company F
Sugar Loaf
Services records indicate two captured dates, February 11, 1865 (near Fort Fisher) and February 16, 1865 (at Fort Fisher). Confined at Point Lookout, Maryland, and released upon taking the Oath of Allegiance on June 3, 1865. Gardiner's capture likely occurred on February 11, along with approximately 60 other 17th NC soldiers, when the Federals advanced against the Sugar Loaf line. This strong Confederate defensive position stretched from the east bank of the Cape Fear River to the southern end of Myrtle Sound. The 17th NC occupied the far left of the line. *NC Troops* incorrectly notes that he was captured at or near Fort Anderson on or about February 16, 1865. During the Wilmington Campaign, the 17th NC, part of Kirkland's Brigade, never served on the west side of the Cape Fear River.
Source: M270; Moore, *The Wilmington Campaign*, 97; *NCT*, VI:249.

▲**Gardner, David D.**, Private, Company E
Sugar Loaf
Captured near Fort Fisher on February 19, 1865. Confined at Point Lookout, Maryland, and released upon taking the Oath of Allegiance on June 27, 1865. Gardner's capture coincided with the Confederate withdrawal from the Sugar Loaf line to a new defensive position several miles back toward Wilmington. *NC Troops* incorrectly notes that he was captured at or near Fort Anderson on or about February 16, 1865.

During the Wilmington Campaign, the 17th NC, part of Kirkland's Brigade, never served on the west side of the Cape Fear River.
Source: M270; Moore, *The Wilmington Campaign*, 117; *NCT*, VI:242; NC Confederate Widow's Pension (Pitt County).

Gardner, Luke E., Private, Company D
Jamesville
Captured at or near Jamesville on February 11, 1865. Confined at Point Lookout, Maryland, and released upon taking the Oath of Allegiance on or about June 27, 1865.
Source: *NCT*, VI:234; M270.

▲**Gaskins, Seth**, Private, Company B
Sugar Loaf
Services records indicate two captured dates, February 11, 1865 (near Wilmington) and February 16, 1865 (at Fort Fisher). Confined at Point Lookout, Maryland, and released upon taking the Oath of Allegiance on June 27, 1865. Gaskin's capture likely occurred on February 11, along with approximately 60 other 17th NC soldiers, when the Federals advanced against the Sugar Loaf line. This strong Confederate defensive position stretched from the east bank of the Cape Fear River to the southern end of Myrtle Sound. The 17th NC occupied the far left of the line.
Source: M270; Moore, *The Wilmington Campaign*, 97; *NCT*, VI:218.

▲**Glisson, Lemuel**, Private, Company F
Sugar Loaf
Services records indicate two captured dates, February 11, 1865 (near Fort Fisher) and February 16, 1865 (at Fort Fisher). Confined at Point Lookout, Maryland, and released upon taking the Oath of Allegiance on June 24, 1865. Glisson's capture likely occurred on February 11, along with approximately 60 other 17th NC soldiers, when the Federals advanced against the Sugar Loaf line. This strong Confederate defensive position stretched from the east bank of the Cape Fear River to the southern end of Myrtle Sound. The 17th NC occupied the far left of the line. *NC Troops* incorrectly notes that he was captured at or near Fort Anderson on or about February 16, 1865. During the Wilmington Campaign, the 17th NC, part of Kirkland's Brigade, never served on the west side of the Cape Fear River.
Source: M270; Moore, *The Wilmington Campaign*, 97; *NCT*, VI:249.

♦**Goodman, Jacob T.**, Private, Company L
Bentonville (Inconclusive)
Wounded at the battle of Bentonville between March 19-21, 1865. According to Surgeon Tanner's "Return of Casualties in Hoke's Div. near Bentonville," Pvt. T. Goodman, Co. F, 17th NC, was severely wounded in the left arm. No T. Goodman is listed on the company rolls. Jacob T. Goodman of Co. L may have been the wounded soldier listed by Tanner. Neither his service records nor *NC Troops* note his wounding at Bentonville. Further research is required.
Source: Tanner (WF), 148; *NCT*, VI:290; M270.

▲ **Gorham, William T.**, Private, Company I
Sugar Loaf
Services records indicate two captured dates, February 11, 1865 (near Fort Fisher) and February 16, 1865 (at Fort Fisher). Confined at Point Lookout, Maryland, and released upon taking the Oath of Allegiance on June 3, 1865. Gorham's capture likely occurred on February 11, along with approximately 60 other 17th NC soldiers, when the Federals advanced against the Sugar Loaf line. This strong Confederate defensive position stretched from the east bank of the Cape Fear River to the southern end of Myrtle Sound. The 17th NC occupied the far left of the line. *NC Troops* incorrectly notes that he was captured at or near Fort Anderson on or about February 16, 1865. During the Wilmington Campaign, the 17th NC, part of Kirkland's Brigade, never served on the west side of the Cape Fear River.
Source: M270; Moore, *The Wilmington Campaign*, 97; *NCT*, VI:275.

♦**Graves, Jesse**, Private, Company F

Bentonville (Inconclusive)
Wounded at the battle of Bentonville between March 19-21, 1865. According to Surgeon Tanner's "Return of Casualties in Hoke's Div. near Bentonville," Pvt. Jesse Graves, Co. F, 17th NC, was severely wounded in the right leg. No, Jesse Graves is listed in the rolls of the 17th NC. Further research is required.
Source: Tanner (WF), 148.

▲**Gray, B. S., Jr.**, Private, Company L
Wise's Forks
Wounded at Wise's Forks on March 10. His service records indicate that he was admitted to GH No. 13 (Pettigrew) in Raleigh on March 11, 1865, with a gunshot wound of the groin. Transferred to a Greensboro hospital on an undetermined date. Paroled at Charlotte on May 3, 1865. According to B. S. Gray Jr.'s Confederate pension application, he was wounded on March 10, 1865, near Kinston by a gunshot in the right side of his groin. In 1901, the ball remained in his body, "between groin and testicle."
Source: M270; NCS (Raleigh), March 29, 1865; WD (Charlotte), April 4, 1865; NCT, VI:290; NC Confederate Pension (Cabarrus County).

▲**Griffin, Franklin M.**, Private, Company E
Wise's Forks
Wounded at the battle of Wise's Forks between March 8-10, 1865. According to Surgeon Tanner's "Return of Casualties near Kinston," Pvt. F. Griffin, Co. E, 17th NC, was severely wounded in the right thigh. *NC Troops* does not note his wounding at Wise's Forks.
Source: Tanner (WF), 138; NCT, VI:242; M270.

Griffin, William A., Private, Company A
Wise's Forks
Captured at Wise's Forks on March 8, 1865. Confined at Point Lookout, Maryland, and released upon taking the Oath of Allegiance on May 13, 1865.
Source: NCT, VI:209; M270; NC Confederate Widow's Pension (Martin County).

▲**Grimes, George W.**, 1st Lieutenant, Company G
Wise's Forks
His service records indicate he was wounded in the chest and captured at the battle of Wise's Forks on March 10, 1865. The U.S. Army Foster GH in New Bern notes Grimes, patient registry no. 6356, was admitted on March 11, 1865, for a "gunshot wound Chest left side" suffered on March 10, 1865. An additional note indicates he had a "ball lodging in cavity of pelvis." He was released from the hospital on May 1, 1865. Grimes indicates on his Confederate pension application that he was wounded "[w]hile charging the enemy works at Wises' Forks." The examining physician noted on the application that the ball, after striking Grimes, "ranged down and is now located near the kidneys."
Source: NCT, VI:254; M270; RG94, Foster General Hospital Registry; NC Confederate Pension (Hertford County).

Gurganus, Daniel, Private, Company E
Wise's Forks
Captured near Kinston on March 11, 1865. Confined at Point Lookout, Maryland, and released upon taking the Oath of Allegiance on June 27, 1865.
Source: NCT, VI:242; M270; NC Confederate Widow's Pension (Martin County).

Gurganus, David, Private, Company E
Wise's Forks
Captured at or near Wise's Forks on March 10, 1865. Confined at Point Lookout, Maryland, and released upon taking the Oath of Allegiance on June 27, 1865.
Source: NCT, VI:242; M270; NC Confederate Widow's Pension (Martin County).

▲**Gurganus, Robert**, Private, Company F
Sugar Loaf

Captured at or near Fort Anderson on or about February 16, 1865. Confined at Point Lookout, Maryland, and released upon taking the Oath of Allegiance on June 27, 1865. Gurganus's capture likely occurred on February 11, along with approximately 60 other 17th NC soldiers, when the Federals advanced against the Sugar Loaf line. This strong Confederate defensive position stretched from the east bank of the Cape Fear River to the southern end of Myrtle Sound. The 17th NC occupied the far left of the line. *NC Troops* incorrectly notes that he was captured at or near Fort Anderson on or about February 16, 1865. During the Wilmington Campaign, the 17th NC, part of Kirkland's Brigade, never served on the west side of the Cape Fear River.
Source: M270; Moore, *The Wilmington Campaign*, 97; *NCT*, VI:249; NC Confederate Widow's Pension (Martin County).

Hadley, William Blount, Private, Company F
Sugar Loaf
Provost Marshal records indicate two dates of capture, both near Fort Fisher: February 11 and February 16, 1865. Confined at Point Lookout, Maryland, and released upon taking the Oath of Allegiance on June 13, 1865. *NC Troops* incorrectly notes that he was captured "at or near Fort Anderson."
Source: *NCT*, VI:250; M270; NC Confederate Pension (Martin County).

Haislip, Alexander, Private, Company E
Wise's Forks
Captured at or near Wise's Forks on March 10, 1865. Confined at Point Lookout, Maryland, and released upon taking the Oath of Allegiance on May 15, 1865.
Source: *NCT*, VI:243; M270.

Haislip, William A., Private, Company E
Wise's Forks
Captured at or near Wise's Forks on March 10, 1865. Confined at Point Lookout, Maryland, and released upon taking the Oath of Allegiance on May 15, 1865.
Source: *NCT*, VI:243; M270.

Hampton, William H., Sergeant, Company H
Wise's Forks
Captured at or near Wise's Forks on March 10, 1865. Confined at Point Lookout, Maryland, and released upon taking the Oath of Allegiance on June 14, 1865.
Source: *NCT*, VI:266; M270; NC Confederate Widow's Pension (Watauga County).

▲Hardee, George W., Private, Company K
Wise's Forks
Wounded at the battle of Wise's Forks between March 8-10, 1865. According to Surgeon Tanner's "Return of Casualties near Kinston," Pvt. G. W. Hardy, Co. K, 17th NC, was slightly wounded in the back. *NC Troops* does not note his wounding at Wise's Forks. His service records indicate that he was admitted to GH No. 13 (Pettigrew) in Raleigh on March 10, 1865, with a gunshot wound on the back. Paroled at Greensboro on April 29, 1865.
Source: Tanner (WF), 138; *NCS* (Raleigh), March 29, 1865; *WD* (Charlotte), April 4, 1865; *WD* (Charlotte), April 4, 1865; *NCT*, VI:284; M270.

▲Hardison, Ebenezar H., Sergeant, Company D
Sugar Loaf
Services records indicate two captured dates, February 11, 1865 (near Fort Fisher) and February 16, 1865 (at Fort Fisher). Confined at Point Lookout, Maryland, and released upon taking the Oath of Allegiance on June 27, 1865. Hardison's capture likely occurred on February 11, along with approximately 60 other 17th NC soldiers, when the Federals advanced against the Sugar Loaf line. This strong Confederate defensive position stretched from the east bank of the Cape Fear River to the southern end of Myrtle Sound. The 17th NC occupied the far left of the line. *NC Troops* incorrectly notes that he was captured at or near Fort

Anderson on or about February 16, 1865. During the Wilmington Campaign, the 17th NC, part of Kirkland's Brigade, never served on the west side of the Cape Fear River.
Source: M270; Moore, *The Wilmington Campaign*, 97; *NCT*, VI:235.

Hardison, Ira T., Private, Company A
Martin County
Captured "at home" in Martin County on February 11, 1865, while recovering from a previous wound (amputated arm). Confined at Point Lookout, Maryland, and released upon taking the Oath of Allegiance on June 6, 1865.
Source: *NCT*, VI:209; M270; NC Confederate Pension (Martin County).

Hardison, James L., Private, Company A
Wise's Forks
Captured at Wise's Forks on March 8, 1865. Confined at Point Lookout, Maryland, and released upon taking the Oath of Allegiance on May 13, 1865.
Source: *NCT*, VI:209; M270; NC Confederate Widow's Pension (Martin County).

♦Harrell, J., Private, Company C
Wise's Forks (Inconclusive)
Surgeon Tanner's "Return of Casualties near Kinston" lists a Pvt. J. Harrell, Co. C, 17th NC, as having suffered a severe wound in the heel at the battle of Wise's Forks between March 8-10, 1865. There are two Harrells with a given name beginning with the letter "J," John and Joseph. Neither of which *NC Troops* indicated they were wounded and later hospitalized in March 1865. Both John and Joseph Harrell obtained Confederate pensions, neither of which mention being wounded in the heel.
Source: Tanner (WF), 137; *NCT*, VI:227; M270; John Harrell, NC Confederate Pension (Edgecombe County); Joseph Harrell, NC Confederate Pension (Martin County).

▲Harrell, Thomas W., Private, Company E
Wise's Forks
Wounded at the battle of Wise's Forks between March 8-10, 1865. According to Surgeon Tanner's "Return of Casualties near Kinston," Pvt. T. W. Harrell, Co. E, 17th NC, was slightly wounded in the head. *NC Troops* does not note his wounding at Wise's Forks.
Source: Tanner (WF), 138; *NCT*, VI:243; M270.

▲Harris, Henry Clay, Private, Company K
Bentonville
Wounded at the battle of Bentonville between March 18-21, 1865. According to Surgeon Tanner's "Return of Casualties in Hoke's Div. near Bentonville," a Pvt. H. C. Harris, Co. K, 17th NC, was dangerously wounded in the left lung. His service records indicate that he was admitted to GH No. 13 (Pettigrew) in Raleigh on March 21, 1865, wounded with a gunshot to his left side.
Source: Tanner (BV), 148; *NCS* (Raleigh), March 29, 1865; *WD* (Charlotte), April 4, 1865; *NCT*, VI:284, 737; M270.

▲Harris, James A., Private, Company K
Wise's Forks
Wounded at the battle of Wise's Forks between March 8-10, 1865. According to Surgeon Tanner's "Return of Casualties near Kinston," Pvt. J. A. Harris, Co. K, 17th NC, was severely wounded in the right thigh. Neither his service records nor *NC Troops* note his wounding at Wise's Forks. Paroled at GH No. 10 in Salisbury on May 2, 1865.
Source: Tanner (WF), 138; *NCT*, VI:284; M270; NC Confederate Widow's Pension (Washington County).

Harrison, Rodman, Private, Company H
Wise's Forks
Captured at or near Wise's Forks on March 10, 1865. Confined at Point Lookout, Maryland, and released upon taking the Oath of Allegiance on June 27, 1865.
Source: *NCT*, VI:266, 737; M270.

▲**Haselip, John**, Private, Company G
Sugar Loaf
Service records indicate that he was captured near Fort Fisher on February 16, 1865. Confined at Point Lookout, Maryland, and released upon taking the Oath of Allegiance on June 13, 1865. Haselip's capture likely occurred along the Sugar Loaf line. This strong Confederate defensive position stretched from the east bank of the Cape Fear River to the southern end of Myrtle Sound. The 17th NC occupied the far left of the line. *NC Troops* incorrectly notes that he was captured at or near Fort Anderson on or about February 16, 1865. During the Wilmington Campaign, the 17th NC, part of Kirkland's Brigade, never served on the west side of the Cape Fear River.
Source: M270; Moore, *The Wilmington Campaign*, 97; *NCT*, VI:258.

▲**Haskell, John**, Private, (Company Unknown)
Sugar Loaf
Services records indicate that he was captured near Fort Fisher on February 19. No further records. Haskell's capture on February 19 coincided with the Confederate withdrawal from the Sugar Loaf line to a new defensive position several miles back toward Wilmington. *NC Troops* incorrectly notes that he was captured at or near Fort Anderson on or about February 16, 1865. During the Wilmington Campaign, the 17th NC, part of Kirkland's Brigade, never served on the west side of the Cape Fear River.
Source: M270; Moore, *The Wilmington Campaign*, 97; *NCT*, VI:294.

Hendricks, William E., Private, Company E
Wise's Forks
Captured at or near Wise's Forks on March 10, 1865. Confined at Point Lookout, Maryland, and released upon taking the Oath of Allegiance on June 27, 1865.
Source: *NCT*, VI:243; M270.

♦**Holliday, Edward D.**, Private, Company K
(Inconclusive)
Edward D. Holliday's Confederate pension indicates that he was wounded in the left arm at Kinston on an unspecified date. His name does not appear on either of Tanner's casualty listings for Bentonville or Wise's Forks. Further research is required.
Source: *NCT*, VI:284; M270; NC Confederate Pension (Pitt County).

▲**Hollis, Edward**, Private, Company E
Bentonville
Wounded at the battle of Bentonville between March 19-21, 1865. According to Surgeon Tanner's "Return of Casualties in Hoke's Div. near Bentonville," Pvt. Ed. Hollis, Co. E, 17th NC, was dangerously wounded in the left thigh. His service records indicate that he was admitted to GH No. 13 (Pettigrew) in Raleigh on March 21, 1865, with a gunshot wound to the left thigh. He died in the hospital on March 28, 1865, of wounds and "erysipelas." He is buried in Oakwood Cemetery in Raleigh, North Carolina.
Source: Tanner (BV), 148; *NCT*, VI:243; M270.

♦**Horn, D. H.**, Private, Company K
Bentonville (Inconclusive)
Wounded at the battle of Bentonville between March 19-21, 1865. According to Surgeon Tanner's "Return of Casualties in Hoke's Div. near Bentonville," Pvt. D. H. Horn, Co. K, 17th NC, was slightly wounded in the abdomen. No D. H. Horn is listed in the National Archives Compiled Service Records for North Carolina Soldiers belonging to the 17th NC. Further research is required.
Source: Tanner (BV), 148; M270.

Hyman, Ebenezer, Private, Company E
Wise's Forks
Captured at or near Wise's Forks on March 10, 1865. Confined at Point Lookout, Maryland, and released upon taking the Oath of Allegiance on May 15, 1865.

Source: *NCT*, VI:243; M270; NC Confederate Pension (Halifax County).

Hyman, Hugh H., Private, Company E
Wise's Forks
Captured at or near Wise's Forks on March 10, 1865. Confined at Point Lookout, Maryland, and released upon taking the Oath of Allegiance on May 15, 1865.
Source: *NCT*, VI:244; M270; NC Confederate Widow's Pension (Martin County).

▲Hyman, Needham Sherrod, Corporal, Company E
Wise's Forks
Wounded at the battle of Wise's Forks between March 8-10, 1865. According to Surgeon Tanner's "Return of Casualties near Kinston," Pvt. N. S. Hyman, Co. E, 17th NC, was slightly wounded in the left ankle. His service records indicate that he was admitted to GH No. 13 (Pettigrew) in Raleigh on March 11, 1865, with a gunshot wound to the left foot. Furloughed for 60 days on March 16, 1865. Neither his service records nor *NC Troops* note his wounding at Wise's Forks.
Source: Tanner (WF), 138; *NCS* (Raleigh), March 29, 1865; *WD* (Charlotte), April 4, 1865; *NCT*, VI:244, 740; M270.

▲Jenkins, George R., Private, Company H
Bentonville
NC Troops notes that Pvt. George R. Jenkins died in North Carolina on March 1, 1865; location and cause of death unknown. According to Surgeon Tanner's "Return of Casualties in Hoke's Div. near Bentonville," a Pvt. G. Jenkins, Co. H, 17th NC, was dangerously wounded in the chest, with the annotation, "since died." In 1885, Pvt. R. K. Cherry, a former member of Co. H, provided a sworn statement on Jenkins's widow's behalf, stating that he "saw him shot down" at Bentonville on or about March 4, 1865. Although Jenkins's widow and R. K. Cherry were unclear on the date of his death in March, both identified Bentonville as the location. Based on Tanner's "Return of Casualties," George R. Jenkins died of wounds suffered at Bentonville.
Source: Tanner (BV), 148; *NCT*, VI:267; M270; NC Confederate Widow's Pension (Martin County).

♦Jenkins, Thomas C., Private, Company C
Bentonville (Inconclusive)
According to Surgeon Tanner's "Return of Casualties in Hoke's Div. near Bentonville," a Pvt. Thos. C. Jenkins, Co. C, 17th NC, was slightly wounded in the face. No Thomas C. Jenkins is listed in the National Archives Compiled Service Records for North Carolina Soldiers belonging to the 17th NC. Further research is required.
Source: Tanner (BV), 148.

▲Johnson, M., Private, Company L
Wise's Forks
Wounded at the battle of Wise's Forks between March 8-10, 1865. According to Surgeon Tanner's "Return of Casualties near Kinston," Pvt. M. Johnson, Co. L, 17th NC, was severely wounded in the left foot. His service records indicate that he was admitted to GH No. 13 (Pettigrew) in Raleigh on March 11, 1865, with a gunshot wound to the left foot. Neither his service records nor *NC Troops* note his wounding at Wise's Forks.
Source: Tanner (WF), 138; *NCS* (Raleigh), March 29, 1865; *WD* (Charlotte), April 4, 1865; *NCT*, VI:290; M270.

▲Keel, Ashley, Private, Company E
Wise's Forks
Wounded at the battle of Wise's Forks between March 8-10, 1865. According to Surgeon Tanner's "Return of Casualties near Kinston," Pvt. A. Keel, Co. E, 17th NC, was severely wounded in the right forearm. Keel's service records indicate that he was admitted to GH No. 13 (Pettigrew) in Raleigh on March 10, 1865, with a gunshot wound to the right arm, and transferred on March 19 to an unspecified hospital. *NC Troops* does not note his wounding at Wise's Forks.

Source: Tanner (WF), 137; M270; *NCS* (Raleigh), March 29, 1865; *WD* (Charlotte), April 4, 1865; *NCT*, VI:244; NC Confederate Widow's Pension (Martin County).

▲Keel, Robert, Private, Company H
Wise's Forks
Wounded at the battle of Wise's Forks between March 8-10, 1865. According to Surgeon Tanner's "Return of Casualties near Kinston," Pvt. R. Keel, Co. H, 17th NC, was slightly wounded in the left thigh. *NC Troops* does not note his wounding at Wise's Forks.
Source: Tanner (WF), 138; *NCS* (Raleigh), March 29, 1865; *NCT*, VI:267; M270; NC Confederate Widow's Pension (Martin County).

♦Kemp, Washington C., Private, Company H
Near Bentonville (Inconclusive)
Washington C. Kemp's service records indicate that he was captured near Bentonville on or about March 14, 1865. Either the date, the location of capture, or both, is incorrect. If the date is correct, the probable location of capture was Kinston. Confined at Point Lookout, Maryland, and released upon taking the Oath of Allegiance on June 28, 1865. Further research is required.
Source: *NCT*, VI:267; M270; NC Confederate Pension (Tyrrell County).

▲Kittrell, Job, Private, Company C
Wise's Forks
Wounded at the battle of Wise's Forks between March 8-10, 1865. According to Surgeon Tanner's "Return of Casualties near Kinston," Pvt. J. Kitrell, Co. C, 17th NC, was severely wounded in the head. No further records. *NC Troops* does not note his wounding at Wise's Forks.
Source: Tanner (WF), 137; *NCT*, VI:228; M270.

Knowles, William F., Sergeant, Company H
Plymouth
Captured at or near Plymouth on March 8, 1865. Confined at Point Lookout, Maryland, and released upon taking the Oath of Allegiance on June 28, 1865.
Source: *NCT*, VI:267; M270; NC Confederate Pension (Tyrrell County).

▲Latham, John W., 1st Sergeant, Company G
Wise's Forks
Wounded at the battle of Wise's Forks between March 8-10, 1865. According to Surgeon Tanner's "Return of Casualties near Kinston," Sgt. J. W. Latham, Co. G, 17th NC, was severely wounded in the right thigh. Latham's service records indicate he was admitted to GH No. 13 (Pettigrew) on March 11, 1865, wounded in the right thigh. He was later transferred to a Charlotte hospital on March 21, 1865. *NC Troops* does not note his wounding at Wise's Forks.
Source: Tanner (WF), 138; *NCS* (Raleigh), March 29, 1865; *WD* (Charlotte), April 4, 1865; *NCT*, VI:259; M270.

♦▲Lee, James W., Private, Company D
Wise's Forks (Inconclusive)
The GH No. 3 (Goldsboro) patient registry lists a Pvt. W. Lee, Co. D, 17th NC, was admitted on March 10, 1865, entry no. 1882, from Kinston for unspecified reasons. A separate No. 3 ledger, titled "Reports of Wounded and Operations," indicates that Pvt. W. Lee, Co. D, 17th NC, was wounded in the left hand "in battle" and admitted on March 10, 1865. The ledger further specifies that he was transferred to Raleigh on an unrecorded date. James W. Lee is probably the same soldier as W. Lee. *NC Troops* does not indicate that he was wounded and hospitalized in March 1865. No further records.
Source: RG109, 6/291:37; NCOAH, CW10, Ledger B, March 1865, entry no. 72; *NCT*, VI:236; M270.

▲Leggett, William W., Private, Company D
Sugar Loaf
Services records indicate two captured dates, February 11, 1865 (near Fort Fisher) and February 16, 1865 (at Fort Fisher). Confined at Point Lookout, Maryland, and released upon taking the Oath of Allegiance on

June 29, 1865. Leggett's capture likely occurred on February 11, along with approximately 60 other 17th NC soldiers, when the Federals advanced against the Sugar Loaf line. This strong Confederate defensive position stretched from the east bank of the Cape Fear River to the southern end of Myrtle Sound. The 17th NC occupied the far left of the line. *NC Troops* incorrectly notes that he was captured at or near Fort Anderson on or about February 16, 1865. During the Wilmington Campaign, the 17th NC, part of Kirkland's Brigade, never served on the west side of the Cape Fear River.
Source: M270; Moore, *The Wilmington Campaign*, 97; NCT, VI:236.

▲**Little, George E.**, Private, Company K
Wise's Forks
Wounded at the battle of Wise's Forks between March 8-10, 1865. According to Surgeon Tanner's "Return of Casualties near Kinston," Pvt. G. E. Little, Co. K, 17th NC, was severely wounded in the left hand. *NC Troops* does not note his wounding at Wise's Forks.
Source: Tanner (WF), 138; *NCT*, VI:285, 745; M270.

▲**Lloyd, William Roland**, Private, Company E
Wise's Forks
Service records indicate that he was captured at or near Wise's Forks on March 10, 1865. Lloyd was admitted to the U.S. Army Foster GH, patient registry no. 6354) in New Bern on March 11, 1865, for a gunshot in his right side that occurred on March 10, 1865. Present at the hospital through April 27, 1865. No further records.
Source: *NCT*, VI:244; M270; RG94, Foster General Hospital Registry, 92.

Long, Thomas, Private, Company C
Wise's Forks
Captured near Kinston on March 10, 1865. Confined at Point Lookout, Maryland, and released upon taking the Oath of Allegiance on June 29, 1865.
Source: *NCT*, VI:228; M270.

▲**Mann, Daniel B.**, Private, Company H
Sugar Loaf
Services records indicate two captured dates, February 11, 1865 (near Fort Fisher) and February 16, 1865 (at Fort Fisher). Confined at Point Lookout, Maryland, and released upon taking the Oath of Allegiance on June 29, 1865. Mann's capture likely occurred on February 11, along with approximately 60 other 17th NC soldiers, when the Federals advanced against the Sugar Loaf line. This strong Confederate defensive position stretched from the east bank of the Cape Fear River to the southern end of Myrtle Sound. The 17th NC occupied the far left of the line. *NC Troops* incorrectly notes that he was captured at or near Fort Anderson on or about February 16, 1865. During the Wilmington Campaign, the 17th NC, part of Kirkland's Brigade, never served on the west side of the Cape Fear River.
Source: M270; Moore, *The Wilmington Campaign*, 97; NCT, VI:268.

▲**Mann, William**, Private, Company H
Sugar Loaf
Services records indicate two captured dates, February 11, 1865 (near Fort Fisher) and February 16, 1865 (at Fort Fisher). Confined at Point Lookout, Maryland, where he died on April 20, 1865, of chronic diarrhea. Mann's capture likely occurred on February 11, along with approximately 60 other 17th NC soldiers, when the Federals advanced against the Sugar Loaf line. This strong Confederate defensive position stretched from the east bank of the Cape Fear River to the southern end of Myrtle Sound. The 17th NC occupied the far left of the line. *NC Troops* incorrectly notes that he was captured at or near Fort Anderson on or about February 16, 1865. During the Wilmington Campaign, the 17th NC, part of Kirkland's Brigade, never served on the west side of the Cape Fear River.
Source: M270; Moore, *The Wilmington Campaign*, 97; NCT, VI:268.

▲**Manning, John W.**, Private, Company H

Sugar Loaf

Services records indicate two captured dates, February 11, 1865 (near Fort Fisher) and February 16, 1865 (at Fort Fisher). Confined at Point Lookout, Maryland, and released upon taking the Oath of Allegiance on June 29, 1865. Manning's capture likely occurred on February 11, along with approximately 60 other 17th NC soldiers, when the Federals advanced against the Sugar Loaf line. This strong Confederate defensive position stretched from the east bank of the Cape Fear River to the southern end of Myrtle Sound. The 17th NC occupied the far left of the line. *NC Troops* incorrectly notes that he was captured at or near Fort Anderson on or about February 16, 1865. During the Wilmington Campaign, the 17th NC, part of Kirkland's Brigade, never served on the west side of the Cape Fear River.
Source: M270; Moore, *The Wilmington Campaign*, 97; *NCT*, VI:268.

Martin, Peyton C., Private, Company F
Bentonville

NC Troops notes that Pvt. Peyton C. Martin was wounded at the battle of Bentonville in March 1865. No further information.
Source: *NCT*, VI:251; M270; NC Confederate Pension (Durham County).

▲May, William H., Private, Company K
Sugar Loaf

Services records indicate two captured dates, February 11, 1865 (near Fort Fisher) and February 16, 1865 (at Fort Fisher). Confined at Point Lookout, Maryland, and released upon taking the Oath of Allegiance on June 29, 1865. May's capture likely occurred on February 11, along with approximately 60 other 17th NC soldiers, when the Federals advanced against the Sugar Loaf line. This strong Confederate defensive position stretched from the east bank of the Cape Fear River to the southern end of Myrtle Sound. The 17th NC occupied the far left of the line. *NC Troops* incorrectly notes that he was captured at or near Fort Anderson on or about February 16, 1865. During the Wilmington Campaign, the 17th NC, part of Kirkland's Brigade, never served on the west side of the Cape Fear River.
Source: M270; Moore, *The Wilmington Campaign*, 97; *NCT*, VI:285.

Melson, William R., Private, Company G
Jamesville

Captured near Jamesville on March 3, 1865. Confined at Point Lookout, Maryland, and released upon taking the Oath of Allegiance on June 29, 1865.
Source: *NCT*, VI:259; M270.

Merideth, Alfred M., Private, Company L
Wise's Forks

Captured at or near Wise's Forks on March 10, 1865. Confined at Point Lookout, Maryland, and released upon taking the Oath of Allegiance on June 29, 1865.
Source: *NCT*, VI:291, 749; M270.

▲Mizell, Mark W., Private, Company D
Sugar Loaf

Services records indicate two captured dates, February 11, 1865 (near Fort Fisher) and February 16, 1865 (at Fort Fisher). Confined at Point Lookout, Maryland, and released upon taking the Oath of Allegiance on June 29, 1865. Mizell's capture likely occurred on February 11, along with approximately 60 other 17th NC soldiers, when the Federals advanced against the Sugar Loaf line. This strong Confederate defensive position stretched from the east bank of the Cape Fear River to the southern end of Myrtle Sound. The 17th NC occupied the far left of the line. *NC Troops* incorrectly notes that he was captured at or near Fort Anderson on or about February 16, 1865. During the Wilmington Campaign, the 17th NC, part of Kirkland's Brigade, never served on the west side of the Cape Fear River.
Source: M270; Moore, *The Wilmington Campaign*, 97; *NCT*, VI:236.

Modlin, Samuel, Private, Company A

Jamesville
Captured at Jamesville on March 3, 1865. Confined at Point Lookout, Maryland, and released upon taking the Oath of Allegiance on May 14, 1865.
Source: *NCT*, VI:212; M270; NC Confederate Widow's Pension (Martin County).

♦▲Moore, J. A., Private, Company K
Wise's Forks (Inconclusive)
Wounded at the battle of Wise's Forks between March 8-10, 1865. According to Surgeon Tanner's "Return of Casualties near Kinston," Pvt. J. A. Moore, Co. K, 17th NC, was dangerously wounded in the left shoulder. The wounded soldier Tanner listed is either John A. Moore or John Arney Moore; both members of Co. K. *NC Troops* does not note either's wounding at Wise's Forks.
Source: Tanner (WF), 138; *NCT*, VI:285, 745; M270.

▲Moore, Joseph A., Private, Company E
Sugar Loaf
Services records indicate two captured dates, February 11, 1865 (near Fort Fisher) and February 16, 1865 (at Fort Fisher). Confined at Point Lookout, Maryland, and released upon taking the Oath of Allegiance on June 23, 1865. Moore's capture likely occurred on February 11, along with approximately 60 other 17th NC soldiers, when the Federals advanced against the Sugar Loaf line. This strong Confederate defensive position stretched from the east bank of the Cape Fear River to the southern end of Myrtle Sound. The 17th NC occupied the far left of the line. *NC Troops* incorrectly notes that he was captured at or near Fort Anderson on or about February 16, 1865. During the Wilmington Campaign, the 17th NC, part of Kirkland's Brigade, never served on the west side of the Cape Fear River.
Source: M270; Moore, *The Wilmington Campaign*, 97; *NCT*, VI:245.

▲Moore, Joseph E., Private, Company E
Sugar Loaf
Services records indicate two captured dates, February 11, 1865 (near Fort Fisher) and February 16, 1865 (at Fort Fisher). Confined at Point Lookout, Maryland, and released upon taking the Oath of Allegiance on June 29, 1865. Moore's capture likely occurred on February 11, along with approximately 60 other 17th NC soldiers, when the Federals advanced against the Sugar Loaf line. This strong Confederate defensive position stretched from the east bank of the Cape Fear River to the southern end of Myrtle Sound. The 17th NC occupied the far left of the line. *NC Troops* incorrectly notes that he was captured at or near Fort Anderson on or about February 16, 1865. During the Wilmington Campaign, the 17th NC, part of Kirkland's Brigade, never served on the west side of the Cape Fear River.
Source: M270; Moore, *The Wilmington Campaign*, 97; *NCT*, VI:245.

▲Moore, Julius, Private, Company H
Sugar Loaf
Services records indicate two captured dates, February 11, 1865 (near Fort Fisher) and February 16, 1865 (at Fort Fisher). Confined at Point Lookout, Maryland, and released upon taking the Oath of Allegiance on June 15, 1865. Moore's capture likely occurred on February 11, along with approximately 60 other 17th NC soldiers, when the Federals advanced against the Sugar Loaf line. This strong Confederate defensive position stretched from the east bank of the Cape Fear River to the southern end of Myrtle Sound. The 17th NC occupied the far left of the line. *NC Troops* incorrectly notes that he was captured at or near Fort Anderson on or about February 16, 1865. During the Wilmington Campaign, the 17th NC, part of Kirkland's Brigade, never served on the west side of the Cape Fear River.
Source: M270; Moore, *The Wilmington Campaign*, 97; *NCT*, VI:268.

▲Nelson, John Randolph, Musician, Company E
Wise's Forks
NC Troops notes that he was wounded at or near Kinston on or about April 1865. This information was obtained from Nelson's Confederate pension application. The *NC Standard* reported a Pvt. J. R. Nelson, Co. E, 17th NC, resent at the GH No. 13 (Pettigrew) in Raleigh, wounded in the right arm in March 1865. The

No. 13 Register of Patients lists a Pvt. J. R. Nelson, Co. E, 17th NC, was admitted (entry no. 2580) on March 11, 1865, with a gunshot wound to his right arm. His service records do not note his hospitalization in March 1865. Based on the date that he was hospitalized for a gunshot wound, John Randolph Nelson was probably wounded at Wise's Forks.
Source: *NCT*, VI:245, 752; NC Confederate Pension (Martin County); *NCS* (Raleigh), March 29, 1865; *WD* (Charlotte), April 4, 1865; GH No. 13 Register of Patients, 6/290:391; M270.

Norman, Nehemiah, Corporal, Company H
Wise's Forks
Captured at or near Wise's Forks on March 10, 1865. Confined at Point Lookout, Maryland, and released upon taking the Oath of Allegiance on June 29, 1865. Norman states in his Confederate pension application that he was slightly wounded in the sternum at Kinston in March 1865.
Source: *NCT*, VI:268; M270; NC Confederate Pension (Washington County).

▲Norris, Ashley, Private, Company D
Sugar Loaf
Services records indicate two captured dates, February 11, 1865 (near Fort Fisher) and February 16, 1865 (at Fort Fisher). Confined at Point Lookout, Maryland, and released upon taking the Oath of Allegiance on June 29, 1865. Norris's capture likely occurred on February 11, along with approximately 60 other 17th NC soldiers, when the Federals advanced against the Sugar Loaf line. This strong Confederate defensive position stretched from the east bank of the Cape Fear River to the southern end of Myrtle Sound. The 17th NC occupied the far left of the line. *NC Troops* incorrectly notes that he was captured at or near Fort Anderson on or about February 16, 1865. During the Wilmington Campaign, the 17th NC, part of Kirkland's Brigade, never served on the west side of the Cape Fear River.
Source: M270; Moore, *The Wilmington Campaign*, 97; *NCT*, VI:236; NC Confederate Pension (Pitt County).

▲Oakley, John, Private, Company F
Wise's Forks
Wounded at the battle of Wise's Forks between March 8-10, 1865. According to Surgeon Tanner's "Return of Casualties near Kinston," Pvt. J. Oakley, Co. F, 17th NC, was severely wounded in the right wrist. Oakley stated in his Confederate pension application that he was wounded in the right wrist at Kinston on March 10, 1865.
Source: Tanner (WF), 138; *NCT*, VI:252; M270; NC Confederate Pension (Person County).

Outterbridge, Andrew J., 1st Sergeant, Company E
Wise's Forks
Captured at or near Wise's Forks on or about March 10, 1865. Confined at Point Lookout, Maryland, and released upon taking the Oath of Allegiance on May 15, 1865.
Source: *NCT*, VI:245, 749; M270.

▲Overton, Henry H., Private, Company D
Sugar Loaf
Services records indicate two captured dates, February 11, 1865 (near Fort Fisher) and February 16, 1865 (at Fort Fisher). Confined at Point Lookout, Maryland, and released upon taking the Oath of Allegiance on June 29, 1865. Overton's capture likely occurred on February 11, along with approximately 60 other 17th NC soldiers, when the Federals advanced against the Sugar Loaf line. This strong Confederate defensive position stretched from the east bank of the Cape Fear River to the southern end of Myrtle Sound. The 17th NC occupied the far left of the line. *NC Troops* incorrectly notes that he was captured at or near Fort Anderson on or about February 16, 1865. During the Wilmington Campaign, the 17th NC, part of Kirkland's Brigade, never served on the west side of the Cape Fear River.
Source: M270; Moore, *The Wilmington Campaign*, 97; *NCT*, VI:237; NC Confederate Pension (Hertford County).

▲Overton, John R., Sergeant, Company I
Sugar Loaf

▲**Overton, William Cooper**, Private, Company C
Sugar Loaf
Services records indicate two captured dates, February 11, 1865 (near Fort Fisher) and February 16, 1865 (at Fort Fisher). Confined at Point Lookout, Maryland, and released upon taking the Oath of Allegiance on June 29, 1865. Overton's capture likely occurred on February 11, along with approximately 60 other 17th NC soldiers, when the Federals advanced against the Sugar Loaf line. This strong Confederate defensive position stretched from the east bank of the Cape Fear River to the southern end of Myrtle Sound. The 17th NC occupied the far left of the line. *NC Troops* incorrectly notes that he was captured at or near Fort Anderson on or about February 16, 1865. During the Wilmington Campaign, the 17th NC, part of Kirkland's Brigade, never served on the west side of the Cape Fear River.
Source: M270; Moore, *The Wilmington Campaign*, 97; *NCT*, VI:229.

▲**Parker, John**, Private, Company C
Sugar Loaf
Services records indicate two captured dates, February 11, 1865 (near Fort Fisher) and February 16, 1865 (at Fort Fisher). Confined at Point Lookout, Maryland, and released upon taking the Oath of Allegiance on June 9, 1865. He was later hospitalized in Petersburg, Virginia, where he died July 4, 1865, of chronic diarrhea. Parker's capture likely occurred on February 11, along with approximately 60 other 17th NC soldiers, when the Federals advanced against the Sugar Loaf line. This strong Confederate defensive position stretched from the east bank of the Cape Fear River to the southern end of Myrtle Sound. The 17th NC occupied the far left of the line. *NC Troops* incorrectly notes that he was captured at or near Fort Anderson on or about February 16, 1865. During the Wilmington Campaign, the 17th NC, part of Kirkland's Brigade, never served on the west side of the Cape Fear River.
Source: M270; Moore, *The Wilmington Campaign*, 97; *NCT*, VI:229.

▲**Parker, Robert**, Private, Company C
Sugar Loaf
Services records indicate two captured dates, February 11, 1865 (near Fort Fisher) and February 16, 1865 (at Fort Fisher). Confined at Point Lookout, Maryland, and released upon taking the Oath of Allegiance on June 17, 1865. Parker's capture likely occurred on February 11, along with approximately 60 other 17th NC soldiers, when the Federals advanced against the Sugar Loaf line. This strong Confederate defensive position stretched from the east bank of the Cape Fear River to the southern end of Myrtle Sound. The 17th NC occupied the far left of the line. *NC Troops* incorrectly notes that he was captured at or near Fort Anderson on or about February 16, 1865. During the Wilmington Campaign, the 17th NC, part of Kirkland's Brigade, never served on the west side of the Cape Fear River.
Source: M270; Moore, *The Wilmington Campaign*, 97; *NCT*, VI:229.

▲**Parker, William K.**, Private, Company A
Wise's Forks
Wounded at the battle of Wise's Forks between March 8-10, 1865. According to Surgeon Tanner's "Return of Casualties near Kinston," Pvt. W. K. Parker, Co. A, 17th NC, was slightly wounded on the left knee. The March 29, 1865 edition of the *NC Standard* listed a Pvt. W. K. Parker, Co. A, 17th NC, wounded in the left knee at GH No. 8 (Peace Institute) in Raleigh. *NC Troops* does not note his wounding at Wise's Forks.
Source: Tanner (WF), 137; *NCS* (Raleigh), March 29, 1865; *WD* (Charlotte), April 4, 1865; *NCT*, VI:212; M270.

▲**Peal, Jesse B.**, Private, Company A
Bentonville
Wounded at the battle of Bentonville between March 19-21, 1865. According to Surgeon Tanner's "Return of Casualties in Hoke's Div. near Bentonville," Pvt. J. B. Peel, Co. A, 17th NC, was slightly wounded in the neck. Peal's Confederate pension application states, "[The] ball went entirely through [the] neck."
Source: Tanner (BV), 148; *NCT*, VI:213; M270; NC Confederate Pension (Martin County).

▲**Peal, William D.**, Private, Company A
Sugar Loaf
Services records indicate two captured dates, February 11, 1865 (near Fort Fisher) and February 16, 1865 (at Fort Fisher). Confined at Point Lookout, Maryland, and released upon taking the Oath of Allegiance on May 14, 1865. Peal's capture likely occurred on February 11, along with approximately 60 other 17th NC soldiers, when the Federals advanced against the Sugar Loaf line. This strong Confederate defensive position stretched from the east bank of the Cape Fear River to the southern end of Myrtle Sound. The 17th NC occupied the far left of the line. *NC Troops* incorrectly notes that he was captured at or near Fort Anderson on or about February 16, 1865. During the Wilmington Campaign, the 17th NC, part of Kirkland's Brigade, never served on the west side of the Cape Fear River.
Source: M270; Moore, *The Wilmington Campaign*, 97; *NCT*, VI:218; *NCT*, VI:213.

Peel, John, Private, Company D
Wise's Forks
Captured near Kinston on March 10, 1865. Confined at Point Lookout, Maryland, and released upon taking the Oath of Allegiance on June 17, 1865.
Source: *NCT*, VI:237; M270.

Peel, John P., Private, Company D
Sugar Loaf
Services records indicate two captured dates, February 11, 1865 (near Fort Fisher) and February 16, 1865 (at Fort Fisher). Confined at Point Lookout, Maryland, and released upon taking the Oath of Allegiance on June 3, 1865. Peel's capture likely occurred on February 11, along with approximately 60 other 17th NC soldiers, when the Federals advanced against the Sugar Loaf line. This strong Confederate defensive position stretched from the east bank of the Cape Fear River to the southern end of Myrtle Sound. The 17th NC occupied the far left of the line. *NC Troops* incorrectly notes that he was captured at or near Fort Anderson on or about February 16, 1865. During the Wilmington Campaign, the 17th NC, part of Kirkland's Brigade, never served on the west side of the Cape Fear River.
Source: M270; Moore, *The Wilmington Campaign*, 97; *NCT*, VI:237; NC Confederate Pension (Chowan County).

Perry, Noah Thomas, Private, Company F
Sugar Loaf
Services records indicate two captured dates, February 11, 1865 (near Fort Fisher) and February 16, 1865 (at Fort Fisher). Confined at Point Lookout, Maryland, and released upon taking the Oath of Allegiance on June 15, 1865. Perry's capture likely occurred on February 11, along with approximately 60 other 17th NC soldiers, when the Federals advanced against the Sugar Loaf line. This strong Confederate defensive position stretched from the east bank of the Cape Fear River to the southern end of Myrtle Sound. The 17th NC occupied the far left of the line. *NC Troops* incorrectly notes that he was captured at or near Fort Anderson on or about February 16, 1865. During the Wilmington Campaign, the 17th NC, part of Kirkland's Brigade, never served on the west side of the Cape Fear River.
Source: M270; Moore, *The Wilmington Campaign*, 97; *NCT*, VI:252, 754; NC Confederate Pension (Martin County).

Perry, William H., Private, Company B
Wise's Forks
Captured near Kinston on March 10, 1865. Confined at Point Lookout, Maryland, and released upon taking the Oath of Allegiance on June 16, 1865.

Source: *NCT*, VI:221; M270.

▲Phelps, James Dallas, Sr., Private, Company H
Sugar Loaf
Services records indicate two captured dates, February 11, 1865 (near Fort Fisher) and February 16, 1865 (at Fort Fisher). Confined at Point Lookout, Maryland, and released upon taking the Oath of Allegiance on June 16, 1865. Phelps's capture likely occurred on February 11, along with approximately 60 other 17th NC soldiers, when the Federals advanced against the Sugar Loaf line. This strong Confederate defensive position stretched from the east bank of the Cape Fear River to the southern end of Myrtle Sound. The 17th NC occupied the far left of the line. *NC Troops* incorrectly notes that he was captured at or near Fort Anderson on or about February 16, 1865. During the Wilmington Campaign, the 17th NC, part of Kirkland's Brigade, never served on the west side of the Cape Fear River.
Source: M270; Moore, *The Wilmington Campaign*, 97; *NCT*, VI:269; NC Confederate Pension (Tyrrell County).

▲Price, William L., Private, Company E
Bentonville
Wounded at the battle of Bentonville between March 19-21, 1865. According to Surgeon Tanner's "Return of Casualties in Hoke's Div. near Bentonville," Pvt. W. E. Price, Co. E, 17th NC, was severely wounded in the left shoulder. The *Daily Progress* reported a Pvt. Wm. Price, Co. E, 17th NC, was present in Raleigh's Episcopal Church Hospital with a wounded right shoulder. Price's service records indicate that he was transferred and admitted to GH No. 11 in Charlotte on April 27, 1865, suffering from a gunshot of the "upper right extremities." Private William L. Price is the same soldier Tanner listed as Pvt. W. E. Price. In his 1905 application for admittance to the North Carolina Soldiers' Home in Raleigh, W. L. Price stated he was wounded at Bentonville.
Source: Tanner (BV), 148; *DP* (Raleigh), March 29, 1865; *WD* (Charlotte), April 4, 1865; *NCT*, VI:245; M270; NC Confederate Pension (Martin County).

▲Purington, Stanley M., Private, Company H
Sugar Loaf
Services records indicate two captured dates, February 11, 1865 (near Fort Fisher) and February 16, 1865 (at Fort Fisher). Confined at Point Lookout, Maryland, and released upon taking the Oath of Allegiance on June 16, 1865. Purington's capture likely occurred on February 11, along with approximately 60 other 17th NC soldiers, when the Federals advanced against the Sugar Loaf line. This strong Confederate defensive position stretched from the east bank of the Cape Fear River to the southern end of Myrtle Sound. The 17th NC occupied the far left of the line. *NC Troops* incorrectly notes that he was captured at or near Fort Anderson on or about February 16, 1865. During the Wilmington Campaign, the 17th NC, part of Kirkland's Brigade, never served on the west side of the Cape Fear River.
Source: M270; Moore, *The Wilmington Campaign*, 97; *NCT*, VI:269.

Ragen, William, Private, Company F
Wise's Forks
Captured at or near Wise's Forks on March 10, 1865. Confined at Point Lookout, Maryland, and released upon taking the Oath of Allegiance on June 14, 1865.
Source: *NCT*, VI:252; M270.

▲Ragen, William Thomas, Private, Company F
Bentonville
Wounded at the battle of Bentonville between March 19-21, 1865. According to Surgeon Tanner's "Return of Casualties in Hoke's Div. near Bentonville," Pvt. W. T. Ragan, Co. F, 17th NC, was slightly wounded in the right hand and shoulder. Confederate pension records indicate that he was wounded on or about March 21, 1865. No further records.
Source: Tanner (BV), 148; *NCT*, VI:252; M270; NC Confederate Pension (Person County).

▲Rawles, John McG., Private, Company A

Sugar Loaf
Services records indicate two captured dates, February 11, 1865 (near Fort Fisher) and February 16, 1865 (at Fort Fisher). Confined at Point Lookout, Maryland, and released upon taking the Oath of Allegiance on May 14, 1865. Rawles's capture likely occurred on February 11, along with approximately 60 other 17th NC soldiers, when the Federals advanced against the Sugar Loaf line. This strong Confederate defensive position stretched from the east bank of the Cape Fear River to the southern end of Myrtle Sound. The 17th NC occupied the far left of the line.
Source: M270; Moore, *The Wilmington Campaign*, 97; *NCT*, VI:213; NC Confederate Pension (Martin County).

▲**Rawlings, Jesse**, Private, Company I
Sugar Loaf
Services records indicate two captured dates, February 11, 1865 (near Fort Fisher) and February 16, 1865 (at Fort Fisher). Confined at Point Lookout, Maryland, and released upon taking the Oath of Allegiance on June 3, 1865. Rawling's capture likely occurred on February 11, along with approximately 60 other 17th NC soldiers, when the Federals advanced against the Sugar Loaf line. This strong Confederate defensive position stretched from the east bank of the Cape Fear River to the southern end of Myrtle Sound. The 17th NC occupied the far left of the line. *NC Troops* incorrectly notes that he was captured at or near Fort Anderson on or about February 16, 1865. During the Wilmington Campaign, the 17th NC, part of Kirkland's Brigade, never served on the west side of the Cape Fear River.
Source: M270; Moore, *The Wilmington Campaign*, 97; *NCT*, VI:278.

Rawlings, William A., Private, Company I
Near Kinston (Post Wise's Forks)
Captured near Wise's Forks on March 10, 1865. Confined at Point Lookout, Maryland, and released upon taking the Oath of Allegiance on June 17, 1865.
Source: *NCT*, VI:278, 756; M270.

▲**Rawls, William C.**, Private, Company A
Sugar Loaf
Services records indicate two captured dates, February 11, 1865 (near Fort Fisher) and February 16, 1865 (at Fort Fisher). Confined at Point Lookout, Maryland, and released upon taking the Oath of Allegiance on May 14, 1865. Rawl's capture likely occurred on February 11, along with approximately 60 other 17th NC soldiers, when the Federals advanced against the Sugar Loaf line. This strong Confederate defensive position stretched from the east bank of the Cape Fear River to the southern end of Myrtle Sound. The 17th NC occupied the far left of the line. *NC Troops* incorrectly notes that he was captured at or near Fort Anderson on or about February 16, 1865. During the Wilmington Campaign, the 17th NC, part of Kirkland's Brigade, never served on the west side of the Cape Fear River.
Source: M270; Moore, *The Wilmington Campaign*, 97; *NCT*, VI:213; NC Confederate Widow's Pension (Martin County).

▲**Ray, Horace E.**, Private, Company H
Sugar Loaf
Services records indicate two captured dates, February 11, 1865 (near Fort Fisher) and February 16, 1865 (at Fort Fisher). Confined at Point Lookout, Maryland, and released upon taking the Oath of Allegiance on June 19, 1865. Ray's capture likely occurred on February 11, along with approximately 60 other 17th NC soldiers, when the Federals advanced against the Sugar Loaf line. This strong Confederate defensive position stretched from the east bank of the Cape Fear River to the southern end of Myrtle Sound. The 17th NC occupied the far left of the line. *NC Troops* incorrectly notes that he was captured at or near Fort Anderson on or about February 16, 1865. During the Wilmington Campaign, the 17th NC, part of Kirkland's Brigade, never served on the west side of the Cape Fear River.
Source: M270; Moore, *The Wilmington Campaign*, 97; *NCT*, VI:269; NC Confederate Pension (Martin County).

Redmond, William, Private, Company I
Kinston (Post Wise's Forks)

Captured at or near Kinston on March 16. 1865. Confined at Point Lookout, Maryland, and released upon taking the Oath of Allegiance on June 17, 1865.
Source: *NCT*, VI:278, 756; M270.

Respess, James H., Private, Company H
Near Goldsboro
Captured near Goldsboro on March 19, 1865. Confined at Point Lookout, Maryland, and released upon taking the Oath of Allegiance on June 17, 1865.
Source: *NCT*, VI:269; M270.

Robason, Benjamin F., Private, Company A
Wise's Forks
Captured at Wise's Forks on March 10, 1865. Confined at Point Lookout, Maryland, and released upon taking the Oath of Allegiance on June 17, 1865.
Source: *NCT*, VI:213; M270.

Roberson, William P., Private, Company A
Wise's Forks
Captured at Wise's Forks on March 8, 1865. Confined at Point Lookout, Maryland, and released upon taking the Oath of Allegiance on May 14, 1865.
Source: *NCT*, VI:213; M270.

▲Robertson, Moses, Private, Company G
Sugar Loaf
Services records indicate two captured dates, February 11, 1865 (near Fort Fisher) and February 16, 1865 (at Fort Fisher). Confined at Point Lookout, Maryland, and released upon taking the Oath of Allegiance on June 17, 1865. Robertson's capture likely occurred on February 11, along with approximately 60 other 17th NC soldiers, when the Federals advanced against the Sugar Loaf line. This strong Confederate defensive position stretched from the east bank of the Cape Fear River to the southern end of Myrtle Sound. The 17th NC occupied the far left of the line. *NC Troops* incorrectly notes that he was captured at or near Fort Anderson on or about February 16, 1865. During the Wilmington Campaign, the 17th NC, part of Kirkland's Brigade, never served on the west side of the Cape Fear River.
Source: M270; Moore, *The Wilmington Campaign*, 97; *NCT*, VI:260.

Rogerson, Nathan, Corporal, Company A
Wise's Forks
Captured at or near Wise's Forks on March 10, 1865. Confined at Point Lookout, Maryland, and released upon taking the Oath of Allegiance on May 14, 1865.
Source: *NCT*, VI:214; M270; NC Confederate Widow's Pension (Martin County).

▲Ruffin, Robert R., Private, Company I
Sugar Loaf
Services records indicate two captured dates, February 11, 1865 (near Fort Fisher) and February 16, 1865 (at Fort Fisher). Confined at Point Lookout, Maryland, and released upon taking the Oath of Allegiance on June 3, 1865. Ruffin's capture likely occurred on February 11, along with approximately 60 other 17th NC soldiers, when the Federals advanced against the Sugar Loaf line. This strong Confederate defensive position stretched from the east bank of the Cape Fear River to the southern end of Myrtle Sound. The 17th NC occupied the far left of the line. *NC Troops* incorrectly notes that he was captured at or near Fort Anderson on or about February 16, 1865. During the Wilmington Campaign, the 17th NC, part of Kirkland's Brigade, never served on the west side of the Cape Fear River.
Source: M270; Moore, *The Wilmington Campaign*, 97; *NCT*, VI:278.

Savage, William Bythel, Private, Company E
Wise's Forks

Captured at or near Wise's Forks on March 10, 1865. Confined at Point Lookout, Maryland, and released upon taking the Oath of Allegiance on June 20, 1865.
Source: *NCT*, VI:246, 758; M270.

Savage, William W., Private, Company E
Wise's Forks
Captured at or near Wise's Forks on March 10, 1865. Confined at Point Lookout, Maryland, and released upon taking the Oath of Allegiance on June 20, 1865.
Source: *NCT*, VI:246; M270.

▲Scoffield, Thomas H., Corporal, Company H
Sugar Loaf
Services records indicate that he was captured at Fort Fisher on February 11, 1865. Confined at Point Lookout, Maryland, and released upon taking the Oath of Allegiance on June 19, 1865. Scoffield's capture likely occurred with approximately 60 other 17th NC soldiers when the Federals advanced against the Sugar Loaf line. This strong Confederate defensive position stretched from the east bank of the Cape Fear River to the southern end of Myrtle Sound. The 17th NC occupied the far left of the line. *NC Troops* incorrectly notes that he was captured at or near Fort Anderson on or about February 11, 1865. During the Wilmington Campaign, the 17th NC, part of Kirkland's Brigade, never served on the west side of the Cape Fear River.
Source: M270; Moore, *The Wilmington Campaign*, 97; *NCT*, VI:270.

▲Sleight, Matthew, Private, Company H
Sugar Loaf
Services records indicate two captured dates at Fort Fisher, February 11 and 16, 1865. Confined at Point Lookout, Maryland, and released on May 12-14, 1865. However, in a March 15, 1865, letter to U.S. Army prison authorities hoping to gain an early release from captivity, Sleight stated that on February 11, 1865, he "came purposedly within the lines of Genl. Terry near Wilmington, N.C." Sleight's desertion likely occurred on the Sugar Loaf line. This strong Confederate defensive position stretched from the east bank of the Cape Fear River to the southern end of Myrtle Sound. The 17th NC occupied the far left of the line. *NC Troops* incorrectly notes that he deserted at or near Fort Anderson on or about February 16, 1865. During the Wilmington Campaign, the 17th NC, part of Kirkland's Brigade, never served on the west side of the Cape Fear River.
Source: M270; Moore, *The Wilmington Campaign*, 97; *NCT*, VI:270, 760.

Snell, Eli, Private, Company G
Wise's Forks
Captured at or near Wise's Forks on March 10, 1865. Confined at Point Lookout, Maryland, and released upon taking the Oath of Allegiance on June 20, 1865.
Source: *NCT*, VI:261; M270.

Spruill, Henry W., Private, Company G
Bentonville
Captured at or near Bentonville on or about March 22, 1865. Confined at Hart's Island, New York Harbor, and released upon taking the Oath of Allegiance on June 17-18, 1865.
Source: *NCT*, VI:261; M270.

▲Taylor, Bythel, Private, Company E
Sugar Loaf
Services records indicate two captured dates, February 11, 1865 (near Fort Fisher) and February 16, 1865 (at Fort Fisher). Confined at Point Lookout, Maryland, and released upon taking the Oath of Allegiance on June 20, 1865. Taylor's capture likely occurred on February 11, along with approximately 60 other 17th NC soldiers, when the Federals advanced against the Sugar Loaf line. This strong Confederate defensive position stretched from the east bank of the Cape Fear River to the southern end of Myrtle Sound. The 17th

NC occupied the far left of the line. *NC Troops* incorrectly notes that he was captured at or near Fort Anderson on or about February 16, 1865. During the Wilmington Campaign, the 17th NC, part of Kirkland's Brigade, never served on the west side of the Cape Fear River.
Source: M270; Moore, *The Wilmington Campaign*, 97; NCT, VI:246.

Taylor, Harvey S., Private, Company A
Wise's Forks
Captured at or near Wise's Forks on March 10, 1865. Confined at Point Lookout, Maryland, and released upon taking the Oath of Allegiance on May 14, 1865.
Source: *NCT*, VI:214; Moore, *The Wilmington Campaign*, 97; M270; NC Confederate Pension (Martin County).

Tonnoffski, George L., Private, Company I
Wise's Forks
Captured at or near Wise's Forks on March 10, 1865. Confined at Point Lookout, Maryland. There is no final disposition record, but he survived the war.
Source: *NCT*, VI:279; M270; Tonnoffski, "My Last Days as a Confederate Soldier," *Confederate Veteran*, 1914, 22:68.

▲Tweedy, Willam Harvey, Private, Company A
Sugar Loaf
Captured near Fort Fisher on or about February 16, 1865. Confined at Point Lookout, Maryland, and released upon taking the Oath of Allegiance on June 20, 1865. Tweedy's capture likely occurred along the Sugar Loaf line. This strong Confederate defensive position stretched from the east bank of the Cape Fear River to the southern end of Myrtle Sound. The 17th NC occupied the far left of the line.
Source: M270; Moore, *The Wilmington Campaign*, 97; *NCT*, VI:215; NC Confederate Pension (Martin County).

▲Walter, Jeremiah A., Private, Company L
Bentonville
His service records indicate that he was admitted to GH No. 13 (Pettigrew) on March 21, 1865, with a gunshot wound to the right thigh. Furloughed from the hospital on April 3, 1865. Paroled at Salisbury on May 12, 1865. J. A. Walter's Confederate pension records indicate that he was wounded by a gunshot "through his upper thigh" at Bentonville in 1865. *NC Troops* notes that he was wounded at Bentonville.
Source: *NCT*, VI:293, 765; *NCS* (Raleigh), March 29, 1865; *WD* (Charlotte), April 4, 1865; M270; NC Confederate Pension (Cabarrus County).

▲Ward, Felton, Private, Company D
Wise's Forks
NC Troops notes that Pvt. Felton Ward was wounded in the foot at or near Kinston on or about March 1, 1865, and was admitted to a Greensboro hospital on March 9, 1865. The GH No. 3 "Register of Wounded and Operations" indicates Pvt. F. Ward, Co. D, 17th NC, was wounded in battle at an unspecified location, and admitted on March 9, 1865, suffering from a gunshot wound to the left foot. His service records and *NC Troops* incorrectly note that Ward was transferred from Kinston to GH No. 3 in Greensboro on March 9, 1865, for unspecified reasons. In National Archives Confederate Record Group 109, General Hospital No. 3's location is erroneously identified as Greensboro. Goldsboro is the correct location. Confederate authorities began relocating GH No. 3 from Goldsboro to High Point on March 11, 1865, as part of the town's evacuation. The hospital resumed operations in High Point on or about March 19, 1865. No further records.
Source: *NCT*, VI:238; M270; NCDAH, GH No. 3 Ledger Book B; Sokolosky, *NC Confederate Hospitals, vol. 2*; NC Confederate Pension (Perquimans County).

Waters, Robert McCoy, Corporal, Company H
Jamesville
Captured at Jamesville on March 3-4, 1865. Confined at Point Lookout, Maryland, and released on May 14, 1865.
Source: *NCT*, VI:271; M270.

▲**Weathington, W. T.**, Private, Company K
Wise's Forks
Wounded at the battle of Wise's Forks between March 8-10, 1865. According to Surgeon Tanner's "Return of Casualties near Kinston," Pvt. W. T. Weathington, Co. K, 17th NC, was severely wounded in the left leg. *NC Troops* does not note his wounding at Wise's Forks. His service records and *NC Troops* incorrectly note that Weathington was transferred from Kinston to GH No. 3 in Greensboro on March 9, 1865, for unspecified reasons. In National Archives Confederate Record Group 109, General Hospital No. 3's location is erroneously identified as Greensboro. Goldsboro is the correct location. Confederate authorities began relocating GH No. 3 from Goldsboro to High Point on March 11, 1865, as part of the town's evacuation. The hospital resumed operations in High Point on or about March 19, 1865. The GH No. 3 Patient Registry lists a Pvt. W. T. Weathington, entry no. 1641, of Co. K, 17th NC. Weathington was later admitted to the U.S. Army, 2nd Division, XXIII Corps Hospital, on May 20, 1865, with a gunshot wound. Took oath on June 7, 1865.
Source: Tanner (WF), 138; *NCT*, VI:287; M270; Sokolosky, *NC Confederate Hospitals, vol. 2*; RG 109, 6/291:37.

▲**Whitaker, Martin**, Private, Company A
Wise's Forks
Wounded at the battle of Wise's Forks between March 8-10, 1865. According to Surgeon Tanner's "Return of Casualties near Kinston," Pvt. W. Whitehead, Co. A, 17th NC, was slightly wounded in the left hip. *NC Troops* does not note his wounding at Wise's Forks. No further information.
Source: Tanner (WF), 137; *NCT*, VI:215; M270; NC Confederate Widow's Pension (Martin County).

Whitehead, John, Private, Company I
Wise's Forks
Captured at or near Wise's Forks on March 10, 1865. Confined at Point Lookout, Maryland, and released upon taking the Oath of Allegiance on June 21, 1865.
Source: *NCT*, VI:280; M270.

▲**Whitehead, Turner**, Private, Company I
Sugar Loaf
Services records indicate two captured dates, February 11, 1865 (near Fort Fisher) and February 16, 1865 (near Fort Fisher). Confined at Point Lookout, Maryland, and released upon taking the Oath of Allegiance on June 3, 1865. Whitehead's capture likely occurred on February 11, along with approximately 60 other 17th NC soldiers, when the Federals advanced against the Sugar Loaf line. This strong Confederate defensive position stretched from the east bank of the Cape Fear River to the southern end of Myrtle Sound. The 17th NC occupied the far left of the line. *NC Troops* incorrectly notes that he was captured at or near Fort Anderson on or about February 16, 1865. During the Wilmington Campaign, the 17th NC, part of Kirkland's Brigade, never served on the west side of the Cape Fear River.
Source: M270; Moore, *The Wilmington Campaign*, 97; *NCT*, VI:280.

▲**Whitehead, Willie**, Private, Company I
Wise's Forks
Wounded at the battle of Wise's Forks between March 8-10, 1865. According to Surgeon Tanner's "Return of Casualties near Kinston," Pvt. W. Whitehead, Co. I, 17th NC, was slightly wounded in the left shoulder. His service records indicate that he was admitted to GH No. 13 (Pettigrew) in Raliegh on March 10, 1865, with a gunshot wound to the left shoulder. Received a 60-day furlough on March 16, 1865. *NC Troops* does not note his wounding at Wise's Forks. The March 29, 1865, edition of the *NC Standard* incorrectly spelled his last name as Whiting.
Source: Tanner (WF), 138; *NCT*, VI:2215; M270; *NCS* (Raleigh), March 29, 1865; NC Confederate Pension (Wilson County).

▲**Wiggins, James R.**, Private, Company L
Sugar Loaf

Service records indicate that he was captured near Fort Fisher on February 16, 1865. Confined at Point Lookout, Maryland, and released upon taking the Oath of Allegiance on May 13, 1865. Wiggin's capture likely occurred along the Sugar Loaf line. This strong Confederate defensive position stretched from the east bank of the Cape Fear River to the southern end of Myrtle Sound. The 17th NC occupied the far left of the line. *NC Troops* incorrectly notes that he was captured at or near Fort Anderson on or about February 16, 1865. During the Wilmington Campaign, the 17th NC, part of Kirkland's Brigade, never served on the west side of the Cape Fear River.
Source: M270; Moore, *The Wilmington Campaign*, 97; *NCT*, VI:293.

▲Wiggins, John Lawrence, Private, Company I
Wise's Forks
Wounded at the battle of Wise's Forks between March 8-10, 1865. According to Surgeon Tanner's "Return of Casualties near Kinston," Pvt. J. L. Wiggins, Co. I, 17th NC, was slightly wounded in the left arm. His service records indicate that he was admitted to GH No. 13 (Pettigrew) in Raliegh on March 11, 1865, with a gunshot wound to the left arm. Received a 60-day furlough on March 14, 1865.
Source: Tanner (WF), 138; *NCS* (Raleigh), March 29, 1865; *WD* (Charlotte), April 4, 1865; *NCT*, VI:280; M270.

▲Wilder, Thomas R., Private, Company D
Bentonville
Wounded at the battle of Bentonville between March 19-21, 1865. According to Surgeon Tanner's "Return of Casualties in Hoke's Div. near Bentonville," Pvt. Thos. R. Wilder, Co. D, 17th NC, was slightly wounded in the left arm. The March 27, 1865 edition of the *Daily Progress* listed Pvt. S. R. Wilder was a patient in the Baptist Church Hospital in Raleigh suffering from a wound to his left arm. The newspaper erred in the spelling of his given name. *NC Troops* notes that he was wounded in the left arm at Bentonville on March 19, 1865.
Source: Tanner (BV), 148; DP (Raleigh), March 27, 1865; *WD* (Charlotte), April 4, 1865; *NCT*, VI:238, 768; M270; NC Confederate Widow's Pension (Chowan County).

▲Wilkerson, W. N., Private, Company L
Sugar Loaf
Services records indicate two captured dates, February 11, 1865 (near Fort Fisher) and February 16, 1865 (at Fort Fisher). Confined at Point Lookout, Maryland, and released upon taking the Oath of Allegiance on June 21, 1865. Wilkerson's capture likely occurred on February 11, along with approximately 60 other 17th NC soldiers, when the Federals advanced against the Sugar Loaf line. This strong Confederate defensive position stretched from the east bank of the Cape Fear River to the southern end of Myrtle Sound. The 17th NC occupied the far left of the line. *NC Troops* incorrectly notes that he was captured at or near Fort Anderson on or about February 16, 1865. During the Wilmington Campaign, the 17th NC, part of Kirkland's Brigade, never served on the west side of the Cape Fear River.
Source: M270; Moore, *The Wilmington Campaign*, 97; *NCT*, VI:293; NC Confederate Pension (Cabarrus County).

Williams, B. B., Private, Company L
Bentonville
Captured at Bentonville on March 19, 1865. Confined at Point Lookout, Maryland, and released upon taking the Oath of Allegiance on June 21, 1865.
Source: *NCT*, VI:293; M270.

♦Williams, E. E., Private, Company D
(Inconclusive)
Admitted to Barbee Wayside Hospital in High Point on March 8, 1865, with a gunshot wound to the right side of his face. The March 29, 1865 edition of the *NC Standard Progress* lists Pvt. E. E. Williams of Co. D, 17th NC, was in GH No. 13 (Pettigrew) in Raleigh, suffering from a wound to the face. No E. E. Williams is found in the National Archives Compiled Service Records for North Carolina Soldiers. Further research is required.
Source: Barbee Wayside Registry, entry no. 5733; *NCS* (Raleigh), March 29, 1865; *WD* (Charlotte), April 4, 1865; M270.

Williams, James W., Private, Company I
Wise's Forks
Captured at or near Wise's Forks on March 8, 1865. Confined at Point Lookout, Maryland, and released upon taking the Oath of Allegiance on June 21, 1865.
Source: *NCT*, VI:281; M270.

Williford, B. L., Private, Company I
Wise's Forks
Captured at or near Wise's Forks on March 10, 1865. Confined at Point Lookout, Maryland, and released upon taking the Oath of Allegiance on June 21, 1865.
Source: *NCT*, VI:281; M270.

▲**Winfield, John D.**, Private, Company G
Wise's Forks
Wounded at the battle of Wise's Forks between March 8-10, 1865. According to Surgeon Tanner's "Return of Casualties near Kinston," Pvt. J. D. Winfield, Co. G, 17th NC, was slightly wounded in the right thigh. Captured on April 13, 1865, while a patient in a Raliegh hospital. No further records. Confederate pension records indicate he was wounded at Kinston, suffering from a gunshot wound in the leg. *NC Troops* incorrectly notes that he was wounded at Bentonville on March 19, 1865.
Source: Tanner (WF), 138; *NCT*, VI:262; M270; NC Confederate Pension (Beaufort County).

▲**Wright, David F.**, Private, Company L
Sugar Loaf
Captured near Fort Fisher on February 11, 1865. Confined at Point Lookout, Maryland, and released upon taking the Oath of Allegiance on May 12-14, 1865. Wright's capture occurred along with approximately 60 other 17th NC soldiers when the Federals advanced against the Sugar Loaf line. This strong Confederate defensive position stretched from the east bank of the Cape Fear River to the southern end of Myrtle Sound. The 17th NC occupied the far left of the line.
Source: M270; *NCT*, VI:293; Moore, *The Wilmington Campaign*, 97; NC Confederate Pension (Rowan County).

Private Edward Hollis
17th Regiment NC Troops
Dangerously wounded in the left thigh during the battle of Bentonville. Hollis died at General Hospital No. 13 in Raleigh on March 28, 1865, and is buried there in Oakwood Cemetery.

(Courtesy of Wade Sokolosky)

General Hospital No. 3
Goldsboro
(First Wartime Location)

In March 1862, following the battle of New Bern, Confederate authorities established a hospital in the Wayne Female College building. In National Archives Confederate Record Group 109, General Hospital No. 3's location is erroneously identified as Greensboro. Either Goldsboro or High Point is the correct location. Confederate authorities began relocating GH No. 3 from Goldsboro to High Point on March 11, 1865, as part of the town's evacuation. The hospital resumed operations in High Point on or about March 19, 1865.

(Wayne County Library, Goldsboro, N.C.)

31st Regiment North Carolina Troops

♦▲Anderson, Moses G., Private, Company E
Wise's Forks (Inconclusive)
The patient registry for GH No. 3 in Goldsboro lists Pvt. M. G. Anderson of Co. E, 31st NC, entry no. 1794, was admitted on March 8, 1865, with a gunshot wound. A separate No. 3 ledger, titled "Reports of Wounded and Operations," indicates he was wounded on the right side "in battle." This wound may have been a previous one suffered in October 1864 in Virginia, where he was hospitalized for a gunshot in the abdomen and right arm. Paroled at Greensboro on May 16, 1865. Confederate pension records read Moses G. Anderson.
Source: RG109, 6/291:36; NCOAH, CW10, Ledger B, March 1865, entry no. 24; *NCT*, VII:465; M270; NC Confederate Pension (Caswell County).

Bullet, Jessie N., Private, Company A
Post Wise's Forks
Captured on the "White Hall Road" on March 14, 1865, and transferred to Kinston. No further records.
Source: *NCT*, VIII:432; M270.

♦▲Burnett, William T., Private, Company F
Bentonville or Wise's Forks
William T. Burnett's Confederate pension records indicate that he was wounded in March 1865 at Bentonville. Burnett stated that he was "struck in [the] head by a fragment of shell." No further records.
Source: *NCT*, VIII:473; M270; NC Confederate Pension (Hyde County).

▲Clark, William R., Sergeant, Company E
Bentonville
Wounded at the battle of Bentonville between March 19-21, 1865. According to Surgeon Tanner's "Return of Casualties in Hoke's Div. near Bentonville," Pvt. W. R. Clark, Co. E, was slightly wounded in the right knee joint. Neither Clark's service records nor *NC Troops* note the wound he received at the battle of Bentonville. Clark's Confederate pension records indicate he was wounded on March 13, 1865. The elderly veteran probably erred in remembering the actual date he suffered the wound.
Source: Tanner, 140; *NCT*, VIII:466; M270; NC Confederate Pension (Durham County).

▲Faucette, George C., First Sergeant, Company E
Bentonville
Wounded at the battle of Bentonville between March 19-21, 1865. According to Surgeon Tanner's "Return of Casualties in Hoke's Div. near Bentonville," Sgt. Geo. Faucett, Co. E, was slightly wounded in the right shoulder. Paroled at Greensboro on May 24, 1865. Neither Faucett's service records nor *NC Troops* note the wound he received at the battle of Bentonville.
Source: Tanner, 140; *NCT*, VIII:466; M270.

▲Francis, Davis, Private, Company G
Wise's Forks
Wounded at the battle of Wise's Forks on March 8, 1865. According to Surgeon Tanner's "Return of Casualties near Kinston," Pvt. David Francis, Co. G, 31st NC, was slightly wounded in the left arm. The GH No. 3 (Goldsboro) patient registry lists Pvt. David Francis, Co. G, 31st NC, (entry no. 1858), was admitted for unspecified reasons on March 10, 1865. A separate No. 3 ledger, titled "Reports of Wounded and Operations," indicates that Pvt. David Francis, Co. G, 31st NC, suffered a gunshot wound "in battle" to the left arm and was admitted on March 10, 1865. The ledger further specifies that he was transferred to another hospital on an unrecorded date. Francis was admitted to GH No. 13 (Pettigrew) in Raleigh on March 10, 1865, with a gunshot wound to the left arm. Transferred to another hospital on March 20, 1865. *NC Troops* does not place his wounding at the battle of Wise's Forks. No further records.
Source: Tanner, 135; RG109, 6/291:37; NCOAH, CW10, Ledger B, March entry no. 62; *NCT*, VIII:483; *NCS* (Raleigh), March 29, 1865; M270.

Hall, Alexander Rankin, Corporal, Company E
Wise's Forks
Captured near Kinston on March 10, 1865. Confined at Point Lookout, Maryland, and released upon taking the Oath of Allegiance on June 6, 1865.
Source: *NCT*, VIII:467; M270; NC Confederate Widow's Pension (Orange County).

▲**Hutchins, Joshua H. T.**, Private, Company F
Wise's Forks
Wounded at the battle of Wise's Forks between March 8-10, 1865. According to Surgeon Tanner's "Return of Casualties near Kinston," Pvt. Jos. Husting, Co. F, 31st NC, was severely wounded in the head. Hospitalized at Raleigh's GH No. 13 (Pettigrew) on March 11, 1865, with a gunshot wound of the head. No further records. *NC Troops* does not note the location where the wound occurred. *NC Standard* incorrectly his name as J. H. F. Hutchings.
Source: Tanner, 135; *NCS* (Raleigh), March 29, 1865; *WD* (Charlotte), April 4, 1865; *NCT*, VIII:476; M270.

Landers, Charles L., Private, Company D
Bentonville
Confederate pension records indicate that he was slightly wounded on the elbow at Bentonville on April 1, 1865. No further records.
Source: *NCT*, VIII:458; M270; NC Confederate Pension Records (Johnston County).

♦**Little, William**, Private, Company D
Bentonville (Inconclusive)
Wounded at the battle of Bentonville between March 19-21, 1865. According to Surgeon Tanner's "Return of Casualties in Hoke's Div. near Bentonville," Pvt. Wm. Little, Co. D, was severely wounded in the left arm. Present at GH No. 7 (Fair Grounds) in Raleigh on March 29, 1865, wounded in the arm. No. William Little is listed on the unit rolls. Further research is required.
Source: Tanner (BV), 140; *NCS* (Raleigh), March 29, 1865; *WD* (Charlotte), April 4, 1865; M270.

Marshburn, D. C., Private, Company E
Wise's Forks
Captured at near Kinston on March 8, 1865. Confined at Point Lookout, Maryland, and released upon taking the Oath of Allegiance on June 29, 1865.
Source: *NCT*, VIII:492; M270; NC Confederate Pension (Wake County).

▲**Mitchell, Edward D.**, Private, Company G
Bentonville
Wounded at the battle of Bentonville between March 19-21, 1865. According to Surgeon Tanner's "Return of Casualties in Hoke's Div. near Bentonville," Pvt. E. D. Mitchell, Co. G, was severely wounded in the left lung. Hospitalized in Raleigh on March 22, 1865, with a gunshot wound to the neck. Mitchell died of wounds on March 26 while a patient at the hospital. *NC Troops* does not note the location where the wound occurred.
Source: Tanner, 140; *NCT*, VIII:485; M270.

New, James Columbus, Private, Company B
Wise's Forks
Confederate pension records indicate that he was wounded in the right arm at Kinston on or about March 1, 1865. No further records.
Source: *NCT*, VIII:444; M270; NC Confederate Pension (Richmond County).

♦▲**Newsom, Leander**, Private, Company G
Wise's Forks (Inconclusive)
Wounded at the battle of Wise's Forks between March 7-10, 1865. The GH No. 3 (Goldsboro) patient registry lists Pvt. L. A. Newsom, Co. G, 31st NC, entry no. 1881, was admitted for unspecified reasons on March 10,

1865. A separate No. 3 ledger, titled "Reports of Wounded and Operations," indicates that Pvt. L. A. Newsom, Co. G, 31st NC, suffered a gunshot wound "in battle" to the right foot and was admitted on March 10, 1865. The ledger further specifies that he was transferred to an unspecified Raleigh hospital on an unrecorded date. Leander Newsom is probably the same soldier as L. A. Newsom. Neither his service records nor *NC Troops* note his wounding at the battle of Wise's Forks and hospitalization. No further records.
Source: RG109, 6/291:37; NCOAH, CW10, Ledger B, March 1865, entry no. 71; *NCT*, VIII:485; M270.

♦Parrish, Putney, Private, Company D
(Inconclusive)
Captured at "Harney" on March 17, 1865. Confined at Point Lookout, Maryland, and released upon taking the Oath of Allegiance on June 16, 1865.
Source: *NCT*, VIII:459; M270.

▲Roberson, Jesse, Private, Company F
Wise's Forks
Wounded at the battle of Wise's Forks between March 8-10, 1865. According to Surgeon Tanner's "Return of Casualties near Kinston," Pvt. Jesse Robinson, Co. F, 17th NC, was dangerously wounded in the left arm, requiring amputation. Hospitalized at Raleigh's GH No. 13 (Pettigrew) on March 11, 1865, with a gunshot wound of the left arm (amputated). Received a 60-day furlough on March 27, 1865.
Source: Tanner, 135; *NCS* (Raleigh), March 29, 1865; *WD* (Charlotte), April 4, 1865; *NCT*, VIII:478; M270.

▲Segraves, Sidney C., Private, Company C
Bentonville
Wounded at the battle of Bentonville between March 19-21, 1865. According to Surgeon Tanner's "Return of Casualties in Hoke's Div. near Bentonville," Pvt. S. C. Seagraves, Co. C, was slightly wounded in the left hip. His Confederate pension records indicate that he suffered a gunshot wound, "struck in the hip," at Bentonville in March 1865.
Source: Tanner, 140; *NCT*, VIII:452; M270; NC Confederate Pension (Wake County).

♦Sewell, William J., Corporal, Company G
(Inconclusive)
His service records and *NC Troops* incorrectly note that he was at Greensboro on March 6, 1865, with a gunshot. Location and date wounded not reported. In National Archives Confederate Record Group 109, General Hospital No. 3's location is erroneously identified as Greensboro. Goldsboro is the correct location. Confederate authorities began relocating GH No. 3 from Goldsboro to High Point on March 11, 1865, as part of the town's evacuation. The hospital resumed operations in High Point on or about March 19, 1865. Further research is required.
Source: VIII:487; M270; Sokolosky, *NC's Confederate Hospitals*, vol. 2.

▲Sexton, Randall R., Private, Company C
Bentonville
Wounded at the battle of Bentonville between March 19-21, 1865. According to Surgeon Tanner's "Return of Casualties in Hoke's Div. near Bentonville," Pvt. R. R. Sexton, Co. C, was dangerously wounded in the breast. Neither Sexton's service records nor *NC Troops* note the wound he received at the battle of Bentonville.
Source: Tanner, 140; *NCT*, VIII:452; M270.

Stewart, Alfred W., Private, Company I
Wise's Forks
Captured at Wise's Forks on March 10, 1865. Confined at Point Lookout, Maryland, and released upon taking the Oath of Allegiance on June 20, 1865.
Source: *NCT*, VIII:503; M270; NC Confederate Pension (Harnett County).

▲Turner, John, Private, Company G

Bentonville
Wounded at the battle of Bentonville between March 19-21, 1865. According to Surgeon Tanner's "Return of Casualties in Hoke's Div. near Bentonville," Pvt. Jno. Turner, Co. G, was severely wounded in the abdomen. Confederate pension records indicate that he was wounded at Bentonville.
Source: Tanner, 140; *NCT*, VIII:487; M270; NC Confederate Pension (Hertford County).

▲**Walker, John W.**, Private, Company B
Bentonville
Wounded at the battle of Bentonville between March 19-21, 1865. According to Surgeon Tanner's "Return of Casualties in Hoke's Div. near Bentonville," Pvt. J. T. Walker, Co. B, was severely wounded in the right shoulder joint. Present at GH No. 7 (Fair Grounds) in Raleigh on March 29, 1865, wounded in the right shoulder. No further records. *NC Troops* does not note his wounding at Bentonville.
Source: Tanner, 140; *NCS* (Raleigh), March 29, 1865; *WD* (Charlotte), April 4, 1865; *NCT*, VIII:446; M270.

City Cemetery
Thomasville, North Carolina
Final resting place of Confederate soldiers who died
while patients at the Thomasville General Hospital.

(Courtesy of Wade Sokolosky)

42nd Regiment North Carolina Troops

Aldridge, Hampton, Corporal, Company C
Wise's Forks
Captured at or near Wise's Forks on March 10, 1865. Confined at Point Lookout, Maryland, and released upon taking the Oath of Allegiance on June 23, 1865.
Source: *NCT*, X:218; M270.

Alexander, Berlin, Private, Company K
Wise's Forks
Captured at or near Wise's Forks on March 10, 1865. Confined at Point Lookout, Maryland, and released upon taking the Oath of Allegiance on June 23, 1865. *Western Democrat* listed him as Vernon Alexander.
Source: *NCT*, X:280; *WD* (Charlotte), March 28, 1865; M270.

Allen, Peter, Private, Company D
Wise's Forks
Captured at or near Wise's Forks on March 10, 1865. Confined at Point Lookout, Maryland, and released upon taking the Oath of Allegiance on June 23, 1865.
Source: *NCT*, X:229; M270; NC Confederate Pension (Davie County).

Allman, Nelson, Private, Company G
Bentonville
Confederate pension records note that he was wounded in the left leg, "between the ankle and knee," at Bentonville in 1865. No further records. His surname is spelled Alman on his pension application.
Source: *NCT*, X:258; M270; NC Confederate Pension (Rowan County).

Almon, John, Private, Company H
Wise's Forks
Captured at or near Wise's Forks on March 10, 1865. Confined at Point Lookout, Maryland, and released upon taking the Oath of Allegiance on June 23, 1865.
Source: *NCT*, X:266; M270.

▲**Armsworthy, J. C.**, Private, Company E
Bentonville
Wounded at the battle of Bentonville on March 19, 1865. According to Surgeon Tanner's "Return of Casualties in Hoke's Div. near Bentonville," Pvt. J. Armstrong, Co. E, was slightly wounded on the right side. Charlotte's *Evening Bulletin* on April 4, 1865, listed Pvt. J. C. Armsworthy, Co. E, as having been wounded on March 19, 1865, at Bentonville. J. C. Armsworthy is probably the same soldier Tanner listed as J. Armstrong of Co. E.
Source: *EB* (Charlotte), April 4, 1865; Tanner (WF), 149; *NCT*, X:241; M270.

▲**Arwood, George**, Private, Company D
Bentonville
Wounded at the battle of Bentonville on March 20, 1865. According to Surgeon Tanner's "Return of Casualties in Hoke's Div. near Bentonville," Pvt. G. Arwood, Co. D, was severely wounded in the left lung. *NC Troops* incorrectly notes that he was present in a Greensboro hospital in March 1865. Admitted to GH No. 3 in High Point, entry no. 2516, between March 21 and April 7, 1865, for unspecified reasons. He later died as a patient on an undetermined date and is buried in the Confederate section of Oakwood Cemetery, High Point, North Carolina.
Source: *EB* (Charlotte), April 4, 1865; Tanner (WF), 149; *NCT*, X:229; M270; RG109, 6/291:50.

Atwell, David A., 1st Sergeant, Company G
Wise's Forks

Captured at or near Wise's Forks on March 10, 1865. Confined at Point Lookout, Maryland, and released upon taking the Oath of Allegiance on June 23, 1865.
Source: *NCT*, X:258; M270.

Bailey, Henry L., Private, Company F
Wise's Forks
Captured at or near Wise's Forks on March 10, 1865. Confined at Point Lookout, Maryland, and released upon taking the Oath of Allegiance on June 24, 1865.
Source: *NCT*, X:250; M270; *DCW* (Salisbury), March 13, 1865; NC Confederate Pension (Davie County).

▲Barba, Gabriel, Corporal, Company H
Bentonville
Charlotte's *Evening Bulletin* reported that Corp. G. Barbee, Co. H, was wounded at Bentonville on March 20, 1865. According to Surgeon Tanner's "Return of Casualties in Hoke's Div. near Bentonville," Corp. G. Barber, Co. H, was severely wounded in the left lung. Corporal Gabriel Barba is probably the same soldier Tanner and the newspaper reported as wounded. *NC Troops* does not note his wounding at Bentonville.
Source: *EB* (Charlotte), April 4, 1865; Tanner (WF), 149; *NCT*, X:266; M270.

Barlow, Wiley, Private, Company E
Wise's Forks
Captured at or near Wise's Forks on March 10, 1865. Confined at Point Lookout, Maryland, and released upon taking the Oath of Allegiance on June 23, 1865.
Source: *NCT*, X:241; *WD* (Charlotte), March 28, 1865; M270.

▲Barringer, Rufus A., Private, Company D
Bentonville
Charlotte's *Evening Bulletin* reported that Pvt. R. A. Barringer, Co. D, was killed at Bentonville on March 20, 1865. Neither his service records nor *NC Troops* note his death at Bentonville.
Source: *EB* (Charlotte), April 4, 1865; *NCT*, X:229; M270.

Black, John W., Sergeant, Company I
Wise's Forks
Captured at or near Wise's Forks on March 8, 1865. Confined at Point Lookout, Maryland, and released upon taking the Oath of Allegiance on June 23, 1865.
Source: *NCT*, X:275; M270; NC Confederate Pension (Davidson County).

Blackwelder, Isaac W., Private, Company B (2nd)
Wise's Forks
Captured at or near Wise's Forks on March 10, 1865. Confined at Point Lookout, Maryland, and released upon taking the Oath of Allegiance on June 23, 1865.
Source: *NCT*, X:208; M270.

Blackwelder, Lawson L., Private, Company C
Wise's Forks
Captured at or near Wise's Forks on March 10, 1865. Confined at Point Lookout, Maryland, and released upon taking the Oath of Allegiance on June 10, 1865.
Source: *NCT*, X:218; M270; NC Confederate Pension (Rowan County).

Blaylock, Benjamin C., Sergeant, Company C
Wise's Forks
Captured at or near Wise's Forks on March 10, 1865. Confined at Point Lookout, Maryland, and released upon taking the Oath of Allegiance on June 23, 1865.
Source: *NCT*, X:218; M270.

Boger, Paul, Private, Company F
Wise's Forks

Captured at or near Wise's Forks on March 8, 1865. Confined at Point Lookout, Maryland, and released upon taking the Oath of Allegiance on June 24, 1865.
Source: *NCT*, X:250; M270; NC Confederate Widow's Pension (Davie County).

Boggs, Arrington G., Sergeant, Company I
Wise's Forks
Captured at or near Wise's Forks on March 10, 1865. Confined at Point Lookout, Maryland, and released upon taking the Oath of Allegiance on May 12, 1865.
Source: *NCT*, X:275; M270.

♦Booe, Jacob, Private, Company F
Wise's Forks (Inconclusive)
The *Daily Carolina Watchmen* listed Pvt. Jacob Booe was missing from the battle of Wise's Forks. *NC Troops* does not his capture, nor does his name appear on U.S. Army prisoner of war records.
Source: *NCT*, X:250; M270; *DCW* (Salisbury), March 13, 1865.

▲Booe, William M., Private, Company F
Wise's Forks
Wounded at the battle of Wise's Forks on March 10, 1865. According to Surgeon Tanner's "Return of Casualties near Kinston," Pvt. W. Boone, Co. F, 42nd NC, was severely wounded in the left hand. Confederate pension records indicate that he was wounded between Kinston and New Bern on March 10, 1865. Booe described that he "had index finger on left hand shot off." Paroled at Salisbury on May 30, 1865.
Source: Tanner (WF), 138; *NCT*, X:250; *DCW* (Salisbury), March 13, 1865; NC Confederate Pension (Rowan County); M270.

Boon, Martin A., Private, Company C
Wise's Forks
Captured at or near Wise's Forks on March 10, 1865. Confined at Point Lookout, Maryland, and released upon taking the Oath of Allegiance on June 23, 1865.
Source: *NCT*, X:219; M270.

♦Bostian, J., Private, Company G
Wise's Forks (Inconclusive)
Wounded at the battle of Wise's Forks between March 8-10, 1865. According to Surgeon Tanner's "Return of Casualties near Kinston," Pvt. J. Bostian, Co. G, 42nd NC, was slightly wounded in the left hand. Multiple soldiers are listed on the unit rolls with the surname of Bostian; none are reported to have been wounded in the left hand.
Source: Tanner (WF), 138; *NCT*, X:259; M270.

Bostian, James M., Private, Company G
Wise's Forks
Captured near Kinston on March 10, 1865. Confined at Point Lookout, Maryland, and released upon taking the Oath of Allegiance on May 15, 1865.
Source: *NCT*, X:259; M270; NC Confederate Pension (Rowan County).

Bosworth, Davidson H., Private, Company C
Wise's Forks
Captured at or near Wise's Forks on March 10, 1865. Confined at Point Lookout, Maryland, and released upon taking the Oath of Allegiance on June 23, 1865.
Source: *NCT*, X:219; M270.

Bowles, B. F., Private, Company F
Wise's Forks
Captured at or near Wise's Forks on March 10, 1865. Confined at Point Lookout, Maryland, and released upon taking the Oath of Allegiance on May 12, 1865.

Source: *NCT*, X:251; M270.

Bowles, G. W., Private, Company F
Wise's Forks
Captured at or near Wise's Forks on March 10, 1865. Confined at Point Lookout, Maryland, and released upon taking the Oath of Allegiance on May 12, 1865.
Source: *NCT*, X:251; M270.

♦Brantley, William W., Sergeant, Company G
Bentonville (Inconclusive)
NC Troops notes that he was captured on an unspecified date after March 21, 1865, and confined at Camp Chase, Ohio, where he died on or about May 15, 1865, of chronic diarrhea.
Source: *NCT*, X:259; M270.

Bratton, Absolum W., Private, Company C
Wise's Forks
Captured at or near Wise's Forks on March 10, 1865. Confined at Point Lookout, Maryland, where he died on May 4, 1865, of acute diarrhea.
Source: *NCT*, X:219; M270; NC Confederate Widow's Pension (Stanly County).

Bridgman, William R., Private, Company G
Wise's Forks
Captured at or near Wise's Forks on March 10, 1865. Confined at Point Lookout, Maryland, and released upon taking the Oath of Allegiance on June 23, 1865.
Source: *NCT*, X:259; M270; NC Confederate Pension (Polk County).

Brown, James L., Private, Company G
Wise's Forks
Captured at or near Wise's Forks on March 10, 1865. Confined at Point Lookout, Maryland, and released upon taking the Oath of Allegiance on June 23, 1865.
Source: *NCT*, X:260; M270.

Bruff, Alfred, Private, Company D
Wise's Forks
Captured at or near Wise's Forks on March 8, 1865. Confined at Point Lookout, Maryland, and released upon taking the Oath of Allegiance on June 24, 1865.
Source: *NCT*, X:230; M270; NC Confederate Widow's Pension (Davidson County).

Bulleboy, Burrell B., Private, Company A
Wise's Forks
Captured at or near Wise's Forks on March 10, 1865. Confined at Point Lookout, Maryland, and released upon taking the Oath of Allegiance on June 23, 1865.
Source: *NCT*, X:195; M270; NC Confederate Pension (Rowan County).

▲Burns, William H., Private, Company B (2nd)
Wise's Forks
Wounded at the battle of Wise's Forks between March 8-10, 1865. According to Surgeon Tanner's "Return of Casualties near Kinston," Pvt. W. H. Brown, Co. B, 42nd NC, was severely wounded in the right hand. *NC Troops* does not his wounding at Wise's Forks.
Source: Tanner (WF), 208; *NCT*, X:208; M270.

Bynum, William S., Sergeant, Company K
Wise's Forks
Captured at or near Wise's Forks on March 10, 1865. Confined at Point Lookout, Maryland, and released upon taking the Oath of Allegiance on June 23, 1865.
Source: *NCT*, X:281; *WD* (Charlotte), March 28, 1865; M270.

Call, Murphy G., Private, Company E
Wise's Forks
Captured at or near Wise's Forks on March 10, 1865. Confined at Point Lookout, Maryland, and released upon taking the Oath of Allegiance on June 26, 1865.
Source: *NCT*, X:242; M270.

▲**Campbell, Benjamin Frank**, Private, Company F
Wise's Forks
Wounded at the battle of Wise's Forks between March 8-10, 1865. According to Surgeon Tanner's "Return of Casualties near Kinston," Pvt. F. Campbell, Co. F, 42nd NC, was slightly wounded in the right shoulder. *NC Troops* does not note his wounding at Wise's Forks.
Source: Tanner (WF), 138; *NCT*, X:251; M270.

Carter, Wilford, Private, Company I
Wilmington
Captured near Wilmington on February 22, 1865. Confined at Point Lookout, Maryland, where he died on April 12, 1865, of "inflammation of the lungs."
Source: *NCT*, X:275; M270.

♦▲**Cauble, Horace G.**, Private, Company B (2nd)
Bentonville (Inconclusive)
Wounded at the battle of Bentonville between March 19-21, 1865. According to Surgeon Tanner's "Return of Casualties in Hoke's Div. near Bentonville," Pvt. G. Cauble, Co. B, suffered a severe contusion on his back. Horace G. Cauble may be the G. Cauble Tanner listed as having been wounded at Bentonville.
Source: Tanner (WF), 148; *NCT*, X:208; M270; NC Confederate Pension (Rowan County).

▲**Cauble, Joseph G.**, Private, Company B (2nd)
Wise's Forks
Captured and wounded in the right lung in an unspecified location on March 12, 1865. Admitted to U.S. Army Foster GH, entry no. 6561, on March 15, 1865, with a gunshot wound [faded record entry, but appears to be "lung."] Released on May 15, 1865.
Source: Tanner (WF), 148; *NCT*, X:208; M270; RG94, Foster General Hospital Registry, 99.

▲**Chaffin, Charles Stanley**, Private, Company H
Wise's Forks
Wounded at the battle of Wise's Forks between March 8-10, 1865. According to Surgeon Tanner's "Return of Casualties near Kinston," Pvt. C. Chaffin, Co. E, 17th NC, was slightly wounded on the right side. *NC Troops* does not note his wounding at Wise's Forks.
Source: Tanner (WF), 138; *NCT*, VI:242; M270.

Charles, Francis W., Private, Company F
Wise's Forks
Captured at or near Wise's Forks on March 10, 1865. Confined at Point Lookout, Maryland, and released upon taking the Oath of Allegiance on June 24, 1865.
Source: *NCT*, X:251; M270; NC Confederate Pension (Rowan County).

Cleaver, Daniel M., Private, Company G
Wise's Forks
Captured at or near Wise's Forks on March 10, 1865. Confined at Point Lookout, Maryland, and released upon taking the Oath of Allegiance on June 24, 1865.
Source: *NCT*, X:260; M270.

Clifford, Franklin A., Private, Company F
Wise's Forks

Captured at or near Wise's Forks on March 10, 1865. Confined at Point Lookout, Maryland, and released upon taking the Oath of Allegiance on June 24, 1865.
Source: *NCT*, X:251; M270.

Clinard, Alexander C., Private, Company A
Wise's Forks
Captured at Wise's Forks on March 8, 1865. Confined at Point Lookout, Maryland, and released upon taking the Oath of Allegiance on June 3, 1865.
Source: *NCT*, X:195; M270; NC Confederate Pension (Davidson County).

Collet, Ezekiel, Private, Company K
Wise's Forks
Wounded and captured at or near Wise's Forks on March 10, 1865. Confined at Point Lookout, Maryland, and released upon taking the Oath of Allegiance on June 21, 1865.
Source: *NCT*, X:282; *WD* (Charlotte), March 28, 1865; M270.

Cooper, David M., Sergeant, Company G
Wise's Forks
Captured at or near Wise's Forks on March 8, 1865. Confined at Point Lookout, Maryland, and released upon taking the Oath of Allegiance on June 24, 1865.
Source: *NCT*, X:260; M270; NC Confederate Pension (Rowan County).

♦Cranfield, Hanes, Private, Company F
(Inconclusive)
NC Troops notes that he was killed in March 1865. The location of death is undetermined.
Source: *NCT*, X:251; M270.

Cranfield, William H., Private, Company E
Sugar Loaf
Captured at or near Sugar Loaf, near Fort Fisher, on or about February 11, 1865. Confined at Point Lookout, Maryland, and released upon taking the Oath of Allegiance on May 13, 1865.
Source: *NCT*, X:243; M270.

♦▲Curlee, Davidson, Private, Company H
Wise's Forks (Inconclusive)
His service records and *NC Troops* incorrectly note that he was admitted to GH No. 3 in Greensboro on March 9, 1865, with a gunshot wound in the right thigh. In National Archives Confederate Record Group 109, General Hospital No. 3's location is erroneously identified as Greensboro. Goldsboro is the correct location. Confederate authorities began relocating GH No. 3 from Goldsboro to High Point on March 11, 1865, as part of the town's evacuation. The hospital resumed operations in High Point on or about March 19, 1865. The patient registry for GH No. 3 in Goldsboro lists Pvt. Davis Curlee of Co. H, 42nd NC, entry no. 1822, was admitted on March 9, 1865, with a gunshot wound in his right thigh. Based on the nature of his wounds and the date of hospitalization, Curlee was probably wounded at the battle of Wise's Forks. No further records.
Source: *NCT*, X:267; M270; Sokolosky, *NC Confederate Hospitals, vol. 2*; RG109, 6/291:36; NC Confederate Pension (Anson County).

Curlee, Joseph Simeon, Private, Company C
Wise's Forks
Captured at or near Wise's Forks on March 10, 1865. Confined at Point Lookout, Maryland, and released upon taking the Oath of Allegiance on June 24, 1865.
Source: *NCT*, X:221; M270; NC Confederate Pension (Stanly County).

Daniel, William Harrison, Private, Company D
Wise's Forks

Captured at or near Wise's Forks on March 10, 1865. Confined at Point Lookout, Maryland, and released upon taking the Oath of Allegiance on May 13, 1865.
Source: *NCT*, X:231; M270; NC Confederate Pension (Davie County).

Danner, Samuel, Private, Company F
Wise's Forks
Captured at or near Wise's Forks on March 10, 1865. Confined at Point Lookout, Maryland, and released upon taking the Oath of Allegiance on June 11, 1865.
Source: *NCT*, X:252; M270.

Davis, Henry H., Private, Company C
Wise's Forks
Captured at or near Wise's Forks on March 10, 1865. Confined at Point Lookout, Maryland, and released upon taking the Oath of Allegiance on May 13, 1865.
Source: *NCT*, X:221; M270.

Deadman, James R., Private, Company F
Wise's Forks
Captured at or near Wise's Forks on March 10, 1865. Confined at Point Lookout, Maryland, and released upon taking the Oath of Allegiance on June 12, 1865.
Source: *NCT*, X:252; M270; NC Confederate Pension (Rowan County).

Deadman, Thomas H., Private, Company F
Wise's Forks
Captured at or near Wise's Forks on March 10, 1865. Confined at Point Lookout, Maryland, and released upon taking the Oath of Allegiance on June 12, 1865.
Source: *NCT*, X:252; M270.

Deal, Samuel, Private, Company G
Wise's Forks
Captured at or near Wise's Forks on March 10, 1865. Confined at Point Lookout, Maryland, and released upon taking the Oath of Allegiance on June 12, 1865.
Source: *NCT*, X:261; M270; NC Confederate Pension (Rowan County).

♦De Berry, William, Private, Company D
(Inconclusive)
Hospitalized at GH No. 11 in Charlotte on February 10, 1865, with a gunshot wound in the lower extremities. Place and date wounded not reported.
Source: *NCT*, X:231; M270.

Drake, John, Jr., Private, Company H
Bentonville
Captured at Bentonville on March 20, 1865. Confined at Point Lookout, Maryland, and released upon taking the Oath of Allegiance on June 26, 1865.
Source: *EB* (Charlotte), April 4, 1865; *NCT*, X:267; M270; NC Confederate Widow's Pension (Stanly County).

Drake, Jordan, Private, Company H
Bentonville
NC Troops notes that he was captured at Bentonville on March 19, 1865. Confined at Point Lookout, Maryland, and released upon taking the Oath of Allegiance on June 26, 1865. Charlotte's *Evening Bulletin* reported that Pvt. Jordan Drake, Co. H, was captured at Bentonville on March 20, 1865.
Source: *NCT*, X:267; M270; *EB* (Charlotte), April 4, 1865.

Dula, Thomas C., Musician, Company K
Wise's Forks

Captured at or near Wise's Forks on March 10, 1865. Confined at Point Lookout, Maryland, and released upon taking the Oath of Allegiance on June 11, 1865. Dula was executed in 1866 for the murder of Laura Foster, which inspired the ballad, "Hang Down Your Head Tom Dooley."
Source: *NCT*, X:282; *WD* (Charlotte), March 28, 1865; M270.

Dula, William L., Private, Company K
Wise's Forks
Captured at or near Wise's Forks on March 10, 1865. Confined at Point Lookout, Maryland, where he died of typhoid fever on June 5, 1865.
Source: *NCT*, X:282; *WD* (Charlotte), March 28, 1865; M270.

Earnheardt, John W., Private, Company D
Wise's Forks
Captured at or near Wise's Forks on March 8, 1865. Confined at Point Lookout, Maryland, and released upon taking the Oath of Allegiance on June 12, 1865.
Source: *NCT*, X:231; M270.

♦Echart, W. W., Private, Company H
Wise's Forks (Inconclusive)
Wounded at the battle of Wise's Forks between March 8-10, 1865. According to Surgeon Tanner's "Return of Casualties near Kinston," Pvt. W. W. Echart, Company H, 42nd NC, was severely wounded in the right shoulder. No W. W. Echart is listed in the National Archives Compiled Service Records for North Carolina Soldiers belonging to the 42nd NC. Further research is required.
Source: Tanner (WF), 138; M270.

Efird, John Jacob, Private, Company C
Wise's Forks
Captured at or near Wise's Forks on March 8, 1865. Confined at Point Lookout, Maryland, and released upon taking the Oath of Allegiance on June 11, 1865.
Source: *NCT*, X:221; M270.

Efird, Martin L., 3rd Lieutenant, Company C
Wise's Forks
Captured at or near Wise's Forks on March 10, 1865. Confined at Point Lookout, Maryland, and then transferred to Washington, D.C., and finally to Fort Delaware, Delaware, and released upon taking the Oath of Allegiance on June 17, 1865.
Source: *NCT*, X:218; M270.

Etchison, Giles B., Private, Company D
Wise's Forks
Captured at or near Wise's Forks on March 10, 1865. Confined at Point Lookout, Maryland, and released upon taking the Oath of Allegiance on June 12, 1865.
Source: *NCT*, X:232; M270; NC Confederate Widow's Pension (Davie County).

Eury, Adam E., Private, Company C
Wise's Forks
Captured at or near Wise's Forks on March 10, 1865. Confined at Point Lookout, Maryland, and released upon taking the Oath of Allegiance on June 12, 1865. Eury indicated on his Confederate pension application that he was wounded by a gunshot in his right knee near Kinston on an unspecified date.
Source: *NCT*, X:221; M270; NC Confederate Pension (Stanly County).

Eury, Eli R., Private, Company C
Wise's Forks

Captured at or near Wise's Forks on March 10, 1865. Confined at Point Lookout, Maryland, and released upon taking the Oath of Allegiance on June 12, 1865. He claimed on his Confederate pension application that he injured his back "carrying heavy pine poles to build winter quarters" at Kinston in September 1863.
Source: *NCT*, X:221; M270; NC Confederate Pension (Lincoln County).

▲Ferribee, Thomas M., Private, Company F
Wise's Forks
NC Troops notes wounded in the left arm at or near Wise's Forks on March 10, 1865. Admitted to U.S. Army Foster GH, entry no. 6357, on March 11, 1865, with a gunshot wound in his left forearm. Released from hospital on April 27, 1865.
Source: *NCT*, X:252; M270; RG94, Foster General Hospital Registry, 92.

▲Fesperman, John A., Private, Company G
Wise's Forks
Wounded at the battle of Wise's Forks between March 8-10, 1865. According to Surgeon Tanner's "Return of Casualties near Kinston," Pvt. J. Fesperman, Co. G, 42nd NC, was slightly wounded in the right arm. Admitted to GH No. 13 (Pettigrew) in Raleigh on March 11, 1865, with a gunshot wound to the right arm.
Source: Tanner (WF), 138; *NCT*, X:261; *NCS* (Raliegh), March 29, 1865; *WD* (Charlotte), April 4, 1865; M270; NC Confederate Widow's Pension (Rowan County).

▲Fink, Moses D., Private, Company B (2nd)
Bentonville
Wounded at the battle of Bentonville on March 19, 1865. According to Surgeon Tanner's "Return of Casualties in Hoke's Div. near Bentonville," Pvt. M. Fink, Co. B, was slightly wounded in the left leg. Charlotte's *Evening Bulletin* on April 4, 1865, listed Pvt. M. D. Fink, Co. B, as having been wounded on March 19, 1865, at Bentonville. *NC Troops* does not note that his wounding at Bentonville.
Source: *EB* (Charlotte), April 4, 1865; Tanner (WF), 148; *NCT*, X:210; M270; NC Confederate Pension (Iredell County).

▲Flinn, Riley, Private, Company G
Bentonville
Wounded at the battle of Bentonville on March 20, 1865. According to Surgeon Tanner's "Return of Casualties in Hoke's Div. near Bentonville," Pvt. R. F. Flinn, Co. G, was severely wounded in the right lung. Flinn was hospitalized in Greensboro in March 1865 with an unspecified complaint.
Source: *EB* (Charlotte), April 4, 1865; Tanner (BV), 149; *NCT*, X:261; M270.

Floyd, Daniel E., Private, Company C
Wise's Forks
Captured at or near Wise's Forks on March 10, 1865. Confined at Point Lookout, Maryland, and released upon taking the Oath of Allegiance on June 26, 1865.
Source: *NCT*, X:221; M270; NC Confederate Pension (Anson County).

Foster, Albert N., Private, Company F
Wise's Forks
Captured at or near Wise's Forks on March 10, 1865. Confined at Point Lookout, Maryland, and released upon taking the Oath of Allegiance on June 11, 1865. The widow's pension application notes the middle initial is M.
Source: *NCT*, X:252; M270; NC Confederate Widow's Pension (Davie County).

Foster, Jackson, Private, Company G
Wise's Forks
Captured at or near Wise's Forks on March 10, 1865. Confined at Point Lookout, Maryland, and released upon taking the Oath of Allegiance on June 26, 1865.
Source: *NCT*, X:261; M270; NC Confederate Pension (Polk County).

Foster, Jahue H., Private, Company K

Wise's Forks

Captured at or near Wise's Forks on March 10, 1865. Confined at Point Lookout, Maryland, and released upon taking the Oath of Allegiance on June 27, 1865. *Western Democrat* listed him as J. Hugh Foster.
Source: *NCT*, X:282; *WD* (Charlotte), March 28, 1865; M270.

Foster, John M., Private, Company F
Wise's Forks

His Confederate pension application indicates that he was injured on March 8, 1865, while "lying down in camp, a tree felled by the soldiers . . . which accidentally fell upon him, breaking his right thigh and badly shivering the left leg from the knee to the hip." Admitted to GH No. 13 (Pettigrew) in Raleigh on March 11, 1865, with a fractured left thigh caused by the fall of a tree. Captured at the hospital on April 13, 1865.
Source: *NCT*, X:252; *NCS* (Raliegh), March 29, 1865; *WD* (Charlotte), April 4, 1865; M270; NC Confederate Pension (Forsyth County).

Fouts, William H., Corporal, Company G
Wise's Forks

Captured at or near Wise's Forks on March 10, 1865. Confined at Point Lookout, Maryland, and released upon taking the Oath of Allegiance on June 26, 1865.
Source: *NCT*, X:261; M270.

Furr, Moses H., Private, Company H
Wise's Forks

Captured at or near Wise's Forks on March 10, 1865. Confined at Point Lookout, Maryland, and released upon taking the Oath of Allegiance on June 26, 1865.
Source: *NCT*, X:268; M270.

Gaither, Milton E., Private, Company D
Sugar Loaf

Captured at or near Wilmington on February 11 or February 16, 1865. Confined at Point Lookout, Maryland, and released upon taking the Oath of Allegiance on June 27, 1865.
Source: *NCT*, X:232; M270.

Garver, Leonard B., Private, Company G
Wise's Forks

Captured at or near Wise's Forks on March 10, 1865. Confined at Point Lookout, Maryland, and released upon taking the Oath of Allegiance on June 27, 1865.
Source: *NCT*, X:261; M270; NC Confederate Widow's Pension (Rowan County).

Gatton John H., Private, Company D
Near Wilmington

Confederate pension records indicate that he was wounded in the left shoulder on Stoney Creek (Northeast River), near Wilmington, on February 22, 1865. Confined at Point Lookout, Maryland, and released upon taking the Oath of Allegiance on June 27, 1865.
Source: *NCT*, X:232; M270; NC Confederate Pension (Iredell County).

▲**Granger, John P.**, Private, Company F
Wise's Forks

Wounded at the battle of Wise's Forks between March 8-10, 1865. According to Surgeon Tanner's "Return of Casualties near Kinston," Pvt. J. Granger, Co. F, 42nd NC, was slightly wounded in the left hand. Paroled at Mocksville on June 6, 1865. *NC Troops* does not note his wounding at Wise's Forks.
Source: Tanner (WF), 138; *NCT*, X:253; M270; NC Confederate Pension (Davie County).

Graves, Albert N., Private, Company E
Wise's Forks

Captured at or near Wise's Forks on March 10, 1865. Confined at Point Lookout, Maryland, and released upon taking the Oath of Allegiance on June 27, 1865.
Source: *NCT*, X:244; M270; NC Confederate Pension (Davie County).

Gray, Thomas, Private, Company F
Wise's Forks
Captured at or near Wise's Forks on March 9, 1865. Confined at Point Lookout, Maryland, and released upon taking the Oath of Allegiance on June 27, 1865.
Source: *NCT*, X:253; M270; NC Confederate Pension (Davie County).

Greene, James M., Sergeant, Company H
Wise's Forks
Captured at or near Wise's Forks on March 10, 1865. Confined at Point Lookout, Maryland, and released upon taking the Oath of Allegiance on June 27, 1865.
Source: *NCT*, X:268; M270.

Grimes, Noah B., Corporal, Company F
Wise's Forks
NC Troops notes that he was killed near Kinston in March 1865. No further records.
Source: *NCT*, X:253; M270.

♦▲Grinner, G. W., Private, Company A
Wise's Forks (Inconclusive)
Admitted to the Barbee Wayside Hospital in High Point on March 11, 1865, with a gunshot wound. He was later paroled at Greensboro on May 6, 1865. No further records. Grinner's name on the patient registry is one of two dozen individuals admitted to the hospital that day, all from units that fought at Wise's Forks. Amongst these soldiers were seven wounded from the battle. Grinner probably suffered his wound at the same battle.
Source: Barbee Wayside Registry, no. 5782; *NCT*, X:198; M270; NC Confederate Pension (Stanly County).

Hampton, David A., Private, Company G
Wise's Forks
Wounded in the left leg and captured at or near Wise's Forks on March 10, 1865. Admitted to U.S. Army Foster GH, entry no. 6564, on March 15, 1865, with a gunshot wound [illegible]. Hampton signed his parole in Salisbury on May 23, 1865. Hampton incorrectly identifies Wilmington as the location of his wounding in March 1865.
Source: *NCT*, X:261; M270; RG94, Foster General Hospital Registry, 99; NC Confederate Pension (Rowan County).

Harkey, Jacob C., Corporal, Company D
Wise's Forks
Captured at or near Wise's Forks on March 10, 1865. Confined at Point Lookout, Maryland, and released upon taking the Oath of Allegiance on May 13, 1865.
Source: *NCT*, X:233; M270.

♦Harris, C. P., 2nd Lieutenant, Company I
Bentonville (Inconclusive)
Wounded at the battle of Bentonville between March 19-21, 1865. According to Surgeon Tanner's "Return of Casualties in Hoke's Div. near Bentonville," Lt. C. P. Harris, Co. I, was severely wounded in the right arm. There is no Lt. C. P. Harris listed on the unit rolls.
Source: Tanner (WF), 149; *NCT*, X:274; M270.

♦Harris, Emsley Lee, 2nd Lieutenant, Company I
Wise's Forks or Bentonville (Inconclusive)

Confederate pension records indicate that he was wounded by a gunshot in the left arm near Kinston on or about March 30, 1865. Charlotte's *Evening Bulletin* reported he was wounded on March 19, 1865. No wound description was provided.
Source: NC Confederate Pension (Randolph County); *NCT*, X:274; *EB* (Charlotte), April 4, 1865; M270.

Hartley, William H., Private, Company E
Bentonville
Wounded and captured at Bentonville on March 19, 1865. Confined at Hart's Island, New York Harbor, and released upon taking the Oath of Allegiance on June 18, 1865. Hartley's Confederate pension indicates "wounded in right hand and right leg."
Source: *NCT*, X:244; M270; NC Confederate Pension (Forsyth County).

▲Hartsell, Isaac A., Musician, Company A
Bentonville
Confederate pension records indicate he was wounded in the "right thigh between hip and knee joint, severing the muscles" at the battle of Bentonville on March 20, 1865. Charlotte's *Evening Bulletin* reported that Pvt. J. A. Hartsell was wounded on March 20, 1865 at Bentonville. The newspaper probably erred in reporting his first initial as "J."
Source: *NCT*, X:192; M270; NC Confederate Pension (Buncombe County); *EB* (Charlotte), April 4, 1865.

Hartsell, Jackson M., Captain, Company H
Wise's Forks
Captured at or near Southwest Creek on March 8, 1865. Confined at Point Lookout, Maryland, and then transferred to Old Capitol Prison, Washington, D.C., and finally to Fort Delaware, Delaware, and released upon taking the Oath of Allegiance on June 17, 1865.
Source: *NCT*, X:266; M270.

Hartsell, Jacob, Sr., Private, Company C
Wise's Forks
Captured at or near Wise's Forks on March 10, 1865. Confined at Point Lookout, Maryland, and released upon taking the Oath of Allegiance on June 27, 1865.
Source: *NCT*, X:222; M270; NC Confederate Pension (Stanly County).

▲Hartsell, Jacob L., Private, Company H
Bentonville
Wounded at the battle of Bentonville on March 20, 1865. According to Surgeon Tanner's "Return of Casualties in Hoke's Div. near Bentonville," Pvt. J. Hartsell, Co. H, was severely wounded in the right thigh. *NC Troops* does not note his wounding at Bentonville.
Source: *EB* (Charlotte), April 4, 1865; Tanner (WF), 149; *NCT*, X:268; M270; NC Confederate Widow's Pension (Stanly County).

▲Hartsell, Jacob M., Private, Company H
Bentonville
Wounded at the battle of Bentonville between March 19-21, 1865. According to Surgeon Tanner's "Return of Casualties in Hoke's Div. near Bentonville," Pvt. J. Hartsell, Co. H, was severely wounded in the right hip. *NC Troops* does not note his wounding at Bentonville.
Source: Tanner (WF), 149; *NCT*, X:268; M270; NC Confederate Widow's Pension (Union County).

Hatley, Alexander, Private, Company C
Wise's Forks
Captured at or near Wise's Forks on March 10, 1865. Confined at Point Lookout, Maryland, and released upon taking the Oath of Allegiance on June 13, 1865.
Source: *NCT*, X:222; M270.

Hatley, John F., Private, Company C

Wise's Forks
Captured at or near Wise's Forks on March 10, 1865. Confined at Point Lookout, Maryland, and released upon taking the Oath of Allegiance on June 13, 1865.
Source: *NCT*, X:222; M270; NC Confederate Pension (Stanly County).

Helms, Eleazar W., Private, Company K
Wise's Forks
Captured at or near Wise's Forks on March 10, 1865. Confined at Point Lookout, Maryland, and released upon taking the Oath of Allegiance on June 28, 1865. His widow identified him as Eli W. Helms on her pension application.
Source: *NCT*, X:283; *WD* (Charlotte), March 28, 1865; M270; NC Confederate Widow's Pension (Union County).

Helms, Hosea James, Private, Company K
Wise's Forks
Captured at or near Wise's Forks on March 10, 1865. Confined at Point Lookout, Maryland, and released upon taking the Oath of Allegiance on June 13, 1865.
Source: *NCT*, X:283; *WD* (Charlotte), March 28, 1865; M270; NC Confederate Widow's Pension (Mecklenburg County).

▲Helms, Joshua, Private, Company K
Wise's Forks
Wounded in the "inferior maxillary" and captured at or near Wise's Forks on March 10, 1865. The *Western Democrat* reported that Pvt. Joshua Helms was wounded and left in the enemy lines on March 10, 1865. Admitted to U.S. Army Foster GH, entry no. 6567, on March 15, 1865, with a gunshot wound [illegible]. The hospital erred in the spelling of the last name. Transferred to and confined at Point Lookout, Maryland, on or about April 27, 1865, and released upon taking the Oath of Allegiance on June 28, 1865.
Source: *NCT*, X:284; *WD* (Charlotte), March 28, 1865; M270; RG94, Foster General Hospital Registry, 99.

Helms, Kinney, Private, Company K
Wise's Forks
Captured at or near Wise's Forks on March 10, 1865. Confined at Point Lookout, Maryland, and released upon taking the Oath of Allegiance on June 13, 1865.
Source: *NCT*, X:284; *WD* (Charlotte), March 28, 1865; M270.

Helms, Osborne, Private, Company C
Wise's Forks
Captured at or near Wise's Forks on March 8, 1865. Confined at Point Lookout, Maryland, and released upon taking the Oath of Allegiance on June 28, 1865. The Western Democrat reported his first name as Uriah.
Source: *NCT*, X:222; *WD* (Charlotte), March 28, 1865; M270.

Henderson, James E., Private, Company D
Sugar Loaf
Captured at or near Town Creek on or about February 18, 1865. Confined at Point Lookout, Maryland, and released upon taking the Oath of Allegiance on May 13, 1865.
Source: *NCT*, X:233; M270.

Hendricks, Nalke, Private, Company E
Wise's Forks
Captured at or near Wise's Forks on March 10, 1865. Confined at Point Lookout, Maryland, and released upon taking the Oath of Allegiance on June 27, 1865.
Source: *NCT*, X:245; M270.

Hendrix, W. G., Private, Company E
Wise's Forks

Captured at or near Wise's Forks on March 10, 1865. Confined at Point Lookout, Maryland, and released upon taking the Oath of Allegiance on May 13, 1865.
Source: *NCT*, X:245; M270.

▲Herrin, Julius H., First Sergeant, Company H
Bentonville
Wounded at the battle of Bentonville on March 20, 1865. According to Surgeon Tanner's "Return of Casualties in Hoke's Div. near Bentonville," Sgt. G. Herring, Co. H, was severely wounded in the "Fr. Radius." Herrin's Confederate pension states that he was wounded at Bentonville on or about March 20, 1865, by a gunshot wound "through the left arm below the elbow." His service records and *NC Troops* incorrectly note that Herrin was hospitalized at GH No. 3 in Greensboro on an unspecified date in March 1865. In National Archives Confederate Record Group 109, General Hospital No. 3's location is erroneously identified as Greensboro. High Point is the correct location. Confederate authorities began relocating GH No. 3 from Goldsboro to High Point on March 11, 1865, as part of the town's evacuation. The hospital resumed operations in High Point on or about March 19, 1865. The No. 3 Patient Registry lists Pvt. J. Herring [sic], Co. H, 42nd NC, entry no. 2442, admitted for unspecified reasons between March 21 and April 7, 1865.
Source: *EB* (Charlotte), April 4, 1865; Tanner (WF), 149; M270; *NCT*, X:269; Sokolosky, *NC's Confederate Hospitals*, vol. 2; NC Confederate Pension (Stanly County); RG109, 6/291:48.

▲Hicks, William H., Sergeant, Company K
Wise's Forks
Wounded in the left thigh and captured at or near Wise's Forks on March 10, 1865. Admitted to U.S. Army Foster GH, entry no. 6360, on March 11, 1865, with a gunshot wound in his left thigh. Later transferred to Camp Hamilton, Virginia, first, and then Newport News, Virginia, and released upon taking the Oath of Allegiance on June 30, 1865.
Source: *NCT*, X:284; *WD* (Charlotte), March 28, 1865; M270; RG94, Foster General Hospital Registry, 92.

▲Hill, John W., Private, Company H
Bentonville
Charlotte's *Evening Bulletin* reported that Pvt. John H. Hill, Co. H, was wounded at the battle of Bentonville on March 20, 1865. The newspaper erred in the spelling of the middle initial. Surgeon Tanner's "Return of Casualties in Hoke's Div. near Bentonville," listed Pvt. J. W. Hill, Co. H, was severely wounded in the right lung. *NC Troops* does not note his wounding at Bentonville.
Source: *EB* (Charlotte), April 4, 1865; Tanner (WF), 149; *NCT*, X:269; M270.

Hinson, Benjamin, Private, Company C
Wise's Forks
Captured at or near Wise's Forks on March 10, 1865. Confined at Point Lookout, Maryland, and released upon taking the Oath of Allegiance on June 13, 1865.
Source: *NCT*, X:222; M270.

Hinson, Wade, Private, Company C
Wise's Forks
Captured at or near Wise's Forks on March 10, 1865. Confined at Point Lookout, Maryland, and released upon taking the Oath of Allegiance on June 27, 1865.
Source: *NCT*, X:223; M270; NC Confederate Widow's Pension (Union County).

▲Hoffman, Henry, Private, Company D
Bentonville
Wounded at the battle of Bentonville on March 20, 1865. According to Surgeon Tanner's "Return of Casualties in Hoke's Div. near Bentonville," Pvt. H. Huffman [sic], Co. D, was severely wounded in the right arm and shoulder. *NC Troops* does not note his wounding at Bentonville.
Source: Tanner (WF), 149; *NCT*, X:233; M270.

Holsouser, Jacob, Private, Company D

Wilmington
Captured at or near Wilmington on February 20, 1865. Confined at Point Lookout, Maryland, and released upon taking the Oath of Allegiance on June 27, 1865.
Source: *NCT*, X:234; M270.

♦▲Honeycutt, J., Private, Company H
Wise's Forks (Inconclusive)
Wounded at the battle of Wise's Forks between March 8-10, 1865. According to Surgeon Tanner's "Return of Casualties near Kinston," Pvt. J. Honeycutt, Co. H, 42nd NC, was slightly wounded on the left side. The soldier may have been Sgt. James W. Honeycutt of Co. H, or one of several other Huneycutts that served in the same company, whose first name begins with the letter J. Further research is required.
Source: Tanner (WF), 138; *NCT*, X:269; M270.

Honeycutt, Noah W., Private, Company H
Wise's Forks
Wounded and captured at Wise's Forks on March 10, 1865. Confined at Point Lookout, Maryland, and released upon taking the Oath of Allegiance on June 13, 1865. His Confederate pension application states that he was wounded in the left shoulder, "struck by a piece of shell and the bones of [the] shoulder were broken or crushed."
Source: *NCT*, X:269; M270; NC Confederate Pension (Cabarrus County).

▲Huneycutt, Solomon S., Private, Company H
Wise's Forks
Wounded in the left leg and thigh and captured at or near Wise's Forks on March 10, 1865. Admitted to U.S. Army Foster GH, entry no. 6359, on March 11, 1865, with a gunshot wound in his left leg and thigh. He later died of wounds on April 16, 1865.
Source: *NCT*, X:270; M270; RG94, Foster General Hospital Registry, 92.

▲Huneycutt, William M., Private, Company H
Wise's Forks
Admitted to the Barbee Wayside Hospital in High Point on March 11, 1865, with a gunshot wound. His Confederate pension application states that he suffered a "gunshot wound in the left hip" on March 10, 1865.
Source: Barbee Wayside Registry, no. 5781; *NCT*, X:270; M270; NC Confederate Pension (Stanly County).

Hunt, David T., Private, Company A
Wise's Forks
Captured at or near Wise's Forks on March 8, 1865. Confined at Point Lookout, Maryland, and released upon taking the Oath of Allegiance on May 12, 1865.
Source: *NCT*, X:199; M270; NC Confederate Pension (Rowan County).

Ingram, James, Private, Company I
Wise's Forks
Captured at or near Wise's Forks on March 8, 1865. Confined at Point Lookout, Maryland, and released upon taking the Oath of Allegiance on June 28, 1865.
Source: *NCT*, X:276; M270; NC Confederate Widow's Pension (Davidson County).

James, John R., Private, Company D
Wise's Forks
Captured at or near Wise's Forks on March 10, 1865. Confined at Point Lookout, Maryland, and released upon taking the Oath of Allegiance on June 28, 1865.
Source: *NCT*, X:234; M270.

Johnson, R. A., Private, Company D
Sugar Loaf

Captured near Fort Fisher on or about February 16, 1865. Confined at Point Lookout, Maryland, and released upon taking the Oath of Allegiance on May 13, 1865.
Source: *NCT*, X:234; M270.

Jones, Ebed, Private, Company F
Wise's Forks
Captured at or near Wise's Forks on March 10, 1865. Confined at Point Lookout, Maryland, and released upon taking the Oath of Allegiance on May 15, 1865.
Source: *NCT*, X:254; M270.

♦Kerfees, John Peter, Private, Company F
Wise's Forks (Inconclusive)
Admitted to GH No. 13 (Pettigrew) on March 11, 1865, with a gunshot wound to the left lung. Furloughed on March 23, 1865, for 60 days. The nature of the wounds and date of hospitalization suggest that he was probably wounded at the battle of Wise's Forks.
Source: *NCT*, X:254; *NCS* (Raleigh), March 29, 1865; *WD* (Charlotte), April 4, 1865; M270.

Kesler, George B., Private, Company D
Wise's Forks
Captured at or near Wise's Forks on March 10, 1865. Confined at Point Lookout, Maryland, and released upon taking the Oath of Allegiance on June 28, 1865.
Source: *NCT*, X:234; M270; NC Confederate Pension (Rowan County).

Kesler, M. F., Private, Company F
Wise's Forks
Captured at or near Wise's Forks on March 10, 1865. Confined at Point Lookout, Maryland, and released upon taking the Oath of Allegiance on July 13, 1865.
Source: *NCT*, X:254; M270.

Ketchie, Benjamin Rufus, Private, Company D
Wise's Forks
Captured at or near Wise's Forks on March 10, 1865. Confined at Point Lookout, Maryland, and released upon taking the Oath of Allegiance on June 28, 1865.
Source: *NCT*, X:235; M270; NC Confederate Pension (Rowan County).

Kimery, D. W., Private, Company C
Wise's Forks
Captured at or near Wise's Forks on March 10, 1865. Confined at Point Lookout, Maryland, and released upon taking the Oath of Allegiance on June 28, 1865.
Source: *NCT*, X:224; M270.

King, Anderson, Private, Company E
Wise's Forks
Confederate pension application indicates that he was killed at the battle of Gum Swamp on March 10, 1865. The reference to Gum Swamp is the same as Wise's Forks.
Source: *NCT*, X:245; M270; NC Confederate Widow's Pension (Davie County).

Kiser, J. H., Sr., Private, Company B (2nd)
Wise's Forks
Captured at or near Wise's Forks on March 10, 1865. Confined at Point Lookout, Maryland, and released upon taking the Oath of Allegiance on May 13, 1865.
Source: *NCT*, X:212; M270; NC Confederate Pension (Lincoln County).

♦▲Klutts, Jesse A., Private, Company G
Bentonville

Charlotte's *Evening Bulletin* reported that Pvt. J. H. Klutts, Co. G, was killed at Bentonville on March 21, 1865. Neither his service records nor *NC Troops* note his death at Bentonville. There is no J. H. Klutts listed on the company rolls. Private Jesse A. Klutts may be the same soldier as J. H. Klutts. Further research is required.
Source: *EB* (Charlotte), April 4, 1865; *NCT*, X:262; M270.

▲Lambert, John L., Private, Company H
Wise's Forks
Wounded at the battle of Wise's Forks between March 8-10, 1865. According to Surgeon Tanner's "Return of Casualties near Kinston," Pvt. L. Lambert, Co. H, 42nd NC, was severely wounded in the left shoulder. Pvt. John L. Lambert of Co. H was admitted to GH No. 13 (Pettigrew) in Raleigh on March 11, 1865, with a gunshot wound in his left shoulder and left leg. Hospital records for No. 13 indicate that he was transferred to Charlotte on March 19, 1865. However, his name does not appear on Charlotte's GH No. 11 patient registry.
Source: Tanner (WF), 138; *NCS* (Raleigh), March 29, 1865; *NCT*, X:270; M270.

▲Lambert, John Q., Corporal, Company H
Bentonville
Wounded at the battle of Bentonville on March 20, 1865. According to Surgeon Tanner's "Return of Casualties in Hoke's Div. near Bentonville," Pvt. J. Lambert, Co. H, was severely wounded in the face. *NC Troops* notes that he was wounded in the left eye at Bentonville between March 19-20, 1865. Admitted to GH No. 13 (Pettigrew) in Raleigh on March 22, 1865, with a gunshot wound to the left eye. The *NC Standard* reported J. Q. Lambert, Co. H., 42n d NC, was present at Raleigh's Wayside Hospital (Ladies' Wayside) on March 29, 1865. His presence at the wayside may have preceded his transfer to another hospital farther west on the railroad. His pension records indicate the gunshot wound blinded him for life in his left eye.
Source: *EB* (Charlotte), April 4, 1865; Tanner (WF), 149; *NCT*, X:270; *NCS* (Raliegh), March 29, 1865; M270; NC Confederate Pension (Stanly County).

Lambert, M., Private, Company H
Wise's Forks
Wounded at the battle of Wise's Forks between March 8-10, 1865. According to Surgeon Tanner's "Return of Casualties near Kinston," Pvt. L. Lambert, Co. H, 42nd NC, was severely wounded in the left shoulder. Admitted to GH No. 13 (Pettigrew) in Raleigh on March 21, 1865, with a gunshot wound to the right knee. Captured on April 13, 1865, while still a patient at the hospital.
Source: Tanner (WF), 138; *NCT*, X:270; *NCS* (Raliegh), March 29, 1865; *EB* (Charlotte), April 4, 1865; M270.

♦▲Lambert, W., Private, Company H
Bentonville (Inconclusive)
Wounded at the battle of Bentonville between March 19-21, 1865. According to Surgeon Tanner's "Return of Casualties in Hoke's Div. near Bentonville," Pvt. W. Lambert, Co. H, was severely wounded in the right leg. He is one of two Lamberts from Co. H that Tanner lists as having been wounded at Bentonville, each having distinct wound descriptions. The other, William W. Lambert, was wounded in the left thigh. The W. Lambert listed by Tanner may have been either William or Wilson C. Lambert of Co. H. Further research is required.
Source: Tanner (WF), 149; *NCT*, X:270; *EB* (Charlotte), April 4, 1865; M270.

▲Lambert, William W., Private, Company H
Bentonville
Wounded at the battle of Bentonville on March 20, 1865. According to Surgeon Tanner's "Return of Casualties in Hoke's Div. near Bentonville," Pvt. W. W. Lambert, Co. H, was dangerously wounded in the left thigh. Neither his service records nor *NC Troops* note his wounding at Bentonville.
Source: *EB* (Charlotte), April 4, 1865; Tanner (WF), 149; *NCT*, X:270; M270.

Lawrence, David A., Private, Company G

Wise's Forks
Captured at or near Wise's Forks on March 10, 1865. Confined at Point Lookout, Maryland, and released upon taking the Oath of Allegiance on May 15, 1865.
Source: *NCT*, X:262; M270.

Layton, Green L., Private, Company C
Wise's Forks
Captured at or near Wise's Forks on March 10, 1865. Confined at Point Lookout, Maryland, and released upon taking the Oath of Allegiance on June 28, 1865.
Source: *NCT*, X:224; M270; NC Confederate Pension (Gaston County).

Ledbetter, Thomas P., Private, Company H
Wise's Forks
Captured at or near Wise's Forks on March 10, 1865. Confined at Point Lookout, Maryland, and released upon taking the Oath of Allegiance on June 28, 1865.
Source: *NCT*, X:270; M270.

Lentz, Daniel Wesley, Private, Company C
Wise's Forks
Captured at or near Wise's Forks on March 10, 1865. Confined at Point Lookout, Maryland, and released upon taking the Oath of Allegiance on June 28, 1865.
Source: *NCT*, X:224; M270; NC Confederate Pension (Rowan County).

♦Leonard, Alexander, Jr., Private, Company I
Wise's Forks (Inconclusive)
NC Troops notes that he suffered a gunshot wound in his lung on an unspecified date and location and was captured and hospitalized in New Bern on March 15, 1865. According to the U.S. Army Foster GH Registry, entry no. 6566, Pvt. Alexander Leonard was admitted on March 15, 1865, due to "inflammation of lungs," not on account of a specific battle wound. He later died on March 18, 1865.
Source: *NCT*, X:277; M270; RG94, Foster General Hospital Registry, 99.

Leonard, Jacob, Private, Company I
Wise's Forks
Captured at or near Wise's Forks on March 10, 1865. Confined at Point Lookout, Maryland, and released upon taking the Oath of Allegiance on June 28, 1865.
Source: *NCT*, X:277; M270.

▲Lewya, Roswell, Private, Company I
Bentonville
Wounded at the battle of Bentonville on March 19, 1865. According to Surgeon Tanner's "Return of Casualties in Hoke's Div. near Bentonville," Pvt. R. Luyan, Co. I, was severely wounded in the left thigh. Present at GH No. 8 (Peace Institute) in Raleigh in March 1865, wounded in the left leg. Roswell Lewya is the same soldier reported by Tanner and the newspaper.
Source: *EB* (Charlotte), April 4, 1865; Tanner (WF), 149; *NCT*, X:277; *NCS* (Raliegh), March 29, 1865; M270.

Linville, John F., Private, Company F
Wise's Forks
Captured at or near Wise's Forks on March 10, 1865. Confined at Point Lookout, Maryland, and released upon taking the Oath of Allegiance on June 28, 1865.
Source: *NCT*, X:254; M270; NC Confederate Pension (Yadkin County).

▲Lipe, James A., Private, Company G
Bentonville

Wounded at the battle of Bentonville on March 20, 1865. According to Surgeon Tanner's "Return of Casualties in Hoke's Div. near Bentonville," Pvt. J. Lipe, Co. G, was severely wounded in the face and neck. Present at GH No. 8 (Peace Institute) in Raleigh in March 1865, wounded in the face. No further records.
Source: *EB* (Charlotte), April 4, 1865; Tanner (WF), 149; *NCT*, X:263; *NCS* (Raliegh), March 29, 1865; M270; NC Confederate Widow's Pension (Iredell County).

Little, Jacob, Private, Company H
Bentonville
Captured at Bentonville on March 20, 1865. Confined at Point Lookout, Maryland, and released upon taking the Oath of Allegiance on June 28, 1865.
Source: *NCT*, X:270; *EB* (Charlotte), April 4, 1865; M270.

Little, James M., Private, Company H
Bentonville
Captured at Bentonville on March 19, 1865. Confined at Point Lookout, Maryland, and released upon taking the Oath of Allegiance on June 28, 1865. Charlotte's *Evening Bulletin* reported that J. M. Little was captured on March 20, 1865.
Source: *NCT*, X:271; *EB* (Charlotte), April 4, 1865; M270; NC Confederate Pension (Mecklenburg County).

Loflin, Wiley J., 1st Sergeant, Company I
Wise's Forks
Captured at or near Wise's Forks on March 10, 1865. Confined at Point Lookout, Maryland, and released upon taking the Oath of Allegiance on June 28, 1865.
Source: *NCT*, X:277; M270.

Love, John E., Private, Company H
Bentonville
Captured at Bentonville on March 19, 1865. Confined at Point Lookout, Maryland, and released upon taking the Oath of Allegiance on June 28, 1865. Charlotte's *Evening Bulletin* reported that Love was captured on March 20, 1865.
Source: *NCT*, X:271; M270; *EB* (Charlotte), April 4, 1865; NC Confederate Pension (Mecklenburg County).

Love, John J., Private, Company H
Wise's Forks
Captured at or near Wise's Forks on March 10, 1865. Confined at Point Lookout, Maryland, and released upon taking the Oath of Allegiance on June 28, 1865.
Source: *NCT*, X:271; M270.

♦Mabrey, Jacob A., Private, Company C
Wise's Forks (Inconclusive)
He was admitted to GH No. 13 (Pettigrew) in Raleigh on March 10, 1865, with a shell wound on his right leg. *NC Standard* incorrectly listed his surname as Mayberry. Transferred on March 19, 1865. No further records. Based on the nature of his wound and the date of hospitalization, he was probably wounded at the battle of Wise's Forks.
Source: *NCT*, X:224; *NCS* (Raliegh), March 29, 1865; *WD* (Charlotte), April 4, 1865; M270.

Mahaley, B. Franklin, Private, Company K
Wise's Forks
Captured at or near Wise's Forks on March 10, 1865. Confined at Point Lookout, Maryland, and released upon taking the Oath of Allegiance on June 29, 1865.
Source: *NCT*, X:285; *WD* (Charlotte), March 28, 1865; M270.

Mann, Jonathan, 2nd Lieutenant, Company H
Wise's Forks

Captured at or near Wise's Forks on March 10, 1865. Confined at Point Lookout, Maryland, and then transferred to Old Capitol Prison, Washington, D.C., and finally to Fort Delaware, Delaware, and released upon taking the Oath of Allegiance on June 17, 1865.
Source: *NCT*, X:266; M270.

Marks, Thomas, Private, Company C
Wise's Forks
NC Troops notes that he was wounded and captured at or near Kinston on or about March 9, 1865. Admitted to U.S. Army Foster GH, entry no. 6562, on March 15, 1865, with a gunshot wound to his shoulder and right hand. He died on March 20, 1865, of wounds.
Source: *NCT*, X:225; M270; RG94, Foster GH Registry, 99; NC Confederate Widow's Pension (Stanly County).

May, William F., Private, Company D
Wise's Forks
Captured at or near Wise's Forks on March 10, 1865. Confined at Point Lookout, Maryland, and released upon taking the Oath of Allegiance on May 14, 1865.
Source: *NCT*, X:235; M270.

▲McDaniel, Alfred C., Private, Company F
Wise's Forks
Admitted to Barbee Wayside Hospital in High Point on March 11, 1865, with a gunshot wound. However, his Confederate pension application states he was "severely hurt at the battle of Kinston" on March 10, 1865, "by a tree falling upon him" damaged by an artillery shell. Based on his Confederate pension records, contrary to *NC Troops*, the correct spelling of his middle initial is "C "rather than "A."
Source: Barbee Wayside Registry, no. 5780; *NCT*, X:254; M270; NC Confederate Pension (Davie County).

McDaniel, Benjamin L., Private, Company F
Wise's Forks
Captured at or near Wise's Forks on March 10, 1865. Confined at Point Lookout, Maryland, and released upon taking the Oath of Allegiance on June 29, 1865.
Source: *NCT*, X:255; M270.

McIntyre, John H., Private, Company C
Wise's Forks
Captured at or near Wise's Forks on March 10, 1865. Confined at Point Lookout, Maryland, and released upon taking the Oath of Allegiance on June 29, 1865.
Source: *NCT*, X:225; M270; NC Confederate Pension (Rowan County).

♦McLenster, M., Private, Company E
Wise's Forks (Inconclusive)
Wounded at the battle of Wise's Forks between March 8-10, 1865. According to Surgeon Tanner's "Return of Casualties near Kinston," Pvt. M. McLenster, Co. E, 42nd NC, was dangerously wounded in the left arm, requiring amputation. The surname is not found on the unit rolls.
Source: Tanner (WF), 138.

Medlin, Jesse, Private, Company I
Bentonville
His widow's pension application indicates that he was "shot through the lungs" at Bentonville and was taken to a Raleigh hospital, where he later died "about six weeks after being wounded."
Source: *NCT*, X:277; M270; NC Confederate Widow's Pension (Guilford County).

♦Melton, Alexander, Private, Company K
Wise's Forks (Inconclusive)
NC Troops notes that Alexander Melton was present on the rolls through February 1, 1865, and on an unspecified date, he was captured and later confined at Point Lookout, Maryland, where he died of rubeola

on June 7, 1865. The Point Lookout Prison Registry indicates Pvt. Alex Martin, Co. K, 42nd NC, was captured near Kinston on March 10, 1865, and died there of rubeola on June 7, 1865. There is no Alex Martin listed on the unit roll. Alexander Melton is probably the same soldier as Alex Martin.
Source: *NCT*, X:285; M270.

Minor, Herbert J., Private, Company K
Wise's Forks
Captured at or near Wise's Forks on March 10, 1865. Confined at Point Lookout, Maryland, and released upon taking the Oath of Allegiance on June 15, 1865.
Source: *NCT*, X:285; *WD* (Charlotte), March 28, 1865; M270.

Morgan, E. D., Private, Company D
Wise's Forks
Captured at or near Wise's Forks on March 10, 1865. Confined at Point Lookout, Maryland, and released upon taking the Oath of Allegiance on May 14, 1865.
Source: *NCT*, X:235; M270.

Morton, David L., Private, Company C
Wise's Forks
Captured at or near Wise's Forks on March 8, 1865. Confined at Point Lookout, Maryland, and released upon taking the Oath of Allegiance on June 29, 1865.
Source: *NCT*, X:225; M270; NC Confederate Widow's Pension (Stanly County).

Motley, M. M., Corporal, Company E
Wise's Forks
Captured at or near Wise's Forks on March 10, 1865. Confined at Point Lookout, Maryland, and released upon taking the Oath of Allegiance on May 14, 1865.
Source: *NCT*, X:247; M270.

Myers, Solomon Wesley, Private, Company E
Wise's Forks
Captured at or near Wise's Forks on March 8, 1865. Confined at Point Lookout, Maryland, and released upon taking the Oath of Allegiance on June 29, 1865.
Source: *NCT*, X:247; *WD* (Charlotte), March 28, 1865; M270.

▲Nail, Thomas, Private, Company F
Wise's Forks
Wounded in the left foot and captured at or near Wise's Forks on March 10, 1865. Admitted to U.S. Army Foster GH, entry no. 6358, on March 11, 1865, with a gunshot wound in his left foot. Released from hospital on April 27, 1865.
Source: *NCT*, X:255; M270; RG94, Foster General Hospital Registry, 92; NC Confederate Pension (Davie County).

Nance, Alexander Greene R., Private, Company H
Wise's Forks
Captured at or near Wise's Forks on March 10, 1865. Confined at Point Lookout, Maryland, and released upon taking the Oath of Allegiance on June 29, 1865.
Source: *NCT*, X:271; M270.

▲Orrell, Robert R., Private, Company D
Bentonville
Wounded at the battle of Bentonville on March 20, 1865. According to Surgeon Tanner's "Return of Casualties in Hoke's Div. near Bentonville," Pvt. R. Orrell, Co. D, was severely wounded in the left hip. No further records. *NC Troops* does not note his wounding at Bentonville.
Source: *EB* (Charlotte), April 4, 1865; Tanner (WF), 149; *NCT*, X:236; M270.

Parker, Julius A., Sergeant, Company D

Sugar Loaf

Captured near Fort Fisher on or about February 16, 1865. Confined at Point Lookout, Maryland, and released upon taking the Oath of Allegiance on June 17, 1865.
Source: *NCT*, X:236; M270.

Penry, Noah, Private, Company K
Wise's Forks
Captured at or near Wise's Forks on March 8, 1865. Confined at Point Lookout, Maryland, where he died of chronic dysentery on May 25, 1865.
Source: *NCT*, X:285; *EB* (Charlotte), April 4, 1865; M270.

Perry, Caswell, Private, Company H
Kinston (Post Wise's Forks)
Captured at or near Kinston on March 20, 1865. Confined at Point Lookout, Maryland, and released upon taking the Oath of Allegiance on June 6, 1865.
Source: *NCT*, X:271; M270.

Pinkston, George W., Corporal, Company D
Wise's Forks
Captured at or near Wise's Forks on March 10, 1865. Confined at Point Lookout, Maryland, and released upon taking the Oath of Allegiance on May 14, 1865.
Source: *NCT*, X:237; M270.

Poplin, John, Sr., Private, Company C
Wise's Forks
Captured at or near Wise's Forks on March 8, 1865. Confined at Point Lookout, Maryland, and released upon taking the Oath of Allegiance on June 17, 1865.
Source: *NCT*, X:225; M270.

Price, William J., Sergeant, Company K
Wise's Forks
Captured at or near Wise's Forks on March 10, 1865. Confined at Point Lookout, Maryland, and released upon taking the Oath of Allegiance on June 17, 1865.
Source: *NCT*, X:286; *WD* (Charlotte), March 28, 1865; M270.

Privett, Ansiel P., Private, Company H
Wise's Forks
Captured at or near Wise's Forks on March 10, 1865. Confined at Point Lookout, Maryland, and released upon taking the Oath of Allegiance on June 16, 1865.
Source: *NCT*, X:271; *WD* (Charlotte), March 28, 1865; M270; NC Confederate Pension (Wilkes County).

▲**Queen, William**, Private, Company E
Bentonville
Charlotte's *Evening Bulletin* erred in reporting that Pvt. Wm. Queen, Co. E, was killed at Bentonville on March 21, 1865. He survived the war and was granted a Confederate pension later in life.
Source: *EB* (Charlotte), April 4, 1865; *NCT*, X:247; M270; NC Confederate Pension (Davidson County).

♦▲**Ragen, William**, Private, Company E
Wise's Forks (Inconclusive)
Captured at or near Wise's Forks on March 10, 1865. Confined at Point Lookout, Maryland, and released upon taking the Oath of Allegiance on June 14, 1865. Maybe the same William Ragen of the 17th NC captured the same day at Wise's Forks. See William Ragen listed on page 114.
Source: *NCT*, X:255; M270.

Redwine, John F., Private, Company E
Wise's Forks

Captured at or near Wise's Forks on March 10, 1865. Confined at Point Lookout, Maryland, and released upon taking the Oath of Allegiance on June 17, 1865.
Source: *NCT*, X:247; M270; NC Confederate Widow's Pension (Davie County).

Ridenhour, John M., Private, Company E
Wise's Forks
Captured at or near Wise's Forks on March 10, 1865. Confined at Point Lookout, Maryland, and released upon taking the Oath of Allegiance on May 14, 1865.
Source: *NCT*, X:248; M270.

Rodgers, Jeremiah, Private, Company G
Wise's Forks
Captured at or near Wise's Forks on March 10, 1865. Confined at Point Lookout, Maryland, and released upon taking the Oath of Allegiance on June 17, 1865.
Source: *NCT*, X:264; M270.

▲**Rough, William M.**, Musician, Company I
Bentonville
Wounded at the battle of Bentonville between March 19-21, 1865. According to Surgeon Tanner's "Return of Casualties in Hoke's Div. near Bentonville," Pvt. W. Rough, Co. I, was slightly wounded in the left arm. The April 4, 1865, edition of the *Western Democrat* lists Rough as wounded and hospitalized in Raleigh.
Source: Tanner (WF), 149; *NCT*, X:278; *WD* (Charlotte), April 4, 1865; M270.

♦**Rufus, R.**, Private, Company F
Wise's Forks (Inconclusive)
Wounded at the battle of Wise's Forks between March 8-10, 1865. According to Surgeon Tanner's "Return of Casualties near Kinston," Pvt. R. Rufus, Co. F, 42nd NC, was severely wounded in the left lung.
Source: Tanner (WF), 138; *NCT*, X:333; M270.

Rumage, E. R., Private, Company C
Wise's Forks
Captured at or near Wise's Forks on March 10, 1865. Confined at Point Lookout, Maryland, and died there on May 31, 1865, of pneumonia.
Source: *NCT*, X:226; M270.

Rumple, James M., Private, Company G
Wise's Forks
Captured at or near Wise's Forks on March 10, 1865. Confined at Point Lookout, Maryland, and released upon taking the Oath of Allegiance on June 3, 1865.
Source: *NCT*, X:264; M270; NC Confederate Pension (Iredell County).

▲**Russell, James S.**, Sergeant, Company C
Wise's Forks
Wounded at the battle of Wise's Forks between March 8-10, 1865. According to Surgeon Tanner's "Return of Casualties near Kinston," Sgt. J. Russell, Co. C, 42nd NC, was severely wounded in the left hand. The patient registry for GH No. 3 in Goldsboro lists Sgt. James Russell, Co. C, 42nd NC, entry no. 1801, was admitted on March 8, 1865, with a gunshot wound.
Source: Tanner (WF), 138; *NCT*, X:226; M270; RG109, 6/291:36.

▲**Sassamon, Christian C.**, Private, Company H
Bentonville
Wounded at the battle of Bentonville on March 20, 1865. According to Surgeon Tanner's "Return of Casualties in Hoke's Div. near Bentonville," Pvt. C. Sasamon, Co. H, was severely wounded in the right thigh. Admitted to GH No. 13 (Pettigrew) on March 21, 1865, with a gunshot wound in the right thigh. Received a 60-day furlough on March 27, 1865. *NC Standard* incorrectly listed his surname as Saperman.

Source: *EB* (Charlotte), April 4, 1865; Tanner (WF), 149; *NCT*, X:272; *NCS* (Raliegh), March 29, 1865; M270.

Scott, John J., Private, Company K
Wise's Forks
Captured at or near Wise's Forks on March 10, 1865. Confined at Point Lookout, Maryland, and released upon taking the Oath of Allegiance on June 20, 1865.
Source: *NCT*, X:286; *WD* (Charlotte), March 28, 1865; M270.

Shoaf, Emanuel, Private, Company I
Wise's Forks
Captured at or near Wise's Forks on March 10, 1865. Confined at Point Lookout, Maryland, and released upon taking the Oath of Allegiance on June 19, 1865.
Source: *NCT*, X:278; M270.

Shuping, John A., Private, Company G
Wise's Forks
Captured at or near Wise's Forks on March 10, 1865. Confined at Point Lookout, Maryland, and released upon taking the Oath of Allegiance on June 20, 1865.
Source: *NCT*, X:265; M270.

Siceliff, Alpheus E., 2nd Lieutenant, Company A
Wise's Forks
Captured at or near Wise's Forks on March 10, 1865. Confined at Point Lookout, Maryland, and then transferred to Old Capitol Prison, Washington, D.C., and finally to Fort Delaware, Delaware, and released upon taking the Oath of Allegiance on June 17, 1865.
Source: *NCT*, X:194; M270.

Simmons, Elijah, Private, Company B (2nd)
Wise's Forks
Mortally wounded at Wise's Forks between March 8-10, 1865. Confederate pension records note that he was wounded at or near Kinston in March 1865 and died on April 1, 1865, of wounds. One former soldier of Simmons recalled that he was "killed in a charge near Kinston, N.C., about 12 March 1865." The location of death is undetermined.
Source: *NCT*, X:215; M270; NC Confederate Widow's Pension (Catawba County).

♦▲Sloan, Charles, Private, Company C
Bentonville (Inconclusive)
Charlotte's *Evening Bulletin* reported that Pvt. Charley Sloan, Co. C, was killed at Bentonville on March 20, 1865. Neither his service records nor *NC Troops* note his death at Bentonville.
Source: *EB* (Charlotte), April 4, 1865; *NCT*, X:226; M270.

Smith, Casper M., Private, Company I
Wise's Forks
Captured at or near Wise's Forks on March 10, 1865. Confined at Point Lookout, Maryland, and released upon taking the Oath of Allegiance on May 14, 1865.
Source: *NCT*, X:279; M270.

▲Smith, J., Private, Company E
Bentonville
Wounded at the battle of Bentonville on March 19, 1865. According to Surgeon Tanner's "Return of Casualties in Hoke's Div. near Bentonville," Pvt. J. Smith, Company E, was severely wounded in the right shoulder.
Source: *EB* (Charlotte), April 4, 1865; Tanner (WF), 149; *NCT*, X:248; M270.

▲Smith, James Douglas, Private, Company E
Bentonville

Reported wounded at the battle of Bentonville on March 19, 1865. *NC Troops* does not note his wounding at Bentonville. Paroled at Mocksville on June 7, 1865.
Source: *EB* (Charlotte), April 4, 1865; *NCT*, X:248; M270; NC Confederate Widow's Pension (Davie County).

▲Smith, John W., Private, Company G
Wise's Forks
Service records indicate that he was wounded in the left leg by a shell and captured at Wise's Forks on March 10, 1865. Admitted to U.S. Army Foster GH, entry no. 6563, on March 15, 1865, with a wound caused by a shell. Survived the war.
Source: Tanner (WF), 149; *NCT*, X:265; M270; RG94, Foster GH, 99; NC Confederate Widow's Pension (Rowan County).

▲Smith, Joseph W., Private, Company G
Bentonville
Wounded at the battle of Bentonville between March 19-21, 1865. According to Surgeon Tanner's "Return of Casualties in Hoke's Div. near Bentonville," Pvt. J. W. Smith, Co. G, was slightly wounded on the right cheek. *NC Troops* does not note his wounding at Bentonville.
Source: Tanner (WF), 149; *NCT*, X:265; M270; NC Confederate Widow's Pension (Rowan County).

Smith, Josiah, Private, Company C
Wise's Forks
Captured at or near Wise's Forks on March 10, 1865. Confined at Point Lookout, Maryland, and released upon taking the Oath of Allegiance on June 20, 1865.
Source: *NCT*, X:227; M270.

▲Smith, Milton M., Private, Company H
Wise's Forks
Wounded at the battle of Wise's Forks between March 7-10, 1865. The GH No. 3 (Goldsboro) patient registry lists Pvt. M. M. Smith, Co. H, 42nd NC, entry no. 1866, was admitted for unspecified reasons on March 10, 1865. A separate No. 3 ledger, titled "Reports of Wounded and Operations," indicates that Pvt. M. M. Smith, Co. H, 42nd NC, suffered a gunshot wound "in battle" to the right arm and was admitted on March 10, 1865. The ledger further specifies that he was transferred to an unspecified Raleigh hospital on an unrecorded date. His service records and *NC Troops* incorrectly note that he was admitted to GH No. 3 in Greensboro on March 10, 1865, for unspecified reasons. In National Archives Confederate Record Group 109, General Hospital No. 3's location is erroneously identified as Greensboro. Goldsboro is the correct location. Confederate authorities began relocating GH No. 3 from Goldsboro to High Point on March 11, 1865, as part of the town's evacuation. The hospital resumed operations in High Point on or about March 19, 1865. Neither his service records nor *NC Troops* note his wounding at Wise's Forks in March 1865. Neither his service records nor *NC Troops* note his wounding at the battle of Wise's Forks.
Source: RG109, 6/291:37; NCOAH, CW10, Ledger B, March 1865, entry no. 67; *NCT*, X:272; M270; Sokolosky, *NC Confederate Hospitals, vol. 2*.

Smith, Moses S., Private, Company H
Wise's Forks
Captured at or near Wise's Forks on March 10, 1865. Confined at Point Lookout, Maryland, and released upon taking the Oath of Allegiance on June 20, 1865.
Source: *NCT*, X:272; M270.

▲Smith, William Harden, Private, Company F
Wise's Forks
Wounded at the battle of Wise's Forks between March 8-10, 1865. According to Surgeon Tanner's "Return of Casualties near Kinston," Pvt. W. H. Smith, Co. F, 42nd NC, was slightly wounded in the left hand. Smith's Confederate pension application indicates the wound occurred in the right hand on March 10, 1865.
Source: Tanner (WF), 138; *NCT*, X:256; M270; NC Confederate Pension (Davie County).

▲Sport, William B., Private, Company F

Bentonville
Wounded at the battle of Bentonville on March 19, 1865. According to Surgeon Tanner's "Return of Casualties in Hoke's Div. near Bentonville," Pvt. W. Short, Co. F, was slightly wounded on the right side. *NC Troops* notes that he was killed at Bentonville in March 1865.
Source: *EB* (Charlotte), April 4, 1865; Tanner (WF), 149; *NCT*, X:256; M270.

Stack, James M., Private, Company D
Wise's Forks
Captured at or near Wise's Forks on March 10, 1865. Confined at Point Lookout, Maryland, and released upon taking the Oath of Allegiance on June 19, 1865.
Source: *NCT*, X:239; M270; NC Confederate Pension (Iredell County).

▲**Stoner, William W.**, Private, Company B (2nd)
Bentonville
Wounded at the battle of Bentonville on March 19, 1865. According to Surgeon Tanner's "Return of Casualties in Hoke's Div. near Bentonville," Pvt. W. Stone, Co. B, was dangerously wounded in the right leg. Admitted to GH No. 13 (Pettigrew) in Raleigh on March 21, 1865, wounded in the right leg. Captured on April 13, 1865, while a patient in the hospital.
Source: *EB* (Charlotte), April 4, 1865; Tanner (WF), 149; *NCT*, X:216; M270; *NCS* (Raliegh), March 29, 1865; *WD* (Charlotte), April 4, 1865; NC Confederate Pension (Rowan County).

Swing, Daniel, Private, Company I
Wise's Forks
Captured at or near Wise's Forks on March 10, 1865. Confined at Point Lookout, Maryland, and released upon taking the Oath of Allegiance on June 20, 1865.
Source: *NCT*, X:279; M270.

▲**Taylor, A. Jackson**, Private, Company B (2nd)
Bentonville
Wounded at the battle of Bentonville on March 19, 1865. According to Surgeon Tanner's "Return of Casualties in Hoke's Div. near Bentonville," Pvt. A. J. Taylor, Co. B, was severely wounded in the face and neck. Taylor's Confederate pension application states that he was "shot through the face, the ball going in below the eye & came out below the ear."
Source: *EB* (Charlotte), April 4, 1865; Tanner (WF), 148; *NCT*, X:216; M270; NC Confederate Pension (Davie County).

▲**Taylor, Edwin**, Private, Company H
Bentonville
Charlotte's *Evening Bulletin* reported that Pvt. E. Taylor, Co. H, was killed at the battle of Bentonville on March 21, 1865. According to Surgeon Tanner's "Return of Casualties in Hoke's Div. near Bentonville," Pvt. Ed. Taylor, Co. H, was dangerously wounded in the head and had "since died." *NC Troops* does not note his wounding at Bentonville.
Source: *EB* (Charlotte), April 4, 1865; Tanner (WF), 149; *NCT*, X:272; M270.

Taylor, William M., Sergeant, Company E
Wise's Forks
Captured at or near Wise's Forks on March 10, 1865. Confined at Point Lookout, Maryland, and released upon taking the Oath of Allegiance on May 15, 1865.
Source: *NCT*, X:248; M270.

Teeter, Whitson A., Private, Company H
Bentonville
Captured at Bentonville on March 20, 1865. Confined at Point Lookout, Maryland, and released upon taking the Oath of Allegiance on June 21, 1865.
Source: *EB* (Charlotte), April 4, 1865; *NCT*, X:272; M270; NC Confederate Widow's Pension (Stanly County).

Templeton, James M., Private, Company D
Wise's Forks
Captured at or near Wise's Forks on March 10, 1865. Confined at Point Lookout, Maryland, and released upon taking the Oath of Allegiance on June 20, 1865.
Source: *NCT*, X:239; M270.

Tomlin, Marshall M., Private, Company D
Wise's Forks
Captured at or near Wise's Forks on March 10, 1865. Confined at Point Lookout, Maryland, and released upon taking the Oath of Allegiance on June 20, 1865.
Source: *NCT*, X:239; M270.

Treddy, George, Private, Company I
Wise's Forks
Captured on the Wilmington Road on March 10, 1865. Turned over to the Federal Provost Marshal at Kinston. No further records. The Wilmington Road (current-day U.S. Highway 258) is approximately three miles from the main Confederate defensive line along Southwest Creek. At the time of the battle of Wise's Forks on March 10, Wilmington Road would have been in the Confederate rear area, making the capture location highly unlikely. The date or location of capture is incorrect.
Source: *NCT*, X:279; M270.

Treece, George, Private, Company H
Bentonville
Captured at Bentonville on March 20, 1865. Confined at Point Lookout, Maryland, and released upon taking the Oath of Allegiance on June 21, 1865. Charlotte's *Evening Bulletin* listed his name as Pvt. J. G. Trice.
Source: *NCT*, X:272; M270; *EB* (Charlotte), April 4, 1865; NC Confederate Widow's Pension (Stanly County).

Trexler, James P., Private, Company D
Wise's Forks
Captured at or near Wise's Forks on March 8, 1865. Confined at Point Lookout, Maryland, and released upon taking the Oath of Allegiance on June 20, 1865.
Source: *EB* (Charlotte), April 4, 1865; *NCT*, X:239; M270; NC Confederate Pension (Rowan County).

Tucker, Leonard G., Private, Company H
Bentonville
Captured at Bentonville on March 19, 1865. Confined at Point Lookout, Maryland, and released upon taking the Oath of Allegiance on June 21, 1865.
Source: *NCT*, X:272; M270.

Upright, William, Private, Company G
Wise's Forks
Captured at or near Wise's Forks on March 10, 1865. Confined at Point Lookout, Maryland, and released upon taking the Oath of Allegiance on June 21, 1865.
Source: *NCT*, X:265; M270; NC Confederate Widow's Pension (Cabarrus County).

Ury, Jacob A., Private, Company H
Wise's Forks
Captured at or near Wise's Forks on March 10, 1865. Confined at Point Lookout, Maryland, and released upon taking the Oath of Allegiance on May 13, 1865.
Source: *NCT*, X:273; M270.

Veach, G. W., Private, Company D
Wise's Forks

Captured at or near Wise's Forks on March 10, 1865. Confined at Point Lookout, Maryland, and died there on or about July 1, 1865, of chronic diarrhea.
Source: *NCT*, X:239; M270.

Walker, George Washington, Corporal, Company F
Wise's Forks
Captured at or near Wise's Forks on March 10, 1865. Confined at Point Lookout, Maryland, and released upon taking the Oath of Allegiance on June 21, 1865.
Source: *NCT*, X:257; M270.

Walls, Lewis, Private, Company D
Wise's Forks
Captured at or near Wise's Forks on March 8, 1865. Confined at Point Lookout, Maryland, and released upon taking the Oath of Allegiance on June 21, 1865.
Source: *NCT*, X:240; M270.

Walser, Spurgeon, Private, Company I
Wise's Forks
Captured at or near Wise's Forks on March 8, 1865. Confined at Point Lookout, Maryland, and released upon taking the Oath of Allegiance on June 21, 1865.
Source: *NCT*, X:279; M270; NC Confederate Pension (Watauga County).

Watkins, William H. G., Private, Company C
Wise's Forks
Captured at or near Wise's Forks on March 10, 1865. Confined at Point Lookout, Maryland, and released upon taking the Oath of Allegiance on June 22, 1865.
Source: *NCT*, X:227; M270; NC Confederate Pension (Stanly County).

Whitley, Ephraim J., Private, Company H
Wise's Forks
Captured at or near Wise's Forks on March 10, 1865. Confined at Point Lookout, Maryland, and released upon taking the Oath of Allegiance on June 21, 1865. According to his Confederate pension application, his middle initial is I.
Source: *NCT*, X:273; M270; NC Confederate Pension (Stanly County).

Whitley, John W., Private, Company H
Bentonville
Captured at Bentonville on March 20, 1865. Confined at Point Lookout, Maryland, and released upon taking the Oath of Allegiance on June 21, 1865.
Source: *NCT*, X:273; M270.

Whitley, Levi H., Private, Company H
Wise's Forks
Captured at or near Wise's Forks on March 10, 1865. Confined at Point Lookout, Maryland, and released upon taking the Oath of Allegiance on June 21, 1865.
Source: *NCT*, X:273; M270.

Whitley, Solomon S., Private, Company H
Bentonville
Captured at Bentonville on March 19, 1865. Confined at Point Lookout, Maryland, and released upon taking the Oath of Allegiance on June 21, 1865.
Source: *EB* (Charlotte), April 4, 1865; *NCT*, X:273; M270.

▲Whitley, Taylor, Private, Company H
Wise's Forks

Wounded in the left thigh at Wise's Forks on March 10, 1865, and captured on an unspecified date. Admitted to U.S. Army Foster GH, entry no. 6565, on March 15, 1865, with a wound [illegible] caused by a shell. He died of wounds on April 12, 1865. According to Federal hospital records, Taylor was 16 years old.
Source: *NCT*, X:273; M270; RG94, Foster General Hospital Registry, 99.

Wilhelm, John C., Corporal, Company G
Wise's Forks
Captured at or near Wise's Forks on March 10, 1865. Confined at Point Lookout, Maryland, and released upon taking the Oath of Allegiance on June 21, 1865.
Source: *NCT*, X:265; M270; NC Confederate Widow's Pension (Rowan County).

Wilkens, Isaac C., Private, Company B (2nd)
Wise's Forks
Captured at or near Wise's Forks on March 10, 1865. Confined at Point Lookout, Maryland, and released upon taking the Oath of Allegiance on May 14, 1865.
Source: *NCT*, X:217; M270.

Williams, Milton, Private, Company F
Wise's Forks
Captured at or near Wise's Forks on March 10, 1865. Confined at Point Lookout, Maryland, and released upon taking the Oath of Allegiance on May 15, 1865.
Source: *NCT*, X:257; M270.

♦Williford, F. H., Private, Company G
Wise's Forks (Inconclusive)
Admitted to Barbee Wayside Hospital in High Point on March 9, 1865, with a gunshot wound in left hand. Place and date not indicated. The next day, March 10, Williford was transferred back to Raleigh's GH No. 13 (Pettigrew) in Raleigh, probably due to the seriousness of the wound. At that time, the Barbee Wayside was a privately operated hospital with local volunteer physicians, not army surgeons. The No. 13 registry notes his admittance for a gunshot wound in the left hand. Furloughed for 60 days on March 11, 1865. Probably wounded at Wise's Forks, based on the fact the Barbee Wayside received 25 wounded soldiers on March 9, 1865; all but one were from units that fought at Wise's Forks.
Source: Barbee Wayside Registry, no. 5749; *NCT*, X:265; *NCS* (Raliegh), March 29, 1865; *WD* (Charlotte), April 4, 1865; *NCT*, X:265; M270.

Willis, Burgess, Private, Company I
Wise's Forks
Captured at or near Wise's Forks on March 10, 1865. Confined at Point Lookout, Maryland, and released upon taking the Oath of Allegiance on May 15, 1865.
Source: *NCT*, X:280; M270.

▲Wood, Harrison W., Private, Company F
Wise's Forks
Wounded at the battle of Wise's Forks between March 8-10, 1865. According to Surgeon Tanner's "Return of Casualties near Kinston," Pvt. H. Wood, Co. F, 42nd NC, was slightly wounded on the right side. Confederate pension application indicates wounded at Kinston in the "right frontal bone" on March 10, 1865
Source: Tanner (WF), 138; *NCT*, X:257; M270; NC Confederate Pension (Forsyth County); NC Confederate Widow's Pension (Forsyth County).

Yow, Henry, Private, Company H
Wise's Forks
Captured at or near Wise's Forks on March 10, 1865. Confined at Point Lookout, Maryland, and released upon taking the Oath of Allegiance on June 22, 1865.
Source: *NCT*, X:274; M270.

General Hospital No. 8
Raleigh
In mid-May 1862, Confederate authorities established a hospital in the semi-complete Peace Institute building. No. 8 was one of three general hospitals established in Raleigh during the war.

(North Carolina Office of Archives and History)

50th Regiment North Carolina Troops

Atkinson, Atlas, 1st Lieutenant, Company B
Fayetteville
Captured at or near Fayetteville on or about March 11, 1865. He was sent to several prison camps for confinement until he was transferred to Johnson's Island, Ohio, on April 9, 1865, and released upon taking the Oath of Allegiance on June 17, 1865.
Source: *NCT*, XII:163; M270; NC Confederate Pension (Robeson County).

Atkinson, E. C., Captain, Company B
Fayetteville
Captured at or near Fayetteville on or about March 11, 1865. He was sent to several prison camps for confinement until he was transferred to Johnson's Island, Ohio, on April 9, 1865, and released upon taking the Oath of Allegiance on June 17, 1865.
Source: *NCT*, XII:163; M270.

Barnes, Richard Rhodes, Corporal, Company B
Fayetteville
Captured at Fayetteville on March 12, 1865. Confined at Point Lookout, Maryland, and released upon taking the Oath of Allegiance on June 24, 1865.
Source: *NCT*, XII:165; M270.

Britt, Colen L., Private, Company B
Fayetteville
Captured at Fayetteville on March 12, 1865. Confined at Point Lookout, Maryland, and released upon taking the Oath of Allegiance on June 24, 1865. His pension application indicates the middle initial is A.
Source: *NCT*, XII:166; M270; NC Confederate Pension (Robeson County).

Britt, Joseph B., Private, Company B
Fayetteville
Captured at Fayetteville on March 12, 1865. Confined at Point Lookout, Maryland, and released upon taking the Oath of Allegiance on June 24, 1865.
Source: *NCT*, XII:167; M270; NC Confederate Pension (Robeson County).

Broadwell, J. H., Private, Company C
Savannah (GA)
Confederate pension records indicate that he was wounded at or near Augusta, Georgia, on January 11, 1865. The 50th NC, assigned to Hardy's Brigade, actively contested preliminary advances by U.S. Army forces into South Carolina before the initiation of the Carolinas Campaign on February 1, 1865. Broadwell may have been wounded at one of several small engagements. No further records.
Source: *NCT*, XII:177; M270; NC Confederate Pension (Johnston County).

Carter, Moses, Private, Company C
Goldsboro (Post Bentonville)
Deserted at Goldsboro on March 24, 1865. Confined at Hart's Island, New York Harbor, and released upon taking the Oath of Allegiance on June 18, 1865.
Source: *NCT*, XII:177; M270.

Cash, Preston, Private, Company A
Rivers Bridge (SC)
Captured at Rivers Bridge, Salkehatchie River, South Carolina, on February 3, 1865. At the time of his battle, Federal soldiers from the U.S. Army XVII Corps discovered him "sick in a house with arms." His widow, Letha Cash, stated on her pension application that he died at a hospital in Columbia, South Carolina. The

Federals may have left him at one of several Confederate hospitals in Columbia before continuing the march northward.
Source: *NCT*, XII:155; M270; NC Confederate Pension (Person County).

Collins, Atlas, 2nd Lieutenant, Company B
Fayetteville
Captured at or near Fayetteville on March 11, 1865. He was sent to several prison camps for confinement until he was transferred to Johnson's Island, Ohio, on April 9, 1865, and released upon taking the Oath of Allegiance on June 18, 1865.
Source: *NCT*, XII:163; M270.

Collins, Samuel S., Private, Company B
Fayetteville
Captured at Fayetteville on March 12, 1865. Confined at Point Lookout, Maryland, and released upon taking the Oath of Allegiance on June 26, 1865.
Source: *NCT*, XII:167; M270.

Corbett, William N., 1st Lieutenant, Company I
Salkehatchie River (SC)
Killed in a fratricide event on January 20, 1865, between the 50th NC and Georgia troops from Fiser's Brigade. "The river flats were heavily timbered and all underwater, at the same time a dense fog prevailed," remembered one soldier from the 50th NC. Because of the adverse conditions, the two Confederate units became disorientated and suddenly encountered one another while wading in waist-deep water. A two-hour skirmish ensued, each supposing the other to be the enemy.
Source: *NCT*, XII:235; Ellington, "Fiftieth Regiment," Clark, *Histories*, 188-89; M270.

Cox, William P., Private, Company B
Fayetteville
Captured at Fayetteville on March 12, 1865. Confined at Point Lookout, Maryland, and released upon taking the Oath of Allegiance on June 26, 1865.
Source: *NCT*, XII:167; M270.

Exum, William D., Private, Company E
Goldsboro (Post Bentonville)
Captured at or near Goldsboro on March 23, 1865. Took the Oath of Allegiance the same day.
Source: *NCT*, XII:199; M270; NC Confederate Pension (Wilson County).

▲Flack, Lewis B., Private, Company G
Bentonville
Killed at Bentonville between March 19-21, 1865. Based on an 1866 listing of Confederate dead buried on the John Harper farm, published in Wilmington's *Daily Journal*, a Pvt. L. B. Flach of the 50th NC was interred there. As reported in the paper, L. B. Flach is probably the same soldier as Lewis B. Flack. Flack's name appears on a monument at Bentonville Battlefield State Historic Site, leading some to assume he is buried in the Confederate mass grave located there.
Source: *NCT*, XII:218; M270; *DJ* (Wilmington, NC), August 8, 1866.

Gilchrist, Charles A., Private, Company F
Bentonville
Confederate pension records indicate that he was wounded in the breast, "struck by a piece of shell," at Bentonville in 1865.
Source: *NCT*, XII:207; M270; NC Confederate Pension (Harnett County).

Goodwin, George, Private, Company E
Goldsboro (Post Bentonville)

Deserted to the enemy at or near Goldsboro on March 24, 1865. Confined at Hart's Island, New York Harbor, on April 10, 1865. Escaped from Hart's Island on or about July 6, 1865.
Source: *NCT*, XII:199; M270.

Hampton, Thomas J., Private, Company K
Bentonville
NC Troops notes that he was killed at Bentonville between March 19-21, 1865. Hampton's name appears on a monument at Bentonville Battlefield State Historic Site, leading some to assume he is buried in the Confederate mass grave located there.
Source: *NCT*, XII:251; M270.

Hamrick, Robert B., Private, Company K
Bentonville
Confederate pension records indicate that he was wounded at Bentonville on March 19, 1865.
Source: *NCT*, XII:251; M270; NC Confederate Pension (Rutherford County).

Hedgepeth, Arch B., Private, Company B
Fayetteville
Captured at Fayetteville on March 12, 1865. Confined at Point Lookout, Maryland, where he died of chronic diarrhea on April 27, 1865.
Source: *NCT*, XII:168; M270.

Hedgepeth, Joel D., Corporal, Company B
Fayetteville
Captured at Fayetteville on March 12, 1865. Transferred to New Bern, arriving on March 26, 1865. No further records.
Source: *NCT*, XII:168; M270.

Jenkins, Elias, Corporal, Company B
Fayetteville
Captured at Fayetteville on March 12, 1865. Confined at Point Lookout, Maryland, and released upon taking the Oath of Allegiance on June 28, 1865.
Source: *NCT*, XII:170; M270.

Jones, Doctor T., Private, Company H
Fayetteville
Captured at or near Fayetteville on March 8, 1865. Confined at Fort Monroe, Virginia, and later Newport News, and released upon taking the Oath of Allegiance on June 30, 1865. Based on Jones's capture date, he was caught before Confederate forces reached Fayetteville ahead of the approaching Federal armies.
Source: *NCT*, XII:231; M270; NC Confederate Pension (Harnett County).

♦Lamb, Hugh, Private, Company B
(Inconclusive)
Hospitalized at Greensboro on February 12, 1865, with a gunshot wound. The date and location of his wounding were not reported. Transferred to another hospital on March 11, 1865. His service records and *NC Troops* incorrectly note that Lamb was hospitalized at GH No. 3 in Greensboro. In National Archives Confederate Record Group 109, General Hospital No. 3's location is erroneously identified as Greensboro. Goldsboro is the correct location. Confederate authorities began relocating GH No. 3 from Goldsboro to High Point on March 11, 1865, as part of the town's evacuation. The hospital resumed operations in High Point on or about March 19, 1865. Lamb's transfer to another hospital was part of the evacuation process. Interestingly, Lamb stated on his pension that he was never wounded during the war. Further research is required.
Source: *NCT*, XII:170; M270; Sokolosky, *NC Confederate Hospitals*, vol. 2; NC Confederate Pension (Robeson County).

Lamb, Michael, Private, Company B

Fayetteville
Captured at Fayetteville on March 12, 1865. Confined at Point Lookout, Maryland, and released upon taking the Oath of Allegiance on June 29, 1865.
Source: *NCT*, XII:170; M270; NC Confederate Widow's Pension (Robeson County).

Lea, S. M., Private, Company A
Savannah (GA)
Confederate pension records indicate that he was wounded in the hip "by a piece of shell" at or near Savannah, Georgia, in January 1865. The 50th NC, assigned to Hardy's Brigade, actively contested preliminary advances by U.S. Army forces into South Carolina before the initiation of the Carolinas Campaign on February 1, 1865. Lea may have been wounded at one of several small engagements. No further records.
Source: *NCT*, XII:159; M270; NC Confederate Pension (Person County).

Ledford, Frederick, Private, Company K
Cheraw (SC)
Captured by U.S. Army forces on an unspecified date and paroled at Cheraw, SC, on March 5, 1865. The fact that Ledford was paroled while the Federals were on the march toward North Carolina suggests he may have been one of an unknown number of sick and wounded Confederate soldiers left behind in the town in temporary hospitals by retreating forces.
Source: *NCT*, XII:253; M270; NC Confederate Pension (McDowell County).

Lewis, Warren A., Sergeant, Company B
Fayetteville
Captured at Fayetteville on March 12, 1865. Confined at Point Lookout, Maryland, and released upon taking the Oath of Allegiance on June 29, 1865.
Source: *NCT*, XII:171; M270.

Long, John A., Private, Company K
Bentonville
NC Troops notes that he was killed at Bentonville between March 19-21, 1865.
Source: *NCT*, XII:253; M270.

Owens, William H., Private, Company E
Bamberg, (SC)
Captured at Bamberg, SC, on February 7, 1865. Confined at Hart's Island, New York Harbor, where he died of pneumonia on May 12, 1865.
Source: *NCT*, XII:201; M270.

Patterson, Robert J., Private, Company H
Savannah (GA)
Confederate pension records indicate that he was wounded in the head near Savannah, Georgia, in January 1865. The 50th NC, part of Hardy's Brigade, actively contested preliminary advances by U.S. Army forces into South Carolina before the initiation of the Carolinas Campaign on February 1, 1865. Lea may have been wounded at one of several small engagements. No further records.
Source: *NCT*, XII:232; M270; NC Confederate Pension (Harnett County).

Pitman, John, Private, Company B
Robeson County
Captured in his native Robeson County on March 4, 1865. Confined at Point Lookout, Maryland, and released upon taking the Oath of Allegiance on June 16, 1865.
Source: *NCT*, XII:172; M270.

Powell, O. D., Private, Company B
Fayetteville

Captured in his native Robeson County on March 4, 1865. Admitted to U.S. Army Foster GH in New Bern on March 28, 1865, suffering from chronic diarrhea and inflammation of the lungs. He later died there on or about May 6, 1865.
Source: *NCT*, XII:172; M270.

Price, Gideon, Private, Company C
Cheraw (SC)
Captured by U.S. Army forces on an unspecified date and paroled at Cheraw, SC, on March 5, 1865. The fact that Price was paroled while the Federals were on the march toward North Carolina suggests he may have been one of an unknown number of sick and wounded Confederate soldiers left behind in the town in temporary hospitals by retreating forces.
Source: *NCT*, XII:184; M270.

Salomon, James P., Private, Company H
Fayetteville
Captured at or near Fayetteville on March 8, 1865. Confined at Fort Monroe, Virginia, and later Newport News, and released upon taking the Oath of Allegiance on June 30, 1865. Based on Solomon's capture date, he was caught before Confederate forces reached Fayetteville ahead of the approaching Federal armies.
Source: *NCT*, XII:233; M270.

Smart, Henry Kerr, Private, Company G
Bentonville
Captured at Bentonville on March 22, 1865. Confined at Hart's Island, New York Harbor, and released upon taking the Oath of Allegiance on June 19, 1865.
Source: *NCT*, XII:223; M270; NC Confederate Pension (Rutherford County).

Smith, Thomas, Private, Company E
Goldsboro (Post Bentonville)
Captured at or near Goldsboro on March 24, 1865. Confined at Point Lookout, Maryland, and released upon taking the Oath of Allegiance on June 20, 1865.
Source: *NCT*, XII:203; M270; NC Confederate Widow's Pension (Wayne County).

Thomas, John M. B., Private, Company C
Near Charleston (SC)
Confederate pension records indicate that he was wounded in the foot near Charleston, South Carolina, on February 14, 1865. His pension application stated, "All of the anterior part of the foot was shot away—leaving only the heel."
Source: *NCT*, XII:212; M270; NC Confederate Pension (Harnett County).

Wall, M. W., _____, Company I
Averasboro
Confederate pension application indicates wounded at Averasboro on or about March 15, 1865. No further records. *NC Troops* notes that the wound occurred on March 16, 1865.
Source: *NCT*, XII:246; M270; NC Confederate Pension (Rutherford County).

Walters, William, Private, Company B
Fayetteville
Captured at Fayetteville on March 12, 1865. Confined at Point Lookout, Maryland, and released upon taking the Oath of Allegiance on June 21, 1865.
Source: *NCT*, XII:174; M270.

Warwick, John J., Private, Company H
Fayetteville

Captured at or near Fayetteville on March 8, 1865. Confined at Point Lookout, Maryland, where he died of "inflammation of the lungs on April 10, 1865. Based on Warwick's capture date, he was caught before Confederate forces reached Fayetteville ahead of the approaching Federal armies.
Source: *NCT*, XII:234; M270; NC Confederate Widow's Pension (Harnett County).

Waters, Jonathan, Private, Company G
Cheraw (SC)
Captured by U.S. Army forces on an unspecified date and paroled at Cheraw, SC, on March 5, 1865. The fact that Waters was paroled while the Federals were on the march toward North Carolina suggests he may have been one of an unknown number of sick and wounded Confederate soldiers left behind in the town in temporary hospitals by retreating forces.
Source: *NCT*, XII:225; M270 NC Confederate Widow's Pension (Cleveland County).

♦Watson, Daniel W., Private, Company G
(Inconclusive)
Captured by U.S. Army forces on an unspecified date and location. Admitted to Foster GH in New Bern on March 30, 1865, where he died of chronic diarrhea on April 3, 1865. Buried in New Bern Cemetery.
Source: *NCT*, XII:225; M270.

Baptist Church Hospital
Raleigh
In early March 1865, Confederate authorities established a temporary hospital in the First Baptist Church to alleviate the stress of overcrowding in Raleigh's three general hospitals.
(North Carolina Office of Archives and History)

51st Regiment North Carolina Troops

Bain, Daniel D., Jr., Private, Company I
Wise's Forks
Captured at or near Wise's Forks on March 10, 1865. Confined at Point Lookout, Maryland, and released upon taking the Oath of Allegiance on June 24, 1865.
Source: *NCT*, XII:368; M270.

Buie, George McD., Private, Company I
Cumberland County
Captured near Fayetteville in his native Cumberland County on March 11, 1865. Confined at Point Lookout, Maryland, and released upon taking the Oath of Allegiance on June 4, 1865.
Source: *NCT*, XII:369; M270.

Buie, Malcolm James, Private, Company I
Cumberland County
Captured at or near Fayetteville in his native Cumberland County on March 11, 1865. Confined at Point Lookout, Maryland, and released upon taking the Oath of Allegiance on June 24, 1865.
Source: *NCT*, XII:370; M270; NC Confederate Widow's Pension (Cumberland County).

Denning, Josiah, Private, Company I
Cumberland County
Captured near Fayetteville in his native Cumberland County on March 16, 1865. Confined at Point Lookout, Maryland, and released upon taking the Oath of Allegiance on June 26, 1865.
Source: *NCT*, XII:371; M270; NC Confederate Pension (Harnett County).

Fields, William B., Private, Company C
Goldsboro
Captured at Goldsboro on March 22, 1865. He was not with the regiment at the battle of Bentonville. See *NC Troops* for more information.
Source: *NCT*, XII:301; M270; NC Soldiers' Home Application (Cumberland County).

▲**Floyd, Faulkner J.**, Sergeant, Company F
Bentonville
Wounded at the battle of Bentonville between March 19-21, 1865. According to Surgeon Tanner's "Return of Casualties in Hoke's Div. near Bentonville," Corp. Floyd J. Faulk, Co. F, was slightly wounded in the right knee. Tanner erred in the transcribing of his name. Private Faulkner Floyd of Company F is the same soldier as Pvt. Floyd S. Faulk. Neither Floyd's service records nor *NC Troops* note the wound he received at the battle of Bentonville.
Source: Tanner (BV), 140; *NCT*, XII:335; M270.

▲**Fulgum, Robert L.**, Private, Company A
Bentonville
Wounded at the battle of Bentonville between March 19-21, 1865. According to Surgeon Tanner's "Return of Casualties in Hoke's Div. near Bentonville," Pvt. R. Fulgum, Co. A, was slightly wounded in the right arm. Private Robert L. Fulgum of Co. A is the soldier as Pvt. R. Fulgum. Neither Fulgum's service records nor *NC Troops* note the wound he received at the battle of Bentonville.
Source: Tanner (BV), 140; *NCT*, XII:282; M270.

▲**Giddens, Henry C.**, Sergeant, Company K
Wise's Forks
Wounded at the battle of Wise's Forks on March 8, 1865. According to Surgeon Tanner's "Return of Casualties near Kinston," Pvt. H. Giddens, Co. K, 51st NC, was severely wounded in the right thigh. *NC Troops* does not note his wounding at Wise's Forks.

Source: Tanner (WF), 135; *NCT*, XII:385; M270.

♦Grady, William Henry, Sergeant, Company C
Wise's Forks (Inconclusive)
The patient registry for GH No. 3 in Goldsboro lists Sgt. W. H. Grady of Co. C, 51st NC, entry no. 1750, was admitted on March 6, 1865, with a gunshot wound. Oddly, he was admitted again to the GH No. 3 on March 9, 1865, entry no. 1814, with a gunshot wound, with the remark "Transferred from Kinston." No further hospital information is found until he is paroled at the end of the war as a patient at Greensboro's Way Hospital No. 2. Grady's Confederate pension application indicates that he was wounded in the "left buttock" at Drewry's Bluff, Virginia, in May 1864. His service records and *NC Troops* incorrectly note that Grady was hospitalized at GH No. 3 in Greensboro. Goldsboro is the correct location. Confederate authorities ordered No. 3's relocation to High Point on March 11, 1865, as part of the Confederate evacuation of Goldsboro. Grady may have been suffering from reoccurring problems with his earlier wounding in Virginia or was wounded during the initial skirmishing before the battle of Wise's Forks.
Source: *NCT*, XVII:301; M270; RG109, 6/291:35, 36; NC Confederate Pension (Duplin County).

▲Guy, Lewis H., Corporal, Company I
Wise's Forks
Wounded at the battle of Wise's Forks on March 8, 1865. According to Surgeon Tanner's "Return of Casualties near Kinston," Pvt. L. Guy, Co. I, 51st NC, was severely wounded in the right thigh. Guy was admitted to GH No. 13 (Pettigrew) on March 11, 1865 (registry no. 2537), with a gunshot wound in the right thigh (fractured). *NC Troops* notes that he was wounded in the right thigh at or near Wise's Forks in March 1865.
Source: Tanner (WF), 135; *NCS* (Raleigh), March 29, 1865; *WD* (Charlotte), April 4, 1865; *NCT*, XII:372; M270.

▲Hayes, Levi C., Private, Co. F
Wise's Forks
Wounded at the battle of Wise's Forks on March 8, 1865. According to Surgeon Tanner's "Return of Casualties near Kinston," Pvt. Levi Hayes, Co. F, 51st NC, was slightly wounded in the right arm and side. His service records and *NC Troops* incorrectly note that he was transferred from Kinston and admitted to GH No. 3 in Greensboro on March 9, 1865, for unspecified reasons. In National Archives Confederate Record Group 109, General Hospital No. 3's location is erroneously identified as Greensboro. Goldsboro is the correct location. Confederate authorities began relocating GH No. 3 from Goldsboro to High Point on March 11, 1865, as part of the town's evacuation. The hospital resumed operations in High Point on or about March 19, 1865. No further records. *NC Troops* does not note that he was wounded at Wise's Forks.
Source: Tanner (WF), 135; *NCT*, XII:336; M270; Sokolosky, *NC Confederate Hospitals*, vol. 2.

▲Lanier, Joseph J., Private, Company C
Bentonville
Captured at or near Bentonville on or about March 21, 1865. Confined at Hart's Island, New York Harbor, and released upon taking the Oath of Allegiance on June 19, 1865.
Source: Tanner (BV), 140; *NCT*, XII:303; M270; NC Confederate Widow's Pension (Duplin County).

♦Laper, M. G., Private, Company H
(Inconclusive)
The March 29, 1865 edition of the *NC Standard* lists a Pvt. M. G. Laper, Co. H, 51st NC, was wounded in the right arm during an unspecified engagement and present in GH No. 13 (Pettigrew) in Raliegh. Not found on the unit rolls.
Source: *NCS* (Raleigh), March 29, 1865; *WD* (Charlotte), April 4, 1865.

♦London, P., Private, Company ___
(Inconclusive)
Present at Baptist Church Hospital in Raleigh on March 27, 1865, wounded in the right hand. Not found in the National Archives Compiled Services Records for North Carolina Confederate Soldiers.

Source: *DP* (Raleigh), March 27, 1865; *WD* (Charlotte), April 4, 1865; M270.

McLean, Angus, Private, Company I
Wise's Forks
Captured at Wise's Forks on March 8, 1865. Confined at Point Lookout, Maryland, and released upon taking the Oath of Allegiance on June 29, 1865.
Source: *NCT*, XII:375; M270; NC Confederate Widow's Pension (Moore County).

McLean, Daniel, Private, Company D
Bentonville
Confederate pension records indicate that he was wounded by a gunshot to the head at Bentonville between March 19-21, 1865. Survived the war.
Source: *NCT*, XII:315; M270; NC Confederate Pension (Robeson County).

▲McLean, Hector R., Private, Company E
Bentonville
Wounded at the battle of Bentonville between March 19-21, 1865. According to Surgeon Tanner's "Return of Casualties in Hoke's Div. near Bentonville," Pvt. H. McLain, Co. E, was slightly wounded in the left hand. Private Hector R. McLean of Co. E is probably the same soldier as Pvt. H. McLain. Neither McLean's service records nor *NC Troops* note the wound he received at the battle of Bentonville. His pension application indicates that he was previously wounded at Cold Harbor, Virginia.
Source: Tanner (BV), 140; *NCT*, XII:326; M270; NC Confederate Pension (Harnett County).

Melvin, Robert D., Private, Company I
Fayetteville
Captured near Fayetteville in his native Cumberland County on March 16, 1865. Confined at Point Lookout, Maryland, and released upon taking the Oath of Allegiance on June 3, 1865.
Source: *NCT*, XII:376; M270; North Carolina Soldier' Home Application (Cumberland County).

Norris, William Indy, Private, Company G
Sugar Loaf
Confederate pension records indicate that he was wounded, "mashed in chest and privates," at Wilmington in February 1864, probably 1865. No further information.
Source: *NCT*, XII:349; M270; NC Confederate Pension (Columbus County).

Nott, William J., Private, Company I
Wise's Forks
Captured at Wise's Forks on March 8, 1865. Confined at Point Lookout, Maryland, and released upon taking the Oath of Allegiance on June 28, 1865.
Source: *NCT*, XII:376; M270; NC Confederate Pension (Cumberland County).

Page, Jesse, Private, Company I
Bentonville
Captured at the battle of Bentonville on March 19, 1865. Confined at Point Lookout, Maryland, and released upon taking the Oath of Allegiance on June 17, 1865.
Source: *NCT*, XII:377; M270; NC Confederate Pension (Harnett County).

▲Pope, Michael S., Private, Company K
Bentonville
According to Surgeon Tanner's "Return of Casualties in Hoke's Div. near Bentonville," Pvt. M. S. Pope, Co. K, was slightly wounded in the right cheek. His pension application indicates wounded at Bentonville on March 19, 1865, and that the right side of his face "exhibits a scar" from the wound. Neither Pope's service records nor *NC Troops* note the wound he received at the battle of Bentonville.
Source: Tanner (BV), 140; *NCT*, XII:388; M270; NC Confederate Pension (Pender County).

▲Porter, Caswell, Private, Company H

Wise's Forks
Wounded at the battle of Wise's Forks on March 8, 1865. According to Surgeon Tanner's "Return of Casualties near Kinston," Pvt. C. Porter, Co. H, 51st NC, was severely wounded in the right foot and reported in Raleigh hospital on March 27, 1865. *NC Troops* incorrectly notes that he was wounded in the right foot at or near Bentonville on or about March 19-21, 1865.
Source: Tanner (WF), 135; *NCT*, XII:362; *WD* (Charlotte), April 4, 1865; M270; NC Confederate Widow's Pension (Columbus County).

▲**Porter, James A.**, Private, Company A
Wise's Forks
Wounded at the battle of Wise's Forks on March 10, 1865. According to Surgeon Tanner's "Return of Casualties near Kinston," Pvt. Jas. A Porter, Co. A, 51st NC, was dangerously wounded in the right shoulder and lung. *NC Troops* does not note his wounding at Wise's Forks. Paroled at Goldsboro on May 6, 1865.
Source: Tanner (WF), 135; *NCT*, XII:285; M270.

Sandy, John A. W., Private, Company I
Cumberland County
Captured in his native Cumberland County on March 13, 1865. Confined at Point Lookout, Maryland, and released upon taking the Oath of Allegiance on June 20, 1865.
Source: *NCT*, XII:378; M270.

♦**Sasser, Matthew G.**, Private, Company H
Wise's Forks (Inconclusive)
NC Troops notes that he was hospitalized at Raleigh on March 16, 1865, with a gunshot wound of the right arm. The location and date are not reported. Captured as a patient in a Raleigh hospital on April 13, 1865. Based on the nature of his wounds and his date of hospitalization, he was probably wounded at the battle of Wise's Forks. Further research is required.
Source: Tanner (BV), 140; *NCT*, XII:363; M270; NC Confederate Widow's Pension (Columbus County).

Sills, Henry Washington, Private, Company K
Sampson County
Captured in his native Sampson County on March 16, 1865. Confined at Hart's Island, New York Harbor, and released upon taking the Oath of Allegiance on June 19, 1865.
Source: *NCT*, XII:389; M270; NC Confederate Pension (Sampson County); North Carolina Soldiers' Home Application (Sampson County).

Sills, William T., Private, Company K
Sampson County
Captured in his native Sampson County on March 16, 1865. Confined at Hart's Island, New York Harbor, and released upon taking the Oath of Allegiance on June 21, 1865.
Source: *NCT*, XII:389; M270; NC Confederate Pension (Sampson County).

Southerland, James, Private, Company C
Kinston (Post Wise Forks)
Captured at or near Kinston on March 20-22, 1865. Confined at Hart's Island, New York Harbor, and released upon taking the Oath of Allegiance on June 18, 1865.
Source: *NCT*, XII:306; M270; NC Confederate Widow's Pension (Cumberland County).

▲**Spivey, John Quincy**, Private, Company F
Wise's Forks
Wounded at the battle of Wise's Forks on March 8, 1865. According to Surgeon Tanner's "Return of Casualties near Kinston," Pvt. Quincy Spivey, Co. F, 51st NC, was slightly wounded in the left shoulder and reported in Raleigh hospital on March 27, 1865. Barbee Wayside Hospital in High Point admitted J. Q.

Spivey, 51st NC, on March 9, 1865, with a gunshot wound. *NC Troops* incorrectly notes that he was wounded in the shoulder at or near Bentonville on or about March 19-21, 1865.
Source: Tanner (WF), 135; Barbee Wayside Registry, no. 5744; *NCT*, XII:339; M270.

Stanley, Alfred C., Private, Company K
Bentonville
Captured at or near Bentonville on or about March 22, 1865. Confined at Hart's Island, New York Harbor, and released upon taking the Oath of Allegiance on June 19, 1865.
Source: *NCT*, XII:389; M270; NC Confederate Pension (Wayne County).

▲Strickland, William T., Private, Company K
Bentonville
Wounded at the battle of Bentonville between March 19-21, 1865. According to Surgeon Tanner's "Return of Casualties in Hoke's Div. near Bentonville," Pvt. W. T. Strickland, Co. K, was slightly wounded in the glut muscle. The March 27, 1865, edition of the *Daily Progress* reported that Pvt. W. G. Stricklin, Co. K, 51st NC, was at the Baptist Church Hospital in Raleigh, wounded in the right hip. *NC Troops* notes that he was wounded in the right hip at the battle of Bentonville on March 20, 1865.
Source: Tanner (BV), 140; *DP* (Raleigh), March 27, 1865; *WD* (Charlotte), April 4, 1865; *NCT*, XII:390; M270.

▲Sullivan, Andrew McI., 2nd Lieutenant, Company C
Wise's Forks
Wounded at the battle of Wise's Forks on March 10, 1865. According to Surgeon Tanner's "Return of Casualties near Kinston," Lt. A. M. Sullivan, Co. C, 51st NC, was severely wounded in the right thigh. *NC Troops* notes that he was wounded at Kinston in March 1865.
Source: Tanner (WF), 135; *NCT*, XII:299; M270.

Taylor, William James, Private, Company I
Cumberland County
Captured in Cumberland County on March 12, 1865. Confined at Hart's Island, New York Harbor, and released upon taking the Oath of Allegiance on June 19, 1865.
Source: *NCT*, XII:379; M270; NC Confederate Widow's Pension (Harnett County).

▲Thigpen, Thomas, Private, Company G
Bentonville
Wounded at the battle of Bentonville between March 19-21, 1865. According to Surgeon Tanner's "Return of Casualties in Hoke's Div. near Bentonville," Pvt. Thos. Thigpen, Co. G, was slightly wounded in the right arm. The March 27, 1865, edition of the *Daily Progress* reported erred in reporting Pvt. Thos. Thigpen was a member of Co. D, 17th NC. Present at the Baptist Church Hospital in Raleigh with a wound to his arm. Neither Thigpen's service records nor *NC Troops* note the wound he received at the battle of Bentonville. His pension application notes two previous wounds he suffered in his legs while serving in Virginia but not the wound in his arm.
Source: Tanner (BV), 140; *DP* (Raleigh), March 27, 1865; *NCT*, XII:352; M270; NC Confederate Pension (Duplin County).

▲Townsend, Jackson, Private, Company E
Wise's Forks
Wounded at the battle of Wise's Forks on March 10, 1865. According to Surgeon Tanner's "Return of Casualties near Kinston," Pvt. Jack Townsend, Co. E, 51st NC, was severely wounded in the right buttock. No further records. *NC Troops* does not note that he was wounded at Wise's Forks.
Source: Tanner (WF), 135; *NCT*, XII:330; M270; NC Confederate Widow's Pension (Cleveland County).

▲Turner, John W., Private, Company A
Bentonville
Wounded at the battle of Bentonville between March 19-21, 1865. According to Surgeon Tanner's "Return of Casualties in Hoke's Div. near Bentonville," Pvt. Jno. Turner, Co. A, was severely wounded in the

abdomen. Private John Turner of Co. A is probably the same soldier as Pvt. Jno. Turner. Neither Turner's service records nor *NC Troops* note the wound he received at the battle of Bentonville.
Source: Tanner (BV), 140; *NCT*, XII:286; M270.

Wade, Clark, Private, Company C
Goldsboro
Captured at or near Goldsboro on March 22, 1865. Provost Marshall's records include the additional "In the Field" remark describing where he was captured. Wade may have been captured during the Confederate withdrawal from Bentonville. Confined at Hart's Island, New York Harbor, and released upon taking the Oath of Allegiance on June 18, 1865.
Source: *NCT*, XII:307; M270.

Watson, Benjamin, Private, Company B
Kinston
Captured at Kinston on March 19, 1865. Based on the date of capture, he may have deserted. No further records.
Source: *NCT*, XII:298; M270.

West, James, Private, Company D
Fayetteville
U.S. Army records indicate that the Cumberland County native deserted on March 11, 1865. Sent to Fort Monroe, Virginia, and later transferred to Washington, D.C. No further records.
Source: *NCT*, XII:319; M270.

White, Stephen, Private, Company H
Bentonville
Confederate pension application indicates wounded at Bentonville in the head and right leg. No further information.
Source: Tanner (BV), 140; *NCT*, XII:366; M270; NC Confederate Pension (Columbus County).

Williford, Sir William T., Private, Company K
Sampson County
Captured in his native Sampson County on March 16, 1865. Confined at Hart's Island, New York Harbor, and released upon taking the Oath of Allegiance on June 21, 1865.
Source: *NCT*, XII:392; M270.

58th Regiment North Carolina Troops

Allred, John L., Sergeant, Company F
Orangeburg (SC)
Captured at Orangeburg, South Carolina on February 12, 1865. Confined at Hart's Island, New York Harbor, and released upon taking the Oath of Allegiance on June 18, 1865.
Source: *NCT*, XIV:344; M270.

Anderson, John Marcus, Private, Company E
Bentonville
The regimental casualty list indicates he was slightly wounded in the knee on March 19, 1865. Anderson's service records do not note hospitalization for the wound that he received at Bentonville.
Source: *DC* (Raleigh), March 29, 1865; *NCT*, XIV:325; M270; NC Confederate Pension (Caldwell County).

▲**Baird, David Franklin**, 2nd Lieutenant, Company D
Bentonville
The regimental casualty list indicates Lt. D. F. Baird of Co. D was dangerously wounded in the breast on March 19, 1865. His service records and *NC Troops* incorrectly note that Baird was hospitalized at GH No. 3 in Greensboro on an unspecified date in March 1865. In National Archives Confederate Record Group 109, General Hospital No. 3's location is erroneously identified as Greensboro. High Point is the correct location. Confederate authorities began relocating GH No. 3 from Goldsboro to High Point on March 11, 1865, as part of the town's evacuation. The hospital resumed operations in High Point on or about March 19, 1865. The No. 3 Patient Registry lists Lt. D. F. Baird, 58th NC, entry no. 2357, was admitted for unspecified reasons between March 21-31, 1865. According to Baird's Confederate pension, he was wounded in the left breast.
Source: *DC* (Raleigh), March 29, 1865; *NCT*, XIV:312; M270; Sokolosky, *NC Confederate Hospitals, vol. 2*; RG109, 6/291:47; NC Confederate Pension (Watauga County).

Buchanan, Abram J., Private, Company B
Columbia (SC)
Deserted near Columbia, South Carolina, on February 19, 1865. Released at Washington, D.C., upon taking the Oath of Allegiance on April 5, 1865.
Source: *NCT*, XIV:293; M270.

Caraway, Elisha, Private, Company A
Orangeburg (SC)
Captured at Orangeburg, South Carolina on February 12, 1865. Confined at Hart's Island, New York Harbor, and released upon taking the Oath of Allegiance on June 19, 1865.
Source: *NCT*, XIV:278; M270.

Coffey, Irwin, Private, Company H
Bentonville
The regimental casualty list indicates Pvt. I. Coffey was slightly wounded in the hand on March 19, 1865. Private Irwin Coffey of Co. H is the same soldier as Pvt. I. Coffey. His service records do not note hospitalization for the wound that he received at Bentonville. *NC Troops* notes that he was wounded at Bentonville on March 19, 1865.
Source: *DC* (Raleigh), March 29, 1865; *NCT*, XIV:377; M270.

▲**Coffey, William C.**, Private, Company E
Bentonville
The regimental casualty list indicates Pvt. W. C. Coffey was slightly wounded in the hand on March 19, 1865. His service records and *NC Troops* incorrectly note that Brown was hospitalized at GH No. 3 in Greensboro on an unspecified date in March 1865. In National Archives Confederate Record Group 109, General Hospital No. 3's location is erroneously identified as Greensboro. High Point is the correct location.

Confederate authorities began relocating GH No. 3 from Goldsboro to High Point on March 11, 1865, as part of the town's evacuation. The hospital resumed operations in High Point on or about March 19, 1865. The No. 3 Patient Registry lists Pvt. W. C. Coffey of Co. E, 58th NC, entry no. 2368, admitted for unspecified reasons between March 21-31, 1865. His Confederate pension indicates that he was wounded in the "left finger & right thumb."
Source: *DC* (Raleigh), March 29, 1865; *NCT*, XIV:329; M270; Sokolosky, *NC Confederate Hospitals, vol. 2*; RG109, 6/291:47; NC Confederate Pension (Watauga County).

▲Coffey, William Columbus, 2nd Lieutenant, Company E
Bentonville
The regimental casualty list indicates Lt. W. C. Coffey was slightly wounded in the breast (contusion from a shell) on March 19, 1865. Present at the Officer's Hospital (Haywood House) in Raleigh on March 24, 1865. His service records do not note his hospitalization for the wound he received at Bentonville.
Source: *DC* (Raleigh), March 29, 1865; *NCS* (Raleigh), March 24, 1865; *DP* (Raleigh), March 27, 1865; *WD* (Charlotte), April 4, 1865; *NCT*, XIV:276, 324; M270.

Crawley, Albert E., Sergeant, Company F
Orangeburg (SC)
Captured at Orangeburg, South Carolina on February 12, 1865. Confined at Hart's Island, New York Harbor, and released upon taking the Oath of Allegiance on June 18, 1865. His pension application indicates his first name is Alberto.
Source: *NCT*, XIV:347; M270; NC Confederate Pension (McDowell County).

Crisp, William L., Corporal, Company H
Edisto River (SC)
Captured at the Edisto River, South Carolina, February 10, 1865. Confined at Point Lookout, Maryland, and released upon taking the Oath of Allegiance on June 26, 1865.
Source: *NCT*, XIV:378; M270; NC Confederate Pension (McDowell County).

▲Faircloth, Michael M., Private, Company F
Bentonville
The regimental casualty list indicates Pvt. M. M. Faircloth of Co. L was seriously wounded in the leg on March 19, 1865. However, *NC Troops* indicates that Pvt. Michael M. Faircloth served in Co. F at the time of the battle, having transferred to the unit in August 1864. His service records and *NC Troops* incorrectly note that Faircloth was hospitalized at GH No. 3 in Greensboro on an unspecified date in March 1865. In National Archives Confederate Record Group 109, General Hospital No. 3's location is erroneously identified as Greensboro. High Point is the correct location. Confederate authorities began relocating GH No. 3 from Goldsboro to High Point on March 11, 1865, as part of the town's evacuation. High Point is the correct location. The No. 3 Patient Registry lists Pvt. W. M. Faircloth of Co. L, 58th NC, entry no. 2580, admitted for unspecified reasons between March 21-31, 1865. Private Michael M. Faircloth is the same soldier as Pvt. W. M. Faircloth. His Confederate pension application indicates he suffered a gunshot wound to the outside of his right leg.
Source: *DC* (Raleigh), March 29, 1865; M270; *NCT*, XIV:348; RG109, 6/291:51; NC Confederate Pension (Ashe County).

Ford, Thomas, Private, Company B
Edisto River (SC)
Captured at the Edisto River, South Carolina, on February 10, 1865. Confined at Point Lookout, Maryland, and released upon taking the Oath of Allegiance on May 15, 1865.
Source: *NCT*, XIV:295; M270.

Fox, Elisha Calvin, Private, Company H
Bentonville
The regimental casualty list indicates Pvt. E. C. Fox was slightly wounded in the hand on March 19, 1865. His service records do not note hospitalization for the wound that he received at Bentonville. Survived the

war. Confederate pension application indicates he was wounded in the right hand, resulting in the loss of his middle finger, at Bentonville on or about March 19, 1865.
Source: *DC* (Raleigh), March 29, 1865; *NCT*, XIV:379; NC Confederate Pension (McDowell County).

Gaddy, Samuel H., Private, Company A
Bentonville
The regimental casualty list indicates Pvt. S. Gaddey was slightly wounded in the head on March 19, 1865. The correct spelling of his surname is Gaddy. His service records do not note hospitalization for the wound that he received at Bentonville. No further records.
Source: *DC* (Raleigh), March 29, 1865; *NCT*, XIV:281; M270.

Gibson, Odom, Private, Company F
Schilling's Bridge (SC)
Captured at Schilling's Bridge, South Carolina, on February 12, 1865. Confined at Hart's Island, New York Harbor, and released upon taking the Oath of Allegiance on June 19, 1865. His Confederate pension states that he was wounded by being "struck in the rim of the belly with a mussel of a gun . . . between Goldsboro and Newbern" in February 1865. It is probable that the incident occurred while being transported to New Bern with other prisoners, which makes March – April 1865 the more appropriate period.
Source: *NCT*, XIV:349; M270; NC Confederate Pension (McDowell County).

Glenn, Simeon, Private, Company D
Bentonville
The regimental casualty list indicates Pvt. S. Glenn was mortally in the head on March 19, 1865, and had "since died." His place and date of his death are unknown. His service records do not note hospitalization for the wound that he received at Bentonville. His widow's pension application indicates that he was killed at Bentonville in April 1865. He may have lingered and died in April.
Source: *DC* (Raleigh), March 29, 1865; *NCT*, XIV:314; M270; NC Confederate Widow Pension (Haywood County).

Green, Augustus F., Private, Company E
Bentonville
The regimental casualty list indicates Pvt. A. F. Green was killed on March 19, 1865. No further records.
Source: *DC* (Raleigh), March 29, 1865; *NCT*, XIV:332.

Green, Fergerson, Private, Company G
Orangeburg (SC)
Captured at Orangeburg, South Carolina on February 12, 1865. Confined at Hart's Island, New York Harbor, and released upon taking the Oath of Allegiance on June 19, 1865.
Source: *NCT*, XIV:363; M270.

Hagaman, Isaac, Jr., Private, Company I
Orangeburg (SC)
Captured at Orangeburg, South Carolina on February 12, 1865. Confined at Hart's Island, New York Harbor, and released upon taking the Oath of Allegiance on June 18, 1865.
Source: *NCT*, XIV:390; M270.

Haney, Daniel W., Private, Company F
Schilling's Bridge (SC)
Captured at Schilling's Bridge, South Carolina, on February 12, 1865. Confined at Hart's Island, New York Harbor, and released upon taking the Oath of Allegiance on June 18, 1865.
Source: *NCT*, XIV:349; M270; NC Confederate Pension (McDowell County).

Harrison, B. Calvin, Private, Company E
Orangeburg (SC)
Captured at Orangeburg, South Carolina on February 12, 1865. Confined at Hart's Island, New York Harbor, and released upon taking the Oath of Allegiance on June 18, 1865.

Source: *NCT*, XIV:333; M270; NC Confederate Pension (Caldwell County).

▲Hurley, Harvey, Private, Company F
Bentonville
The regimental casualty list indicates Pvt. H. Hurley of Co. L was slightly wounded in the thigh on March 19, 1865. His service records and *NC Troops* incorrectly note that he was admitted to GH No. 3 in Greensboro in March 1865 for unspecified reasons. In National Archives Confederate Record Group 109, General Hospital No. 3's location is erroneously identified as Greensboro. Based on his wounding at Bentonville, High Point is the correct location. Confederate authorities began relocating GH No. 3 from Goldsboro to High Point on March 11, 1865, as part of the town's evacuation. The hospital resumed operations in High Point on or about March 19, 1865. The GH No. 3 Patient Registry lists Pvt. Harvey Hurley of Co. L, 58th NC, entry no. 2558, admitted between March 21-31, 1865, for unspecified reasons. He remained hospitalized at the High Point hospital until he was paroled as a patient on May 1, 1865.
Source: *DC* (Raleigh), March 29, 1865; *NCT*, XIV:350; M270; Sokolosky, *NC Confederate Hospitals, vol. 2*; RG109, 6/291:51; M1761.

▲Hurley, Thomas, Private, Company F
Bentonville
The regimental casualty list indicates Pvt. T. Hurley of Co. L was seriously wounded in the knee on March 19, 1865. His service records and *NC Troops* incorrectly note that he was admitted to GH No. 3 in Greensboro in March 1865 for unspecified reasons. In National Archives Confederate Record Group 109, General Hospital No. 3's location is erroneously identified as Greensboro. Based on his wounding at Bentonville, High Point is the correct location. Confederate authorities began relocating GH No. 3 from Goldsboro to High Point on March 11, 1865, as part of the town's evacuation. The hospital resumed operations in High Point on or about March 19, 1865. The No. 3 Patient Registry lists a Pvt. Thomas Hurley of Co. F, 38th NC, entry no. 2564, admitted between March 21-31, 1865, for unspecified reasons. The unit identification was incorrectly written and should read 58th NC. Hurley remained at the High Point hospital until paroled as a patient on May 1, 1865. Unable to leave the hospital, on an undetermined date following his parole, he died and was buried in the Confederate section of Oakwood Cemetery in High Point, North Carolina. The surname Harlen is misidentified on his headstone.
Source: *DC* (Raleigh), March 29, 1865; *NCT*, XIV:350; M270; Sokolosky, *NC Confederate Hospitals, vol. 2*; RG109, 6/291:51; M1761; Purser, *AIANCT*, II:128.

Jarrett, Killian Mills, Private, Company F
Orangeburg (SC)
Captured at Orangeburg, South Carolina on February 12, 1865. Confined at Hart's Island, New York Harbor, and released upon taking the Oath of Allegiance on June 19, 1865.
Source: *NCT*, XIV:350; M270.

Kayler, George, Private, Company F
Schilling's Bridge (SC)
Captured at Schilling's Bridge, South Carolina, on February 12, 1865. Confined at Hart's Island, New York Harbor, and released upon taking the Oath of Allegiance on June 19, 1865.
Source: *NCT*, XIV:351; M270.

Kenney, Simpson, Private, Company E
Orangeburg (SC)
Captured at Orangeburg, South Carolina on February 14, 1865. Confined at Hart's Island, New York Harbor, where he died of pneumonia on April 20, 1865.
Source: *NCT*, XIV:334; M270.

Ledford, William, Private, Company B
Orangeburg (SC)
Captured at Orangeburg, South Carolina on February 14, 1865. Confined at Hart's Island, New York Harbor, where he died of chronic diarrhea on May 26, 1865.

Source: *NCT*, XIV:297; M270.

Mangum, Richard G., Private, Company F
Orangeburg (SC)
Captured at Orangeburg, South Carolina on February 12, 1865. Confined at Hart's Island, New York Harbor, and released upon taking the Oath of Allegiance on June 19, 1865.
Source: *NCT*, XIV:352; M270.

Mathis, Martin, Private, Company F
Orangeburg (SC)
Captured at Orangeburg, South Carolina on February 12, 1865. Confined at Hart's Island, New York Harbor, and released upon taking the Oath of Allegiance on June 18, 1865.
Source: *NCT*, XIV:352; M270.

McCall, Jacob M., Private, Company H
Bentonville
The regimental casualty list indicates Pvt. J. M. McCall of Co. H was slightly wounded in the breast on March 19, 1865. His service records do not note hospitalization for the wound that he received at Bentonville. Survived the war.
Source: *DC* (Raleigh), March 29, 1865; *NCT*, XIV:381; M270.

McKinney, James, Private, Company K
Bentonville
The regimental casualty list indicates Pvt. J. McKinney of Co. K was slightly wounded in the head on March 19, 1865. His service records do not note hospitalization for the wound that he received at Bentonville. Survived the war. *NC Troops* notes that he was wounded at Bentonville on March 19, 1865.
Source: *DC* (Raleigh), March 29, 1865; *NCT*, XIV:402; M270.

Marlin, I. J., Sergeant, Company F
Bentonville
The regimental casualty list indicates Sgt. J. J. Marler of Co. F was slightly wounded in the arm on March 19, 1865. Sergeant I. J. Marlin is probably the same soldier as Sgt. J. J. Marler. *NC Troops Roster* indicates the correct spelling of the surname is Marlin. [Marlin's service records are listed under the surname "Mallen," and it does not indicate hospitalization for the wound that he received at Bentonville.]
Source: *DC* (Raleigh), March 29, 1865; *NCT*, XIV:352; M270.

Miller, Mack, Private, Company A
Bentonville
The regimental casualty list indicates Pvt. M. Miller was slightly wounded in the arm on March 19, 1865. Additionally, both the *Daily Progress* and *NC Standard* incorrectly listed a Pvt. M. Miller of Co. A, 1st Battalion NC Heavy Artillery, as having been wounded in the "left arm" on March 19, 1865, at Bentonville, and present in Raleigh's Baptist Church Hospital. Because no M. Miller is listed on the 1st Battalion rolls, this individual is probably the same soldier as Pvt. Mack Miller of the 58th NC. His service records do not note hospitalization for the wound that he received at Bentonville.
Source: *DC* (Raleigh), March 29, 1865; *DP* (Raleigh), March 27, 1865; *NCS* (Raleigh), March 24, 1865; *NCT*, XIV:285; M270.

Moffitt, John W. L., Corporal, Company F
Columbia (SC)
Captured at Columbia, South Carolina on February 17, 1865. Confined at Hart's Island, New York Harbor, and released upon taking the Oath of Allegiance on June 18, 1865.
Source: *NCT*, XIV:353; M270.

Morgan, Jethro C., Private, Company F
Orangeburg (SC)

Captured at Orangeburg, South Carolina on February 12, 1865. Confined at Hart's Island, New York Harbor, and released upon taking the Oath of Allegiance on June 18, 1865.
Source: *NCT*, XIV:353; M270; NC Confederate Pension (McDowell County).

Murdock, J. C., Private, Company F
Edisto River (SC)
Captured at the Edisto River, South Carolina, on February 12, 1865. Confined at Hart's Island, New York Harbor, where he died of chronic diarrhea on May 31, 1865.
Source: *NCT*, XIV:354; M270.

▲Pearey, Aaron, Private, Company E
Bentonville
The regimental casualty list indicates Pvt. A. Pearce was slightly wounded in the foot on March 19, 1865. Private Aaron Pearey of Co. E is probably the same soldier as Pvt. A. Pearce. His service records and *NC Troops* incorrectly note that he was admitted to GH No. 3 in Greensboro in March 1865 for unspecified reasons. In National Archives Confederate Record Group 109, General Hospital No. 3's location is erroneously identified as Greensboro. Based on his wounding at Bentonville, High Point is the correct location. Confederate authorities began relocating GH No. 3 from Goldsboro to High Point on March 11, 1865, as part of the town's evacuation. The hospital resumed operations in High Point on or about March 19, 1865. The No. 3 Patient Registry lists a Pvt. A. Piercy of Co. E, 58th NC, entry no. 2333, admitted between March 21-31, 1865, for unspecified reasons. Aaron Pearey is the same soldier as A. Piercy. No further records.
Source: *DC* (Raleigh), March 29, 1865; *NCT*, XIV:337; M270; Sokolosky, *NC Confederate Hospitals*, vol. 2; RG109, 6/291:46.

Presnell, Benjamin L., Corporal, Company D
Bentonville
The regimental casualty list indicates Corp. B. L. Presnell was mortally wounded in the abdomen on March 19, 1865. The place and date of death are unknown. His service records do not note hospitalization for the wound that he received at Bentonville.
Source: *DC* (Raleigh), March 29, 1865; *NCT*, XIV:320; M270.

Shehan, Pinkney, Private, Company F
Orangeburg (SC)
Captured at Orangeburg, South Carolina on February 12, 1865. Confined at Hart's Island, New York Harbor, and released upon taking the Oath of Allegiance on June 21, 1865.
Source: *NCT*, XIV:355; M270.

Sherrill, Isaac I., Private, Company E
Bentonville
The regimental casualty list indicates Pvt. I. Sherrell was missing on March 19, 1865. Private Isaac I. Sherrill is the same soldier as Pvt. I. Sherrell. His service records indicate that he was captured at Bentonville on March 22, 1865. Confined at Hart's Island, New York Harbor, where he was released upon taking the Oath of Allegiance on June 19, 1865.
Source: *DC* (Raleigh), March 29, 1865; *NCT*, XIV:339; M270.

▲Shuffler, Jacob C., Private, Company E
Bentonville
The regimental casualty list indicates Pvt. J. C. Shuffler was seriously wounded in the thigh on March 19, 1865. His service records and *NC Troops* incorrectly note that he was admitted to GH No. 3 in Greensboro in March 1865 for unspecified reasons. In National Archives Confederate Record Group 109, General Hospital No. 3's location is erroneously identified as Greensboro. Based on his wounding at Bentonville, High Point is the correct location. Confederate authorities began relocating GH No. 3 from Goldsboro to High Point on March 11, 1865, as part of the town's evacuation. The hospital resumed operations in High Point on or about March 19, 1865. The No. 3 Patient Registry lists a Pvt. J. C. Shuffler, Co. E, 58th NC, entry

no. 2350, admitted between March 21-31, 1865, for unspecified reasons. He was later paroled at Morganton, NC, on May 15, 1865.
Source: *DC* (Raleigh), March 29, 1865; *NCT,* XIV:339; Sokolosky, *NC Confederate Hospitals, vol. 2*; RG109, 6/291:47; M270.

▲Smith, Nelson, Private, Company I
Bentonville
The regimental casualty list indicates Pvt. N. Smith of Co. E was slightly wounded in the foot on March 19, 1865. Private Nelson Smith of Co. I may have been the same soldier as Pvt. N. Smith. His service records do not note hospitalization for the wound that he received at Bentonville. The GH No. 3 (High Point) Patient Registry lists a Pvt. A. Smith, Co. E, 58th NC, entry no. 2349, admitted for unspecified reasons between March 21 and April 7, 1865. There is no A. Smith on the Co. E rolls. Further research is required.
Source: *DC* (Raleigh), March 29, 1865; *NCT,* XIV:394; M270; RG109, 6/291:47.

Sparks, George, Private, Company F
Lynch's Creek (SC)
Captured at Lynch's Creek, South Carolina, on February 12, 1865. Confined at Hart's Island, New York Harbor, and released upon taking the Oath of Allegiance on June 18, 1865.
Source: *NCT,* XIV:356; M270.

Sparks, William M., Sergeant, Company H
Bentonville (not wounded or killed)
He served as the color bearer of the 58th NC at the battle of Bentonville, where he was recognized for "distinguished gallantry."
Source: *NCT,* XIV:384; M270.

Spivey, Jesse, Sergeant, Company F
Bentonville
The regimental casualty list indicates Sgt. J. Spivey of Co. L was mortally wounded in the knee on March 19, 1865, and had "since died." The place and date of his death are unknown. Spivey's service records do not note hospitalization for the wound that he received at Bentonville.
Source: *DC* (Raleigh), March 29, 1865; *NCT,* XIV:356, 415; M270; Purser, II:128.

Stafford, William Henry, Private, Company H
Bentonville
The regimental casualty list indicates Pvt. H. Stafford of Co. H was slightly wounded in the arm on March 19, 1865. Private William Henry Stafford of Co. H is the same soldier as Pvt. H. Stafford. His service records do not note hospitalization for the wound that he received at Bentonville. *NC Troops* notes his wounding at Bentonville on March 19, 1865.
Source: *DC* (Raleigh), March 29, 1865; *NCT,* XIV:385; M270.

Strickland, Moore, Private, Company D
Bentonville
The regimental casualty list indicates Pvt. M. Strickland of Co. D was slightly wounded in the shoulder on March 19, 1865. His Tennessee Confederate pension indicates that he was wounded in the "right side and/or shoulder by a shell." Strickland's service records do not note hospitalization for the wound that he received at Bentonville. Confederate pension records indicate that he was "disabled by an exploding shell at [or] near Goldsboro."
Source: *DC* (Raleigh), March 29, 1865; *NCT,* XIV:321; M270; Tennessee Confederate Pension (Washington County).

Turbyfield, James Pickney, Private, Company B
Bentonville
The regimental casualty list indicates Pvt. J. B. Turbeyfill was slightly wounded in the foot on March 19, 1865. Pvt. James Pickney Turbyfield of Co. B is the same soldier as Pvt. J. B. Turbeyfill. He later applied for

a pension in both North Carolina and Tennessee using the surname of Turbeyfill. Turbyfield's service records do not note hospitalization for the wound that he received at Bentonville.
Source: *DC* (Raleigh), March 29, 1865; *NCT*, XIV:300; M270; NC Confederate Pension (Mitchell County).

Turnmire, John N., Private, Company H
Bentonville
The regimental casualty list indicates Pvt. J. Turnmire of Co. H was slightly wounded in the groin on March 19, 1865. Private John N. Turnmire is probably the same soldier as Pvt. J. Turnmire. His service records do not note hospitalization for the wound that he received at Bentonville.
Source: *DC* (Raleigh), March 29, 1865; *NCT*, XIV:385; M270.

White, A. J., Private, Company F
Orangeburg (SC)
Captured at Orangeburg, South Carolina on February 12, 1865. Confined at Hart's Island, New York Harbor, and released upon taking the Oath of Allegiance on June 19, 1865.
Source: *NCT*, XIV:357; M270.

♦Wilson, John W., Private, Company C
(Inconclusive)
His Confederate pension indicates that he was wounded at Milledgeville, Georgia, on February 1, 1865. No U.S. Army forces were present in that region of Georgia in early 1865. Further research is required.
Source: *NCT*, XIV:310; M270; NC Confederate Pension (Yancy County).

60th Regiment North Carolina Troops

Alexander, Joseph B., ____, (Company Unknown)
Bentonville
Slightly wounded at the battle of Bentonville between March 19-21, 1865.
Source: *NCT*, XIV:591; Clarks, *Histories*, III:496; M270.

Cauble, Adam L., Private, Company K
Bentonville
NC Troops notes that he was wounded in the left hip at Bentonville on March 19, 1865. Present in Baptist Church Hospital in Raleigh, wounded in the right arm. His service records do not note his wounding or hospitalization in March 1865. His Confederate pension records note that he was "struck by a ball in his left hip, "immediately under the hip joint," during a charge at Bentonville. Paroled at Asheville on May 11, 1865.
Source: *NCS* (Raleigh), March 24, 1865; *DP* (Raleigh), March 27, 1865; *WD* (Charlotte), April 4, 1865; *NCT*, XIV:584; M270; NC Confederate Pension (Buncombe County).

Reno, John Ed., Corporal, Company A
Bentonville
Clark's *Histories* states that Ed Reno was slightly wounded at the battle of Bentonville on March 19-21, 1865. There is only one soldier in the unit with Reno as his surname: John Ed. Reno is the soldier noted in the regimental history as Ed Reno. There are no further records.
Source: *NCS* (Raleigh), March 24, 1865; *NCT*, XIV:512; Clarks, *Histories*, III:496; M270.

Roberts, Melville B., Sergeant, Company C
Bentonville
NC Troops notes that he was wounded in the right thigh at Bentonville on March 19, 1865. His Confederate pension records indicate that he suffered a gunshot wound in the "right leg above the knee."
Source: *NCS* (Raleigh), March 24, 1865; *NCT*, XIV:529; M270; NC Confederate Pension (Buncombe County).

Robeson, M. A., Private, Company K
Bentonville
NC Troops notes that he was wounded in the left hand at Bentonville between March 19-21, 1865. His Confederate pension records indicate his left index finger was shot off at the "first joint" and lost his fourth finger at the "knuckle joint."
Source: *NCS* (Raleigh), March 24, 1865; *NCT*, XIV:589; M270; Tennessee Confederate Pension (Greene County).

Wilson, James E., Private, Company C
Bentonville
Captured at Bentonville on March 22, 1865. Confined at Hart's Island, New York Harbor, and released upon taking the Oath of Allegiance on June 19, 1865.
Source: *NCS* (Raleigh), March 24, 1865; *NCT*, XIV:530; M270; NC Confederate Pension (Caldwell County).

Colonel William S. Devane
Commander, 61st Regiment NC Troops
Acting Commander of Clingman's Brigade, Hoke's Division
Wounded in the neck at Bentonville on March 21, 1865

(Histories of Several Regiments and Battalions from North Carolina in the Great War)

61st Regiment North Carolina Troops

▲**Biggs, John Dawson, Sr.**, Captain, Company H
Bentonville
Wounded at the battle of Bentonville between March 19-21, 1865. According to Surgeon Tanner's "Return of Casualties in Hoke's Div. near Bentonville," Capt. J. D. Biggs, Company H, was slightly wounded in the right thigh. Present in Raleigh's Wayside Hospital (Ladies' Wayside) on March 29, 1865, suffering from a wound in his right leg. His service records and *NC Troops* incorrectly note that he was admitted to GH No. 3 in Greensboro in April 1865 for unspecified reasons. In National Archives Confederate Record Group 109, General Hospital No. 3's location is erroneously identified as Greensboro. Based on his wounding at Bentonville, High Point is the correct location. Confederate authorities began relocating GH No. 3 from Goldsboro to High Point on March 11, 1865, as part of the town's evacuation. The hospital resumed operations in High Point on or about March 19, 1865. Survived the war.
Source: Tanner (BV), 140; *NCS* (Raleigh), March 29, 1865; *WD* (Charlotte), April 4, 1865; *NCT*, XIV:727; Sokolosky, *NC Confederate Hospitals, vol. 2*; RG109, 6/291:53; M270.

▲**Blevens, Thomas J.**, Private, Company I
Bentonville
Wounded at the battle of Bentonville between March 19-21, 1865. According to Surgeon Tanner's "Return of Casualties in Hoke's Div. near Bentonville," Pvt. T. Blevins, Company I, was slightly wounded in the right shoulder. Private Thomas J. Blevens, Company I, is the same soldier as Pvt. T. Blevins. Neither his service records nor *NC Troops* note his wounding in March 1865.
Source: Tanner (BV),140; *NCT*, XIV:740; M270.

Blevins, Isom, Private, Company I
Wise's Forks
Captured near Kinston on March 10-11, 1865. Confined at Point Lookout, Maryland, and released upon taking the Oath of Allegiance on May 15, 1865.
Source: *NCT*, XIV:740; M270.

Blount, Sherman J., Private, Company A
Bentonville
Mortally wounded at the battle of Bentonville between March 19-21, 1865. According to Surgeon Tanner's "Return of Casualties in Hoke's Div. near Bentonville," Sgt. Maj. S. Blunt, Field & Staff, was dangerously wounded in the head, which proved mortal. Sherman J. Blount is the same soldier Tanner listed as S. Blunt. *NC Troops* notes that he was killed at Bentonville. The name T. J. Blount, Co. A, 61st NC, appears on a monument at Bentonville Battlefield State Historic Site, leading some to assume he is buried in the Confederate mass grave located there. Despite the discrepancy regarding rank, Sherman J. Blount is probably the same soldier, T. J. Blount, identified on the monument. There is a marker for Sherman J. Blount in the Blount Cemetery in Clinton, North Carolina. The marker may be just a memorial for Blount, not his burial site.
Source: Tanner (BV), 140; *NCT*, XIV:655; M270.

Brackens, Adam, Private, Company I
Wise's Forks
NC Troops notes that he was wounded in the abdomen, right leg, and right thigh at Kinston on or about March 10, 1865. Admitted to GH No. 13 (Pettigrew) in Raleigh on March 11, 1865, with a gunshot wound to the right leg and thigh. Brackens died there of wounds on March 12, 1865, and is buried in Oakwood Cemetery in Raliegh, North Carolina.
Source: *NCT*, XIV:740; *NCS* (Raleigh), March 29, 1865; *WD* (Charlotte), April 4, 1865; M270.

Braddy, William B., Private, Company B
Wise's Forks

Captured near Kinston on March 10, 1865. Confined at Point Lookout, Maryland, where he died of acute dysentery on or about May 12, 1865.
Source: *NCT,* XIV:663; M270; NC Confederate Pension (Beaufort County).

Carmack, Thomas, Private, Company C
Kinston (Post Wise's Forks)
Captured at Kinston on March 19, 1865. Released on an unspecified date.
Source: *NCT,* XIV:670; M270; NC Confederate Pension (Craven County).

▲**Carroll, Francis Marion**, 3rd Lieutenant, Company A
Bentonville
Wounded at the battle of Bentonville between March 19-21, 1865. According to Surgeon Tanner's "Return of Casualties in Hoke's Div. near Bentonville," Lt. F. M. Carroll, Company A, was slightly wounded in the head. Present in Officer's Hospital (Haywood House) in Raleigh on March 24, 1865. His Confederate pension records indicate that he was wounded at Bentonville in the head.
Source: Tanner, 140; *NCS* (Raleigh), March 24, 1865; *DP* (Raleigh), March 27, 1865; *WD* (Charlotte), April 4, 1865; *NCT,* XIV:654; M270; NC Confederate Pension (Sampson County).

Creech, Benjamin P., Private, Company E
Wise's Forks
Captured near Kinston on March 10, 1865. Confined at Point Lookout, Maryland, and released upon taking the Oath of Allegiance on June 26, 1865.
Source: *NCT,* XIV:695; M270.

Devane, William Stewart, Colonel, Field & Staff
Bentonville
Wounded at the battle of Bentonville between March 19-21, 1865. According to Surgeon Tanner's "Return of Casualties in Hoke's Div. near Bentonville," Col. W. S. Devane, Field & Staff, was dangerously wounded in the neck. *NC Troops* noted that he was wounded in the neck on March 21, 1865, while commanding Clingman's Brigade. His service records incorrectly note that he was admitted to GH No. 3 in Greensboro in April 1865 for unspecified reasons. In National Archives Confederate Record Group 109, General Hospital No. 3's location is erroneously identified as Greensboro. Based on his wounding at Bentonville, High Point is the correct location. Confederate authorities began relocating GH No. 3 from Goldsboro to High Point on March 11, 1865, as part of the town's evacuation. The hospital resumed operations in High Point on or about March 19, 1865. The GH No. 3 (High Point) Patient Registry lists a Col. W. S. Devane, no entry number listed, as having been admitted on or after April 1, 1865, for unspecified reasons. His service records indicate he was later hospitalized at General Hospital No. 10 in Salisbury, where he was paroled as a patient on May 2, 1865.
Source: Tanner (BV), 140; *NCT,* XIV:651; Sokolosky, *NC Confederate Hospitals, vol. 2*; RG109, 6/291:53; M270.

Edwards, Granville Billing, Private, Company I
Wise's Forks
NC Troops notes that he was wounded in the left arm (fracture) and captured at Kinston on March 10, 1865. Admitted to U.S. Army Foster GH in New Bern on March 15, where he died of wounds on April 4, 1865.
Source: *NCT,* XIV:743; M270; RG 94, Foster General Hospital Registry, 99.

Estep, William, Private, Company I
Wise's Forks
Captured at Kinston on March 10, 1865. Confined at Point Lookout, Maryland, where he died of acute dysentery on May 15, 1865.
Source: *NCT,* XIV:743; M270.

Harper, Bright, Private, Company E
Wise's Forks

Captured near Kinston on March 8, 1865. Confined at Point Lookout, Maryland, and released upon taking the Oath of Allegiance on June 13, 1865.
Source: *NCT*, XIV:697; M270; GA Confederate Widow's Pension (Houston County).

Howard, Willie J., Private, Company F
Wise's Forks
Captured near Kinston on March 10, 1865. Confined at Point Lookout, Maryland, where he died of acute dysentery on June 27, 1865.
Source: *NCT*, XIV:709; M270.

Littleton, Dexter B., Private, Company E
Wise's Forks
NC Troops notes that he was wounded in the neck at Kinston on or about March 10, 1865. Admitted to GH No. 13 (Pettigrew) in Raleigh on March 10, 1865, with a gunshot wound to the neck. He was later admitted to Charlotte's GH No. 11 on April 27, 1865. Transferred to an unidentified hospital the next day.
Source: *NCT*, XIV:700; *NCS* (Raliegh), March 29, 1865; *WD* (Charlotte), April 4, 1865; M270.

Mallett, Edward, Lieutenant Colonel, Field & Staff
Bentonville
Wounded at the battle of Bentonville between March 19-21, 1865. According to Surgeon Tanner's "Return of Casualties in Hoke's Div. near Bentonville," Lt. Col. Ed. Mallett, Field & Staff, was dangerously wounded in the left lung, "since died." The *Daily Confederate* published a death notice, "Killed in the battle near Bentonville." He is buried in Old Chapel Hill Cemetery, Chapel Hill, North Carolina. His tombstone marks his date of death as March 21, 1865. Mallett's name appears on a monument at Bentonville Battlefield State Historic Site, leading some to assume he is buried in the Confederate mass grave located there.
Source: Tanner (BV), 140; *DC* (Raleigh), March 27, 1865; *NCT*, XIV:651; M270.

Moore, Isaiah, Private, Company H
Wise's Forks
NC Troops notes that he was wounded in the left buttock and captured at Kinston on March 9, 1865. Admitted to U.S. Army Foster GH in New Bern on March 15, 1865, where he died of typhoid fever on March 24, 1865.
Source: *NCT*, XIV:733; M270; RG 94, Foster General Hospital Registry, 99.

Newsom, Nicholas H., Sergeant, Company C
Wise's Forks
Captured near Kinston on March 10, 1865. Confined at Point Lookout, Maryland, and released upon taking the Oath of Allegiance on June 29, 1865.
Source: *NCT*, XIV:674; M270; NC Confederate Pension (Davidson County).

Orr, Timothy C., Corporal, Company G
Goldsboro
Deserted to the enemy at Goldsboro on March 22, 1865. Sent to Washington, D.C., and released upon taking the Oath of Allegiance on or about the same day.
Source: *NCT*, XIV:722; M270.

Owens, Stephen D., 1st Sergeant, Company B
Wise's Forks
Captured near Kinston on March 10, 1865. Confined at Point Lookout, Maryland, where he died of acute dysentery on June 29, 1865.
Source: *NCT*, XIV:666; M270.

Parrish, Thomas, Private, Company C
New Hope (Post Wise's Forks)
Deserted to the enemy at New Hope on March 17, 1865. No further records.

Source: *NCT*, XIV:674; M270; NC Confederate Pension (Lenoir County).

▲Paschall, Joseph P., Private, Company C
Wise's Forks
Wounded at the battle of Wise's Forks on March 10, 1865. According to Surgeon Tanner's "Return of Casualties near Kinston," Pvt. Jos. Paschal, Company C, 51st NC, was severely wounded in the right cheek. The Barbee Wayside Hospital in High Point admitted an unidentified soldier from the 61st NC on March 9, 1865, with a gunshot to his mouth. This shoulder may be James Paschal, whose wound description is very similar. Neither his service records nor *NC Troops* note his wounding in March 1865. His Confederate pension records indicate that he was wounded at Swift Creek near Kinston on March 11, 1865.
Source: Tanner (WF), 135; Barbee Wayside Registry, no. 5752; *NCT*, XIV:674; M270; NC Confederate Pension (Durham County).

Perry, John J., Private, Company D
Wise's Forks
Admitted to GH No. 13 (Pettigrew) in Raleigh on March 10, 1865, suffering from two separate gunshots, one fracturing his jaw bone and the other, his left thumb. Transferred to an unidentified hospital on March 16, 1865. No further records.
Source: *NCT*, XIV:687; *WD* (Charlotte), April 4, 1865; M270.

♦Sims, John, Private, (Company Unknown)
Bentonville (Inconclusive)
Deserted to the enemy on or about March 20, 1865. Confined at Washington, D.C., and released upon taking the Oath of Allegiance on or about April 6, 1865.
Source: *NCT*, XIV:759; M270.

Skeen, John H., Private, Company E
Kinston (Post Wise's Forks)
Deserted to the enemy on March 15, 1865 at Kinston. No further records.
Source: *NCT*, XIV:702; M270.

▲Smith, John W., Private, Company K
Bentonville
Wounded at the battle of Bentonville between March 19-21, 1865. According to Surgeon Tanner's "Return of Casualties in Hoke's Div. near Bentonville," Pvt. Jno. Smith, Company K, was dangerously wounded in the head. A Pvt. John Smith, Co. K, 61st NC, was reported present in Raleigh's Wayside Hospital (Ladies' Wayside) suffering from a wound to his head. He was later admitted to GH No. 13 (Pettigrew) in Raleigh on March 25, 1865, with a gunshot to his left back that resulted in paralysis of his left side. No. 13 records indicate that he died that same day. Smith is buried in Oakwood Cemetery, Grave No. 311, Raleigh, North Carolina.
Source: Tanner (BV), 140; *NCS* (Raleigh), March 29, 1865; *WD* (Charlotte), April 4, 1865; *NCT*, XIV:757; M270.

▲Sugg, Joshua Parrott, Corporal, Company E
Wise's Forks
Wounded at the battle of Wise's Forks on March 10, 1865. According to Surgeon Tanner's "Return of Casualties near Kinston," Pvt. J. P. Suggs, Company E, 51st NC, was severely wounded in the right thigh. Corporal Joshua Parrot Sugg of Co. E is the same soldier Tanner listed as Suggs. No further records. Neither his service records nor *NC Troops* note his wounding in March 1865.
Source: Tanner (WF), 135; *NCT*, XIV:704; M270.

Williams, Henry A., Private, Company K
Wise's Forks
Captured near Kinston on March 8, 1865. Confined at Point Lookout, Maryland, and released upon taking the Oath of Allegiance on June 21, 1865.
Source: *NCT*, XIV:758; M270; NC Confederate Pension (Lenoir County).

Wood, William Jackson, Private, Company I
Wise's Forks
Captured near Kinston on March 8, 1865. Confined at Point Lookout, Maryland, and released upon taking the Oath of Allegiance on June 22, 1865. His Confederate pension records indicate a shell struck him, the date and location unspecified.
Source: *NCT*, XIV:748; M270; NC Confederate Pension (Franklin County).

Captain John D. Biggs, Sr.
Company H, 61st Regiment NC Troops
Wounded at Bentonville
Patient at the Ladies' Wayside Hospital in Raleigh before transferred to General Hospital No. 3 in High Point.

(Histories of Several Regiments and Battalions from North Carolina in the Great War)

Private Richard B. Carrington
Company A, 66th Regiment NC Troops
Captured at Wise's Forks on March 10, 1865

(Histories of Several Regiments and Battalions from North Carolina in the Great War)

66th Regiment North Carolina Troops

▲Alford, John, Private, Company B
Wise's Forks
Wounded at Wise's Forks on March 10, 1865. According to Surgeon Kinyoun's "Register of Sick, Killed and Wounded 66th N.C. Regt., March 1865," Pvt. J. Alford, Co. B, was severely wounded by an artillery shell (bruised on the left knee) and transferred that same day to "General Hospital Goldsboro." Surgeon Tanner's "Return of Casualties near Kinston" also lists him as wounded. Admitted to GH No. 13 (Pettigrew) in Raleigh on March 11, 1865, with a contusion to his left knee caused by a shell. No further records. His Confederate pension records indicate that he was wounded in the left knee by a shell at Wise's Forks on March 10, 1865.
Source: Houts, *A Darkness Ablaze*, 280; Tanner (WF), 139; *NCS* (Raliegh), March 29, 1865; *DP* (Raleigh), March 28, 1865; *WD* (Charlotte), April 4, 1865; *NCT*, XV:329; M270; NC Confederate Pension (Franklin County).

Anderson, Perry, Corporal, Company C
Wise's Forks
Captured at or near Kinston on or about March 7-10, 1865. Confined at Hart's Island, New York Harbor, and released upon taking the Oath of Allegiance on June 19, 1865.
Source: *NCT*, XV:337; M270; NC Confederate Pension (Wayne County).

Arnold, John Stanley, Private, Company D
Wise's Forks
Captured near Kinston on March 10, 1865. Confined at Point Lookout, Maryland, and released upon taking the Oath of Allegiance on June 23, 1865.
Source: *NCT*, XV:345; M270; NC Confederate Pension (Craven County).

Ashworth, Rufus, Private, Company F
Wise's Forks
Captured near Kinston on March 8, 1865. Confined at Point Lookout, Maryland, and released upon taking the Oath of Allegiance on June 23, 1865.
Source: *NCT*, XV:361; M270; NC Confederate Pension (Buncombe County).

Baber, Leonard A., Private, Company I
Wise's Forks
Captured at or near Kinston on March 8, 1865. Confined at Point Lookout, Maryland, and released upon taking the Oath of Allegiance on June 23, 1865.
Source: *NCT*, XV:385; M270; NC Confederate Pension (Rutherford County).

Badgett, Burrill R., 3rd Lieutenant, Company G
Wise's Forks
Captured at Kinston on March 10, 1865. First confined at Old Capitol Prison, Washington, D.C., transferred to Fort Delaware, Delaware, and released upon taking the Oath of Allegiance on June 17, 1865.
Source: *NCT*, XV:369; M270.

Bailey, John H., Private, Company K
Wilmington
Captured at Wilmington on February 22, 1865. Confined at Point Lookout, Maryland, and released upon taking the Oath of Allegiance on June 24, 1865.
Source: *NCT*, XV:394; M270.

Bailey, William W., Private, Company K
Wise's Forks
Captured near Kinston on March 10, 1865. Confined at Point Lookout, Maryland, and released upon taking the Oath of Allegiance on June 8, 1865.
Source: *NCT*, XV:394; M270.

▲Barbee, James, Private, Company E
Wise's Forks
Wounded at Wise's Forks on March 10, 1865. According to Surgeon Kinyoun's "Register of Sick, Killed and Wounded 66th N.C. Regt., March 1865," Pvt. J. Barbee, Co. E, was severely wounded in the outer part of the right thigh by a gunshot and sent to "General Hospital Goldsboro" that same day. Surgeon Tanner's "Return of Casualties near Kinston" also lists him as wounded. Paroled at Greensboro on May 5, 1865. Neither *NC Troops* nor his service records note his wounding in March 1865. There is an NC Confederate Pension for a Pvt. James M. Barbee, Co. C, 66th NC. However, he does not state that he was wounded during the war.
Source: Houts, *A Darkness Ablaze,* 280; Tanner (WF), 139; M270; *NCT*, XV:317, 354; M270; NC Confederate Pension (Wake County).

▲Barrow, William H., Private, Company A
Wise's Forks
Wounded and captured on March 10, 1865. His service records indicate that he was admitted to the U.S. Army Foster GH in New Bern on March 15, 1865, with a wound to his left arm, requiring amputation. He later died of typhoid fever on April 3, 1865. Son of William J. Barrow of Co. A, 66th North Carolina.
Source: *NCT*, XV:317; M270; RG 94, Foster General Hospital Registry, 99; *Raleigh News* (NC), April 11, 1878.

Barrow, William J., Sergeant, Company A
Wise's Forks
Captured at Kinston on March 10, 1865. Confined at Point Lookout, Maryland, and released upon taking the Oath of Allegiance on June 24, 1865. Father of William H. Barrow of Co. A, 66th North Carolina.
Source: *NCT*, XV:317; M270; *Raleigh News* (NC), April 11, 1878.

♦Bartholomew, Benjamin B., Private, Company B
Bentonville or Wise's Forks (Inconclusive)
Confederate pension records (1903) state that he was wounded in the heel at Smithfield in March 1865. However, a 1909 pension application notes that he suffered the wound at Kinston in the Spring of 1865.
Source: *NCT*, XV:329; M270; NC Confederate Pension (Franklin County).

Batchelor, Merrit, Private, Company B
Wise's Forks
Captured at Kinston on March 8, 1865. Confined at Point Lookout, Maryland, and released upon taking the Oath of Allegiance on June 7-8, 1865. *NC Troops* identifies the surname as "Bachelor" in Volume V of the series, which, according to the compilers, may be incorrect.
Source: *NCT*, XV:329; M270.

Boon, Franklin, Private, Company E
Moseley Hall (Post Bentonville)
Captured at Moseley Hall on March 27, 1865. Confined at Hart's Island, New York Harbor, and released upon taking the Oath of Allegiance on June 19, 1865.
Source: *NCT*, XV:354; M270.

Bostic, John M, Private, Company H
Wise's Forks
Captured near Kinston on March 10, 1865. Confined at Point Lookout, Maryland, and released upon taking the Oath of Allegiance on June 24, 1865.
Source: *NCT*, XV:378; M270; NC Confederate Widow's Pension (Duplin County).

▲Boswell, John A., Private, Company K
Bentonville
Wounded on March 20, 1865, at Bentonville. According to Surgeon Kinyoun's "Register of Sick, Killed and Wounded 66th N.C. Regt., March 1865," Pvt. J. A. Boswell, Co. K, was seriously wounded by a gunshot in

the left thigh (fractured). Surgeon Tanner's "Return of Casualties in Hoke's Div. near Bentonville" also listed him as wounded. Admitted to GH No. 3 (High Point), registry no. 2392, for unspecified reasons between March 21 and April 7, 1865. Paroled as a patient there on May 1, 1865. Boswell was later hospitalized at Goldsboro on May 4, 1865, with remittent fever. He was released on May 9, 1865.
Source: Houts, *A Darkness Ablaze*, 281; Tanner (BV), 149; RG109, 6/291:47; *NCT*, XV:395; M270; NC Confederate Pension (Wilson County).

Bowden, Robert T. D., Private, Company B
Wise's Forks
Captured at Kinston on March 8, 1865. Confined at Point Lookout, Maryland, where he was released upon taking the Oath of Allegiance on June 23, 1865.
Source: *NCT*, XV:330; M270.

Braswell, Joseph R., Private, Company B
Wise's Forks
Captured at Kinston on March 10, 1865. Confined at Point Lookout, Maryland, where he was released upon taking the Oath of Allegiance on June 23, 1865.
Source: *NCT*, XV:330; M270; NC Confederate Widow's Pension (Nash County).

▲Braxton, Jesse W., Private, Company E
Bentonville
Wounded on March 20, 1865, at Bentonville. According to Surgeon Kinyoun's "Register of Sick, Killed and Wounded 66th N.C. Regt., March 1865," Pvt. J. Braxten, Co. E, was severely wounded by a gunshot through his right arm (fractured) on March 20, 1865. Surgeon Tanner's "Return of Casualties in Hoke's Div. near Bentonville" also listed him as wounded. Present at Raleigh's Baptist Church Hospital. Based on Surgeon Kinyoun's registry entry of March 20, *NC Troops* is incorrect in indicating that he was wounded on March 19, 1865, at Bentonville. His Confederate pension application indicates that he was wounded in the "right arm between the elbow and shoulder, "breaking all to pieces."
Source: Houts, *A Darkness Ablaze*, 281; Tanner (BV), 149; *DP* (Raleigh), March 27, 1865; *WD* (Charlotte), April 4, 1865; *NCT*, XV:354; M270; NC Confederate Pension (Pitt County).

Britton, Owen W. Private, Company H
Wise's Forks
Captured at Kinston on March 10, 1865. Confined at Point Lookout, Maryland, and released upon taking the Oath of Allegiance on June 23, 1865.
Source: *NCT*, XV:379; M270.

▲Brown, Burton, Private, Company G
Bentonville
Wounded on March 20, 1865, at Bentonville. According to Surgeon Kinyoun's "Register of Sick, Killed and Wounded 66th N.C. Regt., March 1865," Pvt. B. Brown, Co. G, was severely wounded by a gunshot on the right side of his back. Surgeon Tanner's "Return of Casualties in Hoke's Div. near Bentonville" also listed him as wounded. Admitted to Raleigh's Episcopal Church Hospital on an unspecified date in March 1865, wounded on the right side. Confederate pensions records indicate Bentonville, but the date was incorrectly listed as April 1865.
Source: Houts, *A Darkness Ablaze*, 281; Tanner (BV), 149; *NCS*, (Raleigh), March 24, 1865; *WD* (Charlotte), April 4, 1865; *NCT*, XV:370; M270; NC Confederate Pension (Davie County).

Brown, Franklin, Corporal, Company E
Kinston (Post Wise's Forks)
Captured at Kinston on March 14, 1865, and sent to New Bern. No further records.
Source: *NCT*, XV:354; M270; NC Confederate Pension (Bladen County).

Brown, Owen M. Private, Company H
Sugar Loaf

Captured at or near Fort Fisher on February 16, 1865. Confined at Point Lookout, Maryland, and released upon taking the Oath of Allegiance on June 23, 1865. He later died on the U.S. Army Hospital Steamer *Connecticut* on July 25, 1865, while being transported to a hospital in Washington, D.C. Cause of death not reported.
Source: *NCT*, XV:379; M270; NC Confederate Widow's Pension (Onslow County).

Brown, William, Sergeant, Company G
Wise's Forks
Captured near Kinston on March 8, 1865. Confined at Point Lookout, Maryland, and released upon taking the Oath of Allegiance on June 23, 1865.
Source: *NCT*, XV:370; M270.

Bryan, Frederick J., Private, Company D
Wise's Forks
Captured at Kinston on March 10, 1865. Confined at Point Lookout, Maryland, and released upon taking the Oath of Allegiance on June 24, 1865.
Source: *NCT*, XV:346; M270.

▲Bunting, James V., 3rd Lieutenant, Company B
Wise's Forks
Wounded at Wise's Forks on March 8, 1865. According to Surgeon Kinyoun's "Register of Sick, Killed and Wounded 66th NC Regiment, March 1865," Lt. J. V. Bunting, Co. B, was shot severely on the right side of his head. Described by the surgeon as "scalped." Transferred to "General Hospital Goldsboro" on March 9, 1865. Surgeon Tanner's "Return of Casualties near Kinston" also lists him as wounded. His service records do not note his wounding in March 1865.
Source: Houts, *A Darkness Ablaze*, 278; Tanner (WF), 139; *NCT*, XV:328; M270.

Calloway, Joseph A., Private, Company I
Wise's Forks
Captured near Kinston on March 8, 1865. Confined at Point Lookout, Maryland, and released upon taking the Oath of Allegiance on June 24, 1865.
Source: *NCT*, XV:386; M270.

Carrington, Richard B., Private, Company A
Wise's Forks
Captured near Kinston on March 10, 1865. Confined at Point Lookout, Maryland, and released upon taking the Oath of Allegiance on June 26, 1865.
Source: *NCT*, XV:319; M270; NC Confederate Widow's Pension (Durham County).

▲Carter, Samuel Sidney, 1st Lieutenant, Company F
Wise's Forks
Wounded at Wise's Forks on March 10, 1865. According to Surgeon Kinyoun's "Register of Sick, Killed and Wounded 66th N.C. Regt., March 1865," Lt. S. S. Carter, Co. F, was wounded in the right arm below the elbow by a "grape shot," requiring amputation, and sent to "General Hospital Goldsboro" that same day. Surgeon Tanner's "Return of Casualties near Kinston" also lists him as wounded. Admitted to GH No. 13 (Pettigrew) in Raleigh on March 11, 1865, with an amputated right arm. The No. 13 patient registry incorrectly noted the cause of his wounding as a gunshot. Furloughed on March 25, 1865. Confederate pension application indicates that he was shot in the right arm, requiring amputation below the elbow.
Source: Houts, *A Darkness Ablaze*, 280; Tanner (WF), 139; *NCS* (Raliegh), March 29, 1865; *WD* (Charlotte), April 4, 1865; *NCT*, XV:361; M270; NC Confederate Pension (Anson County).

Cherry, Willis W., 1st Lieutenant, Company H
Clinton
Captured at Clinton on March 20, 1865. In confinement at New Berne on March 29, 1865. No further records.
Source: *NCT*, XV:378; M270.

▲**Christian, James Newton**, Private, Company A
Wise's Forks
Wounded at Wise's Forks on March 8, 1865. According to Surgeon Kinyoun's "Register of Sick, Killed and Wounded 66th NC Regiment, March 1865," Pvt. J. N. Christian, Co. A, was severely wounded in the right knee by a gunshot, fracturing the patella, and sent to GH No. 3 in Goldsboro on March 9, 1865, and transferred the next day to GH No. 13 (Pettigrew) in Raleigh. Furloughed on March 16 for 60 days. His service records and *NC Troops* incorrectly note that Christian was hospitalized at GH No. 3 in Greensboro on March 9, 1865, with an unspecified complaint. Goldsboro is the correct location. Confederate authorities ordered No. 3's relocation to High Point on March 11, 1865, as part of the Confederate evacuation of Goldsboro.
Source: Houts, *A Darkness Ablaze,* 278; Tanner (WF), 138; *NCS* (Raliegh), March 29, 1865; *DP* (Raleigh), March 28, 1865; *DB* (Charlotte), April 4, 1865; *NCT*, XV:319; M270.

Colbert, John H., Private, Company B
Wise's Forks
Captured near Kinston on March 8, 1865. Confined at Point Lookout, Maryland, and was released upon taking the Oath of Allegiance on June 24, 1865.
Source: *NCT*, XV:330; M270; NC Confederate Pension (Franklin County).

Cook, William Stephen, Private, Company B
Wise's Forks
Captured at Kinston on March 8, 1865. Confined at Point Lookout, Maryland, where he died of unspecified reasons on May 6, 1865.
Source: *NCT*, XV:331; M270; NC Confederate Widow's Pension (Franklin County).

Coppedge, George W., Private, Company B
Wise's Forks
Captured at Kinston on March 8, 1865. Confined at Point Lookout, Maryland, and released upon taking the Oath of Allegiance on June 24, 1865.
Source: *NCT*, XV:331; M270.

Coppedge, Jordan, Private, Company B
Wise's Forks
Captured at Kinston on March 8, 1865. Confined at Point Lookout, Maryland, and released upon taking the Oath of Allegiance on June 24, 1865.
Source: *NCT*, XV:331; M270.

Coppedge, Joseph, Private, Company B
Wise's Forks
Captured at Kinston on March 8, 1865. Confined at Point Lookout, Maryland, and released upon taking the Oath of Allegiance on June 24, 1865.
Source: *NCT*, XV:331; M270.

Couch, Nathan, Private, Company A
Wise's Forks
NC Troops notes that he was wounded in the right arm at Kinston on March 10, 1865. Admitted to GH No. 13 (Pettigrew) in Raleigh on March 10, 1865, wounded in the right arm. Furloughed on March 16th for 60 days. *NC Standard* incorrectly lists him as a member of the 42nd NC.
Source: *DB* (Charlotte), March 28, 1865; *NCT*: XV:320; M270; *NCS* (Raleigh), March 29, 1865; *DC* (Raleigh). April 4, 1865.

Coxey, J. William, Private, Company F
Wise's Forks
Captured near Kinston on March 10, 1865. Confined at Point Lookout, Maryland, and released upon taking the Oath of Allegiance on June 26, 1865. According to his Confederate pension records, he was wounded

in the left hand and left side in North Carolina on or about March 8, 1865, and imprisoned at Point Lookout, Maryland.
Source: *NCT*, XV:363; M270; NC Confederate Pension (Swain County).

Crabtree, William R., Private, Company E
Wise's Forks
Captured near Kinston on March 10, 1865. Confined at Point Lookout, Maryland, and released upon taking the Oath of Allegiance on June 26, 1865.
Source: *NCT*, XV:355; M270.

Crews, Henry H., Private, Company G
Wise's Forks
Captured near Kinston on March 10, 1865. Confined at Point Lookout, Maryland, and released upon taking the Oath of Allegiance on June 24, 1865.
Source: *NCT*, XV:371; M270.

Culpepper, James M., Private, Company B
Wise's Forks
Captured at Kinston on March 10, 1865. Confined at Point Lookout, Maryland, and released upon taking the Oath of Allegiance on June 24, 1865.
Source: *NCT*, XV:331; M270.

Davis, John, Private, Company C
Goldsboro (Post Bentonville)
Captured at Goldsboro on March 31, 1865. Confined at Hart's Island, New York Harbor, and released upon taking the Oath of Allegiance on June 19, 1865.
Source: *NCT*, XV:339; M270.

Dennis, William N., 1st Lieutenant, Company E
Wise's Forks
Captured near Kinston on March 8, 1865. Confined at Fort Delaware, Delaware, and released upon taking the Oath of Allegiance on June 7, 1865.
Source: *NCT*, XV:353; M270.

Dorsey, Ephraim, Private, Company B
Wise's Forks
Captured at Kinston on March 10, 1865. Confined at Point Lookout, Maryland, and released upon taking the Oath of Allegiance on June 12, 1865.
Source: *NCT*, XV:331; M270; NC Confederate Pension (Franklin County).

▲Eudy, John M., Private, Company G
Wise's Forks
Wounded at Wise's Forks on March 8, 1865. According to Surgeon Kinyoun's "Register of Sick, Killed and Wounded 66th NC Regiment, March 1865," Pvt. J. M. Euda, Co. G, was slightly wounded in the right arm above the elbow by a gunshot and transferred to "Goldsboro thence to G.H. in Raleigh" on March 11, 1865. Surgeon Tanner's "Return of Casualties near Kinston" also lists him as wounded. His service records do not note his wounding. No further records.
Source: Houts, *A Darkness Ablaze*, 278; Tanner (WF), 139; *NCT*, XV:372; M270.

Farmer, Phillip R., Sergeant, Company K
Wise's Forks
Captured near Kinston on March 10, 1865. Confined at Point Lookout, Maryland, and released upon taking the Oath of Allegiance on June 26, 1865.
Source: *NCT*, XV:396; M270; NC Confederate Widow's Pension (Edgecombe County).

Fuller, James H., Private, Company B
Wise's Forks
Captured at Kinston on March 8, 1865. Confined at Point Lookout, Maryland, and released upon taking the Oath of Allegiance on June 26, 1865.
Source: *NCT*, XV:331; M270.

Garrett, Skidmore J., Private, Company A
Wise's Forks
Captured near Kinston on March 10, 1865. Confined at Point Lookout, Maryland, and released upon taking the Oath of Allegiance on June 27, 1865.
Source: *NCT*, XV:321; M270; NC Confederate Pension (Durham County); NC Confederate Widow's Pension (Durham County).

Gay, Thomas L., Private, Company B
Wise's Forks
Captured at Kinston on March 8, 1865. Confined at Point Lookout, Maryland, and released upon taking the Oath of Allegiance on June 27, 1865.
Source: *NCT*, XV:332; M270.

Giles, William T., Private, Company I
Wise's Forks
Captured near Kinston on March 8, 1865. Confined at Point Lookout, Maryland, and released upon taking the Oath of Allegiance on June 27, 1865.
Source: *NCT*, XV:386; M270.

Greene, James P., Private, Company G
Wise's Forks
Captured near Kinston on March 10, 1865. Confined at Point Lookout, Maryland, and released upon taking the Oath of Allegiance on June 27, 1865.
Source: *NCT*, XV:372; M270.

Griffin, James D., Private, Company B
Wise's Forks
Captured at Kinston on March 8, 1865. Confined at Point Lookout, Maryland, and released upon taking the Oath of Allegiance on June 27, 1865.
Source: *NCT*, XV:332; M270; NC Confederate Pension (Franklin County).

Guess, William C., Private, Company A
Wise's Forks
Captured at Kinston on March 10, 1865. Confined at Point Lookout, Maryland, and released upon taking the Oath of Allegiance on June 27, 1865.
Source: *NCT*, XV:322; M270; North Carolina Soldiers' Home Application.

Harper, Franklin, Sergeant, Company H
Wise's Forks
Captured near Kinston on March 10, 1865. Confined at Point Lookout, Maryland, and released upon taking the Oath of Allegiance on June 27, 1865.
Source: *NCT*, XV:380; M270.

Harper, Joseph, Private, Company B
Wise's Forks
Captured at Kinston on March 10, 1865. Confined at Point Lookout, Maryland, and released upon taking the Oath of Allegiance on June 27, 1865.
Source: *NCT*, XV:332; M270.

Herring, James B., Private, Company C

Wise's Forks
Captured at Kinston on March 10, 1865. Confined at Point Lookout, Maryland, and released upon taking the Oath of Allegiance on May 13, 1865.
Source: *NCT*, XV:340; M270.

Hill, Lemuel H., Private, Company I
Goldsboro (Post Bentonville)
Deserted at Goldsboro on March 24, 1865. Confined at Fort Monroe, Virginia, until released at Washington, D.C., upon taking the Oath of Allegiance on April 5, 1865.
Source: *NCT*, XV:387; M270.

Hill, Leonidas, Private, Company I
Goldsboro (Post Bentonville)
Deserted at Goldsboro on March 25, 1865. Confined at Fort Monroe, Virginia, until released at Washington, D.C., upon presumably taking the Oath of Allegiance on April 26, 1865. He submitted his Confederate pension application using his earlier service in Co. F, 10th NC (1st NC Artillery).
Source: *NCT*, XV:387; M270; NC Confederate Pension (Lenoir County).

Hill, Parrott N., Private, Company I
Goldsboro (Post Bentonville)
Deserted at Goldsboro on March 27, 1865. Took the Oath of Allegiance the same day.
Source: *NCT*, XV:387; M270.

♦**Hill, Robert P.**, Private, Company E
(Inconclusive)
Admitted to Barbee Wayside Hospital in High Point on March 4, 1865, with an amputated right leg. The result of a gunshot wound. The place and date of the wound were not reported; however, it was probably from a previous battle in Virginia or possibly near Wilmington. No further records. His widow's pension application indicated that his middle initial was "R."
Source: *NCT*, XV:356; M270; NC Confederate Widow's Pension (Craven County).

Hill, Robert R., Sergeant, Company E
Kinston (Post Wise's Forks)
Captured at Kinston on March 14, 1865. No further records.
Source: *NCT*, XV:357; M270.

▲**Hines, Henry A.**, Private, Company B
Wise's Forks
Wounded at Wise's Forks on March 10, 1865. According to Surgeon Kinyoun's "Register of Sick, Killed and Wounded 66th N.C. Regt., March 1865," Pvt. H. A. Hines, Co. B, was slightly wounded (bruised) on his back by a shell and sent to "General Hospital Goldsboro" that same day. Surgeon Tanner's "Return of Casualties near Kinston" also lists him as wounded. Neither *NC Troops* nor his service records note his wounding in March 1865.
Source: Houts, *A Darkness Ablaze,* 280; Tanner (WF), 139; M270; *NCT*, XV:332; M270.

Hines, J. Ivey, Private, Company C
Goldsboro (Post Bentonville)
Captured at Goldsboro on March 27, 1865. Confined at Hart's Island, New York Harbor, and released upon taking the Oath of Allegiance on June 18, 1865.
Source: *NCT*, XV:340; M270.

Holland, Charles, Private, Company H
Kinston (Post Wise's Forks)
Captured at Kinston on March 15, 1865, while listed as a deserter. No further records.
Source: *NCT*, XV:380; M270.

Holland, John, Private, Company H
Kinston (Post Wise's Forks)
Captured at Kinston on March 15, 1865, while listed as a deserter. No further records.
Source: *NCT*, XV:380; M270; NC Confederate Pension (Duplin County).

Humphrey, John, Private, Company H
Wise's Forks
Captured near Kinston on March 10, 1865. Confined at Point Lookout, Maryland, prison camp. *NC Troops* notes that "he arrived at Point Lookout under an assumed name or assumed one for the purpose of being transferred, exchanged, or released."
Source: *NCT*, XV:381; M270.

Humphrey, Lewis D., Private, Company H
Wise's Forks
Captured near Kinston on March 10, 1865. Confined at Point Lookout, Maryland, and released upon taking the Oath of Allegiance on June 28, 1865.
Source: *NCT*, XV:381; M270.

James, John T., Corporal, Company A
Wise's Forks
Captured at Kinston on March 10, 1865. Confined at Point Lookout, Maryland, and released upon taking the Oath of Allegiance on June 28, 1865.
Source: *DB* (Charlotte), March 28, 1865; *NCT*, XV:323; M270; *NCS* (Raleigh), March 24, 1865; *DC* (Raleigh), April 4, 1865.

Jones, James B., Private, Company I
Goldsboro (Post Bentonville)
Captured at Goldsboro on March 24, 1865. Confined at Hart's Island, New York Harbor, and released upon taking the Oath of Allegiance on June 19, 1865.
Source: *NCT*, XV:388; M270; NC Confederate Widow's Pension (Lenoir County).

Jones, Reddick H., Sergeant, Company H
Goldsboro
Captured near Goldsboro on March 20, 1865. Confined at Hart's Island, New York, and released upon taking the Oath of Allegiance on June 19, 1865.
Source: *NCT*, XV:381; M270.

Karlott, W. R., ____, Company A
NC Troops indicates that he was wounded in the hip at Bentonville on March 19, 1865. Present in Raleigh's Baptist Church Hospital, wounded in the hip.
Source: *WD* (Charlotte), April 4, 1865; *NCT*, XV:323; *NCS* (Raleigh), March 24, 1865; *DC* (Raleigh), April 4, 1865.

Kennedy, William H., Private, Company H
Wise's Forks
Captured near Kinston on March 10, 1865. Confined at Point Lookout, Maryland, and released upon taking the Oath of Allegiance on May 13, 1865.
Source: *NCT*, XV:381; M270; NC Confederate Pension (Duplin County).

Lamm, Jonas, Private, Company K
Wilmington
Captured near Wilmington on February 22, 1865. Confined at Point Lookout, Maryland, and released upon taking the Oath of Allegiance on June 28, 1865.
Source: *NCT*, XV:398; M270.

♦Lane, John, Private, Company K
(Inconclusive)

Provost Marshal records indicate captured at Goldsboro on March 15, 1865. Confined at Hart's Island, New York Harbor, and released upon taking the Oath of Allegiance on June 19, 1865. However, Federal forces were not near Goldsboro on March 15, making his location of capture more probable near Kinston.
Source: *NCT*, XV:398; M270.

♦Lane, John W., Corporal, Company K
In the Field or Clinton (Inconclusive)
Provost Marshal records indicate two locations and dates of capture or desertion: "In the field," deserted on March 14, 1865, and captured at Clinton on March 20, 1865. Confined at New Bern on or about March 29, 1865. No further records.
Source: *NCT*, XV:398; M270.

Layton, Franklin A., Sergeant, Company G
Wise's Forks
Captured near Kinston on March 10, 1865. Confined at Point Lookout, Maryland, and released upon taking the Oath of Allegiance on June 28, 1865.
Source: *NCT*, XV:374; M270.

Leitner, Edward E., Private, Company C
Wise's Forks
Wounded and captured at Wise's Forks on March 10, 1865. Admitted to U.S. Army Foster General Hospital in New Bern on March 15, 1865, wounded in the left calf by a gunshot. Released on April 21, 1865. No further records.
Source: *NCT*, XV:341; M270; RG94, Foster General Hospital Registry, no. 6571, 99.

Mariner, J. B., Private, Company D
Wise's Forks
Captured at Kinston on March 8, 1865. Confined at Point Lookout, Maryland, and released upon taking the Oath of Allegiance on June 29, 1865.
Source: *NCT*, XV:349; M270.

▲Mathis, Noel, Private, Company K
Wise's Forks
Wounded at Wise's Forks on March 10, 1865. According to Surgeon Kinyoun's "Register of Sick, Killed and Wounded 66th N.C. Regt., March 1865," Pvt. N. Matthews [sic], Co. K, was wounded in the left arm above the elbow by a gunshot wound, requiring amputation, and sent to "General Hospital Goldsboro" that same day. His service records do not indicate that he was wounded in March 1865. Confederate pension application indicates that he "lost his left arm near shoulder joint" at Wise's Forks on or about March 10, 1865.
Source: Houts, *A Darkness Ablaze*, 280; Tanner (WF), 139; *NCT*, XV:399; M270; NC Confederate Pension (Wilson County).

McCoy, Frederick, Private, Company D
Mosely Hall (Post Bentonville)
Captured at Mosely Hall on March 23, 1865. Confined at Point Lookout, Maryland, and released upon taking the Oath of Allegiance on June 26, 1865.
Source: *NCT*, XV:349; M270.

McFarlin, Simeon, Private, Company A
Wise's Forks
Surgeon Kinyoun's "Register of Sick, Killed and Wounded 66th N.C. Regt. Kirkland's Brigade March 1865" listed a soldier by only the surname of McFarlin, with no rank or company assignment, who was wounded on March 10, 1865, and transferred to "General Hospital Goldsboro." The same individual is not listed on Tanner's registry. The rolls for Company A, 66th N.C. Infantry lists a Pvt. Simeon McFarlin, last reported as a carpenter, detailed at Wilmington through October 31, 1864. A Simeon McFarland, Co. A, 66th NC, indicated on Confederate pension application that he was wounded in the breast, "struck by [a] piece of

bomb shell," near Kinston in April 1864. Although the date is misidentified, Simeon McFarland is the same soldier Kinyoun listed as McFarlin.
Source: Houts, *A Darkness Ablaze*, 280; *DB* (Charlotte), March 28, 1865; *NCT*, XV:324; M270; *NCS* (Raleigh), March 24, 1865; *DC* (Raleigh), April 4, 1865; NC Confederate Pension (Durham County).

Milliard, James J., Private, Company K
Piney Grove
Deserted at or near Piney Grove on March 19, 1865. Confined at Hart's Island, New York Harbor, and later hospitalized at David's Island, New York Harbor, with chronic diarrhea. He died at David's Island on or about April 21, 1865, of typhoid fever.
Source: *NCT*, XV:399; M270.

Monk, Henderson, Private, Company A
Wise's Forks
His service records report that he was admitted on March 15, 1865, to U.S. Army Foster General Hospital (New Bern) with a gunshot wound. Hospital records note the date of death as March 16, 1865. Buried in the Confederate Vault at Ceder Grove Cemetery in New Bern, North Carolina. "Find a Grave" identifies him as Alexander Monk Henderson, with a date of death of March 17, 1865.
Source: NARA, RG; *DB* (Charlotte), March 28, 1865; *NCT*, XV:324; M270; *NCS* (Raleigh), March 24, 1865; *DC* (Raleigh), April 4, 1865; Find a Grave.

Morrow, John S., Private, Company I
Wise's Forks
Captured near Kinston on March 10, 1865. Confined at Point Lookout, Maryland, and released upon taking the Oath of Allegiance on May 15, 1865. *NC Troops*, XV:389, incorrectly notes Clinton as the location of capture. His service records state "near Kinston."
Source: *NCT*, XV:389; M270.

Murphrey, John, Private, Company H
Wise's Forks
Captured at or near Kinston on March 10, 1865. Confined at Point Lookout, Maryland, and released upon taking the Oath of Allegiance on June 29, 1865.
Source: *NCT*, XV:381; M270.

Myers, William A., Corporal, Company G
Wise's Forks
Captured near Kinston on March 10, 1865. Confined at Point Lookout, Maryland, and released upon taking the Oath of Allegiance on June 15, 1865.
Source: *NCT*, XV:375; M270; NC Confederate Pension (Rowan County).

Newman, James, ____, Company E
Sugar Loaf
Wounded by artillery fire below Wilmington at Sugar Loaf on or about February 11, 1865. The *Daily Journal* reported that his leg was amputated. No further records.
Source: *DJ* (Wilmington, NC), February 13, 1865; *NCT*, XV:358; M270.

Oadum, Nathan L., Private, Company K
Wise's Forks
His Confederate pension records indicate that he was slightly wounded by the "concussion of [a] shell which exploded" near his head at Kinston in March 1865. *NC Troops* indicates the correct spelling of his surname may be Odum.
Source: *NCT*, XV:399; M270; NC Confederate Pension (Wayne County).

Oliver, Asa W., Private, Company K
Wise's Forks

Captured near Kinston on March 10, 1865. Confined at Point Lookout, Maryland, and released upon taking the Oath of Allegiance on June 29, 1865.
Source: *NCT*, XV:399; M270; NC Confederate Pension (Johnston County).

♦Overcash, William A., Private, Company G
Near Kinston (Inconclusive)
Captured near Kinston on February 10, 1865. Confined at Point Lookout, Maryland, and released upon taking the Oath of Allegiance on June 29, 1865. If the capture date is correct, the general location of his capture would have been closer to New Bern in February 1865. Further research is required.
Source: *NCT*, XV:375; M270.

Parham, H. E., Private, Company F
Wise's Forks
Captured near Kinston on March 8, 1865. Confined at Point Lookout, Maryland, and released upon taking the Oath of Allegiance on June 16, 1865.
Source: *NCT*, XV:366; M270; NC Confederate Pension (Buncombe County).

Parker, John C., Corporal, Company D
Mosely Hall
Captured (or deserted) at Mosely Hall on March 27, 1865. Confined at Hart's Island, New York, and released upon taking the Oath of Allegiance on June 18, 1865.
Source: *NCT*, XV:350; M270.

Pate, Gatlin, Private, Company E
Mosely Hall
Captured at Mosely Hall on March 27, 1865. Confined at Hart's Island, New York, and released upon taking the Oath of Allegiance on June 18, 1865.
Source: *NCT*, XV:358; M270.

Pate, Lenoir, Private, Company E
Wise's Forks
Captured near Kinston on March 10, 1865. Confined at Point Lookout, Maryland, and released upon taking the Oath of Allegiance on May 14, 1865.
Source: *NCT*, XV:358; M270.

♦▲Patton, L. L., Private, Company F
Bentonville or Wise's Forks (Inconclusive)
Wounded on March 19, 1865, at Bentonville. According to Surgeon Kinyoun's "Register of Sick, Killed and Wounded 66th N.C. Regt., March 1865," L. M. Paton, Co. F, was severely wounded by a gunshot to his right hip. Surgeon Tanner's "Return of Casualties in Hoke's Div. near Bentonville" also lists a Pvt. L. M. Payton, Co. I, 66th NC, was severely wounded in the right hip. However, the *Daily Confederate* of March 29, 1865, reported a Pvt. L. L. Patton, Co. F, 66th NC, was wounded at or near Kinston on or about March 10, 1865. *NC Standard* reported his name as L. L. Patten.
Source: Houts, *A Darkness Ablaze,* 281; Tanner (WF), 149; *NCS* (Raliegh), March 29, 1865; *DC* (Raleigh), March 29, 1865; *WD* (Charlotte), April 4, 1865; *NCT*, XV:366; M270.

Potts, Milton, Private, Company G
Wise's Forks
Captured near Kinston on March 8, 1865. Confined at Point Lookout, Maryland, and released upon taking the Oath of Allegiance on June 16, 1865.
Source: *NCT*, XV:375; M270; NC Confederate Pension (Davidson County).

Powell, James Alfred, Private, Company E
Kinston (Post-Wise's Forks)

Federal Provost Marshal Officer records indicate he was captured as a deserter at Kinston on March 15, 1865. No further records.
Source: *NCT*, XV:358; M270; NC Confederate Pension (Pamlico County).

Quinn, John W., Private, Company C
Wise's Forks
Federal Provost Marshal records indicate that he was captured on Wilmington Road near Kinston on March 10, 1865. Confined at Point Lookout, Maryland, where he died of pneumonia on May 21, 1865. The Wilmington Road (current-day U.S. Highway 258) is approximately three miles from the main Confederate defensive line along Southwest Creek. At the time of the battle of Wise's Forks on March 10, Wilmington Road would have been in the Confederate rear area, making the capture location highly unlikely. The date or location of capture is incorrect.
Source: *NCT*, XV:342; M270.

Rhodes, George A., Private, Company A
Wise's Forks
Captured near Kinston on March 10, 1865. Confined at Point Lookout, Maryland, and released upon taking the Oath of Allegiance on June 30, 1865. Confederate pension records indicate that he was wounded in the head from a shell at Kinston on March 9, 1865. The artillery shell "exploded just over his head knocking him down and rendering him unconscious for twenty four hours."
Source: *NCT*, XV:325; M270; NC Confederate Pension (Durham County).

♦Riley, Thomas Jefferson, Private, Company E
(Inconclusive)
Captured on an unspecified date and location. Admitted to the U.S. Army Foster General Hospital in New Bern on March 31, 1865, with acute diarrhea. He died in the hospital on April 29, 1865, and is buried in the National Cemetery in New Bern, North Carolina. Further research is required.
Source: *NCT*, XV:358; M270.

Riley, William L., Private, Company E
Wise's Forks
Captured near Kinston on March 10, 1865. Confined at Point Lookout, Maryland, and released upon taking the Oath of Allegiance on June 17, 1865.
Source: *NCT*, XV:358; M270.

▲Ross, T. McGilbert, Private, Company E
Wise's Forks
Wounded at Wise's Forks on March 10, 1865. According to Surgeon Kinyoun's "Register of Sick, Killed and Wounded 66th N.C. Regt., March 1865," Pvt. T. M. Ross, Co. E, was wounded in the left arm above the elbow by a gunshot, requiring amputation, and sent to "General Hospital Goldsboro" that same day. Surgeon Tanner's "Return of Casualties near Kinston" also lists him as wounded. Neither *NC Troops* nor his service records note his wounding in March 1865.
Source: Houts, *A Darkness Ablaze,* 280; Tanner (WF), 139; M270; *NCT*, XV:359; M270.

Rowe, John G., Private, Company K
Wise's Forks
Captured near Kinston on March 8, 1865. Confined at Point Lookout, Maryland, and released upon taking the Oath of Allegiance on June 19, 1865.
Source: *NCT*, XV:400; M270.

Sanderson, Lewis, Private, Company H
Wise's Forks
Captured at Kinston on March 10, 1865. Confined at Point Lookout, Maryland, and released upon taking the Oath of Allegiance on June 20, 1865. Confederate pension records note that he was wounded on his back and hip at Wyse's Fork on March 2, 1865, "by a tree falling across him[,] that was shot off by a Ball."

Source: *NCT*, XV:382; M270; NC Confederate Pension (Duplin County).

Scarlett, James C., Private, Company A
Wise's Forks
Captured at Kinston on March 10, 1865. Confined at Point Lookout, Maryland, where he was released upon taking the Oath of Allegiance on June 20, 1865.
Source: *NCT*, XV:325 M270.

Scarlett, William R., Sergeant, Company A
Bentonville
Wounded on March 20, 1865, at Bentonville. According to Surgeon Kinyoun's "Register of Sick, Killed and Wounded 66th N.C. Regt., March 1865," Sgt. W. R. Scarlett, Co. A, was severely wounded by a gunshot to his right hip. Surgeon Tanner's "Return of Casualties in Hoke's Div. near Bentonville" also listed him as wounded. Neither his service records nor *NC Troops* note his wounding in March 1865. No further records.
Source: Houts, *A Darkness Ablaze*, 280; Tanner, 149; *NCT*, XV:326; M270.

Shuping, Henry Jeremiah, Private, Company G
Wise's Forks
Captured near Kinston on March 10, 1865. Confined at Point Lookout, Maryland, and released upon taking the Oath of Allegiance on June 20, 1865.
Source: *NCT*, XV:376; M270.

Simpson, Charles, Private, Company A
Bentonville
Confederate pension records indicate that he was wounded in the left hand and left knee at the battle of Bentonville. Simpson's service records do not note his wounding in March 1865.
Source: *NCT*, XV:326; M270; NC Confederate Pension (Granville County).

♦**Solomon, William S.**, Private, Company G
Kinston (Inconclusive)
Confederate pension records note that he was wounded in the left arm at Kinston on an unspecified date.
Source: *NCT*, XV:376; M270; NC Confederate Pension (Stanly County).

♦**Spencer, William Jesse**, Private, Company K
(Inconclusive)
Captured near Smithfield on an unspecified date while still identified as a deserter. Paroled on April 12, 1865.
Source: *NCT*, XV:401; M270.

Strickland, Cyrus, Private, Company E
Kinston (Post Wise's Forks)
His service records indicate he was captured at Kinston on March 15, 1865. No further records.
Source: *NCT*, XV:359; M270.

▲**Stroud, Isaac**, Private, Company C
Bentonville
Wounded on March 20, 1865, at Bentonville. According to Surgeon Kinyoun's "Register of Sick, Killed and Wounded 66th N.C. Regt., March 1865," Pvt. J. Stroud, Co. C, was seriously wounded by a gunshot on the right side of his head, "with fracture." Surgeon Tanner's "Return of Casualties in Hoke's Div. near Bentonville" also listed him as wounded. Admitted to GH No. 3 in High Point for unspecified reasons between March 31 and April 7, 1865. Paroled there as a patient on May 1, 1865.
Source: Houts, *A Darkness Ablaze*, 281; *NCT*, XV:343; M270.

Sutton, Daniel, Private, Company D
Mosely Hall

Captured at Mosely Hall on March 25, 1865. Confined at Hart's Island, New York, and released upon taking the Oath of Allegiance on June 19, 1865.
Source: *NCT*, XV:351; M270.

Sutton, Thomas, Sergeant, Company D
Mosely Hall
Captured at Mosely Hall on March 28, 1865. Confined at Hart's Island, New York, and released upon taking the Oath of Allegiance on June 19, 1865.
Source: *NCT*, XV:351; M270.

Tate, Elias, Private, Company I
Wise's Forks
Captured near Kinston on March 10, 1865. Confined at Point Lookout, Maryland, and released upon taking the Oath of Allegiance on June 21, 1865.
Source: *NCT*, XV:391; M270.

Tate, Jesse, Private, Company I
Wise's Forks
Captured near Kinston on March 10, 1865. Confined at Point Lookout, Maryland, and released upon taking the Oath of Allegiance on June 21, 1865.
Source: *NCT*, XV:391; M270.

Taylor, John P., Private, Company I
Goldsboro (Post Bentonville)
Captured at Goldsboro on March 28, 1865. Confined at Hart's Island, New York Harbor, and released upon taking the Oath of Allegiance on June 19, 1865.
Source: *NCT*, XV:391; M270.

Thomas, Charles G., Private, Company H
Wise's Forks
Captured near Kinston on March 10, 1865. Confined at Point Lookout, Maryland, and released upon taking the Oath of Allegiance on June 21, 1865.
Source: *NCT*, XV:384; M270; NC Confederate Pension (Duplin County).

Thomason, W. T., Private, Company G
Wise's Forks
Captured near Kinston on March 10, 1865. Confined at Point Lookout, Maryland, and released upon taking the Oath of Allegiance on June 20, 1865.
Source: *NCT*, XV:376; M270.

Turner, Cicero F., Private, Company D
Wise's Forks
Captured near Kinston on March 10, 1865. Confined at Point Lookout, Maryland, and released upon taking the Oath of Allegiance on June 21, 1865.
Source: *NCT*, XV:351; M270.

Vickers, Moses, Private, Company A
Wise's Forks
Captured near Kinston on March 10, 1865. Confined at Point Lookout, Maryland, and released upon taking the Oath of Allegiance on June 21, 1865.
Source: *NCT*: XV; M270; NC Confederate Pension (Guilford County).

Wade, Drew H., Musician, Field and Staff
Kinston (Post Wise's Forks)
Captured at Kinston on March 14, 1865. No further records. Survived the war.
Source: *NCT*, XV:316, M270; NC Confederate Pension (Lenoir County).

Warren, Chesley P., Private, Company A
Wise's Forks
According to Surgeon Kinyoun's "Register of Sick, Killed and Wounded 66th NC Regiment March 1865," Pvt. C. P. Warren, Co. A, was treated for a slight wound caused by a spent ball striking his stomach on either March 8 or 9 (date eligible), 1865, and was then transferred to "Goldsboro General Hospital" on March 11, 1865, and later that same day, transferred to a Raleigh hospital. Private Warren was very fortunate as Houts noted the bullet only struck him on the stomach and "did not enter." He is also listed in Surgeon Tanner's "Return of Casualties near Kinston. His service records indicate that he was admitted to General Hospital No. 3 (Goldsboro) from Kinston on March 10, 1865. Although Houts annotated that Private Warren was transferred to a Raleigh hospital, he may have been admitted to one of the several established temporary hospitals where no formal records exist. *NC Troops* notes that he survived the war.
Source: *NCT*, XV:327; M270.

Waters, Elisha, Company D
Wise's Forks
Captured near Kinston on March 10, 1865. Confined at Point Lookout, Maryland, and released upon taking the Oath of Allegiance on June 21, 1865.
Source: *NCT*, XV:351; M270; NC Confederate Pension (Onslow County).

Watson, Spencer O., Private, Company E
Wise's Forks
Captured at Kinston on or about March 10, 1865, and was sent to New Bern. No further records.
Source: *NCT*, XV:360; M270.

Whaley, Frederick, Private, Company H
Wise's Forks
Wounded on the left side of the neck and captured at Wise's Forks on March 10, 1865, and admitted to U.S. Army Foster General Hospital in New Bern on March 11, 1865. He later died of wounds on March 31, 1865.
Source: *NCT*, XV:384; M270; RG94, Foster General Hospital Registry, no. 6361, 92.

♦▲**Whitaker, Joseph A.**, Private, Company A
Wise's Forks
Wounded at Wise's Forks on March 8, 1865. According to Surgeon Kinyoun's "Register of Sick, Killed and Wounded 66th NC Regiment, March 1865," Pvt. J. Whitaker, Company A, was slightly wounded (bruised) on the back by a shell and sent to GH No. 3 in Goldsboro. Surgeon Tanner's "Return of Casualties near Kinston" also listed him as wounded. His service records and *NC Troops* incorrectly note that he was admitted to GH No. 3 in Greensboro on March 10, 1865, for unspecified reasons. In National Archives Confederate Record Group 109, General Hospital No. 3's location is erroneously identified as Greensboro. Goldsboro is the correct location. Confederate authorities began relocating GH No. 3 from Goldsboro to High Point on March 11, 1865, as part of the town's evacuation. The hospital resumed operations in High Point on or about March 19, 1865. Neither his service records nor *NC Troops* note his wounding at Wise's Forks in March 1865. Whitaker was discharged and returned to his unit on an undetermined date before March 20, 1865.

Bentonville
Wounded on March 20, 1865, at Bentonville. According to Surgeon Kinyoun's "Register of Sick, Killed and Wounded 66th N.C. Regt., March 1865," Pvt. J. Whitaker, Co. A, was seriously wounded in the mouth by a gunshot, "breaking [the] right upper jaw bone." Surgeon Tanner's "Return of Casualties in Hoke's Div. near Bentonville" also listed him as wounded. Neither his service records nor *NC Troops* note his wounding at Bentonville in March 1865. No further records.
Source: Houts, *A Darkness Ablaze*, 278; ibid., 281; Tanner (WF), 139; ibid., 149; *NCT*, XV:327; M270; Sokolosky, *NC Confederate Hospitals, vol. 2*; NC Confederate Widow's Pension (Orange County).

White, Needham M., Private, Company F
Wise's Forks
Wounded at Wise's Forks on March 10, 1865. According to Surgeon Kinyoun's "Register of Sick, Killed and Wounded 66th N.C. Regt., March 1865," Pvt. N. White, Co. F, was severely wounded on the top of his head by a gunshot wound and sent to "General Hospital Goldsboro" that same day. Surgeon Tanner's "Return of Casualties near Kinston" also lists him as wounded. His service records do not note his wounding in March 1865. No further records.
Source: Houts, *A Darkness Ablaze,* 280; Tanner, 139; *NCT,* XV:368; M270; NC Confederate Widow's Pension (Jones County).

Whitman, William, Private, Company H
Wise's Forks
Captured near Kinston on March 10, 1865. Confined at Point Lookout, Maryland, and released upon taking the Oath of Allegiance on June 21, 1865.
Source: *NCT,* XV:384; M270; NC Confederate Pension (Duplin County).

▲**Wiggs, James J.**, First Sergeant, Company B
Wise's Forks
Wounded at Wise's Forks on March 8, 1865. According to Surgeon Kinyoun's "Register of Sick, Killed and Wounded 66th NC Regiment, March 1865," Sgt. J. J. Wiggs was shot severely in the right thigh and then transferred to "General Hospital Goldsboro" on March 9, 1865. Surgeon Tanner's "Return of Casualties near Kinston" also lists him as wounded. His service records and *NC Troops* incorrectly note that Wiggs was hospitalized at GH No. 3 in Greensboro on March 9, 1865. In National Archives Confederate Record Group 109, General Hospital No. 3's location is erroneously identified as Greensboro. Goldsboro is the correct location. Confederate authorities began relocating GH No. 3 from Goldsboro to High Point on March 11, 1865, as part of the town's evacuation. The hospital resumed operations in High Point on or about March 19, 1865. Transferred to Raleigh and admitted to GH No. 13 (Pettigrew) on March 13, 1865. Received a 60-day furlough on March 20, 1865.
Source: Houts, *A Darkness Ablaze,* 278; Tanner: 138; *NCS* (Raliegh), March 29, 1865; *Daily Progress* (Raleigh), March 28, 1865; *WD* (Charlotte), April 4, 1865; *NCT,* XV:336; M270; Sokolosky, *NC Confederate Hospitals, vol. 2.*

Wilson, Elbert W., Private, Company D
Wise's Forks
Captured at Kinston on March 10, 1865. Confined at Point Lookout, Maryland, and released upon taking the Oath of Allegiance on June 21, 1865.
Source: *NCT,* XV:352; M270.

Winborn, David, Private, Company K
Wise's Forks
Captured near Kinston on March 10, 1865. Confined at Point Lookout, Maryland, and released upon taking the Oath of Allegiance on May 14, 1865.
Source: *NCT,* XV:402; M270.

Witherington, James G., Sergeant, Company E
Wise's Forks
Captured near Kinston on March 10, 1865. Confined at Point Lookout, Maryland, and released upon taking the Oath of Allegiance on June 21, 1865.
Source: *NCT,* XV:360; M270.

Wofford, William W., Private, Company A
Fayetteville
Captured at Fayetteville on March 18, 1865. Confined at Hart's Island, New York, and released upon taking the Oath of Allegiance on June 19, 1865.
Source: *DB* (Charlotte), March 28, 1865; *NCT,* XV:327; M270; NC Confederate Widow's Pension (Mecklenburg County).

Wood, Bennett, Private, Company B
Wise's Forks
Wounded and captured on March 10, 1865, and admitted to U.S. Army Foster General Hospital (New Bern) with a gunshot in the right lumbar region on March 15, 1865. No further records.
Source: *NCT*, XV:336; M270; RG94, Foster General Hospital Registry, no. 6570, 99.

▲Wooten, Allen, Corporal, Company I,
Bentonville
Wounded on March 19, 1865, at Bentonville. According to Surgeon Kinyoun's "Register of Sick, Killed and Wounded 66th N.C. Regt., March 1865," Corp. A. Wooten, Co. I, was mortally wounded by a gunshot to his neck, breaking the spinal column. Surgeon Tanner's "Return of Casualties in Hoke's Div. near Bentonville" also lists him as wounded. Admitted to GH No. 13 (Pettigrew) in Raleigh on March 21, 1865, paralyzed throughout his whole body, and died there on March 28, 1865. Buried in Oakwood Cemetery in Raleigh, North Carolina. Wooten's name also appears on a monument at Bentonville Battlefield State Historic Site, leading some to assume he is buried in the Confederate mass grave located there.
Source: Houts, *A Darkness Ablaze*, 281; Tanner (BV), 149; *NCT*, XV:393; M270.

Wooten, Council, Private, (Company Unknown)
Bentonville
According to Clark's *Histories*, "the young gallant Council Wooten, a young man from near Kinston, who was killed suddenly while bravely and defiantly waving the colors of the regiment in front of the enemy."
Source: Clark's *Regiments*, III: 698; *NCT*, XV:408.

Worlie, David M., Private, Company E
Sugar Loaf
Captured near Wilmington on February 16, 1865. Confined at Point Lookout, Maryland, and released upon taking the Oath of Allegiance on May 14, 1865. *NC Troops* notes that the correct spelling of the surname may be Worley. His Confederate pension application uses the surname of "Worley."
Source: *NCT*, XV:360; M270; NC Confederate Pension (Lenoir County).

Kirkland's Brigade Monument
Wyse Fork Battlefield
17th, 42nd, and 66th NC Regiments
Includes the names of those soldiers captured, killed, and wounded during the battle in March 1865.

(Courtesy of Dennis Harper)

67th Regiment North Carolina Troops

Andrews, Macon, Private, Company L
Kinston (Post Wise's Forks)
Captured at Kinston on March 13, 1865. Confined at Point Lookout, Maryland, and released upon taking the Oath of Allegiance on June 23, 1865.
Source: *NCT*, XV:506; M270.

Barfield, Mills T., Private, Company C
Cox's Bridge
Wounded in the left breast and captured at Cox's Bridge on or about March 18, 1865. Admitted to a U.S. Army of the Ohio field hospital that same day. *NC Troops* notes that he survived the war.
Source: *NCT*, XV:443; M270.

Bass, Augustus, Private, Company D
Goldsboro (Post Bentonville)
Captured at Goldsboro on March 31, 1865. Confined at Hart's Island, New York Harbor, and released upon taking the Oath of Allegiance on June 19, 1865.
Source: *NCT*, XV:450; M270; NC Confederate Pension (Wilson County).

Bell, George, Private, Company D
Kinston (Post Wise's Forks)
Deserted at Kinston on March 18, 1865. The Kinston Provost Marshall listed Bell as a deserter. No further records.
Source: *NCT*, XV:450; M270.

Bell, Ottaway S., Private, Company K
Wise's Forks
Confederate pension records indicate that he was wounded in the left forearm at Kinston on March 8, 1865, requiring the removal of "seven (7) inches" of bone. Admitted to GH No. 13 (Pettigrew) in Raleigh on March 11, 1865, entry no. 2573, suffering from a gunshot wound to the arm. Transferred to Charlotte's GH No. 11 on March 19, 1865. No further records.
Source: NC Confederate Pension (New Hanover County); RG109, 6/290:391; *NCT*, XV:501; *NCS* (Raliegh), March 29, 1865; M270; *WD* (Charlotte), April 4, 1865.

Britt, James, Private, Company B
Goldsboro (Post Bentonville)
Deserted at Goldsboro on March 24, 1865. Confined at Washington, D.C., on April 5, 1865, and released upon taking the Oath of Allegiance on or about the same date.
Source: *NCT*, XV:450; M270.

Carr, Titus William, 2nd Lieutenant, Company K
Hookerton
Captured at Hookerton on March 31, 1865. Confined at Hart's Island, New York Harbor, and released upon taking the Oath of Allegiance on June 17, 1865.
Source: *NCT*, XV:500; M270.

Chase, Henry, Private, Company B
Goldsboro (Post Bentonville)
Captured at Goldsboro on March 26, 1865. Confined at Hart's Island, New York Harbor, and released upon taking the Oath of Allegiance on June 18, 1865.
Source: *NCT*, XV:437; M270; NC Confederate Pension (Greene County).

Cummings, Marshall, Private, Company D
Kinston (Post Wise's Forks)

Federal Provost Marshal records indicate that he was a deserter captured on Wilmington Road on March 14, 1865. The Wilmington Road (current-day U.S. Highway 258) is approximately three miles from the main Confederate defensive line along Southwest Creek. By March 14, the Confederates were evacuating Kinston toward Goldsboro, and Federal cavalry patrols probably picked up Cummings. No further records.
Source: *NCT*, XV:451; M270.

Cutler, George B., 2nd Lieutenant, Company G
Mosely Hall (Post Bentonville)
Captured at Mosely Hall on March 28, 1865, and sent to the provost marshal in Goldsboro. No further records. *NC Troops* notes that he survived the war.
Source: *NCT*, XV:473; M270.

Dail, Christopher C., Private, Company D
Goldsboro (Post Bentonville)
Captured at Goldsboro on March 22, 1865, as a deserter. Took the Oath of Allegiance the next day.
Source: *NCT*, XV:451; M270.

Dail, Elbert, Private, Company C
Mosely Hall (Post Bentonville)
Captured at Mosely Hall on March 31, 1865. Confined at Hart's Island, New York, and released upon taking the Oath of Allegiance on June 18, 1865. The Goldsboro Provost Marshal records included the letter "D," probably an abbreviation for deserter.
Source: *NCT*, XV:444; M270.

Darden, John G., Private, Company D
Goldsboro (Post Bentonville)
Captured at Goldsboro on March 22, 1865, as a deserter. Took the Oath of Allegiance the next day.
Source: *NCT*, XV:451; M270; NC Confederate Pension (Wake County).

▲Fisher, J. C., Private, Company H
Wise's Forks
The GH No. 3 (Goldsboro) patient registry lists a Pvt. J. C. Fisher, Co. L, 67th NC, entry no. 1885, admitted on March 10, 1865, from Kinston for an unspecified complaint. A separate No. 3 ledger, titled "Reports of Wounded and Operations," indicates that Pvt. J. C. Fisher, Co. L, 67th NC, suffered a contusion "in battle" by an artillery shell and was admitted on March 10, 1865. The ledger further specifies that he was transferred to Raleigh on an unrecorded date. No further records. *NC Troops* does not note his hospitalization on account of being injured in March 1865. His Confederate pension records state that he was wounded at Jackson's Mill in 1865, which is the battle of Wise's Forks.
Source: RG109, 6/291:37; NCOAH, CW10, Ledger B, March 1865, entry no. 74; *NCT*, XV:483; M270; NC Confederate Pension (Duplin County).

Forrest, Jesse T., Private, Company C
Wise's Forks
Captured near Kinston on March 8, 1865. Confined at Point Lookout, Maryland, and released upon taking the Oath of Allegiance on June 27, 1865.
Source: M270; *NCT*: XV:444.

♦▲Fulcher, Joseph A., Private, Company A
Wise's Forks (Inconclusive)
The patient registry for General Hospital No. 3 in Goldsboro lists Pvt. I. A. Fulcher of Company A, 67th North Carolina, entry no. 1815, was transferred from Kinston and admitted on March 8, 1865, with a gunshot wound in his right arm. A J. A. Fulchier, Co. A, 67th NC, was admitted to GH No. 13 (Pettigrew) in Raleigh on March 10, 1865, entry no. 2434, wounded in the right arm. Although GH No. 13's patient registry indicates that he was transferred to Charlotte on March 19, 1865, his name does not appear on GH

No. 11's patient registry. No further records. Joseph A. Fulcher is probably the same soldier spelled with slight differences between the two hospital registries. *NC Troops* does not note the wounding and hospitalization in March 1865. Further research is required.
Source: RG109, 6/291:36; RG109, 6/290:391; *NCT*, XV:431; M270.

Grant, Lewis, Private, Company C
Kinston (Post Wise's Forks)
Captured at Kinston on March 18, 1865. The Goldsboro Provost Marshal records included the letter "D," probably an abbreviation for deserter. However, his Confederate pension records indicate that he served till the end of the war.
Source: *NCT*, XV:444; M270; NC Confederate Pension (Duplin County).

▲Hardison, Council W., Private, Company A
Kinston (Accidental Wound)
The GH No. 3 (Goldsboro) patient registry lists a Pvt. C. Hardison, Co. A, 67th NC, admitted on March 7, 1865, from Kinston with a fractured left leg. A separate No. 3 ledger, titled "Reports of Wounded and Operations," indicates that Pvt. C. Hardison, Co. A, 67th NC, was injured in the left leg because of an "accident." The ledger further notes that he was transferred to Raleigh on an unspecified date. No further records. *NC Troops* does not note his hospitalization on account of being injured in March 1865.
Source: RG109, 6/291:35; NCOAH, CW10, Ledger B, March entry no. 22; *NCT*, XV:431; M270; NC Confederate Widow's Pension (Craven County).

♦Hardy, Parrott M., Private, Company G
Kinston or Mosely Hall (Post Bentonville)
Provost Marshal records indicate two separate locations and dates of capture: Kinston on March 25, 1865, and Mosely Hall on March 28, 1865. The latter entry includes the letter "D," possibly an abbreviation for a deserter. Confined at Hart's Island, New York, and released upon taking the Oath of Allegiance on June 18, 1865.
Source: *NCT*, XV:475; M270; NC Confederate Pension (Duplin County).

▲Hart, Jesse, Private, Company D
Wise's Forks
The GH No. 3 (Goldsboro) patient registry lists a Pvt. Jessie Hart, Co. D, 67th NC, entry no. 1879, was admitted on March 10, 1865, from Kinston with a fractured left leg. A separate No. 3 ledger, titled "Reports of Wounded and Operations," indicates that Pvt. Jesse Hart, Co. D, 67th NC, was shot "in battle" in the right leg and admitted on March 10, 1865. The ledger further specifies that he was transferred to Raleigh on an unrecorded date. No further records. *NC Troops* notes Hart as a member of Co. C, not D, and it does not note his hospitalization on account of being injured in March 1865.
Source: RG109, 6/291:37; NCOAH, CW10, Ledger B, March entry no. 70; *NCT*, XV:445, 452; M270; NC Confederate Widow's Pension (Pitt County).

▲Hatch, James R., Private, Company G
Wise's Forks
Confederate pension records indicate that he was shot above the left eye at "Cobb Mill below Kinston" in February 1865, resulting in the loss of eyesight. Cobb's Mill is an alternative name to the battle of Wise's Forks. His service records note that he was later captured. Provost Marshal records indicate two separate locations and dates of capture: Snow Hill on March 22, 1865, and Mosely Hall on March 28, 1865. Confined at Hart's Island, New York Harbor, and released upon taking the Oath of Allegiance on June 18, 1865.
Source: NC Confederate Pension (Jones County); *NCT*, XV:476; M270.

Henly, Joseph, Private, Company H
Kinston
Federal Provost Marshal records indicate that he was captured as a deserter on the Wilmington Road on March 10, 1865. The Wilmington Road (current-day U.S. Highway 258) is approximately three miles from

the main Confederate defensive line along Southwest Creek. At the time of the battle of Wise's Forks on March 10, Wilmington Road would have been in the Confederate rear area, making the capture location highly unlikely. The date or location of capture is incorrect.
Source: *NCT*, XV:485; M270.

Hines, David, Private, Company C
Wise's Forks
Wounded at Wise's Forks between March 7-10, 1865. Admitted to GH Hospital No. 13 (Pettigrew) in Raleigh on March 11, 1865, with a gunshot wound to the right thigh. Captured at the hospital as a patient on April 13, 1865. His Confederate pension records indicate that he was wounded in the right leg, "ball going clean through his thigh," at Kinston in March 1865.
Source: *NCT*, XV:445; M270; *NCS* (Raliegh), March 29, 1865; *WD* (Charlotte), April 4, 1865; NC Confederate Pension (Pitt County).

Humphrey, C., Private Company F
Near Faison's Depot
Deserted on an unspecified date in March 1865. Took the oath at Headquarters, U.S. Army X Corps at Faison's Depot, where he took the Oath of Allegiance on March 31, 1865. No further records.
Source: *NCT*, XV:470; M270.

Ives, John Lewis, Private Company G
Wise's Forks
Captured near Kinston on March 8, 1865. Confined at Point Lookout, Maryland, and released upon taking the Oath of Allegiance on June 3, 1865.
Source: *NCT*, XV:476; M270.

Jones, McG., ____, Company G
Wise's Forks
NC Troops notes that he was wounded in the right ankle at Kinston on March 10, 1865. Admitted to GH No. 13 (Pettigrew) in Raleigh, where he died of wounds on April 4, 1865.
Source: *NCT*, XV:476; M270; *NCS* (Raliegh), March 29, 1865; *WD* (Charlotte), April 4, 1865.

King, Frederick, Private, Company H
Kinston
Federal Provost Marshal records indicate that he was captured as a deserter on the Wilmington Road on March 8, 1865. Took the Oath of Allegiance on or about the same date. The Wilmington Road (current-day U.S. Highway 258) is approximately three miles from the main Confederate defensive line along Southwest Creek. At the time of the battle of Wise's Forks on March 8, Wilmington Road would have been in the Confederate rear area, making the capture location highly unlikely. The date or location of capture is incorrect.
Source: *NCT*, XV:486; M270.

King, Hill Ennett, Private, Company H
Bentonville
Confederate pension records indicate that he was "slightly wounded in [the] hip" at Bentonville. No further records.
Source: *NCT*, XV:486; M270; NC Confederate Pension (Wake County).

▲Kinsall, John, Private, Company A
Wise's Forks
The GH No. 3 (Goldsboro) patient registry lists Pvt. John Kinsaw, Co. A, 67th NC, was admitted on March 9, 1865, entry no. 1847, from Kinston for an unspecified complaint. A separate No. 3 ledger, titled "Reports of Wounded and Operations," indicates that Pvt. John Kinsaw, Co. A, 67th NC, was wounded "in battle" in the face, "Infr. Max.," and admitted on March 9, 1865. The ledger further specifies that he was transferred to Raleigh on an unrecorded date. No further records. John Kinsall is the same soldier listed in the hospital

records as John Kinsaw. *NC Troops* does not note his hospitalization on account of being injured in March 1865.
Source: RG109, 6/291:37; NCOAH, CW10, Ledger B, March 1865, entry no. 60; *NCT*, XV:432; M270.

▲Kittrel, Alex, Private, Company E
Wise's Forks
The GH No. 3 (Goldsboro) patient registry lists a Pvt. A. Kittrell, Co. E, 67th NC, entry no. 1871, admitted on March 10, 1865, from Kinston for an unspecified complaint. A separate No. 3 ledger, titled "Reports of Wounded and Operations," indicates that Pvt. Alex Kittrell, Co. E, 67th NC, was wounded "in battle" on the left side of the face by a gunshot and admitted on March 10, 1865. The ledger further specifies that he was transferred to Raleigh on an unrecorded date. No further records. *NC Troops* does not note his hospitalization on account of being injured in March 1865.
Source: RG109, 6/291:37; NCOAH, CW10, Ledger B, March entry no. 68; *NCT*, XV:462; M270.

Lassitter, William B., Private, Company C
Mosely Hall (Post Bentonville)
Captured at Mosely Hall on March 31, 1865. The Goldsboro Provost Marshal records included the letter "D," probably an abbreviation for deserter. Confined at Hart's Island, New York, and released upon taking the Oath of Allegiance on June 19, 1865.
Source: *NCT*, XV:446; M270.

Little, Francis Marion, Private, Company G
Wise's Forks
Wounded at or near Kinston on or about March 10, 1865. Admitted to GH Hospital No. 13 (Pettigrew) in Raleigh on March 11, 1865, with a gunshot wound to the left thigh. Transferred to GH No. 3 in High Point, entry no. 2649, at some point on or after April 9, 1865, where he was admitted for unspecified causes. His service records incorrectly note that Little was hospitalized at GH No. 3 in Greensboro in April 1865 with an unspecified complaint. In National Archives Confederate Record Group 109, General Hospital No. 3's location is erroneously identified as Greensboro. High Point is the correct location. Confederate authorities began relocating GH No. 3 from Goldsboro to High Point on March 11, 1865, as part of the town's evacuation. The hospital resumed operations in High Point on or about March 19, 1865. No further records. *NC Troops* notes that he survived the war.
Source: *NCT*, XV:477; M270; *NCS* (Raliegh), March 29, 1865; *WD* (Charlotte), April 4, 1865; Sokolosky, *NC Confederate Hospitals, vol. 2*; RG109, 6/291:52; NC Confederate Widow's Pension (Pitt County).

McCotter, George Badger, 2nd Lieutenant, Company G
Snow Hill (Post Bentonville)
Captured at Snow Hill on March 28, 1865. First, confined at Hart's Island, New York Harbor, transferred in April to Fort Delaware, Delaware, and released upon taking the Oath of Allegiance on June 17, 1865.
Source: *NCT*, XV:474; M270.

McKindler, James, Private, Company D
Goldsboro (Post Bentonville)
Captured as a deserter at Goldsboro on March 23, 1865. Took the Oath of Allegiance the same day. The Goldsboro Provost Marshal records included the letter "D," probably an abbreviation for deserter.
Source: *NCT*, XV:454; M270.

Miller, John W., Private, Company L
Hookerton (Post Bentonville)
Captured at Hookerton on March 31, 1865. Confined at Hart's Island, New York, and released upon taking the Oath of Allegiance on June 18, 1865.
Source: *NCT*, XV:507; M270.

▲Parker, William F., Private, Company D
Wise's Forks

The GH No. 3 (Goldsboro) patient registry lists a Pvt. W. F. Parker, Co. D, 67th NC, entry no. 1823, was admitted on March 9, 1865, from Kinston for unspecified reasons. A separate No. 3 ledger, titled "Reports of Wounded and Operations," indicates that Pvt. W. F. Parker, Co. D 67th NC, was wounded in the left arm "in battle" and admitted on March 9, 1865. The ledger further specifies that he was transferred to Raleigh on an unrecorded date. No further records. *NC Troops* notes that he was wounded in the left leg by a shell at Kinston on March 8, 1865. However, the source of this information is not recorded. Furthermore, his service records and *NC Troops* incorrectly note that Parker was hospitalized at GH No. 3 in Greensboro on March 9, 1865, with an unspecified complaint. In National Archives Confederate Record Group 109, General Hospital No. 3's location is erroneously identified as Greensboro. Goldsboro is the correct location. Confederate authorities began relocating GH No. 3 from Goldsboro to High Point on March 11, 1865, as part of the town's evacuation. The hospital resumed operations in High Point on or about March 19, 1865. Paroled at Goldsboro on May 8, 1865.
Source: RG109, 6/291:36; NCOAH, CW10, Ledger B, March 1865, entry no. 38; *NCT*, XV:455; M270; Sokolosky, *NC Confederate Hospitals, vol. 2*.

Parks, Benjamin, Private, Company H
Mosely Hall (Post Bentonville)
Deserted at Mosely Hall on March 27, 1865. Confined at Hart's Island, New York, and released upon taking the Oath of Allegiance on June 19, 1865.
Source: *NCT*, XV:488; M270.

Pate, Hutching P., Private, Company G
Wise's Forks
Confederate pension records indicate that he was wounded in the face, neck, and eye at Wise's Forks in 1865. By 1901, he was blind in his left eye. His service records note his capture at Kinston on March 15, 1865. *NC Troops* notes that his surname's correct spelling may be Hutchings or Hutchins.
Source: *NCT*, XV:478; M270; NC Confederate Pension (Greene County).

Pate, William H., Private, Company D
Goldsboro (Post Bentonville)
Captured at Goldsboro on March 24, 1865, possibly a deserter. Hospitalized at U.S. Army Foster General Hospital in New Bern for measles before being sent to Newport News, Virginia, and released upon taking the Oath of Allegiance on June 30, 1865.
Source: *NCT*, XV:455; M270; NC Confederate Pension (Lenoir County).

Patrick, James B., Private, Company C
Beaufort County
Captured in Beaufort County on February 19, 1865. Confined at Point Lookout, Maryland, and released upon taking the Oath of Allegiance on June 16, 1865. No details regarding the circumstances of his capture.
Source: M270; *NCT*: XV: 446.

Rives, Peter Richard, Company K
Greenville
Captured at Greenville on February 18, 1865. Confined at Point Lookout, Maryland, and released upon taking the Oath of Allegiance on June 15, 1865.
Source: *NCT*, XV:504; M270; NC Confederate Pension (Martin County).

Sheppard, James Henry, Private Company H
Bentonville
Confederate pension records indicate he was wounded in the right hand and right hip at Bentonville in March 1865. No further records.
Source: *NCT*, XV:489; M270; NC Confederate Pension (Lenoir County).

Skinner, Richard, Private, Company C
Mosely Hall (Post Bentonville)

Captured at Mosely Hall on March 31, 1865. The Goldsboro Provost Marshal records included the letter "D," probably an abbreviation for deserter. Confined at Hart's Island, New York, and released upon taking the Oath of Allegiance on June 19, 1865.
Source: *NCT*, XV:447; M270.

Slaughter, William James, Private, Company G
Kinston (Post Wise's Forks)
Federal Provost Marshal records indicate that he was captured as a deserter at Kinston on March 19, 1865. No further records.
Source: *NCT*, XV:478; M270.

Sparrow, Thomas Gideon, III, 2nd Lieutenant, Company K
Hookerton
Captured at Hookerton on March 31, 1865. Confined at Fort Delaware, Delaware, and released upon taking the Oath of Allegiance on May 30, 1865.
Source: *NCT*, XV:501; M270.

Stafford, Gaston, Private, Company D
Goldsboro (Post Bentonville)
Captured at Goldsboro on March 30, 1865. Confined at Hart's Island, New York, and released upon taking the Oath of Allegiance on June 19, 1865. The Goldsboro Provost Marshal records included the letter "D," probably an abbreviation for deserter.
Source: *NCT*, XV:456; M270; NC Confederate Pension (Wake County).

♦Stevens, Josiah, Private Company D
Bentonville or Goldsboro (Inconclusive)
Captured at or near Bentonville on March 22, 1865, or near Goldsboro on March 24, 1865. Confined at Hart's Island, New York Harbor, and released upon taking the Oath of Allegiance on June 19, 1865.
Source: *NCT*, XV:456; M270.

Strickland, Jerry, Private, Company D
Mosely Hall (Post Bentonville)
Captured at Mosely Hall on or about March 24, 1865. The Goldsboro Provost Marshal records included the letter "D," probably an abbreviation for deserter. Confined at Hart's Island, New York, and released upon taking the Oath of Allegiance on June 18, 1865.
Source: *NCT*, XV:456; M270.

Sugg, John Patrick, Company C
Wise's Forks
Captured near Kinston on March 8, 1865. Confined at Point Lookout, Maryland, and released upon taking the Oath of Allegiance on June 20, 1865.
Source: *NCT*, XV:447; M270; NC Confederate Pension (Greene County).

♦Sugg, Reuben, Corporal, Company G
Goldsboro (Post Wise's Forks) (Inconclusive)
U.S. Army prisoner of war records indicate that he was captured at Goldsboro on March 13, 1865. Confined at Hart's Island, New York, and released upon taking the Oath of Allegiance on June 19, 1865. On March 13, 1865, Confederate forces still occupied Goldsboro. If the capture date is correct, the more probable location would be Kinston. Further research is required.
Source: *NCT*, XV:478; M270; NC Confederate Pension (Pitt County); NC Soldiers' Home Application.

Sumerlin, L. D., Private Company D
Bentonville
Captured at or near Bentonville on March 22, 1865, on March 22, 1865. Confined at Hart's Island, New York Harbor, and released upon taking the Oath of Allegiance on June 19, 1865.

Source: *NCT*, XV:456; M270.

♦Thigpen, Stephen Miller, Private, Company L
(Inconclusive)
His 1903 Confederate pension records indicate that he was wounded at Kinston on or about February 20, 1865, suffering from a flesh wound on the inside of his right leg. No further records.
Source: *NCT*, XV:507; M270; NC Confederate Pension (Lenoir County).

Tyson, Benjamin F., Private, Company G
Mosely Hall (Post Bentonville)
Captured at Mosely Hall on or about March 31-April 1, 1865. The Goldsboro Provost Marshal records included the letter "D," probably an abbreviation for deserter. Confined at Hart's Island, New York, and released upon taking the Oath of Allegiance on June 19, 1865.
Source: *NCT*, XV:479; M270.

Tyson, Sherrod, Private, Company G
Mosely Hall (Post Bentonville)
Captured at Mosely Hall on or about March 31-April 1, 1865. The Goldsboro Provost Marshal records included the letter "D," probably an abbreviation for deserter. Confined at Hart's Island, New York, and released upon taking the Oath of Allegiance on June 19, 1865.
Source: *NCT*, XV:479; M270.

Wells, William B., Private Company L
Wise's Forks
His Confederate pension records indicate he was wounded in the right arm near Kinston on March 8, 1865, "necessitating the amputation of the arm near the shoulder."
Source: *NCT*, XV:507; M270; NC Confederate Pension (Duplin County).

Wigtine, John C., Private, Company G
Kinston (Post Wise's Forks)
Federal Provost Marshal records indicate that he was captured as a deserter at Kinston on March 19, 1865. No further records.
Source: *NCT*, XV:479; M270.

Wilkerson, Elisha, Private, Company H
White Oak River
Captured at the White Oak River on March 11, 1865. Confined at Point Lookout, Maryland, and released upon taking the Oath of Allegiance on June 21, 1865.
Source: *NCT*, XV:491; M270.

Wilson, B. Frank, Private, Company H
Kinston (Post Wise's Forks)
Captured as a deserter at Kinston on March 13, 1865. The Goldsboro Provost Marshal records included the letter "D," probably an abbreviation for deserter. No further records. In early 1865, he was detailed as a wheelwright with the Quartermaster Department in Kinston.
Source: *NCT*, XV:492; M270.

Wilson, John A., Private, Company H
Kinston (Post Wise's Forks)
Captured at Kinston on March 13, 1865. The Goldsboro Provost Marshal records included the letter "D," probably an abbreviation for deserter. No further records. In early 1865, he was detailed as a wheelwright with the Quartermaster Department in Kinston.
Source: *NCT*, XV:492; M270.

68th Regiment North Carolina Troops

Baum, Abraham, Private, Company B
North River
Captured on the North River on March 11, 1865. Confined at Point Lookout, Maryland, and released upon taking the Oath of Allegiance on June 21, 1865. He was a resident of Currituck County when he enlisted in 1863. It is assumed that he was captured on the North River in the northeastern part of the state, not the North River in Carteret County.
Source: *NCT*, XV:535; M270.

▲**Brinkly, James M.**, Private, Company D
Kinston (Accidental Wound)
The GH No. 3 (Goldsboro) patient registry lists a Pvt. J. M. Brinkly, Co. B, 67th NC, admitted on March 9, 1865, entry no. 1864, from Kinston for an unspecified reason. A separate No. 3 ledger, titled "Reports of Wounded and Operations," indicates that Pvt. J. M. Brinkly, Co. B, 67th NC, was wounded "in battle" by a gunshot to the right leg. The ledger further specifies that he was transferred to an unspecified hospital on an unrecorded date. His service records and *NC Troops* incorrectly note that he was admitted to GH No. 3 in Greensboro on March 9, 1865, from Kinston, for unspecified reasons. In National Archives Confederate Record Group 109, General Hospital No. 3's location is erroneously identified as Greensboro. Goldsboro is the correct location. Confederate authorities began relocating GH No. 3 from Goldsboro to High Point on March 11, 1865, as part of the town's evacuation. The hospital resumed operations in High Point on or about March 19, 1865. Neither his service records nor *NC Troops* note his wounding at Wise's Forks in March 1865. Paroled at Goldsboro on May 3, 1865. No further records.
Source: RG109, 6/291:37; NCOAH, CW10, Ledger B, March 1865, entry no. 56; *NCT*, XV:546; M270; Sokolosky, *NC Confederate Hospitals, vol. 2*.

Carter, William H., Private, Company I
Wise's Forks
His Confederate pension records indicate that he was wounded in the right eye near Kinston in March 1865, which resulted in "total blindness." No further records.
Source: *NCT*, XV:575; M270; NC Confederate Pension (Gates County).

Cook, Robert, Private, Company K
Wise's Forks
The Barbee Wayside Hospital in High Point patient registry lists Pvt. Robert Cook, Co. K, 68th NC, was admitted on March 9, 1865, with a gunshot wound in the left hand. His Confederate pension records indicate that he was wounded in the left hand, resulting in the "loss of [the] second finger" at Kinson in April 1865. Cook erred in his memory of the month.
Source: Barbee Wayside Registry, entry no. 5737; *NCT*, XV:270; NC Confederate Pension (Northampton County).

▲**Early, John A.**, Private, Company E
Wise's Forks
The Barbee Wayside Hospital in High Point patient registry lists Pvt. Jno. Early, Co. E, 68th NC, was admitted on March 9, 1865, with a gunshot wound in the left hand. Confederate pension records note that he was wounded in the left leg, "fractured," at Kinston on March 8, 1865.
Source: Barbee Wayside Registry, entry no. 5747; *NCT*, XV:554; M270; NC Confederate Pension (Bertie County).

Earnhart, Henry L., Private, Company B
Wise's Forks
Confederate pension records note that he was shot in the left side of the breast, "breaking two ribs," at Kinston in March 1865.
Source: *NCT*, XV:536; M270; NC Confederate Pension (Rowan County).

Foster, John, Private, Company B

Tarboro
Deserted near Tarboro on or about March 3, 1865, and captured March 24, 1865. No further records.
Source: *NCT*, XV:536; M270.

▲Grant, Newitt, Private, Company K
Wise's Forks
Admitted to GH No. 13 (Pettigrew) in Raleigh on March 10, 1865, wounded in the right leg. Received a 60-day furlough on March 16, 1865. No further records.
Source: *NCT*, XV:583; *WD* (Charlotte), April 4, 1865; M270; NC Confederate Widow's Pension (Northampton County).

Hall, Gustavus, P., Corporal, Company H
Wise's Forks
NC Troops notes that he was wounded in the right leg at or near Kinston on March 10, 1865. Admitted to GH No. 13 (Pettigrew) in Raleigh on March 10, 1865, wounded in the right leg. No further records.
Source: *NCT*, XV:571; *WD* (Charlotte), April 4, 1865; M270.

♦Ham, William H., Private, (Company Unknown)
Goldsboro (Post Wise's Forks) (Inconclusive)
Deserted at Goldsboro on March 13, 1865. Transferred to Washington, D.C., on April 5, 1865, via Fort Monroe, Virginia, and released upon taking the Oath of Allegiance on or about the same date. On March 13, 1865, Confederate forces still occupied Goldsboro. If the capture date is correct, the more probable location would be Kinston. Further research is required.
Source: *NCT*, XV:585; M270.

♦Kirby, William C., Private, Company H
Wise's Forks (Inconclusive)
NC Troops notes that he was wounded at Kinston in March 1865. No further records. *NC Troops* notes that he survived the war. No further records. Based on the date, he was probably wounded at Wise's Forks. Further research is required.
Source: *NCT*, XV:572; *WD* (Charlotte), April 4, 1865; M270.

♦▲Lineberrier, David, Private, Company B
(Inconclusive)
Both his service Records and *NC Troops* incorrectly note that he was admitted to GH No. 3 in Greensboro on February 12, 1865, with a gunshot wound; *NC Troops* also misidentified the date as February 22. In National Archives Confederate Record Group 109, General Hospital No. 3's location is erroneously identified as Greensboro. Goldsboro is the correct location. Confederate authorities began relocating GH No. 3 from Goldsboro to High Point on March 11, 1865, as part of the town's evacuation. The hospital resumed operations in High Point on or about March 19, 1865. Returned to duty on February 19, 1865. He was later paroled at Salisbury on May 13, 1865.
Source: *NCT*, XV:538; Sokolosky, *NC's Confederate Hospitals*, vol. 2; M270.

▲Reid, William H., Private, Company I
Wise's Forks
Wounded at Kinston on March 8, 1865. The Barbee Wayside Hospital in High Point patient registry lists Pvt. W. H. Read [sic], Co. I, 68th NC, was admitted on March 9, 1865, with a gunshot wound in the left arm. Survived the war.
Source: *NCT*, XV:579; Barbee Wayside Registry, entry no. 5743; M270.

Sasser, Edward, Private, Company C
Wise's Forks
The Barbee Wayside Hospital in High Point patient registry lists Pvt. Edward Saucer, Co. C, 68th NC, was admitted on March 9, 1865, with a gunshot wound in the left arm. His Confederate pension records indicate that he was shot "through the left arm" at Kinston on an unspecified date.

Source: Barbee Wayside Registry, entry no. 5742; *NCT*, XV:582; M270; NC Confederate Pension (Johnston County).

Trueblood, John T., Private, Company A
Wise's Forks
Confederate pension records note that he was wounded in the chest by "a spent bullet" at Kinston on an unspecified date.
Source: *NCT*, XV:533; M270; NC Confederate Pension (Perquimans County).

Thomas, John M., Private, Company A
Mosely Hall (Post Bentonville)
Captured as a deserter at Mosely Hall on March 28, 1865, and sent to the Goldsboro Provost Marshall. No further records.
Source: *NCT*, XV:533; M270.

Captain William J. McDugald
McDugald's Company was attached to the 1st Battalion NC Heavy Artillery during the battle of Bentonville, where he was wounded on March 19, 1865. He died later at GH No. 13 (Pettigrew) in Raleigh during the week ending April 7, 1865. Buried in Oakwood Cemetery in Raleigh, North Carolina.

(Courtesy of Wade Sokolosky)

Captain James M. McDugald's Company[3]

▲**Cowan, James K.**, Private, McDugald's Company
Bentonville
Surgeon Hanahan's "Return of Wounded" for Hagood's Brigade from the battle of Bentonville listed Pvt. J. K. P. Cowan, Co. A, 1st Battalion NC, was slightly wounded in his right leg on March 19, 1865. His name also appears on Surgeon Tanner's "Return of Casualties in Hoke's Div. near Bentonville." Both surgeons erred in listing Cowan as a member of 1st Battalion NC. Cowan was a member of McDugald's Company, temporarily attached to the battalion during the battle of Bentonville.
Source: Hanahan, 3; Tanner, 146; *DC* (Raleigh), April 7, 1865; *NCT*, XIX:429; M270; NC Confederate Pension (Pender County).

▲**Hall, James O.**, Private, McDugald's Company
Bentonville
Surgeon Hanahan's "Return of Wounded" for Hagood's Brigade from the battle of Bentonville listed Pvt. J. O. Hall, Co. A, 1st Battalion NC, was severely wounded in his left foot on March 20, 1865. His name also appears on Surgeon Tanner's "Return of Casualties in Hoke's Div. near Bentonville." Both surgeons erred in listing Hall as a member of the 1st Battalion NC. Hall was a member of McDugald's Company, temporarily attached to the battalion during the battle of Bentonville. Admitted to GH No. 13 (Pettigrew) in Raleigh on March 21, 1865, with a gunshot wound to the left foot. On an unspecified date in April 1865, he was transferred to GH No. 3 in High Point. No further records.
Source: Hanahan, 1; Tanner, 146; *DC* (Raleigh), April 7, 1865; *NCT*, XIX:431; M270; RG109, 6/291:52; NC Confederate Pension (Guilford County).

▲**Jones, Silas**, Private, McDugald's Company
Bentonville
Surgeon Hanahan's "Return of Wounded" for Hagood's Brigade from the battle of Bentonville listed Pvt. S. Jones, "Capt. McDudle's Co.," 1st Battalion NC, was severely wounded in his left shoulder joint on March 19, 1865. His name also appears on Surgeon Tanner's "Return of Casualties in Hoke's Div. near Bentonville."
Private Silas Jones, McDougald's Company, is the same soldier as Pvt. S. Jones. Neither his service records nor *NC Troops* notes his wounding at Bentonville.
Source: Hanahan, 4; Tanner, 146; *DC* (Raleigh), April 7, 1865; *NCT*, XIX:432; M270.

▲**McDugald, William J.**, Captain, McDugald's Company
Bentonville
Surgeon Hanahan's "Return of Wounded" for Hagood's Brigade from the battle of Bentonville listed Capt. W. J. McDudle [sic], 1st Battalion NC, suffered a fractured left arm and flesh wound on March 19, 1865. His name also appears on Surgeon Tanner's "Return of Casualties in Hoke's Div. near Bentonville." Both surgeons erred in listing McDougald as a member of 1st Battalion NC. McDougald's Company was temporarily attached to the battalion during the battle of Bentonville. His service records indicate that Capt. W. J. McDugald died during the week ending April 7, 1865, while a patient at General Hospital No. 13 (Pettigrew) in Raleigh. McDugald is buried in Oakwood Cemetery, Raleigh, North Carolina, grave no. 38.
Source: Hanahan, 4; Tanner, 146; M270; *DC* (Raleigh), April 7, 1865; *NCT*, XIX:427; M270.

---

[3] This company was designated at various times as Captain Buie's Company, NC Troops; Company A, City Battalion, Garrison of Wilmington, North Carolina Troops; Lieutenant Baldwin's Company, North Carolina Troops; and Captain W. J. McDugald's Company, Unattached Company of North Carolina Troops. On an undetermined date in 1865, McDugald's Company was attached to the 1st Battalion North Carolina Heavy Artillery and may have fought with the battalion at the battle of Wise's Forks. Compiled Service Records of Confederate Soldiers Who Served in Organizations from the State of North Carolina, 1861-1865 (M270), RG109, NA.

Patterson, Neill, Private, McDugald's Company
Bentonville
Captured at the battle of Bentonville on March 20, 1865. Confined at Hart's Island, New York Harbor, where he died of chronic diarrhea on May 18, 1865.
Source: *NCT*, XIX:434; M270.

Pridgen, John O., Private, McDugald's Company
Bentonville
Captured at the battle of Bentonville on March 20, 1865. Confined at Hart's Island, New York Harbor, where he died of nostalgia on June 4, 1865.
Source: *NCT*, XIX:434; M270.

158th Anniversary of the Battle of Bentonville
4,133 lighted candles honor the soldiers captured, killed, or wounded at the battle.
(Courtesy of Bentonville Battlefield State Historic Site)

PART IV
(Reserves)

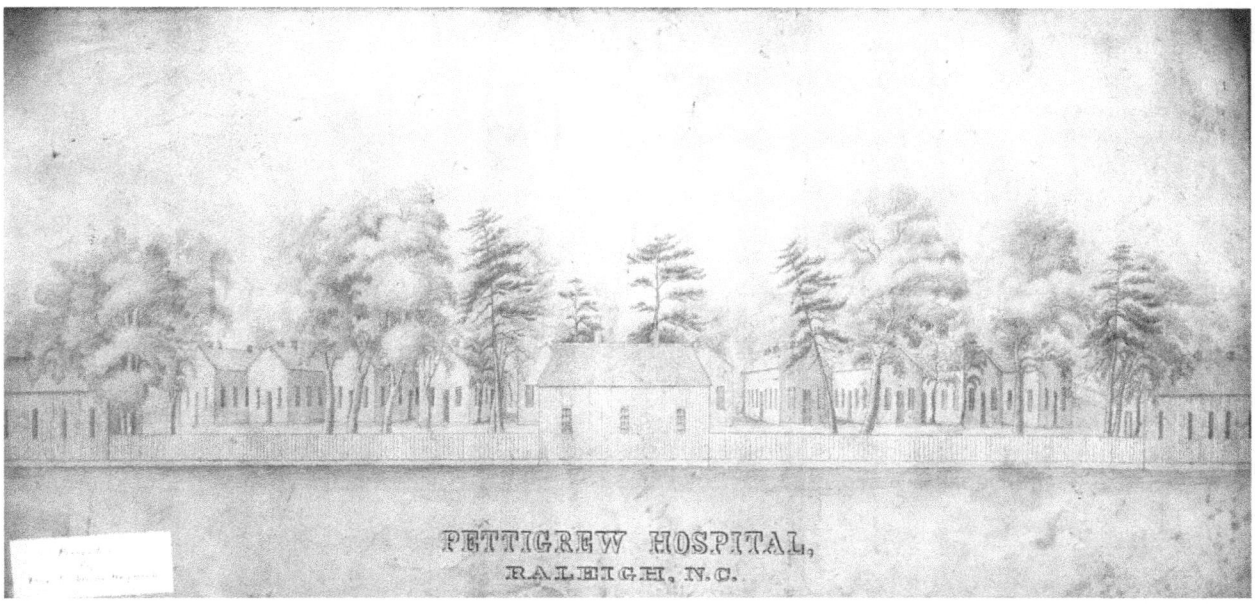

General Hospital No. 13 (Pettigrew Hospital) Raleigh
It opened in the spring of 1864 and was one of three pavilion-style hospitals built by the Confederate Medical Department in North Carolina.

(Sketch by S. A. Partridge, North Carolina Office of Archives and History)

1st Battalion North Carolina Junior Reserves

Burgin, Samuel D., Sergeant, Company A
Bentonville
According to Surgeon Tanner's "Return of Casualties in Hoke's Div. near Bentonville," Sgt. S. D. Burgin, Co. A, was slightly wounded in the right thigh on an unspecified date between March 19-21, 1865.
Source: Tanner (BV), 150; *NCT*, XVII:122; M270.

▲**Carter, William T.**, Private, Company E
Bentonville
Wounded at the battle of Bentonville between March 19-21, 1865. According to Surgeon Tanner's "Return of Casualties in Hoke's Div. near Bentonville," Pvt. Wm. Carter, Co. E, was severely wounded in the right hand on an unspecified date between March 19-21, 1865.
Source: Tanner (BV), 150; Clark, *Histories*, IV:394; *NCT*, XVII:145; M270.

▲**Douthit, James B.**, 1st Lieutenant, Company E
Wise's Forks
NC Troops notes that he was shot in the lower right leg at Kinston between March 8, 1865, "while gallantly leading, and cheering his men." The GH No. 3 (Goldsboro) patient registry lists a Lt. J. B. Douthirst, Co. E, 1st NC Jr., entry no. 1836, was admitted on March 9, 1865, for unspecified reasons. A separate No. 3 ledger, titled "Reports of Wounded and Operations," indicates that a Lt. J. B. Dauthis, Co. E, 1st NC Jr., suffered a gunshot wound "in battle" to the right leg, "bone broken," and was admitted on March 9, 1865. The ledger further specifies that he was transferred to another unspecified hospital on an unrecorded date. He later died of wounds in the hospital at Goldsboro on March 23, 1865. James B. Douthit of 1st Battalion NC Jr. Reserves is the same officer listed above, with various spellings of his surname and the incorrect unit designation.
Source: *NCT*, XVII:145; *People's Press* (Salem, NC), April 6, 1865; WD (Charlotte), April 4, 1865; RG109, 6/291:36; NCOAH, CW10, Ledger B, March 1865, entry no. 50; M270.

Hill, John, Private, Company C
Bentonville
NC Troops notes that Hill's pension records indicate that he was "wounded at Bentonville in March 1865." Private John Hill's name does not appear on Surgeon Tanner's "Return of Casualties in Hoke's Div. near Bentonville."
Source: *NCT*, XVII:137; M270; NC Confederate Pension (Rutherford County).

▲**Hill, William R.**, Corporal, Company D
Wise's Forks
NC Troops notes that Corp. William R. Hill was wounded in the left breast at Kinston between March 8-9, 1865. Admitted to GH No. 13 (Pettigrew) in Raleigh on March 11, 1865, with a gunshot wound in the left breast. Died in a hospital in Raleigh on March 26, 1865.
Source: Clark, 4:393; *NCT*, XVII:142; M270.

♦▲**Kurfes, John**, Private, Company E
Wise's Forks (Inconclusive)
The GH No. 3 (Goldsboro) patient registry lists a Pvt. John Kurfes, Co. E, 1st Batt. Jr., was admitted on March 8, 1865, with a gunshot wound. The date and location of the wounding were not recorded. A separate No. 3 ledger, titled "Reports of Wounded and Operations," indicates that Pvt. Jno. Kerfes, Co. E, 1st Batt Jr., suffered a gunshot wound to the nose and right hand "in battle" and was admitted on March 9, 1865. The ledger further specifies that he was transferred to Raleigh on an unrecorded date. There is no soldier listed on the unit rolls with the surname of "Kurfes." There are two soldiers found with the surname of Kerfeese, both of Co. E, John G., and John W., neither of which *NC Troops* notes as having been wounded. According to *NC Troops*, the surname may be Kerfees or Kurfees.
Source: RG109, 6/291:36; NCOAH, CW10, Ledger B, March 1865, entry no. 30; *NCT*, XVII:147; M270.

Lane, William C. Preston, Captain, Company C
Wise's Forks
NC Troops notes that Capt. William C. Lane was shot through the breast near Kinston on March 8, 1865. No further records. Survived the war.
Source: *NCT*, XVII:134; M270; NC Confederate Pension (Henderson County).

▲Lewis, James Whittington, Private, Co. B
Bentonville
Wounded at the battle of Bentonville between March 19-21, 1865. According to Surgeon Tanner's "Return of Casualties in Hoke's Div. near Bentonville," Pvt. J. Lewis, Co. B, was severely wounded in the left arm. Admitted to GH No. 11 in Charlotte on April 28, 1865, with a gunshot wound of the "upper extremities" and paroled there as a patient in May 1865.
Source: Tanner (BV), 150; *NCT*, XVII:131; M270.

▲Lineberry, Edwin Culver, 3rd Lieutenant, Company E
Wise's Forks
NC Troops notes that he was wounded at Wise's Forks between March 8-9, 1865. Admitted to GH No. 13 (Pettigrew) in Raleigh on March 11, 1865, with a gunshot wound to the right hip. Died two weeks later, on March 25, 1865. No further records. He is buried in Oakwood Cemetery, Raliegh, North Carolina.
Source: *NCT*, XVII:145; *WD* (Charlotte), April 4, 1865.

Liner, A. Joseph, 2nd Lieutenant, Company C
Wise's Forks
Clark's *Histories* states that Lt. Joseph A. Liner was wounded at Kinston between March 8-9, 1865. No further records. Survived the war. According to *NC Troops*, Liner's Confederate gravestone indicates that his given name was Joseph James.
Source: Clark, *Histories*, 4:393; *NCT*, XVII:134; M270.

♦Stephenson, J. A., Private, Company D
Bentonville (Inconclusive)
Private Stephenson was admitted to GH No. 13 (Pettigrew) in Raleigh on March 21, 1865, with a gunshot wound to the left middle finger. Received a 21-day furlough on March 23, 1865. Private J. A. Stephenson's name does not appear on Surgeon Tanner's "Return of Casualties in Hoke's Div. near Bentonville."
Source: *NCT*, XVII:143; M270.

♦▲Whitaker, Jesse, Private, Company A
Bentonville (Inconclusive)
His Confederate pension records indicate wounded in the jaw at Smithfield on or about March 18, 1865. This may refer to Bentonville. Whitaker's services records incorrectly note that he was admitted to GH No. 3 in Greensboro on an unspecified date in March 1865. In National Archives Confederate Record Group 109, General Hospital No. 3's location is erroneously identified as Greensboro. High Point is the correct location. Confederate authorities began relocating GH No. 3 from Goldsboro to High Point on March 11, 1865, as part of the town's evacuation. High Point is the correct location. The GH No. 3 Patient Registry lists Pvt. J. Whitaker, Co. A, 1st NC Res., (no. 2394), was admitted on an unspecified date between March 19 and April 7, 1865. No further records. *NC Troops* also erred by noting the hospital's location as Goldsboro.
Source: NC Confederate Pension (Buncombe County); M270; Sokolosky, *NC's Confederate Hospitals*, vol. 2; RG109, 6/291:47; *NCT*, XVII:127; M270.

1st Regiment North Carolina Junior Reserves[4]
(70th Regiment North Carolina)

Calhoun, W., Private, Company F
Bentonville
Wounded at the battle of Bentonville between March 19-21, 1865. According to Surgeon Tanner's "Return of Casualties in Hoke's Div. near Bentonville," Pvt. W. Calhoun, Co. F, 17th NC, was severely wounded in the head. No W. Calhoun is listed in the rolls of the 17th NC. However, a Pvt. Wm. Calhoun, Co. F., 1st NC Jr. Reserves, was admitted to GH No. 3 in High Point on an unrecorded date between March 21 and April 7, 1865, for unspecified reasons. He later died at the hospital and is buried in the Confederate section of Oakwood Cemetery in High Point, North Carolina.
Source: Tanner (WF), 148; RG109, 6/291:50.

▲**Cheek, Noah**, Private, Company H
Wise's Forks
Wounded at the battle of Wise's Forks between March 7-9, 1865. The patient registry for GH No. 3 in Goldsboro lists Pvt. Noah Cheek, Co. H, 1st NC Jr., entry no. 1829, who was transferred from Kinston and admitted on March 8, 1865, for unspecified reasons. However, a separate No. 3 ledger, titled "Reports of Wounded and Operations," indicates that Pvt. Noah Cheek, Co. H, 1st NC Jr., suffered a gunshot wound to the left shoulder "in battle" and was admitted on March 9, 1865. The ledger further specifies that he was transferred to Raleigh on an unrecorded date. *NC Troops* notes that Noah Cheek was hospitalized in Raleigh after March 10, 1865. The Raliegh hospital's identification is not indicated. No further records.
Source: RG109, 6/291:36; NCOAH, CW10, Ledger B, March 1865, entry no. 44; *NCT*, XVII:212; M270.

Dowdy, Dennis, Corporal, Company H
Wise's Forks
Wounded at the battle of Wise's Forks on an unspecified date between March 7-10, 1865. Admitted to GH No. 13 (Pettigrew) in Raleigh on March 10, 1865, with a gunshot wound in the left thigh. Received a 60-day furlough on March 16, 1865.
Source: RG109, 6/291:36; *NCT*, XVII:213; M270.

▲**Dowdy, James D.**, Private, Company H
Wise's Forks
Wounded at the battle of Wise's Forks on March 8, 1865. Dowdy's services records and *NC Troops* incorrectly note that he was admitted to GH No. 3 in Greensboro from Kinston on March 8, 1865, suffering from a gunshot wound. Goldsboro is the correct location. Confederate authorities ordered GH No. 3's relocation from Goldsboro to High Point on March 11, 1865, as part of the Confederate evacuation of the town. A separate GH No. 3 ledger, titled "Reports of Wounded and Operations," indicates that Pvt. J. D. Dowdy, Co. H, 1st NC Jr., suffered a gunshot wound in the left thigh "in battle" and was admitted on March 9, 1865. The ledger further specifies that he was transferred to Raleigh on an unrecorded date. His Confederate pension records indicate that he was shot through the thigh on or about March 8, 1865. No further records. Further research is required regarding the discrepancy between the date of admittance to GH No. 3.
Source: RG109, 6/291:36; NCOAH, CW10, Ledger B, March 1865, entry no. 28; *NCT*, XVII:213; M270; NC Confederate Pension (Chatham County).

♦▲**Eddinger, D.**, Private, Company C
Bentonville

---

[4] The unit designations 70th, 71st, and 72nd North Carolina are post-war identifications assigned by John W. Moore, ed. *Roster of North Carolina Troops in the War Between the States*, 4 vols., and copied by Walter Clark's *Histories of the several regiments and Battalions from North Carolina in the Great War 1861-'65*.

Wounded at the battle of Bentonville on an unspecified date between March 19-21, 1865. According to Surgeon Tanner's "Return of Casualties in Hoke's Div. near Bentonville," Pvt. D. Edinger, Co. C, was dangerously wounded in the chest. There are two Eddinger's in Co. C, both with a given name beginning with the letter D, Daniel, and David. Neither soldiers' service records nor *NC Troops* note their wounding at Bentonville. A patient registry entry (no. 2575) for GH No. 3 in High Point lists a Pvt. D. A. Ediger, Co. C, 1st NC, admitted on an unspecified date between March 21 and April 7, 1865. Both Daniel and David Eddinger were paroled at Greensboro on May 6, 1865. Further research is required.
Source: Tanner (BV), 150; *NCT*, XVII:172; RG109, 6/291:50; M270.

▲**Edwards, Phil**, Private, Company A
Bentonville
Wounded at the battle of Bentonville on an unspecified date between March 19-21, 1865. According to Surgeon Tanner's "Return of Casualties in Hoke's Div. near Bentonville," Pvt. P. Edwards, Co. A, was severely wounded in the right arm. Neither his service records nor *NC Troops* note his wounding at Bentonville. No further records. Survived the war.
Source: Tanner (BV), 150; *NCT*, XVII:154; M270.

▲**Gross, Thomas**, Private, Company H
Bentonville
Wounded at the battle of Bentonville on an unspecified date between March 19-21, 1865. According to Surgeon Tanner's "Return of Casualties in Hoke's Div. near Bentonville," Pvt. T. Gross, Co. H, was slightly wounded in the finger. Neither his service records nor *NC Troops* note his wounding at Bentonville. No further records.
Source: Tanner (BV), 150; *NCT*, XVII:214; M270; NC Confederate Pension (Lee County).

Harward, R. E., _____, Company B
Bentonville
Confederate pension records indicate that he was wounded, breaking his leg, at Bentonville. No further records.
Source: *NCT*, XVII:164; NC Confederate Pension (Durham County).

♦**Hedrick, William F.**, Private, Company C
Wise's Forks (Inconclusive)
Service records indicate that he was admitted to General Hospital No. 13 (Pettigrew) on March 13, 1865, with a gunshot wound to the left thigh. He died on March 25, 1865, of tetanus "on amputation of left thigh." No further records. He is buried in Oakwood Cemetery, Raleigh, North Carolina.
Source: *NCT*, XVII:173; M270.

Holder, W. H., Private, Company D
Bentonville
Confederate pension records indicate that he was shot in the ankle at Bentonville. No further records.
Source: *NCT*, XVII:182; NC Confederate Pension (Caldwell County).

Howard, W. A., Private, Company B
Bentonville
Confederate pension records indicate that he was wounded in the right shoulder, "broken," at Bentonville. No further records.
Source: *NCT*, XVII:165; NC Confederate Pension (Franklin County).

▲**Huff, Obediah L.**, Private, Company C
Wise's Forks
Wounded at the battle of Wise's Forks between March 7-9, 1865. His services records and *NC Troops* incorrectly note that he was admitted to GH No. 3 in Greensboro from Kinston on March 9, 1865, for unspecified reasons. In National Archives Confederate Record Group 109, General Hospital No. 3's location is erroneously identified as Greensboro. Goldsboro is the correct location. Confederate authorities

began relocating GH No. 3 from Goldsboro to High Point on March 11, 1865, as part of the town's evacuation. The hospital resumed operations in High Point on or about March 19, 1865. He is also listed in a separate No. 3 ledger, titled "Reports of Wounded and Operations," wounded from battle in the right arm and admitted on March 9, 1865. The ledger further specifies that he was transferred to Raleigh on an unrecorded date. Paroled at Greensboro on May 6, 1865. No further records. Neither his service records nor *NC Troops* notes his wounding in March 1865.
Source: RG109, 6/291:36; NCOAH, CW10, Ledger B, March 1865, entry no. 40; Sokolosky, *NC's Confederate Hospitals*, vol. 2; *NCT*, XVII:173; M270.

▲**Jackson, George W.**, Private, Company A
Wise's Forks
Wounded at the battle of Wise's Forks on March 8, 1865. His Tennessee Confederate pension records indicate that he was "shot in the right leg, one inch above the knee" and wounded in the left side by a "bayonet" at Kinston on March 8, 1865. Jackson's services records incorrectly note that he was admitted to GH No. 3 in Greensboro from Kinston on March 9, 1865, suffering from a gunshot wound to his right knee. In National Archives Confederate Record Group 109, General Hospital No. 3's location is erroneously identified as Greensboro. Goldsboro is the correct location. Confederate authorities began relocating GH No. 3 from Goldsboro to High Point on March 11, 1865, as part of the town's evacuation. The hospital resumed operations in High Point on or about March 19, 1865. He is also listed in a separate No. 3 ledger, titled "Reports of Wounded and Operations," wounded from battle in the left leg and admitted on March 9, 1865. The ledger further specifies that he was transferred to Raleigh on an unrecorded date. No further records.
Source: RG109, 6/291:36; NCOAH, CW10, Ledger B, March 1865, entry no. 36; *NCT*, XVII:155; M270; Sokolosky, *NC Confederate Hospitals*, vol. 2; Tennessee Confederate Pension (Bedford County).

▲**Lamb, C. W.**, Private, Company F
Bentonville
Wounded at the battle of Bentonville on an unspecified date between March 19-21, 1865. According to Surgeon Tanner's "Return of Casualties in Hoke's Div. near Bentonville," Pvt. C. Lamb, Co. F, was severely wounded in the face. Lamb's services records incorrectly note that he was admitted to GH No. 3 in Greensboro on an unspecified date in March 1865. In National Archives Confederate Record Group 109, General Hospital No. 3's location is erroneously identified as Greensboro. High Point is the correct location. Confederate authorities began relocating GH No. 3 from Goldsboro to High Point on March 11, 1865, as part of the town's evacuation. The hospital resumed operations in High Point on or about March 19, 1865. A patient registry entry (no. 2434) for GH No. 3 in High Point lists a Pvt. C. W. Lamb, Co. F, 1st NC Batt, admitted on an unspecified date between March 21 and April 7, 1865. The reference to the 1st NC Battalion (Broadfoot's) on the registry pertains to Lamb's original enlistment in the unit before the consolidation of it and the 6th NC Battalion to form the 1st Regiment NC Junior Reserves in early July 1864. See *NC Troops*, XVII:34, for more information. Paroled at Greensboro on May 9, 1865. Neither Lamb's service records nor *NC Troops* note his wounding at Bentonville. No further records.
Source: Tanner (BV), 150; M270; Sokolosky, *NC's Confederate Hospitals*, vol. 2; RG109, 6/291:48; *NCT*, XVII:199.

▲**Lee, E. J.**, Private, Company I
Bentonville
Wounded at the battle of Bentonville on March 19, 1865. According to Surgeon Tanner's "Return of Casualties in Hoke's Div. near Bentonville," Pvt. J. Lea, Co. I, was severely wounded in the left leg. Lee's Confederate pension application indicates that he was wounded at Bentonville on March 19, 1865. E. J. Lee is the same soldier Tanner incorrectly identified as J. Lea. His Confederate pension records indicate that he was wounded by a "ball from a shell passing through [his] right leg," which suggests an exploding artillery case shot. No further records.
Source: Tanner (BV), 150; *NCT*, XVII:223; M270; NC Confederate Pension (Durham County).

♦**Leonard, Lorenzo**, Private, Company C
Goldsboro (Post Wise's Forks) (Inconclusive)

Service records indicate he was captured in Goldsboro on March 17, 1865; however, the Confederates still controlled the town to that date. Confined at Hart's Island, New York Harbor, and released upon taking the Oath of Allegiance on June 14, 1865.
Source: *NCT*, XVII:174; M270.

▲**Martin, George D.**, Private, Company D
Wise's Forks
Wounded at the battle of Wise's Forks on an unspecified date between March 7-8, 1865. Martin's service records and *NC Troops* incorrectly note that he was admitted to GH No. 3 in Greensboro from Kinston on March 8, 1865, entry no. 1802, suffering from a gunshot wound. In National Archives Confederate Record Group 109, General Hospital No. 3's location is erroneously identified as Greensboro. Goldsboro is the correct location. Confederate authorities began relocating GH No. 3 from Goldsboro to High Point on March 11, 1865, as part of the town's evacuation. The hospital resumed operations in High Point on or about March 19, 1865. A separate GH No. 3 ledger, titled "Reports of Wounded and Operations," indicates that Pvt. G. D. Martin, Co. D, 1st NC Jr., was wounded in the chin and left hand "in battle" and was admitted on March 9, 1865. The ledger further specifies that he was transferred to Raleigh on an unrecorded date. GH No. 13 (Pettigrew) records indicate that he was admitted on March 10, 1865, with a gunshot wound to his chin and left hand. Received a 60-day furlough on March 13, 1865. His Confederate pension records indicate that he was wounded both in the hand and chin.
Source: RG109, 6/291:36; NCOAH, CW10, Ledger B, March 1865, entry no. 29; *NCT*, XVII:183; M270; *WD* (Charlotte), April 4, 1865; Sokolosky, *NC Confederate Hospitals, vol. 2*; NC Confederate Pension (Wake County).

♦**Maynard, Brinkley**, Private, Company D
Unspecified Location (Inconclusive)
Service records indicate he was captured at an unspecified location on February 22, 1865. Confined at Hart's Island, New York Harbor, and released upon taking the Oath of Allegiance on June 18, 1865.
Source: *NCT*, XVII:183; M270; NC Confederate Widow's Pension (Durham County).

♦**Pope, J. A.**, Private, Company C
(Inconclusive)
Raleigh's *Daily Conservative* reported Pvt. J. A. Pope was present in GH No. 7 (Fair Grounds) with a wounded left hand. The date and location of the wounding are undetermined. Paroled at Thomasville General Hospital on May 1, 1865. Neither his service records nor *NC Troops* note his wounding.
Source: *DC* (Raleigh), March 29, 1865; *NCT*, XVII:176; Thomasville General Hospital Paroles; M270.

▲**Price, George W.**, Private, Company A
Wise's Forks
Wounded at the battle of Wise's Forks between March 7-9, 1865. His services records and *NC Troops* incorrectly note that he was admitted to GH No. 3 in Greensboro from Kinston on March 9, 1865, for unspecified reasons. In National Archives Confederate Record Group 109, General Hospital No. 3's location is erroneously identified as Greensboro. Goldsboro is the correct location. Confederate authorities began relocating GH No. 3 from Goldsboro to High Point on March 11, 1865, as part of the town's evacuation. The hospital resumed operations in High Point on or about March 19, 1865. He is also listed in a separate No. 3 ledger, titled "Reports of Wounded and Operations," admitted on March 9, 1865, suffering from a gunshot wound "in battle" on the right side of his back. The ledger further specifies that he was transferred to Raleigh on an unrecorded date. No further records. Neither his service records nor NC Troops notes his wounding and hospitalization in March 1865.
Source: *NCT*, XVII:157; M270; Sokolosky, *NC Confederate Hospitals, vol. 2*; RG109, 6/291:36; NCOAH, CW10, Ledger B, March 1865, entry no. 42.

Pruden, William Dossey, Jr., 1st Lieutenant, Company K
Bentonville
NC Troops notes that the United Daughters of the Confederacy records indicate that he was wounded at Bentonville on March 19, 1865. No further records.

Source: *NCT*, XVII:228.

▲Richardson, Cornelius J., Captain, Company D
Bentonville
Wounded at the battle of Bentonville on an unspecified date between March 19-21, 1865. According to Surgeon Tanner's "Return of Casualties in Hoke's Div. near Bentonville," Capt. C. J. Richardson, Co. D, was slightly wounded in the thigh. Admitted to GH No. 13 (Pettigrew) in Raleigh on March 23, 1865, with a contusion in the left thigh caused by an artillery shell. Furloughed on March 27, 1865. No further records.
Source: Tanner (BV), 150; *NCT*, XVII:179; *WD* (Charlotte), April 4, 1865; M270.

▲Short, William P., Private, Company A
Bentonville
Wounded at the battle of Bentonville on an unspecified date between March 19-21, 1865. According to Surgeon Tanner's "Return of Casualties in Hoke's Div. near Bentonville," Pvt. W. P. Short, Co. A, was slightly wounded in the right hand. Neither his service records nor *NC Troops* note his wounding at Bentonville. No further records.
Source: Tanner (BV), 150; *NCT*, XVII:158; M270.

♦Smith, T. C., Private, Company D
Wise's Forks and/or Bentonville (Inconclusive)
His Confederate pension records indicate, albeit confusing, that he was wounded at "Kingston Bentonville on or about March 28, 1864. Based on the wording of his pension application, he may have been wounded in both battles. No further records.
Source: *NCT*, XVII:185; NC Confederate Pension (Wake County).

♦Stephenson, J. H., _____, (Company Unknown)
(Inconclusive)
The *Daily Confederate* reported he was hospitalized in Raleigh with a wounded left hand. No further records.
Source: *DConf* (Raleigh), March 29, 1865; *NCT*, XVII:233.

♦Treadaway, Z. T., Private, Company I
Bentonville (Inconclusive)
Confederate pension records indicate that he was wounded in the breast at Smithfield, probably Bentonville. No further records.
Source: *NCT*, XVII:226; NC Confederate Pension (Anson County).

▲Weaver, Benjamin F., 2nd Lieutenant, Company I
Bentonville
Wounded at the battle of Bentonville on an unspecified date between March 19-21, 1865. According to Surgeon Tanner's "Return of Casualties in Hoke's Div. near Bentonville," Lt. B. F. Weaver, Co. I, was severely wounded in the left thigh. Admitted to GH No. 13 (Pettigrew) in Raleigh on March 23, 1865, with a gunshot wound to the left hip. Furloughed for 21 days beginning March 27, 1865. No further records. National Archives Compiled Service Records identify his middle name as "Frank."
Source: Tanner (BV), 150; *NCT*, XVII:219; *DC* (Raleigh), March 29, 1865; *WD* (Charlotte), April 4, 1865; M270.

Woodlief, J. O., _____, Company A
Bentonville
Confederate pension records indicate that he was wounded (flesh wound) in the left leg below the knee at Bentonville. No further records. He goes by "A. O. Woodlief" on his Confederate pension. *NC Troops* lists him as J. O. Woodliff.
Source: *NCT*, XVII:160; NC Confederate Pension (Vance County).

York, Alfred R., Private, Company F
Wise's Forks

Confederate pension records indicate that he was injured in the left knee, "twisted and dislocated," at Jackson's Creek in March 1865. No further records.
Source: *NCT*, XVII:201; NC Confederate Pension (Guilford County).

Private William F. Hedrick
1st Regiment NC Junior Reserves

He was admitted to General Hospital No. 13 (Pettigrew) in Raleigh on March 13, 1865, with a gunshot to his left thigh, resulting in amputation. He later died of tetanus as a patient on March 25, 1865. He is buried in Oakwood Cemetery in Raleigh, North Carolina. Although undetermined, based on the date of hospitalization, Hedrick probably suffered his wound during the battle of Wise's Forks.

(Courtesy of Wade Sokolosky)

2nd Regiment North Carolina Junior Reserves
(71st Regiment North Carolina)

♦Barwick, W. M., Private, Company G
Wise's Forks (Inconclusive)
NC Troops notes that his Roll of Honor application indicates that he was wounded in the leg, imprisoned at Kinston, and paroled in May 1865. The surname may have been Bowick. No further records.
Source: *NCT*, XVII:293; M270.

♦Beaman, John Allen, Corporal, Company A
Bentonville (Inconclusive)
His Confederate pension and United Daughters of the Confederacy records indicate that Beaman was captured at the battle of Bentonville on March 19, 1865. However, U.S. Army records do not note his capture and later detention as a prisoner. According to Beaman's service records, he was paroled while a patient in a hospital in Greensboro in April 1865.
Source: *NCT*, XVII:237; M270; NC Confederate Pension (Sampson County).

Brown, George T., Private, Company G
Kinston (Post Wise's Forks)
NC Troops notes that he was captured at Kinston on March 19, 1865. No further records.
Source: *NCT*, XVII:294; M270.

♦▲Cherry, J. L., Private, Company K
Bentonville (Inconclusive)
Wounded at the battle of Bentonville on an unspecified date between March 19-21, 1865. According to Surgeon Tanner's "Return of Casualties in Hoke's Div. near Bentonville," Pvt. J. L. Cherry, Co. K, was severely wounded in the head. No J. L. Cherry is listed on the Co. K rolls, only a Pvt. A. Cherry. However, a Pvt. Joshua Cherry is found on the Co. I roster. Neither soldiers' service records nor *NC Troops* note having been wounded at Bentonville. Further research is required.
Source: Tanner (BV), 150; *NCT*, XVII:309, 315; M270.

▲Clark, J. B., Private, Company B
Bentonville
Wounded at the battle of Bentonville on an unspecified date between March 19-21, 1865. According to Surgeon Tanner's "Return of Casualties in Hoke's Div. near Bentonville," Pvt. J. B. Clark, Co. B, was slightly wounded in the nose. Clark's services records incorrectly note that he was admitted to GH No. 3 in Greensboro on an unspecified date in March 1865. In National Archives Confederate Record Group 109, General Hospital No. 3's location is erroneously identified as Greensboro. High Point is the correct location. Confederate authorities began relocating GH No. 3 from Goldsboro to High Point on March 11, 1865, as part of the town's evacuation. The hospital resumed operations in High Point on or about March 19, 1865. High Point is the correct location. Confederate authorities ordered GH No. 3's relocation from Goldsboro to High Point on March 11, 1865, as part of the town's evacuation. A patient registry entry (no. 2435) for GH No. 3 in High Point lists a Pvt. J. B. Clark, Co. B, 2nd NC Batt, admitted on an unspecified date between March 21 and April 7, 1865. The reference to the 2nd NC Battalion (Anderson's) on the registry pertains to Lamb's original enlistment in the unit before the consolidation of it and the 5th NC Battalion to form the 2nd Regiment NC Junior Reserves in early July 1864. See *NC Troops*, XVII:34, for more information. Paroled at Charlotte on May 15, 1865. Neither Clark's service records nor *NC Troops* note his wounding at Bentonville. No further records.
Source: Tanner (BV), 150; M270; Sokolosky, *NC's Confederate Hospitals*, vol. 2; *NCT*, XVII:247; RG109, 6/291:48.

▲Cobb, L. L., Private, Company D
Wise's Forks

Wounded at the battle of Wise's Forks between March 7-9, 1865. The patient registry for GH No. 3 in Goldsboro lists Pvt. L. L. Cobb, Co. D, 2nd NC Jr., entry no. 1798, who was transferred from Kinston and admitted on March 8, 1865, for unspecified reasons. However, a separate No. 3 ledger, titled "Reports of Wounded and Operations," indicates that Pvt. L. L. Cobb, Co. D, 2nd NC Jr., suffered a gunshot wound to the right side of the head "in battle" on March 9, 1865. The ledger further specifies that he was transferred to Raleigh on an unrecorded date. Neither his service records nor *NC Troops* note his wounding and hospitalization in March 1865. Further research is required regarding the discrepancy between the date of admittance to GH No. 3.
Source: RG109, 6/291:36; NCOAH, CW10, Ledger B, March 1865, entry no. 25; *NCT*, XVII:269; M270.

Daniel, John D., Private, Company A
Goldsboro
Captured at Goldsboro on March 22, 1865. Paroled and released upon taking the Oath of Allegiance that same day.
Source: *NCT*, XVII:239; M270.

Downs, John S., Private, Company D
Bentonville
His Confederate pension application indicates he was shot in the left hand at Bentonville on March 20, 1865. The gunshot "passed through [the] middle of left hand ranging outward destroying half of the underside of hand & two fingers." No further records.
Source: *NCT*, XVII:270; M270; NC Confederate Pension (Cleveland County).

♦Durham, Richard John, 2nd Lieutenant, Company D
(Inconclusive)
The March 29, 1865 edition of the *Daily Confederate* listed Durham as present in a Raleigh hospital. Neither his service records nor *NC Troops* note his wounding in March 1865.
Source: *DC* (Raleigh), March 29, 1865; *NCT*, XVII:268; M270.

▲Green, N. E., Private, Company D
Bentonville
Wounded at the battle of Bentonville on an unspecified date between March 19-21, 1865. According to Surgeon Tanner's "Return of Casualties in Hoke's Div. near Bentonville," Pvt. N. E. Green, Co. D, was severely wounded in the right thigh. Neither Green's service records nor *NC Troops* note his wounding at Bentonville. No further records.
Source: Tanner (BV), 150; *NCT*, XVII:271; M270.

Hargrove, John A., Private, Company A
Sampson County (Post Bentonville)
Captured in his native Sampson County on March 26, 1865. Paroled at Raleigh on April 22, 1865.
Source: *NCT*, XVII:240; M270.

Helms, Evan A., Private, Company F
Wise's Forks
His Confederate pension application indicates that he was slightly wounded in the right arm near Kinston on March 10, 186[5]. No further records.
Source: *NCT*, XVII:288; M270; NC Confederate Pension (Cabarrus County).

Hill, Egbert Washington, Private, Company G
Kinston (Post Wise's Forks)
Captured at Kinston on March 18, 1865. The Goldsboro Provost Marshal records included the letter "D," probably an abbreviation for deserter. No further records.
Source: *NCT*, XVII:295; M270.

♦Howell, Freeman, Private, Company A

Goldsboro (Possibly Wise's Forks) (Inconclusive)
According to Howell's service records, he was captured on two separate dates, March 8 and March 27, 1865, both at Goldsboro. Confined at Hart's Island, New York Harbor, released upon taking the Oath of Allegiance on June 18, 1865. If the former date, it is probable that he was captured at the battle of Wise's Forks, as Federal forces did not occupy Goldsboro until March 21, 1865. Regarding the later date, Freeman was a Wayne County resident at the time of his enlistment. Confederate forces were encamped in the Smithfield area following the battle of Bentonville, so he may have been captured trying to visit home. Further research is required.
Source: *NCT*, XVII:241; M270.

King, M. H., Private, Company C
Bentonville
NC Troops notes that a postwar roster indicates that he was wounded in the toe at Bentonville. No further records. NC Troops indicates that he may also be the same soldier as Hamilton King of Co. C.
Source: *NCT*, XVII:263; M270.

Madra, E. N., Private, Company K
Bentonville
His Confederate pension application indicates that he was wounded at Bentonville in March 1865. No further records.
Source: *NCT*, XVII:316; M270; NC Confederate Pension (Nash County).

♦▲Neville, W., Private, Company K
Bentonville (Inconclusive)
Wounded at the battle of Bentonville on an unspecified date between March 19-21, 1865. According to Surgeon Tanner's "Return of Casualties in Hoke's Div. near Bentonville," Pvt. W. Nevill, Co. K, was dangerously wounded in the abdomen. Private W. Nevill of Co. K listed by Tanner is probably one of two Nevilles listed on the unit rolls, either T. William or West T. Neither soldiers' service records nor *NC Troops* note having been wounded at Bentonville. Further research is required.
Source: Tanner (BV), 150; *NCT*, XVII:316; M270.

Page, Wiley M., Private, Company A
Sampson County (Post Wise's Forks)
Captured in his native Sampson County on March 16, 1865. Confined at Hart's Island, New York Harbor, and released upon taking the Oath of Allegiance on June 21, 1865.
Source: *NCT*, XVII:243; M270; NC Confederate Pension (Cumberland County).

▲Parker, Young R., Private, Company F
Bentonville
Wounded at the battle of Bentonville on an unspecified date between March 19-21, 1865. According to Surgeon Tanner's "Return of Casualties in Hoke's Div. near Bentonville," Pvt. J. H. Parker, Co. F, was slightly wounded in the left shoulder. Parker's Confederate pension application indicates that he was wounded in the left shoulder at Bentonville. No further records.
Source: Tanner (BV), 150; *NCT*, XVII:289; M270; NC Confederate Pension (Union County).

Pate, Sherrard H., Private, Company A
Goldsboro (Post Bentonville)
Captured at Goldsboro on March 23, 1865. Took the Oath of Allegiance that same day.
Source: *NCT*, XVII:243; M270.

♦Pendleton, J. M. P., Private, Company C
Bentonville or Wise's Forks (Inconclusive)
His Confederate pension application indicates that an exploding shell at "Stanly Creek near Kinston" wounded him in the chest on or about March 20, 1865. The date suggests Bentonville. Further research is required. *NC Troops* notes that he may be the same soldier as Puckett Pendleton of Co. C.

Source: *NCT*, XVII:264; M270; NC Confederate Pension (Lincoln County).

♦▲Putman, Rufus, Private, Company D
Wise's Forks (Inconclusive)
The GH No. 3 (Goldsboro) patient registry lists a Pvt. Sol. Putman, Co. D, 2nd NC Jr., entry no. 1805, was admitted on March 8, 1865, with a gunshot wound. The date and location of the wounding was not recorded. There is no Sol. Putman listed on the unit rolls. However, a separate No. 3 ledger, titled "Reports of Wounded and Operations," indicates that Pvt. R. Putman, Co. D, 2nd NC Jr., suffered a gunshot wound in the right arm, near the wrist, "in battle" and was admitted on March 9, 1865. The ledger further specifies that he was transferred to Raleigh on an unrecorded date. *NC Troops* lists two Putman's in the regiment, including a Pvt. Rufus Putman (Co. D) and a Pvt. Putman, whose first name was unknown, served in Co. C. Pvt. Rufus Putman of Co. D is probably the same soldier admitted to GH No. 3. Neither his service records nor *NC Troops* note his wounding and hospitalization in March 1865. Further research is required regarding the discrepancy between the date of admittance to GH No. 3.
Source: RG109, 6/291:36; NCOAH, CW10, Ledger B, March 1865, entry no. 27; *NCT*, XVII:276; M270.

♦Roberts, Robert M., Private, Company E
Bentonville (Inconclusive)
His Confederate pension application indicates that he was wounded in the head at Smithfield on March 15, 1865. No further records.
Source: *NCT*, XVII:283; M270; NC Confederate Pension (Cabarrus County).

Rogers, John H., Private, Company A
Bentonville
His Confederate pension application indicates that he was wounded in the right arm at Bentonville on March 19, 1865. No further records.
Source: *NCT*, XVII:243; M270; NC Confederate Pension (Wayne County).

♦▲Sykes, A. F., Corporal, Company B
Bentonville (Inconclusive)
Wounded at the battle of Bentonville on an unspecified date between March 19-21, 1865. According to Surgeon Tanner's "Return of Casualties in Hoke's Div. near Bentonville," Sgt. ___, Sikes, Co. B, was dangerously wounded in the chest and had "since died." Corporal A. F. Sykes, Co. B, is probably the same soldier as Sergeant Sikes of Co. B. Neither his service records nor *NC Troops* indicate that he was mortally wounded at Bentonville. The location and date of death are undetermined. Further research is required.
Source: Tanner (BV), 150; *NCT*, XVII:254; M270.

Weddington, Washington Taylor, Private, Company E
Wise's Forks
Confederate pension records indicate that he was wounded at Kinston on March 9, 1865. The examining physician for his pension wrote the gunshot passed "through the right shoulder, breaking the shoulder blade and through the right lung[,] partially paralyzing his right arm." Admitted to GH No. 13 (Pettigrew) in Raleigh on March 11, 1865, with a gunshot wound to the right shoulder. No further records.
Source: *NCT*, XVII:284; M270; *WD* (Charlotte), April 4, 1865; NC Confederate Pension (Mecklenburg County).

▲Yarborough, Aphus, Private, Company C
Bentonville (Possibly Wise's Forks as well)
Wounded at the battle of Bentonville on an unspecified date between March 19-21, 1865. According to Surgeon Tanner's "Return of Casualties in Hoke's Div. near Bentonville," Pvt. A. Yarborough, Co. A, was slightly wounded in the right leg. The patient registry for GH No. 3 in High Point lists Pvt. A. Yarborough of Co. C, 2nd NC, entry no. 2303, was admitted on an unspecified date between March 31–April 7, 1865. Complaint not reported. The hospital erred in not fully recording his unit designation. Private Aphus Yarborough of Co. C is the same soldier as Pvt. A. Yarborough. Neither his service records nor *NC Troops* note his wounding at Bentonville and later hospitalization at High Point. NC Troops notes that a postwar

roster stated that he was "wounded through the leg at Kinston." If so, Yarborough would have been wounded twice in his legs in less than two weeks.
Source: Tanner (BV), 150; *NCT*, XVII:267; M270; RG109, 6/291:46.

Archway to the Confederate Cemetery Section
Oakwood Cemetery in Raleigh, North Carolina

(Courtesy of Wade Sokolosky)

Confederate Mass Grave
Willow Dale Cemetery, Goldsboro, North Carolina
Final resting place for soldiers who died in Goldsboro's hospitals throughout the war.

(Courtesy of Stacey Jones)

3rd Regiment North Carolina Junior Reserves
(72nd Regiment North Carolina)

▲**Barringer, Andrew L.**, Private, Company F
Bentonville
Wounded at the battle of Bentonville on an unspecified date between March 19-21, 1865. According to Surgeon Tanner's "Return of Casualties in Hoke's Div. near Bentonville," Pvt. A. L. Barringer, Co. F, was slightly wounded in the chest. Paroled at Greensboro on May 1, 1865. Barringer's Confederate pension records indicate that he was wounded in the breast on or about March 19, 1865, by a "spent ball."
Source: Tanner (BV), 150; *NCT*, XVII:355, 446; M270; NC Confederate Pension (Iredell County).

▲**Beach, Joseph Lawson**, Private, Company G
Bentonville
Wounded at the battle of Bentonville on an unspecified date between March 19-21, 1865. According to Surgeon Tanner's "Return of Casualties in Hoke's Div. near Bentonville," Pvt. J. H. Parker, Co. F, was slightly wounded in the shoulder. Beach's Confederate pension records indicate that he was wounded in the left arm at Bentonville (1914 application) and "flesh wound in the shoulder" at Bentonville (1921 application). No further records.
Source: Tanner (BV), 150; *NCT*, XVII:360, 461; M270; NC Confederate Pension (Caldwell County).

Benton, William, Private, Company G
Wise's Forks
The March 29, 1865, edition of the *NC Standard* reported that Pvt. Wm. Benton, Co. G, 3rd NC Junior Reserves, was at General Hospital No. 8 (Peace Institute) in Raleigh, suffering from a wound to his right arm. His Confederate pension records indicate that he was shot "in the right arm at [the] elbow joint . . . cutting the muscle of the arm" at Gum Swamp on March 8, 1865.
Source: *NCS* (Raleigh), March 29, 1865; *NCT*, XVII:360; M270; *WD* (Charlotte), April 4, 1865; NC Confederate Pension (Burke County).

♦**Boswell, William M.**, Private, Company B
Wise's Forks (Inconclusive)
Boswell's Confederate pension records indicate that he was wounded in the ankle at Gum Swamp in April 1864. Boswell erred in the date because his enlistment date, May 27, 1864, occurred after the indicated period of his wounding. He was probably wounded near Kinston, which is near Gum Swamp, in March 1865.
Source: *NCT*, XVII:327, 392; M270; NC Confederate Pension (Alamance County).

Bowden, Albert Monroe, Private, Company C
Bentonville
Confederate pension records indicate that he was wounded by an exploding artillery shell near his head at Bentonville, causing deafness. No further records.
Source: *NCT*, XVII:334; M270; NC Confederate Pension (Orange County).

Bowden, J. J., Private, Company D
Wise's Forks
Wounded at Wise's Forks between March 7-10, 1865. According to Col. Jno. W. Hinsdale's casualty list from the battle of Southwest Creek [Wise's Forks], Pvt. J. Bowden, Co. D, was wounded in the hand. Paroled at Greensboro on May 1, 1865.
Source: *DConf* (Raleigh), March 31, 1865; *NCT*, XVII:342; M270.

▲**Bowser, John W.**, Sergeant, Company B
Wise's Forks
Wounded at Wise's Forks between March 7-9, 1865. According to Col. Jno. W. Hinsdale's casualty list from the battle of Southwest Creek [Wise's Forks], Sgt. J. Bower, Co. B, wounded in the arm. The patient registry

for General Hospital No. 3 in Goldsboro lists Sgt. S. W. Bowser of Co. B, 3rd NC Junior Reserves, entry no. 1797, was admitted on March 8, 1865, with a gunshot wound. The hospital erred in the spelling of his given name in the registry because a separate No. 3 ledger, titled "Reports of Wounded and Operations," indicates that Sgt. J. W. Bowser, Co. B 3rd NC Jr., suffered a gunshot wound to the left arm near the wrist "in battle" and was admitted on March 9, 1865. The ledger further specifies that he was transferred to Raleigh on an unrecorded date. No further records. Further research is required regarding the discrepancy between the date of admittance to GH No. 3.
Source: RG109, 6/291:36; NCOAH, CW10, Ledger B, March 1865, entry no. 26; *NCT*, XVII:327; M270.

▲Chrisman, James M., Corporal, Company A
Wise's Forks
Wounded at the battle of Wise's Forks between March 7-9, 1865. The GH No. 3 (Goldsboro) patient registry lists a Pvt. James Christian, Co. A, 3rd NC Jr., entry no. 1883, was admitted on March 10, 1865, from Kinston for unspecified reasons. A separate No. 3 ledger, titled "Reports of Wounded and Operations," indicates that Pvt. James Chrisman, Co. A, 3rd NC Jr., suffered a contusion from an artillery shell "in battle" and was admitted on March 10, 1865. The ledger further specifies that he was transferred to an unspecified Raleigh hospital on an unrecorded date. No further records. He was paroled in Salisbury on May 13, 1865. Before his parole, he was promoted to corporal. His service records and *NC Troops* incorrectly note that he was admitted to GH No. 3 in Greensboro on March 10, 1865, for unspecified reasons. In National Archives Confederate Record Group 109, General Hospital No. 3's location is erroneously identified as Greensboro. Goldsboro is the correct location. Confederate authorities began relocating GH No. 3 from Goldsboro to High Point on March 11, 1865, as part of the town's evacuation. The hospital resumed operations in High Point on or about March 19, 1865. Neither his service records nor *NC Troops* note his wounding at Wise's Forks in March 1865.
Source: RG109, 6/291:37; NCOAH, CW10, Ledger B, March 1865, entry no. 73; *NCT*, XVII:321; *WD* (Charlotte), April 4, 1865; M270; Sokolosky, *NC Confederate Hospitals, vol. 2*; NC Confederate Widow's Pension (Guilford County).

Denton, W., Private, Company D
Wise's Forks
Wounded at Wise's Forks between March 7-10, 1865. According to Col. Jno. W. Hinsdale's casualty list from the battle of Southwest Creek [Wise's Forks], Pvt. W. Denton, Co. D, was wounded in the arm. Paroled at Greensboro on May 1, 1865.
Source: *DConf* (Raleigh), March 31, 1865; *NCT*, XVII:343; M270.

♦Foster, W., Private, Company G
Inconclusive
Reported in hospital at Greensboro on March 27, 1865, with a gunshot wound of the left hand. The date and location are undetermined. Further research is required.
Source: *NCT*, XVII:361.

▲Fowler, Rufus C., Private, Company B
Wise's Forks
Wounded at the battle of Wise's Forks between March 7-9, 1865. The GH No. 3 (Goldsboro) patient registry lists a Pvt. R. C. Fowler, Co. B, 3rd NC Jr., entry no. 1843, was admitted on March 9, 1865, from Kinston for unspecified reasons. A separate No. 3 ledger, titled "Reports of Wounded and Operations," indicates that Pvt. R. C. Fowler, Co. B, 3rd NC Jr., suffered a gunshot wound "in battle" to the right foot and was admitted on March 9, 1865. The ledger further specifies that he was transferred to another unspecified hospital on an unrecorded date. Fowler's service records note that he was admitted to GH No. 13 (Pettigrew) in Raleigh on March 10, 1865, with a gunshot wound in the right foot. Received a 60-day furlough on March 13, 1865.
Source: RG109, 6/291:37; NCOAH, CW10, Ledger B, March 1865, entry no. 57; *NCT*, XVII:328; *WD* (Charlotte), April 4, 1865; M270.

♦Fowler, S. H., Private, Company A
Bentonville (Inconclusive)

Wounded at the battle of Bentonville on an unspecified date between March 19-21, 1865. According to Surgeon Tanner's "Return of Casualties in Hoke's Div. near Bentonville," Pvt. S. H. Fowler, Co. A, was dangerously wounded in the scalp. There is no S. H. Fowler listed on the rolls. Further research is required.
Source: Tanner (BV), 150.

Hamlin, Frank M., 1st Lieutenant, Field and Staff
Wise's Forks
Wounded at Wise's Forks between March 7-10, 1865. According to Col. Jno. W. Hinsdale's casualty list from the battle of Southwest Creek [Wise's Forks], Lt. F. M. Hamlin, acting as adjutant, was slightly wounded in the arm. Neither his service records nor *NC Troops* note his wounding at Wise's Forks.
Source: *DConf* (Raleigh), March 31, 1865; *NCT*, XVII:319; M270.

Harper, John Witherow, Sergeant, Company G
Wise's Forks
Wounded at Wise's Forks between March 7-10, 1865. According to Col. Jno. W. Hinsdale's casualty list from the battle of Southwest Creek [Wise's Forks], Lt. J. W. Harper, Co. G, was mortally wounded. See *NC Troops*, XVII:362, regarding the difference in his reported rank versus his service records. Buried in Caldwell County.
Source: *DC* (Raleigh), March 29, 1865; Clark, *Histories*, IV:42; *NCT*, XVII:360, 362; M270; https://www.geni.com/people/Pvt-CSA-John-Witherow-Harper/6000000018711889113.

Huffman, Julius M., Private, Company E
Wise's Forks
Wounded at Wise's Forks between March 7-10, 1865. According to Col. Jno. W. Hinsdale's casualty list from the battle of Southwest Creek [Wise's Forks], Pvt. J. M. Hoffman, Co. E, was slightly wounded in the hip. Admitted to GH No. 13 (Pettigrew) on March 11, 1865, with a gunshot wound. Furloughed for 21 days on March 27, 1865. No further records.
Source: *DConf* (Raleigh), March 29, 1865; *NCT*, XVII:351; *WD* (Charlotte), April 4, 1865; M270; NC Confederate Widow's Pension (Lincoln County).

▲Johnston, David, Private, Company B
Wise's Forks
NC Troops notes that Pvt. David Johnston was wounded in the arm at Southwest Creek, near Kinston, March 7-10, 1865, and his surname may have been Johnson. Southwest Creek is an alternative name for the battle of Wise's Forks. The patient registry for General Hospital No. 3 in Goldsboro lists Pvt. David Johnson of Co. B, 3rd NC Junior Reserves, entry no. 1816, was admitted on March 9, 1865, with a gunshot wound in his left arm. Neither his service record nor *NC Troops* note his hospitalization in Goldsboro. *NC Troops* notes that the surname may have been Johnson.
Source: *NCT*, XVII:329; M270; RG109, 6/291:36.

▲Jones, John Willie, Sergeant, Company K
Wise's Forks
Wounded at Wise's Forks between March 7-9, 1865. According to Col. Jno. W. Hinsdale's casualty list from the battle of Southwest Creek [Wise's Forks], Sgt. J. W. Jones, Co. K, was wounded in the foot. Admitted to the Barbee Wayside Hospital in High Point on March 9, 1865, with a gunshot wound in the foot. Paroled at Greensboro on May 8, 1865. Neither his service records nor *NC Troops* note his hospitalization in High Point.
Source: *DConf* (Raleigh), March 31, 1865; Barbee Wayside Hospital Registry, entry no. 5738; *NCT*, XVII:380; M270; NC Confederate Pension (Rockingham County).

▲McGee, William, Private, Company I
Bentonville
Wounded at the battle of Bentonville on an unspecified date between March 19-21, 1865. According to Surgeon Tanner's "Return of Casualties in Hoke's Div. near Bentonville," Pvt. S. D. Stanaland, Co. D, was

severely wounded in the right leg. Paroled while a patient at Thomasville General Hospital on May 1, 1865. Neither his service records nor *NC Troops* note his wounding at Bentonville.
Source: Tanner (BV), 150; *NCT*, XVII:375; M270; RG109, M1761, Thomasville General Hospital Paroles.

Michael, J. W., Private, Company A
Bentonville
Captured at Bentonville on February 22, 1865, probably March 22, 1865, at Bentonville. Confined at Hart's Island, New York Harbor, and died of chronic diarrhea on June 18, 1865.
Source: *NCT*, XVII:324; M270.

▲Stanaland, D. B., Private, Company D
Bentonville
Wounded at the battle of Bentonville on an unspecified date between March 19-21, 1865. According to Surgeon Tanner's "Return of Casualties in Hoke's Div. near Bentonville," Pvt. S. D. Stanaland, Co. D, was severely wounded in the right leg. Paroled while a patient at Thomasville General Hospital on May 1, 1865. Neither his service records nor *NC Troops* note his wounding at Bentonville.
Source: Tanner (BV), 150; *NCT*, XVII:346; M270; RG109, M1761, Thomasville General Hospital Paroles.

Turner, J. R., Private, Company K
Wise's Forks
Wounded at Wise's Forks between March 7-10, 1865. According to Col. Jno. W. Hinsdale's casualty list from the battle of Southwest Creek [Wise's Forks], Pvt. J. R. Turner, Co. K, was slightly wounded in the side. Paroled at Greensboro on May 9, 1865.
Source: *DConf* (Raleigh), March 31, 1865; *NCT*, XVII:382; M270.

▲Watkins, Richard R., Private, Company K
Wise's Forks
Wounded at Wise's Forks on March 8, 1865. According to Col. Jno. W. Hinsdale's casualty list from the battle of Southwest Creek [Wise's Forks], Pvt. R. R. Watkins, Co. K, was wounded in the hand. Private R. R. Watkins, Co. K, 3rd NC, was admitted to the Barbee Wayside Hospital in High Point on March 9, 1865, with a gunshot wound in the hand. Paroled at Greensboro on May 8, 1865. His Confederate pension records indicate that he was wounded in the hand at Kinston on March 8, 1865. Neither his service records nor *NC Troops* note his hospitalization in High Point.
Source: *DConf* (Raleigh), March 31, 1865; Barbee Wayside Hospital Registry, entry no. 5736; *NCT*, XVII:382; M270; NC Confederate Pension (Rockingham County).

♦Waugh, George M., Private, Company F
Inconclusive
The *Heritage of Iredell* County, I:539, notes that George Musentine Waugh of Iredell County was killed in the war on March 16, 1865. No records of alleged death in his service records.
Source: *NCT*, XVII:359; M270.

Williams, Richard, Private, Company G
Wise's Forks
Wounded at Wise's Forks on March 8, 1865. According to Col. Jno. W. Hinsdale's casualty list from the battle of Southwest Creek [Wise's Forks], Pvt. R. Williams, Co. G, was slightly wounded in the shoulder.
Source: *DConf* (Raleigh), March 31, 1865; *NCT*, XVII:366; M270; NC Confederate Pension (Burke County).

Wright, D. F., Private, Company I
Wise's Forks
Confederate pension records indicate that he was wounded in the right thigh at Kinston in March 1865. No further records.
Source: *NCT*, XVII:378; M270; NC Confederate Pension (Columbus County).

▲Wyatt, William B., Private, Company B

Wise's Forks
Wounded at the battle of Wise's Forks between March 7-9, 1865. According to Col. Jno. W. Hinsdale's casualty list from the battle of Southwest Creek [Wise's Forks], Pvt. W. Wyatt, Co. D, was wounded in the leg. The patient registry for General Hospital No. 3 in Goldsboro lists Pvt. Wm. Wyatt of Co. B, 3rd NC Junior Reserves, entry no. 1820, was admitted on March 9, 1865, with a gunshot wound in his left leg. A separate No. 3 ledger, titled "Reports of Wounded and Operations," indicates that Pvt. Wm. Wyatt, Co. B, 3rd NC Jr., suffered a gunshot wound in the left leg "in battle" and was admitted on March 9, 1865. The ledger further specifies that he was transferred to Raleigh on an unrecorded date. GH No. 13 (Pettigrew) in Raliegh admitted Wyatt on March 10, 1865. Received a 60-day furlough on March 13, 1865. No further records.
Source: *DConf* (Raleigh), March 31, 1865; RG109, 6/291:36; NCOAH, CW10, Ledger B, March 1865, entry no. 35; *NCT*, XVII:333; *WD* (Charlotte), April 4, 1865; M270.

Farquhard C. Smith House, "Lebanon"
Battle of Averasboro
Confederate headquarters and field hospital during the battle.

(Courtesy of Wade Sokolosky)

7th Regiment North Carolina Senior Reserves[5]
(77th Regiment North Carolina)

Blalock, John M., Lieutenant, Capt. R. S. Davie's Company
Bentonville
Captured at Bentonville on March 19, 1865. Confined first at Point Lookout, Maryland, and later Johnson's Island, near Sandusky, Ohio, and released upon taking the Oath of Allegiance on June 17, 1865.
Source: *NCT*, XVIII:337; M270.

Haley, Thomas, Private, Capt. W. B. Johnson's Company
South Carolina
Deserted to the enemy on February 20-21, 1865, at an unspecified location in South Carolina. Confined first in the Citadel, Charleston, South Carolina, and later at Hilton Head, awaiting transfer to the Provost Marshal General, New York City, New York. No further records.
Source: *NCT*, XVIII:311; M270.

Nelson, William, Private, Capt. W. P. William's Company
South Carolina
His Confederate pension records indicate that he was wounded in South Carolina on or about February 1, 1865. He was later hospitalized in Columbia, South Carolina, where he died on an undetermined date. No further records. If his widow's statement regarding the date and location of his wounding is correct, Nelson was probably wounded along the Salkehatchie River Confederate defensive line.
Source: *NCT*, XVIII:327; M270; NC Confederate Widow's Pension (Rockingham County).

♦**Rumley, Edward**, Private, Capt. W. S. Bradshaw's Company (Company A)
Inconclusive
His Confederate pension records indicate that he was wounded in the left leg "just above the ankle." No further records.
Source: *NCT*, XVIII:300; M270; NC Confederate Pension (Rockingham County).

---

[5] The unit designation 77th North Carolina is a post-war identification assigned by John W. Moore, ed. *Roster of North Carolina Troops in the War Between the States*, 4 vols., and copied by Walter Clark's *Histories of the several regiments and Battalions from North Carolina in the Great War 1861-'65.*

Bibliography

Newspapers

Carolina Watchman (Salisbury, NC)
Daily Bulletin (Charlotte, NC)
Daily Confederate (Raleigh, NC)
Evening Bulletin (Charlotte, NC)
Daily Confederate (Raleigh, NC)
Daily Conservative (Raleigh, NC)
Daily Progress (Raleigh, NC)
Daily Standard (Raleigh, NC)
Fayetteville Observer (NC)
Fayetteville Semi-Weekly Observer (NC)
Fayetteville Weekly Observer (NC)
Goldsboro Argus (NC)
Greensboro Patriot (NC)
New Bern Times (NC)
North Carolina Standard (Raleigh, NC)
North Carolina Weekly Standard (Raleigh, NC)
Peoples Press (Salem, NC)
Weekly Conservative (Raliegh, NC)
Weekly Progress (Raleigh, NC)
Weekly Raleigh Register (NC)
Weekly Sentinel (Raliegh, NC)
Western Democrat (Charlotte, NC)
Wilmington Journal (NC)

Manuscripts and Collections

Bentonville Battlefield State Historic Site
    Friends of Bentonville Battlefield Association Papers
    John W. Taylor, copies of family letters, biography, etc.

High Point Public Library, North Carolina Collection, High Point, NC
    Barbee Hotel Confederate Hospital Registry (1863–1865)

Library of Virginia, Richmond, VA
    Kate S. (Sarah Catherine) Sperry Diary, 1861–1865

National Archives and Records Administration, Washington, D.C.
    RG 109: War Department Collection of Confederate Records
        Chap. VI: Medical Department
            Vol. 280: Statistical Reports of Patients and Attendants, Office of the Medical Director of Hospitals in North Carolina, 1863–65
            Vol. 281: A Register of Patients, General Hospital No. 11 (Charlotte), May 15, 1864 –

April 28, 1865
Vol. 290: A Register of Patients, General Hospital No. 13 (Raleigh), June 1864 – April 1865
Vol. 291: A Register of Patients, General Hospital No. 3 (Greensboro), January 1 – March 20, 1865 [should read Goldsboro/High Point]

Microfilm M251: Compiled Service Records of Confederate Soldiers Who Served in Organizations from the State of Florida
Microfilm M270: Compiled Service Records of Confederate Soldiers Who Served in Organizations from the State of North Carolina
Microfilm M1761: Muster Rolls and Lists of Confederate Troops Paroled in North Carolina

North Carolina Office of Archives and History, Raleigh, NC
John Douglas Taylor Papers
Military Collection-Civil War
William S. Wade Papers-Ledger Books
CW10, Ledger B, General Hospital No. 3

University of North Carolina at Chapel Hill, Wilson Library, Southern Historical Collection
Earnest Haywood Collection of Haywood Family Papers
William A. Holt Papers

Virginia Museum of History & Culture, Richmond, VA
Isaac S. Tanner,
"Return of casualties near Kinston, N.C. March 8th & 10th, 1865"
"Return of casualties in Hoke's Div. near Bentonville, N.C. March 1865"

Private Collections

Wade Sokolosky, Isaac Tanner Personal Papers

Government Publications

United States War Department. *The War of the Rebellion: A Compilation of the Official Records of the Union and Confederate Armies*. 128 volumes. Washington, D.C.: Government Printing Office, 1880–1891.

Articles and Books

Bradley, Mark L. *Last Stand in the Carolinas: The Battle of Bentonville*. Campbell, CA: Savas Publishing Co., 1995.
Clark, Walter, ed. *Histories of the Several Regiments and Battalions from North Carolina in the Great War 1861-'65*. 5 vols. Goldsboro, NC: Nash Brothers, 1901.
Fonvielle, Chris E., Jr. *The Wilmington Campaign: Last Rays of Departing Hope*. Campbell, CA: Savas Publishing, 1997.
_____. *Fort Anderson: Battle for Wilmington*. Mason City, IA: Savas Publishing Co., 1999.

Hardy, Michael C. *The Fifty-Eighth North Carolina Troops: Tar Heels in the Army of Tennessee.* Jefferson, NC: McFarland & Co., Inc., 2010.

Houts, Joseph K., Jr., ed. *A Darkness Ablaze: The Civil War Medical Diary and Wartime Experiences of Dr. John Hendricks Kinyoun, Sixty-Sixth North Carolina Infantry Regiment.* St. Joseph, MO: Platte Purchase Publishers, 2005.

Keith, H. James. *3rd Battalion North Carolina Light Artillery: "Moore's Battalion", C.S.A..* Morrisville, NC: Lulu Enterprises, Inc., 2006.

Manarin, Louis H., Weymouth T. Jordan, Jr., Matthew M. Brown, and Michael W. Coffey, comps. *North Carolina Troops 1861-1865 A Roster,* 22 vols. to date. Raleigh, NC: Division of Archives and History, Department of Cultural Resources,1966-.

Moore, Mark A. *Moore's Historical Guide to The Wilmington Campaign and the Battles for Fort Fisher.* Mason City, IA: Savas Publishing Co., 1999.

Purser, Charles E., Jr. *Additional Information and Amendments to the North Carolina Troops 1861-1865 Seventeen Volume Roster.* Wake Forest, NC: The Scuppernong Press, 2010.

_____. *Additional Information and Amendments to the North Carolina Troops 1861-1865 Eighteen Volume Roster – Volume II.* Wake Forest, NC: The Scuppernong Press, 2014.

Rich, William M. "Confederate Cemetery, Thomasville, N.C." Confederate Veteran 16 (October 1908): 514.

Smith Mark A. and Wade Sokolosky, *No Such Army Since the Days of Julius Caesar, Sherman's Carolinas Campaign: from Fayetteville to Averasboro.* Fort Mitchell, KY: Ironclad Publishing, 2005.

Sokolosky, Wade, *North Carolina's Confederate Hospitals, 1861 1863,* vol. 1. Burlington, NC: Fox Run Publishing, 2022.

Sokolosky, Wade and Mark A. Smith. *To Prepare for Sherman's Coming: The Battle of Wise's Forks, March 1865.* El Dorado Hills, CA: Savas Beatie, 2015.

Internet Sources

Family Search, accessed on January 13, 2025, https://www.familysearch.org/ark:/61903/3:1:3Q9M-CST7-S7CS-P?view=index.

Find a Grave, https://www.findagrave.com.

Index

A

Adams, J. H., 91
Albertson, Joshua L., 37
Alderman, John A., 3
Aldridge, Hampton, 127
Alexander, Berlin, 127
Alexander, Joseph B., 177
Alford, John, 185
Alfred, John L., 169
Allen, Peter, 127
Allison, John A., 91
Allison, Joseph E., 75
Allman, Nelson, 127
Almon, John, 127
Anders, Franklin James, 27
Anderson, John Marcus, 169
Anderson, Moses G., 123
Anderson, Perry, 185
Andrews, George H., 91
Andrews, Macon, 203
Armsworthy, J. C., 127
Arnold, John Stanley, 185
Arwood, George, 127
Arrington, Benjamin R., 91
Ashworth, Rufus, 185
Atkinson, Atlas, 157
Atkinson, E. C., 157
Atwell, David A., 127
Ausban, Jefferson J., 91
Ausbon, William James, 92
Austin, John E. W., 61
Avery, Jason, 92

B

Baber, Leonard A., 185
Badgett, Burrill R., 185
Baggot, William, 83
Bailey, Henry L., 128
Bailey, John H., 185
Bailey, William W., 185
Bain, Daniel D., Jr., 163
Baird, David Franklin, 169
Baker, Bryant, 92
Baker, John W., 3
Baldwin, John K., 27
Ball, G. W., 37
Ball, J. W., 37
Ball, Niles, 37
Barba, Gabriel, 128
Barbee, James, 186
Barber, Murdock, 67
Barden, Arthur, 92
Barden, William E., 3
Barfield, Horace E., 92
Barfield, Mills T., 203
Barfield, Thomas, 92
Barlow, John, 75
Barlow, Wiley, 128
Barnes, Christopher C.,
Barnes, John, 37
Barnes, Richard Rhodes, 157
Barnhart, J. M., 37
Barringer, Andrew L., 233
Barringer, Rufus A., 128
Barrow, William H., 186
Barrow, William J., 186
Bartholomew, Benjamin B., 186
Barwick, W. M., 227
Bass, Augustus, 203
Bass, Robert John, 93
Batchelor, James K. P., 67
Batchelor, Merrit, 186
Baucom, Henry T., 61
Baucom, Lewis R., 61
Baum, Abraham, 211
Baum, Thomas T., 93
Beach, Joseph Lawson, 233
Beaman, John Allen, 227
Bell, George, 203

Bell, Ottaway S., 203
Bennett, Calvin R., 93
Bennett, Milton N., 93
Benton, Jesse Morris, 61
Benton, William, 233
Bentonville Battlefield State
    Historic Site, *photos*, 80, 82, 216
Berry, Christopher S., 38
Berry, William W., 93
Best, J. W., 3
Best, Richard W., 23
Best, W. T., 23
Best, William H., 3
Biggs, Absalom D., 3
Biggs, John Dawson, Sr., 179; *photo*, 183
Biggs, Levi W., 93
Bishop, Riley M., 4
Bivens, William, 61
Black, John W., 128
Blackburn, W. W., 4
Blackman, William, 4
Blackwelder, Isaac W., 128
Blackwelder, Lawson L., 128
Blackwelder, William R., 93
Blackwood, John Turner, 94
Blalock, John M., 239
Blaylock, Benjamin C., 128
Blevens, Thomas J., 179
Blevins, Isom, 179
Blount, Sherman J., 179
Boger, Paul, 128
Boggs, Arrington G., 129
Boney, Gabriel J., 38
Bonner, Macon, 38
Booe, Jacob, 129
Booe, William M., 129
Boon, Franklin, 186
Boon, Martin A., 129
Boone, David C., 71
Bostian, J., 129
Bostic, John M., 186
Boswell, John A., 186
Boswell, William M., 233

Bosworth, Davidson H., 129
Bowden, Albert Monroe, 233
Bowden, J. J., 233
Bowden, Robert T. D., 187
Bowen, Martin Van Buren, 67
Bowers, John, 38
Bowers, William R., 94
Bowles, B. F., 129
Bowles, G. W., 130
Bowser, John W., 233
Brackens, Adam, 179
Braddy, William B., 179
Bradford, William, 38
Bradley, W. Cornelius, 94
Bradshaw, John Pope, 83
Brafford, Nathan, 23
Brantley, S., 67
Brantley, William W., 130
Braswell, Joseph R., 187
Bratton, Absolum W., 130
Braxton, Jesse W., 187
Bray, William, 83
Brewer, Munro, 23
Brickhouse, Franklin L., 33
Bridgman, William R., 130
Bridgeman, John L, 38
Briley, William Stephen, 94
Brinkley, James M., 211
Britt, Colen L., 157
Britt, George C., 38
Britt, James, 203
Britt, Joseph B., 157
Britt, Noah, 23
Britt, Thomas, 23
Britton, Owen W., 187
Broadwell, J. H., 157
Brockwell, Hutson, 23
Brooks, Iverson J. W., 38
Brooks, William F., 27
Brothers, Richard T., 87
Brown, Burton, 187
Brown, C., 94
Brown, Duncan, 4

Brown, Elam, 75
Brown, Franklin, 187
Brown, George T., 227
Brown, Henry C., 38
Brown, James L., 130
Brown, James M., 94
Brown, John L., 67
Brown, Owen M., 187
Brown, William, 188
Brown, William A., 4
Brown, William H., 39
Brown, William Henry, 5
Bruff, Alfred, 130
Bryan, Joseph B., 67
Bryan, Joseph E., 71
Bryan, Frederick, 188
Bryant, *See also*: Bryan.
Buchanan, Abram J., 169
Buie, George McD., 163
Buie, Malcolm James, 163
Bulleboy, Burrell B., 130
Bullet, Jessie N., 123
Bullock, Henry G., 27
Bundy, James A., 87
Bunting, James V., 188
Burgin, Samuel D., 219
Burnett, Drew D., 75
Burney, Daniel H., 27
Burnett, William T., 123
Burns, William H., 130
Bush, Abram T., 33
Bynum, William S., 130
Byrd, Josiah Miller, 39

C

Caison, Hillory R., 71
Cain, Joseph G., 95
Calhoun, O. D., 39
Calhoun, W., 221
Call, Murphy G., 131
Callaway, Elijah E., 39
Callaway, Jesse R., 39

Calloway, Joseph A., 188
Campbell, Benjamin Frank, 131
Capps, Henry G., 24
Carawan, William M., 95
Caraway, Elisha, 169
Carmack, Thomas, 180
Carney, Robert H., 95
Carr, Titus William, 203; *photo*, 264
Carrington, Richard B., 188; *photo*, 184
Carroll, Francis Marion, 180
Carter, Amos, 39
Carter, Moses, 157
Carter, Samuel Sidney, 188
Carter, Wilford, 131
Carter, William, 219
Carter, William H., 211
Cash, Preston, 157
Cauble, Adam L., 177
Cauble, Horace G., 131
Cauble, Joseph G., 131
Causey, Frank, 95
Chaffin, Charles Stanley, 131
Chambers, James F., 40
Chappell, Benjamin, 95
Charles, Francis W., 131
Chase, Henry, 203
Cheek, Noah, 221
Cherry, J. L., 227
Cherry, John L., 95
Cherry, William A., 95
Cherry, Willis W., 188
Chesson, John B. J., 96
Chewning, Thomas, 40
Chippewater, Joseph F., 33
Chrisman, James M., 234
Christian, James Newton, 189
City Cemetery, Thomasville, *photo*, 126
Clapp, David, 87
Clapp, Peter, 40
Clark, Daniel, 96
Clark, J. B., 227
Clark, Robert G., 40
Clark, William, 40

Clark, William R., 123
Clayton, Thomas T., 96
Cleaver, Daniel M., 131
Clifford, Franklin A., 131
Clinard, Alexander C., 132
Cobb, Alexander M., 5
Cobb, L. L., 227
Coble, Elias, 40
Coffey, Irwin, 169
Coffey, William C., 169
Coffey, Willam Columbus, 170
Coffield, Thomas T., 96
Coffield, Zachariah, 67
Colbert, John H., 189
Collet, Ezekiel, 132
Collins, Atlas, 158
Collins, Benjamin F., 40
Collins, Samuel S., 158
Coltrain, Alfred M., 96
Colvin, Aaron M., 5
Conder, William, 61
Congleton, Ashley, 41
Cook, David A., 41
Cook, J. B., 96
Cook, Robert, 211
Cook, William Stephen, 189
Cooper, David M., 132
Cooper, Gilbert Y., 96
Copeland, Timothy Quincy, 97
Coppedge, George W., 189
Coppedge, Jordan, 189
Coppedge, Joseph, 189
Corbett, William N., 158
Couch, Nathan, 189
Cowan, James K., 215
Cowan, Thomas W., 5
Cowen. *See also*: Cowan.
Cowen, William Henry, 97
Cox, Abram R., 41
Cox, William P., 158
Coxey, J. William, 189
Crabtree, William R., 190
Craddock, James H., 97

Craddock, William A., 97
Craft, Elder James, 97
Craft, Richard A., 41
Cranfield, Hanes, 132
Cranfield, William H., 132
Crawley, Albert E., 170
Creech, Benjamin P., 180
Crews, Henry H., 190
Crisp, William L., 170
Cromartie, Addison A., 83
Cross, Lazarus, 97
Cross, William T., 97
Culpepper, James M., 190
Cummings, Marshall, 203
Curlee, Davidson, 132
Curlee, Joseph Simeon, 132
Curtis, John H., 68; *photo*, 66
Curtis, M. A., 15
Curtis, Samuel A., 68
Cushing, William M., 98
Cutler, George B., 204

D

Dail, Christopher C., 204
Dail, Elbert, 204
Daniel, John D., 228
Daniel, William Harrison, 132
Danner, Samuel, 133
Darden, John G., 204
Davenport, Hezekiah H., 98
Davenport, Jerome B., 98
Davis, Ashley, 98
Davis, Henry H., 133
Davis, James L. G., 98
Davis, John, 190
Davis, John Z., 41
Deadman, James R., 133
Deadman, Thomas H., 133
Deal, Samuel, 133
De Berry, William, 133
Deneale, William H., 41
Denning, Josiah, 163

Dennis, William N., 190
DeRosset, Armand L., 83
Denton, W., 234
Devane, William Stewart, 180; *photo*, 178
Dickson, John F., 75
Dodd, W. M., 33
Dorsey, Ephraim, 190
Doughty, Charles H., 41
Douthit, James B., 219
Dowdy, Dennis, 221
Dowdy, Harman H., 42
Dowdy, James D., 221
Downs, John S., 228
Drake, John R., 133
Drake, Jordan, 133
Dula, Thomas C., 133
Dula, William L., 134
Duncan, Isaac T., 98
Durham, Richard John, 228
Dyson, William J., 28

E

Eagles, Benjamin F., 42
Eakins, Robert, 5
Early, John A., 211
Early, Thomas, 75
Earnhart, Henry L., 211
Earnheardt, John W., 134
Eason, Willis, 42
Eastwood, William D., 98
Echart, W. W., 134
Eddinger, D., 221
Edwards, Granville Billing, 180
Edwards, Phil, 222
Efird, John Jacob, 134
Efird, Martin L., 134
Ellis, Zacheus, 6
English, Enoch D., 99
Ermul, Paschal H., 42
Estep, William, 180
Etchison, Giles B., 134
Eudy, John M., 190

Eury, Adam E., 134
Eury, Eli R., 134
Evans, Isaac, 99
Evans, J. Albert, 99
Evans, James M., 99
Evans, Smith, 68
Evans, Theophilus, 99
Everett, John H., 99
Everett, Simon Turner, 99
Everett, Staten, 99
Everett, William C., 68
Exum, William D., 158

F

Faircloth, Michael M., 170
Farmer, John D., 42
Farmer, Moses, 42
Farmer, Phillip R., 190
Farmer, Sameul B., 42
Faucette, George C., 123
Faw, Amos, 75
Felton, Howell, 43
Ferribee, Thomas M., 135
Fesperman, John A., 135
Feutrel, Lawrence, 28
Fields, William B., 163
Fink, Moses D., 135
Fisher, J. C., 204
Flack, Lewis B., 158
Flinn, Riley, 135
Florida Military Units: 1st Florida Infantry, 4
Flowers, Abner, 43
Flowers, Hugh, 6
Flowers, Robert W., 43
Floyd, Daniel E., 135
Floyd, Faulkner J., 163
Flythe, George Washington, 71
Fodry, A. Fulford, 43
Foley, Staten W., 100
Forbes, Samuel Harney, 68
Forbis, Larkin, V., 62

Ford, Thomas, 170
Forrest, Jesse T., 204
Foster, Albert N., 135
Foster, Jackson, 135
Foster, Jahue H., 135
Foster, John, 211
Foster, John M., 135
Foster, W., 234
Fouts, William H., 136
Fowler, Rufus, C., 234
Fowler, S. H., 234
Fowler, William S., 62
Fox, Elisha Calvin, 170
Fulcher, Joseph A., 204
Furr, Moses H., 136
Francis, Davis, 123
Frank, Philip, 43
Freeman, William T., 100
French, Beverly Tucker, 6
Fronley, W. H., 100
Fulgum, Robert L., 163
Fuller, James H., 191

G

Gaddy, Samuel H., 171
Gaither, Milton E., 136
Gallagher, James, 43
Gardiner, David C., 100
Gardner, David D., 100
Gardner, Luke E., 101
Garrett, Skidmore J., 191
Garrison, Robert J., 43
Garver, Leonard B., 136
Gaskins, Seth, 101
Gatton, John H., 136
Gay, Thomas L., 191
Gibson, Odom, 171
Gibson, Thomas L., 33
Giddens, Henry C., 163
Gilchrist, Charles A., 158
Gilchrist, John A., 6
Gilchrist, William C., 6

Giles, William T., 191
Gillespie, D., 7
Gillespie, G. D., 7
Gillespie, John W., 7
Glazener, Benjamin N., Sr., 76
Glenn, Simeon, 171
Glisson, Lemuel, 101
Goodman, Jacob T., 101
Goodson, Peter M., 62
Goodwin, George, 158
Gordon, W., 43
Gore, Christopher, 28
Gorham, William T., 101
Gosset, William J., 76
Grady, William Henry, 164
Graham, Hugh, 7
Graham, Thomas S., 7
Granger, John P., 136
Granger, William, 71
Grant, Lewis, 205
Grant, Newitt, 212
Graves, Albert N., 136
Graves, Jesse, 101
Gray, B. S., Jr., 102
Gray, Thomas, 137
Green, Augustus F., 171
Green, Fergerson, 171
Green, N. E., 228
Greene, James M., 137
Greene, James P., 191
Greene, Robert, 44
Gregory, James N., 62
Grice, William D., 83
Griffin, Franklin M., 102
Griffin, James D., 191
Griffin, William A., 102
Griffin, William C., 28
Grimes, George W., 102
Grimes, Noah B., 137
Grinner, G. W., 137
Gross, Thomas, 222
Guess, William C., 191
Gulledge, Elisha, 44

Gulledge, W. D., 44
Gurganus, Daniel, 102
Gurganus, David, 102
Gurganus, Robert, 102
Guthrie, Thomas C., 28
Guy, Lewis H., 164

H

Hadley, William Blount, 103
Hagaman, Isaac, Jr., 171
Haislip, Alexander, 103
Haislip, William A., 103
Haley, Thomas, 239
Hall, Alexander Rankin, 124
Hall, Calton, 28
Hall, Gustavus P., 212
Hall, J. H., 2
Hall, James O., 215
Hall, James T., 83
Hall, Livingston, 84
Ham, Benjamin, 44
Ham, William H., 212
Hamlin, Frank M., 235
Hampson, Joseph M., 24
Hampton, David A., 137
Hampton, Thomas J., 159
Hampton, William H., 103
Hamrick, Robert B., 159
Haney, Daniel W., 171
Hansley, Thomas, 44
Hardee, George W., 103
Hardin, A., 76
Hardin, W., 76
Hardison, Council W., 205
Hardison, Ebenezar H., 103
Hardison, Ira T., 104
Hardison, James L., 104
Hardy, Parrott M., 205
Hargrove, John A., 228
Hargrove, John C., 71
Harkey, Jacob C., 137
Harper, Bright, 180

Harper, Franklin, 191
Harper, John Witherow, 235
Harper, Joseph, 191
Harrell, J., 104
Harrell, Thomas W., 104
Harris, C. P., 137
Harris, Calvin G., 62
Harris, Emsley Lee, 137
Harris, Henry Clay, 104
Harris, Henry F., 71
Harris, James A., 104
Harris, James Edward, 63
Harris, James F., 71
Harris, Joseph P., 8
Harris, Taylor, 44
Harrison, B. Calvin, 171
Harrison, Rodman, 104
Hart, Jesse, 205
Hartley, William H., 138
Hartsell, Isaac A., 138
Hartsell, Jackson M., 138
Hartsell, Jacob, Sr., 138
Hartsell, Jacob L., 138
Hartsell, Jacob M., 138
Harward, R. E., 222
Haselip, John 105
Haskell, John, 105
Hatch, James R., 205
Hatley, Alexander, 138
Hatley, John F., 138
Hawkins, James, 87
Hayes, Levi C., 164
Heath, William A., 8
Hedgepeth, Arch B., 159
Hedgepeth, Joel D., 159
Hedrick, John J., 44; *photo*, 36
Hedrick, William F., 222; *photo*, 226
Hellen, Joseph F., 45
Helms, Elezar W., 139
Helms, Evan A., 228
Helms, Hosea James, 139
Helms, John, 63
Helms, Kinney, 139

Helms, Osborne, 139
Hemby, Amos, 63
Henderson, James E., 139
Hendricks, Nalke, 139
Hendricks, William E., 105
Hendrix, W. G., 139
Henly, Joseph, 205
Henry, James A., 8
Herrin, Julius H., 140
Herring, James B., 191
Herring, John D., 8
Herrington, John E., 84; *photo*, 85
Hicks, William H., 140
Higgins, John M., 45
Higgs, Joseph Benjamin, 28
Hight, Alexander, 87
Hill, Atlas, 87
Hill, Egbert Washington, 228
Hill, Lemuel H., 192
Hill, John, 219
Hill, John Hampden, 45
Hill, John W., 140
Hill, Leonidas, 192
Hill, Parrott N., 192
Hill, Reuben, 76
Hill, Robert P., 192
Hill, Robert R., 192
Hill, William E., 45
Hill, William R., 219
Hines, Benjamin H., 45
Hines, David, 206
Hines, Henry A., 192
Hines, J. Ivey, 192
Hines, James A., 45
Hines, William S., 8
Hinson, Benjamin, 140
Hinson, Wade, 140
Hobson, Richard, 87
Hodges, D., 8
Hodges, Thomas B., 33
Hodges, William T., 9
Hoffman, Henry, 140
Holder, W. H., 222

Holland, Blueman, 84
Holland, Charles, 192
Holland, John, 193
Holliday, Edward D., 105
Hollis, Edward, 105; *photo*, 121
Hollowell, Marshall H., 24
Holsouser, Jacob, 140
Honeycutt, J., 141
Honeycutt, Noah W., 141
Hood, Robert B., 24
Hood, Solomon P., 24
Horn, D. H., 105
Horne, John, 29
hospitals,
    General Hospital No. 3 (Raleigh), *photo*, 122
    General Hospital No. 8 (Raleigh), *photo*, 156
    General Hospital No. 13 (Raleigh), *photo*, 218
    Cobb House (Wise's Forks), *photo*, 35
    First Baptist Church (Raleigh), *photo*, 162
    Harper House (Bentonville), *photo*, 80
    "Lebanon" (Averasboro), *photo*, 238
Howard, W. A., 222
Howard, Willie J., 181,
Howell, Calvin, 45
Howell, Freeman, 229
Howell, Kedar, 24
Howell, Robert, 24
Howell, W. S., 87
Hoyle, J. C., 45
Hudnell, Willis B., 46
Huff, Obediah L., 222
Huffman, Julius M., 235
Hughes, N. A., 9
Hughes, Robert, 9
Humphrey, C., 206
Humphrey, John, 193

Humphrey, Lewis D., 193
Huneycutt, Solomon S., 141
Huneycutt, William M., 141
Hunt, David T., 141
Hunter, Benjamin F., 33
Hunter, Henry D., 46
Hunter, Samuel Benjamin, 29
Hurley, Harvey, 172
Hurley, Thomas, 172
Hutchins, Joshua H. T., 124
Hyman, Ebenezer, 195
Hyman, Hugh H., 106
Hyman, Needham Sherrod, 106

I

Ingram, James, 141
Ives, John Lewis, 206

J

Jackson, Asa, 46
Jackson, Bracy E., 46
Jackson, Cornelius, 46
Jackson, George W., 223
Jackson, Lewis, 9
Jackson, Thomas, 46
James, John R., 141
James, John T., 193
James, John W., 9
Jarrett, Killian Mills, 172
Jarrett, Obediah B., 76
Jenkins, David Frank, 265
Jenkins, Elias, 159
Jenkins, George R., 106
Jenkins, Thomas C., 106
Jewett, Richard B., 9
Job, William L., 68
Johnson, A., 10
Johnson, Fleet, 84
Johnson, James, 24
Johnson, M., 196
Johnson, R. A., 141

Johnston, David, 235
Jones, Calvin E., 47
Jones, Doctor T., 159
Jones, Ebed, 142
Jones, George R., 10
Jones, George W., 47
Jones, Haywood, 47
Jones, James B., 193
Jones, John Willie, 235
Jones, Jonas, 72
Jones, McG., 206
Jones, Reddick H., 193
Jones, Robert B., 47
Jones, Silas, 215
Jones, Thaddeus L., 47
Jones, Walter J., 47
Jones, William T., 10
Jordan, William H., 47
Judge, Stephen M., 10

K

Karlott, W. R., 193
Kayler, George, 172
Keel, Ashley, 106
Keel, Robert, 107
Kelly, Henry H., 10
Kelly, James A., 29
Kemp, Washington C., 107
Kennedy, L., 10
Kennedy, Levi T., 10
Kennedy, Richard M., 47
Kennedy, Stiles, 88; *photo*, 86
Kennedy, William H., 193
Kenney, Simpson, 172
Kerfees. *See also*: Kurfes.
Kerfees, John Peter, 142
Kerman, James M., 48
Kesler, George B., 142
Kesler, M. E., 142
Ketchie, Benjamin Rufus, 142
Ketchum, Christopher, 48
Kick, George, 48

Kimery, D. W., 142
King, Anderson, 142
King, Everett, 11
King, Frederick, 206
King, Hill Ennett, 206
King, James, 72
King, James S., 25
King, M. H., 229
King, Solomon O., 11
Kinsall, John, 206
Kirby, William C., 212
Kirkland Brigade Monument, *photo*, 202
Kiser, J. H., Sr., 142
Kitchen, John, 11
Kittrel, Alex, 207
Kittrell, Job, 107
Klutts, Jesse A., 142
Knowles, William E., 107
Kurfes, John, 219

L

Lamb, C. W., 223
Lamb, Hugh, 159
Lamb, Michael, 159
Lamb, William R., 11
Lambert, John L., 143
Lambert, John Q., 143
Lambert, M., 143
Lambert, W., 143
Lambert, William W., 143
Lamm, Jonas, 193
Lancaster, Lawrence, 48
Lance, William H., 77
Landers, Charles L., 124
Lane, John, 193
Lane, John W., 194
Lane, William C. Preston, 220
Langston, John, 25
Lanier, Joseph J., 164
Laper, M. G., 164
Larkin, Eli, 11
Larkins, James R., 33

Lassitter, William B., 207
Latham, David C., 77
Latham, James, 77
Latham, John W., 107
Lawrence, David A., 143
Lawrence, William G., 77
Layton, Franklin, 194
Layton, Green L., 144
Layton, John A., 29
Lea, S. M., 160
Lea, William A., 68
Leach, Henry C., 63
Ledbetter, Thomas P., 144
Ledford, Frederick, 160
Ledford, William, 172
Lee, E. J., 223
Lee, Elam, 48
Lee, James W., 48, 107
Lee, Joel, 48
Lee, Sedulus D., 48
Leggett, John E., 48
Leggett, William W., 107
Leitner, Edward E., 194
Lentz, Daniel Wesley, 144
Leonard, Alexander, Jr., 144
Leonard, Jacob, 144
Leonard, John W., 33
Leonard, Lorenzo, 223
Leslie, Neil. *See*: Lesley L.
Lesley, L., 12
Lewis, James Whittington, 220
Lewis, Warren A., 160
Lewya, Roswell, 144
Lineberrier, David, 212
Lineberry, Edwin Culver, 220
Liner, A. Joseph, 220
Linville, John F., 144
Lipe, James A., 144
Little, Francis Marion, 207
Little, George E., 108
Little, Jacob, 145
Little, James M., 145
Little, William, 124

Littleton, Dexter B., 181
Littleton, Edward J., 34
Lloyd, William Roland, 108
Locke, William, 49
Loflin, Wiley J., 145
London, P., 164
Long, Edward, 49
Long, John A., 160
Long, Thomas, 108
Long, Wilson N., 49
Looper, Temolin, 88
Love, John E., 145
Love, John J., 145
Lucas, Henry D., 49

M

Mabrey, Jacob A., 145
Madra, E. N., 229
Mahaley, B. Franklin, 145
Mallett, Edward, 181
Mangum, Richard G., 173
Mann, Daniel B., 108
Mann, Jonathan, 145
Mann, William, 108
Manning, John W., 108
Mariner, J. B., 194
Marks, Thomas, 146
Marlin, I. J., 173
Marshburn, D. C., 124
Martin, George D., 224
Martin, Peyton C., 109
Mason, William T., 49
Mathis, Martin, 173
Mathis, Noel, 194
Maultsby, Henry C., 29; *photo*, 26
Maurice, Samuel, 49
May, William F., 146
May, William H., 109
Maynard, Brinkley, 224
Mayo, Charles E. S., 49
Mayo, William, 68
McAchin, V. *See*: McEachin, Evander

McCall, Duncan D., 12
McCall, Jacob M., 173
McCall, John T., 12
McCauley, John A., 49
McCauley, Samuel S., 63
McCotter, George Badger, 207
McCoy, Frederick, 194
McCoy, Kenneth, 12
McCullen, Lewis M., 50
McDaniel, Alfred C., 146
McDaniel, Benjamin L., 146
McDonald, L., 29
McDuffie, Luther Calvin, 12
McDuffie, Robert John, 13
McDugald, William J., 215; *photo*, 214
McEachin, Evander, 13
McFarlin, Simeon, 194
McFayden, H. L., 30
McGee, William, 235
McGuire, John K., 13
McIntyre, John H., 146
McKay, James A., 13
McKee, David James, 30
McKellar, James, 13
McKindler, James, 207
McKinney, James, 173
McKinnon, Daniel, 72
McLauchlin, James W., 50
McLaughlin, Archibald J., 14
McLaughlin, Kenneth, 30
McLean, Angus, 165
McLean, Daniel, 165
McLean, Daniel L., 14
McLean, Hector R., 165
McLenster, M., 146
McLeod, Archibald, 84
McNeill, Daniel Evander, 14
McNeill, John B., 50
McPhaul, James, 50
McPhaul, John A., 14
McPhaul, Maloy, 14
Medlin, Jesse, 146
Melson, William R., 109

Melton, Alexander, 146
Melvin, Joseph M., 30
Melvin, Robert D., 165
Mendenhall, Julian C., 64
Merideth, Alfred M., 109
Michael, J. W., 236
Millard, Luther R., 30
Miller, John W., 88, 207
Miller, M., 15
Miller, Mack, 173
Milliard, James J., 195
Minor, Herbert J., 147
Mitchell, E., 77
Mitchell, Edward D., 124
Mizell, Mark W., 109
Mizell, William, 34
Mock, David, 50
Modlin, Samuel, 109
Moffitt, John W. L., 173
Monds, Lemuel, 34
Monds, William M., 34
Monk, Henderson, 195
Moore, D. F., 69
Moore, Hezekiah W., 15
Moore, Isaiah, 181
Moore, J. A., 110
Moore, Jordan M., 64
Moore, Joseph A., 110
Moore, Joseph E., 110
Moore, Julius, 110
Morgan, E. D., 147
Morgan, Jethro C., 173
Morgan, Oliver C., 77
Morrow, John S., 195
Morse, James, 88
Morton, David L., 147
Motley, M. M., 147
Murdock, J. C., 174
Murphy, John, 69
Murphey, William D., 50
Murphrey, John, 195
Murray, Alphonso H., 50
Murray, Murdock W., 15

Myers, Solomon Wesley, 147
Myers, William A., 195

N

Nail, Thomas, 147
Nance, Alexander Greene R., 147
Nance, James H., 69
Neagle, John P., 77
Neely, Albert Jefferson, 78
Nelson, John Randolph, 110
Nelson, William, 239
Neville, W., 229
New, James Columbus, 124
Newberry, Demetrius W., 34
Newell, Samuel T., 50
Newman, James, 195
Newman, William S., 51
Newsom, Leander, 124
Newson, Nicholas H., 181
Newton, Nathan W., 15
Nivens, Dunkin, 51
Nixon, James A., 34
Nixon, John E., 34
Noah, Humphrey, 69
Norman, Nehemiah, 111
Norris, Ashley, 111
Norris, William Indy, 165
North Carolina Military Units:
    See Table of Contents
Nott, William J., 165

O

Oadum, Nathan L., 195
Oakdale Cemetery, Wilmington, 16, 17
Oakley, John 111
Oast, W. T., 51
O'Connell, John, 51
Odum, Benjamin D., 69
Oliver, Asa W., 195
Only, Richard M., 34
Orr, Timothy C., 181

Orrell, Robert R., 147
Outterbridge, Andrew J., 111
Overcash, William A., 196
Overton, Henry H., 111
Overton, John R., 111
Overton, William Cooper, 112
Owen, David A., 51
Owen, Jacob S., 52
Owens, Stephen D., 181
Owens, William H., 160
Oakwood Cemetery, High Point, 4, 26, 29, 84, 85, 127, 172, 221
Oakwood Cemetery, Raleigh, 19, 20, 89, 105, 105, 121, 179, 182, 202, 214, 215, 220, 222, 226; *photo*, 231

P

Page, Jesse, 165
Page, W. Riley, 88
Page, Wiley M., 229
Parham, H. E., 196
Parker, James N., 69
Parker, John, 112
Parker, John C., 196
Parker, Julius A., 147
Parker, Robert, 112
Parker, William F., 207
Parker, William K., 112
Parker, Young R., 229
Parks, Benjamin, 208
Parks, Harvey Baxter, 64
Parrish, Nathaniel H., 78
Parrish, Putney, 125
Parrish, Thomas, 181
Paschall, Joseph P., 182
Pate, Gatlin, 196
Pate, Hutching P., 208
Pate, Lenoir, 196
Pate, James A., 25
Pate, Robert, 52
Pate, Sherrard H., 229
Pate, William H., 208

Patrick, James B., 208
Patterson, Neill, 215
Patterson, Robert J., 160
Patton, L. L., 196
Peal, Jesse B., 113
Peal, William D., 113
Pearey, Aaron, 174
Peel, John, 113
Peel, John P., 113
Pendleton, J. M. P., 229
Penry, Noah, 148
Perry, Caswell, 148
Perry, John J., 182
Perry, Noah Thomas, 113
Perry, William H., 113
Peterson, Laban, 72
Phelps, James Dallas, Sr., 114
Philips, Reuben, 52
Phillips, Frank, 52
Phillips, James W., 15
Pigott, James F., 31
Pinkston, George W., 148
Pitman, John, 160
Pope, J. A., 224
Pope, Michael S., 165
Poplin, John, Sr., 148
Porter, Caswell, 165
Porter, James A., 166
Potter, A. Gustavus, 15
Potter, John L., 52
Potts, Milton, 196
Powell, Isham, 84
Powell, James, 84
Powell, James Alfred, 196
Powell, O. D., 160
Powers, George G., 16
Powers, Kitchen F., 16
Powers, Nicaner William, 16
Presnell, Benjamin L., 174
Price, George W., 224
Price, Gideon, 161
Price, William J., 148
Price, William L., 114

Pridgen, John O., 216
Privett, Ansiel P., 148
Privett, Samuel, 34
Pruden, William Dossey, Jr., 224
Pullin, J. L., 52
Purington, Stanley M., 114
Purser, James R., 52
Purser, Jesse D., 52
Putman, Rufus, 230

Q

Quaite, William, 64
Quinn, John W., 197
Queen, William, 148

R

Rabon, Armand, 16
Ragen, William, 114, 148
Ragen, William Thomas, 114
Ramsey, William J., 53
Rankin, John T., 16
Rankin, Robert George, 17; *photo*, 22
Rasberry, Alex J., 53
Rawles, John McG., 114
Rawlings, Jesse, 115
Rawlings, William A., 115
Rawls, William C., 115
Ray, A. H., 78
Ray, C. L., 53
Ray, George W., 78
Ray, Horace, 115
Ray, Hilton H., 78
Ray, James J., 78
Ray, James M., 79
Ray, John A., 79
Ray, W., 17
Raybon, Richard, 31
Reasons, Joseph T., 17
Redmond, William, 115
Redwine, John F., 148
Reese, Aaron, 79

Reid, William H., 212
Reno, John Ed., 177
Respess, James H., 116
Reynolds, Lewis, 17
Rhea, Robert C., 79
Rhodes, George A., 197
Rich, Lewis W., 53
Richardson, Cornelius J., 225
Ricks, A. E., 53
Ricks, R., 54
Riddick, Job, 35
Ridenhour, John M., 149
Riley, Thomas Jefferson, 197
Riley, William L., 197
Rivenbark, Matthew J., 17
Riverside Cemetery, Smithfield, *photo*, 90
Rives, Peter Richard, 208
Robason, Alfred, 54
Robason, Benjamin F., 116
Roberson, Jesse, 125
Roberson, William P., 116
Roberts, D. M., 88
Roberts, Joseph L., 54
Roberts, Melville B., 177
Roberts, Robert M., 230
Robertson, John C., 54
Robertson, Moses, 116
Robeson, David G., 17
Robeson, M. A., 177
Robinson, Abner, 84
Robinson, Frederick G., 31
Robinson, Henry, 25
Rodger, Jeremiah, 149
Rodgers, William B., 18
Rogers, John H., 230
Rogerson, Nathan, 116
Ross, John Riley, 54
Ross, T. McGilbert, 197
Rough, William M., 149
Rowe, James M., 70
Rowe, John G., 197
Ruffin, Robert R., 116

Rufus, R., 149
Rumage, E. R., 149
Rumley, Edward, 239
Rumple, James M., 149
Rushing, Elijah J., 54
Russ, William, 31
Russ, William Henry, 18
Russell, James S., 149
Russell, Nicholas A., 54
Ryland, Noah, 54

S

Salomon, James P., 161
Sanders, John A. T., 79
Sanderson, Lewis, 197
Sandy, John A. W., 166
Sassamon, Christian C., 149
Sasser, Edward, 212
Sasser, John A. W., 166
Savage, William Bythel, 116
Savage, William W., 117
Scarlett, James C., 198
Scarlett, William R., 198
Scoffield, Thomas H., 117
Scott, John J., 150
Seagraves, Sidney C., 125
Sewell, William J., 125
Sexton, Randall R., 125
Shehan, Pinkney, 174
Sheppard, James Henry, 208
Sherrill, Isaac I., 174
Shoaf, Emanuel, 150
Short, William P., 225
Shown, James W., 79
Shuffler, Jacob C., 174
Shuping, Henry Jeremiah, 198
Shuping, John A., 150
Siceliff, Alpheus E., 150
Sikes, George W., 18
Sikes, James T., 55
Sills, Henry Washington, 166
Sills, William T., 166

Simmons, Elijah, 150
Simmons, Lemuel, 55
Simmons, Saunders, 72
Simmons, Wiley King, 31
Simpson, Charles, 198
Simpson, John O., 18
Sims, John, 182
Skeen, John H., 182
Skinner, Richard, 208
Slaughter, William James, 209
Sleight, Matthew, 117
Sloan, Charles, 150
Smart, Henry Kerr, 161
Smith, Casper M., 150
Smith, J., 150
Smith, James Douglas, 150
Smith, John W., 151, 182
Smith, Joseph W., 151
Smith, Josiah, 151
Smith, Milton M., 151
Smith, Moses S., 151
Smith, Nelson, 175
Smith, T. C., 225
Smith, Thomas, 161
Smith, William Harden, 151
Smith, William S., 72
Snell, Eli, 117
Solomon, William S., 198
Southerland, James, 166
Sparks, George, 175
Sparks, William M., 175
Sparrow, Thomas Gideon, III, 209
Spencer, William Jesse, 198
Spivey, Jesse, 175
Spivey, John Quincy, 166
Sport, William B., 151
Spruill, Henry W., 117
Southerland, Wiley T., 55
Sowers, Jacob, 70
Spry, Gregory, 64
Stack, James M., 152
Stanaland, D. B., 236
Stafford, Gaston, 209

Stafford, William Henry, 175
Stafford, William W., 55
Stanley, Alfred C., 167
Staton, *See*: Staten.
Staten, William, 64
Stedman, David M., 85
Stephenson, J. A., 220
Stephenson, J. H., 225
Stevens, Josiah, 209
Stevenson, James C., 31
Steward, *See also*: Stewart.
Stewart, Alfred W., 125
Stewart, C. E., 18
Stokely, Charles L., 88
Stokes, George A., 55
Stone, Duncan E., 19
Stoner, William W., 152
Strayhorn, Isaac R., 55
Strickland, Cyrus, 198
Strickland, J. H., 25
Strickland, Jerry, 209
Strickland, Moore, 175
Strickland, William T., 167
Stroud, Isaac, 198
Sugg, George W., 55
Sugg, John Patrick, 209
Sugg, Joshua Parrott, 182
Sugg, Reuben, 209
Sullivan, Andrew McI., 167
Sumerlin, L. D., 209
Sutton, Daniel, 198
Sutton, John A., 19
Sutton, Thomas, 199
Sutton, William Hardy, 56
Swing, Daniel, 152
Sykes, A. F., 230

T

Tarlton, John W., 56
Tate, Elias, 199
Tate, Jesse, 199
Tate, William N., 56

Taylor, A. Jackson, 152
Taylor, Bythel, 117
Taylor, Edwin, 152
Taylor, Gilbert C., 19
Taylor, Harvey S., 118
Taylor, Jacob W., 19
Taylor, John Douglas, 32
Taylor, John P., 199
Taylor, John William, 19; *photo*, 2
Taylor, Lewis, 20
Taylor, Major J., 20
Taylor, William James, 167
Taylor, William M., 152
Teeter, Whitson A., 152
Templeton, James M., 153
Thigpen, A. Marion, 65
Thigpen, Stephen Miller, 210
Thigpen, Thomas, 167
Thomas, Charles G., 199
Thomas, John A., Jr., 56
Thomas, John M., 213
Thomas, John M. B., 161
Thomason, W. T., 199
Thornton, Isaac Ingram, 25
Thornton, Moore Lee, 20
Tomlin, Marshall M., 153
Tommer, Alexander, 56
Tonnoffski, George L., 118
Townsend, Jackson, 167
Trueblood, John T., 213
Turner, Cicero F., 199
Turner, John W., 167
Treadaway, Z. T., 225
Treddy, George, 153
Treece, George, 153
Trexler, James P., 153
Tucker, Leonard G., 153
Turbyfield, James Pickney, 175
Turner, J. R., 236
Turner, James, 65
Turner, John, 125
Turnmire, John N. 176
Tuten, Thomas A. E., 56

Tuten, Wilson, 57
Tweedy, William Harvey, 118
Tyson, Benjamin F., 210
Tyson, Sherrod, 210

U

Underhill, John, 20
Underwood, William M., 65
Upright, William, 153
Ury, Jacob A., 153
USS Connecticut, hospital steamer, 188

V

Vann, Albert C., 57
Vause, Robert Bond, 57; *photo*, 59
Veach, G. W., 153
Vick, William B., 57
Vickers, Moses, 199
Vinson, Nathan, 25

W

Wade, Clark, 168
Wade, Drew H., 199
Walker, George Washington, 154
Walker, John W., 126
Wall, M. W., 161
Walls, Lewis, 154
Walser, Spurgeon, 154
Walsh, William, 80
Walsh, William A., 25
Walter, Jeremiah A., 118
Walters, John F., 70
Walters, William, 161
Walton, George D., 65
Ward, Felton, 118
Warren, Chesley P., 200
Warwick, John J., 161
Waters, Elisha, 200
Waters, George W., 57
Waters, Jonathan, 162

Waters, Robert McCoy, 118
Watkins, Lewis A., 70
Watkins, Richard R., 236
Watkins, William H. G., 154
Watson, Benjamin, 168
Watson, Daniel W., 162
Watson, Guilford H., 57
Watson, Spencer O., 200
Watts, Guilford, 72
Watts, Josiah T., 57
Watts, Lewis, 21
Watts, William, 72
Waugh, George M., 236
Weathersbee, Francis Joseph, 32
Weathington, W. T., 119
Weaver, Benjamin F., 225
Webb, David, 57
Webb, William Jeptha, 35
Weddington, Washington Taylor, 230
Welborn, James M., 65
Wells, William B., 210
West, James, 168
Whaley, Frederick, 200
Whitaker, Jesse, 220
Whitaker, Joseph P., 200
Whitaker, Martin, 119
Whitaker, William, 58
White, A. J., 176
White, Needham M., 201
White, Stephen, 168
Whitehead, John, 119
Whitehead, Turner, 119
Whitehead, Willie, 119
Whitehurst, Charles C., 58
Whitley, Ephraim J., 154
Whitley, John W., 154
Whitley, Levi H., 154
Whitley, Solomon S., 154
Whitley, Taylor, 154
Whitman, William, 201
Wiggins, James R., 119
Wiggins, John Lawrence, 120
Wiggs, James J., 201

Wigtine, John C., 210
Wilder, Thomas R., 120
Wilhelm, John C., 155
Wilkerson, Elisha, 210
Wilkerson, W. N., 120
Wilkins, Isaac C., 155
Williams, B. B., 120
Williams, E. E., 120
Williams, Henry A., 182
Williams, Hezekiah, 35
Williams, James W., 121
Williams, Milton, 155
Williams, Patrick J., 25
Williams, Richard, 236
Williamson, Obediah H., 32
Williford, B. L., 121
Williford, F. H., 155
Williford, Sir William T., 168
Willis, Burgess, 155
Willis, John W., 58
Willow Dale Cemetery, Goldsboro, *photo*, 232
Wilson, Amzi R., 21
Wilson, B. Frank, 210
Wilson, Calvin D., 58
Wilson, Elbert W., 201
Wilson, Francis M., 21
Wilson, James E., 177
Wilson, John A., 210
Wilson, John W., 176
Wilson, Peter, 58
Winborn, David, 201
Winborn, Woodard, 59
Windley, James T., 59
Winfield, John D., 121
Winfry, J. G., 21
Winningham, James N., 59
Witherington, James G., 201
Wofford, William W., 201
Wolfe, John N., 65
Wood, Bennett, 202
Wood, Harrison W., 155
Wood, Thomas, 32

Wood, William Jackson, 183
Woodlief, J. O., 225
Wooten, Allen, 202
Wooten, Council, 202
Workman, George W., 59
Worlie, David M., 202
Wright, D. F., 236
Wright, David E., 121
Wyatt, William B.,

Y

Yarborough, Aphus, 230
York, Alfred R., 225
Yow, Henry, 155

About the Authors

Wade Sokolosky

Colonel Wade Sokolosky (Ret.), a native of Beaufort, North Carolina, is a graduate of East Carolina University and a 25-year veteran of the U.S. Army. He is one of North Carolina's leading experts on the 1865 Carolinas Campaign. Wade has lectured nationwide, speaking to roundtables, various societies, organizations, and historical sites. He is the author of the two-volume series *North Carolina's Confederate Hospitals*. Wade is also co-author (with Mark A. Smith) of *"To Prepare for Sherman's Coming": The Battle of Wise's Forks, March 1865,* and *"No Such Army Since the Days of Julius Caesar": Sherman's Carolinas Campaign from Fayetteville to Averasboro.*

He is the recipient of the 2024 North Carolina Division of the United Daughters of the Confederacy Jefferson Davis Historical Gold Medal for his publishing and lecturing excellence on Confederate history. Raleigh Civil War Round Table's 2017 T. Harry Gatton Award for his important efforts to study, preserve, and share the Civil War heritage of his native North Carolina.

Stacey Jones

North Carolinian Stacey Jones is a Wayne Community College, Mount Olive College, and Campbell University Divinity School graduate in studies ranging from agricultural and animal sciences to business management and Christian education. He worked 30 years in the swine industry, performing at different levels of management, has served in church ministry, and is currently employed as the CEO of a small credit union. His love of studying genealogy and local and Civil War history has compelled his strong passion for a hobby of researching deeper into those subjects. Jones currently serves as the treasurer for the Wyse Fork Battlefield Commission.

Sergeant Reddick H. Jones
Company H, 66th NC Troops
Captured near Goldsboro on March 20, 1865

(Courtesy of Stacey Jones)

Additional Information Not Previously Found

Jenkins, David Frank, Private, Company E, 42nd North Carolina
Sugar Loaf
Service records indicate that he was wounded by a shell on an unspecified date and admitted to GH No. 4 in Wilmington on February 12, 1865. He was later transferred to GH No. 6 in Fayetteville on February 18, 1865. No further medical information. He signed his Oath of Allegiance on June 7, 1865, at Mocksville, North Carolina. He is not listed in *NC Troops*.
Source: M270.

Additional Information Submission

The authors realize that while *Final Roll Call* is the most complete compiled source to date, more information may become available through other sources. They hope such opportunities arise to build on the present work with additional information that others may be able to provide. If anyone possesses knowledge not contained within this volume, please use the contacts below to submit to the authors for review and consideration for future editions.

To Submit by Email:

wadesokolosky@gmail.com

stayjones02@gmail.com

To Submit by Mail:

Wade Sokolosky

175 Shore Drive

Beaufort, NC 28516